THE CHANGING FACES OF FAMILIES

With a focus on nine different national contexts, this book explores contemporary family diversity. With attention to the different welfare states and cultures of care in each setting, it problematizes the pre-eminence of research and policy centered on heteronormative families, showing the extent to which family diversity exists cross-nationally in relation to different gendered and "family-friendly" policies. Considering variations in family forms, including differences in the number and marital status of parents, their gender, sexual orientation and biological relationship to the children (adoption), multicultural families, and families created by technological assistance or surrogacy, it presents demographic information, alongside quantitative and qualitative research, across a number of advanced countries. A contribution to our understanding of the diversity of family forms, how diversity is lived in families, and what family diversity means in various international policy contexts. *The Changing Faces of Families* will appeal to scholars with interests in the sociology of the family.

Marina A. Adler is Professor in the Department of Sociology, Anthropology and Public Health at the University of Maryland, Baltimore County, US and the co-editor of *Father Involvement in the Early Years: An International Comparison of Policy and Practice*.

Karl Lenz is Professor of Microsociology at the TU Dresden, Germany and the co-editor of *Father Involvement in the Early Years: An International Comparison of Policy and Practice*.

Routledge Studies in Family Sociology

This series presents the latest research on the sociology of the family, with particular attention to family dynamics, changing family forms and the impact of events in the life-course and societal transformation on family practices.

Titles in the series:

Father Involvement and Gender Equality in the United States
Contemporary Norms and Barriers
Richard J. Petts

Family Violence and Social Change in the Pacific Islands
Edited by Loïs Bastide & Denis Regnier

The Changing Faces of Families
Diverse Family Forms in Various National Policy Contexts
Edited by Marina A. Adler and Karl Lenz

THE CHANGING FACES OF FAMILIES

Diverse Family Forms in
Various Policy Contexts

Edited by
Marina A. Adler and Karl Lenz

We acknowledge support for the Open Access publication by the Saxon State
Digitization Program for Science and Culture.

Routledge
Taylor & Francis Group
LONDON AND NEW YORK

Designed cover image: © Shutterstock

First published 2023
by Routledge
2 Park Square, Milton Park, Abingdon, Oxon OX14 4RN

and by Routledge
605 Third Avenue, New York, NY 10158

Routledge is an imprint of the Taylor & Francis Group, an informa business

British Library Cataloguing-in-Publication Data
A catalogue record for this book is available from the British Library

ISBN: 978-1-032-04503-0 (hbk)
ISBN: 978-1-032-04502-3 (pbk)
ISBN: 978-1-003-19350-0 (ebk)

DOI: 10.4324/9781003193500

Typeset in Bembo
by codeMantra

CONTENTS

TABLES

CONTRIBUTORS

Marina A. Adler is Professor in the Department of Sociology, Anthropology and Public Health, University of Maryland, Baltimore County, US.

Vicente Díaz-Gandasegui is Lecturer at Universidad Carlos III de Madrid, Spain.

Anne-Laure Garcia is Interim Chair of Microsociology at TU Dresden, Germany.

Ursula Henz is Associate Professor in the Department of Sociology, London School of Economics, UK.

Barbara Hobson is Professor in the Department of Sociology, Stockholm University, Sweden.

Karl Lenz is Professor of Microsociology at TU Dresden, Germany.

Lun Li is Postdoctoral Research Fellow at Gerontology Research Centre, Simon Fraser University, Canada.

Aušra Maslauskaitė is Professor in the Department of Sociology, Vytautas Magnus University, Lithuania.

Gerardo Meil is Professor in the Department of Sociology, Universidad Autónoma de Madrid, Spain.

Barbara A. Mitchell is Professor in the Department of Sociology/Anthropology and Department of Gerontology, Simon Fraser University, Canada.

Livia Sz. Oláh is Associate Professor in the Department of Sociology, Stockholm University, Sweden.

Jesús Rogero-García is Lecturer at Universidad Autónoma de Madrid, Spain.

Glenn Sandström is Associate Professor in the Department of Historical, Philosophical and Religious Studies, CEDAR, Umeå University, Sweden.

Tino Schlinzig is Postdoctoral Research Fellow at ETH Wohnforum – ETH Centre for Research on Architecture, Society & the Built Environment, ETH Zürich, Switzerland.

Takashi Yamashita is Professor in the Department of Sociology, Anthropology and Public Health, University of Maryland, Baltimore County, US.

1

BEYOND STANDARD FAMILIES IN ADVANCED COUNTRIES

Marina A. Adler and Karl Lenz

Who is considered family in the 21st century? Among countries and even within countries, there is no clear consensus on this question, but some common changes involving unions, parents, and children in "post-modern" families are evident. Over the past five decades, a dramatic proliferation and diversification of family forms has occurred across advanced countries. Increasing individualization processes and the rise of the women's and LGBTQA+ (lesbian, gay, bisexual, transsexual, queer, asexual, plus) movements opened the door for new relationship forms, new ways of living together, as well as increasing trends of living alone and living without children. The nuclear family consisting of a married, heterosexual couple with joint (biological) children has experienced a sharp decline relative to other forms of "doing family." Based on the bourgeois family ideal that emerged in the 18th century, the nuclear family was long considered the hegemonic standard, and the only normatively appropriate and aspirational family form. The heteronormative nuclear family dominated not only in public and policy discourses but also in social research, where deviations from this norm were interpreted as deficient and incomplete. However, over time it became increasingly evident that this standard family form does not guarantee a happy family life, the well-being of children, or gender equality. Consequently, as the popularity of the nuclear family waned, more alternative, non-traditional family forms have emerged and increased in significance.

This diversification of what families look like, how families are created and how family is "done" every day has progressed significantly in advanced countries, reflecting what Cherlin (2004) refers to as a de-institutionalization process. The de-institutionalization of marriage involves an increasing instability of couple relationships and a growing acceptance of sexual orientations beyond compulsory heterosexuality. Forming a union without marriage can

DOI: 10.4324/9781003193500-1

take the form of non-marital cohabitation or a living-apart-together relationship (LAT). Relationship biographies have changed, and now it is increasingly rare for people to marry their first partners and stay with them for the rest of their lives. Instead, it is common practice to have a series of relationships, to live in them in different ways over the life course, and to have children with different partners (multi-partner fertility). Hence, a family can include more than one household, family members are linked not only by biological ties, and membership in a family is subjective and fluid and can change over time. Same-sex relationships, marriage, and parenthood have been de-criminalized and are even legally sanctioned in many advanced countries. In addition to these changes in couple relationships, migration processes and resulting ethnic heterogeneity of the population as well as advances in reproductive medicine have created the space for a rapid diversification of family forms (see Harris, 2008, for a review).

The waning popularity of marriage as the only option for union formation, increased cohabitation, changes in divorce and remarriage rates, and the growing acceptance of same-sex unions, medically assisted reproductive methods, adoption, and voluntarily not having children reflect a broadening range of family definitions and practices. Not only has the structural family composition undergone major changes, so have family members' perceptions of who is part of their family, where and how family is done, and what family relationships mean to them (Seltzer, 2019). These processes also have far-reaching consequences for social science research: Household composition and common living arrangements have become inadequate criteria for defining what constitutes a family and for understanding the meanings assigned to being a family by its members. Family diversity can be researched as empirical variations in family composition and through an interpretative or constructionist lens as differences in the understanding of family relationships (Harris, 2008).

And yet, the diverse strategies of reproduction and family formation largely remain unscripted terrain (Nordqvist, 2021), and it appears that there is a cultural lag between alternative pathways to becoming family and the traditional normative understandings of what a family is. The observed trends in family diversity also raise family policy-related questions, such as which types of families are or should be privileged by government support (Cherlin, 2020). It has also to be recognized that the standard heteronormative family tends to remain privileged in the policies and laws of advanced countries. Historically, while a variety of family forms have coexisted with the standard family, depending on social and economic conditions, they have long remained invisible, often stigmatized, and discriminated and have only recently been acknowledged. This family diversity emerges in societies from the social context and social forces that construct families (Baca Zinn & Wells, 2000). Consequently, we examine the current state of knowledge regarding the compositional, interpretative, and policy dimensions of family diversity in several advanced countries.

Forms of parenthood

While family formation remains one of the most significant life course events, the timing, constellation, and strategies have diversified. In the 21st century, numerous alternative pathways to parenthood have proliferated, becoming more accepted and legitimized in the policy arena of advanced nations (see Furstenberg et al., 2020). According to Vaskovics (2011), parenthood can be differentiated into biological, genetic, legal, and social parenthood. Biological parenthood refers to fertilization/conception, pregnancy, and birth of an offspring; in everyday language, it is common to speak of "biological" mothers, fathers, and children. The emergence of reproductive medicine (Passet-Wittig & Bujard, 2021) has made it necessary to distinguish biological from genetic parenthood because sperm and/or egg cells can originate from, or be implanted into, a third person. Although there are strictly only two biological parents, these need not always be known, and given further technical advances in reproductive medicine, the number of genetic parents may be unlimited (Eggen, 2020).

Adoption expands the opportunities for family formation beyond biological and genetic relationships to legal relationships. Legal parenthood involves assigning rights and responsibilities to an adult to care for someone, usually a child. In order to legally become a parent, whether through birth or adoption, mothers and fathers have to be legally registered by state authorities. The visibility of pregnancy and birth link biological motherhood directly to legal parenthood. However, child abandonment and child relinquishment illustrate that there are ways to avoid legal biological motherhood. Biological fatherhood is less directly linked to legal fatherhood, and while paternity can reliably be determined, this involves distrust and additional action.

Social parenthood refers to the assumption of parental responsibility and everyday care for a child that relates to the position of father or mother. When a child grows up with both birth parents, social and biological parenthood coincide. However, in adoptive and reconstituted (step) families, parental duties are performed by non-biological caregivers. Social parenthood also reveals that the birth of a child per se does not create a family; families are established only when at least one person accepts the position as parent. A motherhood or fatherhood becomes socially relevant only when it is recognized as such, that is, when it is transformed into a "lived" parenthood. There can be families without biological (and without legal) parenthood, but not families without social parenthood (see Lenz, 2013).

The separation of biological and social parenthood also creates the possibility that a child has more than two (social) parents. After relationship dissolution, in reconstituted families (or stepfamilies or blended families or multiple partner families), the new partners can take on the parental role fully or partially. Thus, in these families, there are typically multiple parents, who often live in multiple locations because the families span more than one household.

Beyond "standard" families

Family forms that diverge from the "traditional family standard" in one or more central characteristics are collectively referred to here as diverse family forms.

1. *One-parent families and cohabiting families*

One-parent families include one parent who is single, married but separated, widowed or divorced, and who lives with one or more children in the same household. Mother-only families are significantly more common than father-only families. One-parent families result from relationship dissolution, either before or after marriage, before or after the birth of a child. The de-institutionalization of marriage has also meant an increase in the number of families in which the parents remain unmarried. These cohabiting families can be lived as a prelude to marriage or constitute a permanent living arrangement.

2. *Reconstituted families (stepfamilies)*

In reconstituted families (e.g., stepfamilies), biological and social parenthood generally diverge in the case of one parent. While until the middle of the 20th century, these families were almost exclusively formed after the death of one parent, today they result mostly from separation or divorce. After relationship dissolution, a new family is formed when one of the two parents enters into a new relationship. This can take the form of a marriage, a non-marital partnership, or a long-distance relationship. If both separated (biological) parents enter new couple relationships, the child has two reconstituted families, one primary and one secondary. The primary stepfamily is where the child lives most of the time, whereas the child lives only sporadically (e.g., on weekends) in the secondary stepfamily. Because children most often remain with their mothers after relationship dissolution, primary stepfamilies tend to be step-father families. Finally, a distinction is made between simple, composite, and complex reconstituted families. In simple stepfamilies, only one adult brings children of their own into the relationship. In a composite stepfamily, also referred to as a patchwork family, both adults bring in their own children. A complex stepfamily includes, in addition to the stepchild(ren), joint new children of the couple.

The introduction of joint custody arrangements and the increased efforts of separated fathers to engage with their children has created a new living arrangement in which the child/children live in approximately equal parts in both separate parental households. In some cases, the children remain in a household in which each parent alternately co-resides with them. This living arrangement is referred to as the "dual residence arrangement."

3. *Adoptive and foster families*

Unlike foster care, adoption legally establishes parental rights. Through adoption, the parent gains complete and permanent legal parenthood. It is important to distinguish adoption of a stepchild from a third-party adoption. In the case of stepchild adoption, biological, legal, and social parenthood continue to coincide for one parent but for the other partner, social parenthood is supplemented by legal parenthood. In third-party adoption, both relinquishing parents lose their legal parenthood. There are cross-national differences in how adoptions occur. Recently, the recognition of children's right to information about their own roots has led to more open forms of adoption.

Fostering involves the placement of a child into a household for a limited period of time. The biological parents can retain legal parenthood, provided the child has not been removed from their care. Also, during the foster placement, contacts between the child and the biological parent(s) usually continue. The foster parents have social parenthood status during the time of the placement, but not legal parenthood status.

4. *Families created by medically assisted reproduction (MAR)*

According to Zegers-Hochschild et al. (2017), MAR is the umbrella term for various technologies and interventions to treat infertility. This involves fertility treatments and procedures that use eggs, sperm, or embryos (Sunderam et al., 2022), such as in vitro fertilization (IVF), egg and embryo donation, and surrogacy. Although assisted insemination and hormonal treatments enable an infertile woman to become a mother, they are not considered assisted reproductive technology (ART), and thus, not much data and research are available on them. Third-party reproduction involves the eggs, sperm, or embryos of a donor (i.e., a third person) (Thoma et al., 2014). While homologous insemination uses eggs and sperm of one couple, heterologous insemination involves third persons in the form of sperm or egg donation. A surrogacy may involve oocyte and sperm from a couple; however, in this case, biological motherhood is transferred to another woman. Significant differences exist among countries as to which forms of reproductive medicine are legally permissible.

MAR has made it possible to dissolve the biological reproductive triad (woman, man, and their offspring) (Eggen, 2020; Passet-Wittig & Bujard, 2021). While every child has a biological mother and father, there is a difference between biological and genetic parenthood. The woman from whom the egg or parts of it originate is the genetic mother; the biological mother is the woman in whose uterus the (artificially) fertilized egg matures and who gives birth to the child. The genetic father is the man (or men) whose sperm is used for fertilization, so that biological paternity coincides with genetic paternity. The option of being a mere sperm donor shows that genetic paternity does not have to involve legal or social parenthood.

5. *Sex and gender minority families (SGM)*

According to Reczek (2020), sex and gender minority (SGM) families include lesbian, gay, bisexual, transgender, queer, asexual, intersex, pansexual, multiamorous, and other LGBTQA+ families. Moore and Stambolis-Ruhstorfer (2013, p. 492) add that "sexual minority refers broadly to individuals whose sexual identity/behavior is marginalized by heterosexually prescribed norms." Due to the weakening of heteronormativity and the gender binary, the legal status and social acceptance of non-heterosexual relationships have improved significantly in some countries. Increasingly, it is also legally and socially accepted for same-sex couples to become parents. SGM families can include biological, step, adopted, or foster children, as well as children resulting from MAR.

6. *Multicultural and migrant families*

Global migration processes also make a significant contribution to the diversity of family forms. While in some countries ethnic heterogeneity has a long history, in others strong migratory movements have only started after the Second World War or have taken on a new quality. While the term immigrant family refers to families residing in a receiving country together, transnational families are those with family members residing in different countries. Although it is common to compare migrant families with non-migrant families, it is generally true that migrant families cannot be regarded as a separate form of family (Baykara-Krumme, 2015). Rather, these families are characterized by enormous heterogeneity. There are considerable differences in the contexts of origin, individual migration experiences, duration of residence, intermarriage patterns, and social and legal status, and in many cases, these differences are greater than among families without migration experiences (van Hook & Glick, 2020).

De-traditionalization of living arrangements and doing family

Not only have family forms diversified, family life in general has become less self-evident (Cherlin, 2020). The options for individual lifestyles have become greater; this has increased the scope for action, but also the constraints on making biographical decisions. At the same time, the contexts of families have become more diverse and demanding. In many cases, working life is accompanied by high demands for flexibility in terms of time and space, which have to be reconciled with family life (Perry-Jenkins & Gerstel, 2020). The care and educational facilities for children require a high degree of attention and cooperation. Normative expectations of a child-centered family life and responsible parenthood, linked with the demands of good relationship quality and gender egalitarianism in the relationship, put increasing pressure on parents.

Formerly a social institution with strict cultural norms for the genders and generations, family is now a place of constant negotiation among the family members. The everyday existence and continuity of families can no longer be taken for granted, but must be continuously established in the interactions of family members (Jurczyk & Meysen, 2020). "Doing family" implies reflexive family practices, which "exist in the routine talk about family—family obligations, family duties, family constraints" (Morgan, 1999, p. 29). Organizationally, everyday family life also must be coordinated by continuously clarifying who does what, when, and how.

In addition to overcoming these practical challenges, doing family also extends to the level of meaning-making. It requires identity-supporting efforts to convince people that the family has commonalities and forms a cohesive group. Widmer's (2021, p. 62) "configurational perspective" assumes that the individual family members "co-construct a feeling of being part of a family 'we' or 'we-ness' ... Such a 'we' is based on the individual members' feelings of intimacy with other family members, and the mutual commitments they develop over time ..." Hence, various family configurations are considered alternatives to the heteronormative nuclear family. The creation of a sense of "we" and processes of inclusion and exclusion from the family unit are as much a part of doing family as the external presentation as a family ("displaying family") (Finch, 2007).

While all families are confronted with everyday practical tasks, the construction of commonalities poses a particular challenge for non-traditional family forms. Naples (2001, p. 33) argues that the work of doing family is even more crucial to non-standard families:

> Family must be achieved and constructed on a daily basis. ... [Those] who do not fit into the normative heterosexual-family model understand this well. But all of us, regardless of the family form we inherit or create, must work to sustain these relationships.

Thus, Nelson (2006) for example describes how single mothers "perform family" and negotiate the meanings of family identity and family membership within various economic, cultural, and normative constraints while still considering the standard family as the ideal and aspirational family form. Post-divorce families also express a need for legitimation in terms of presenting themselves as a "real" family to the outside world. This need of non-traditional families for recognition and justification reflects the strong normative pressures to conform. Non-traditional family forms are continuously confronted with the standard family as hegemonic norm and have to permanently prove that they are also real families.

The concept of parenthood remains an important basis for doing family in non-traditional family forms (Buschner & Bergold, 2017). While families involving biological relationships can rely on self-evident definitions of who is the mother or father, non-traditional families require clarifications and definitions of family membership and positions. In addition, while parenting concepts include negotiation processes about the responsibilities and tasks in everyday family life, even in a biological mother-father-child triad, this is not as self-evident as it may seem. The possible strategies of withdrawing from parental roles show that even biological parenthood has to be accepted in order to become social. Furthermore, the discussions on active fatherhood reveal that despite cultural mandates, father engagement can take on very different forms (Adler & Lenz, 2016). For non-traditional families, notions of the standard family create numerous challenges. For example, there are no normative specifications for the position of stepfathers, and thus, the competencies and responsibilities required for dealing with a stepchild are unclear. Should stepfathers assume a conventional parental role or the role of a parental friend? Should they be addressed by their first name or as father? The mother's new partner also does not necessarily become part of the family—they can remain merely a household member. For the children involved, the establishment of a new family also involves great uncertainty. Both rivalry and loyalty conflicts are possible.

Family policy and welfare state regimes

We conceive of family policy as embedded in the overall framework of welfare state regimes. A broad conceptualization of family policy refers to

> what government does to and for children and their families, in particular those public policies (laws, regulations) that are designed to affect the situation of families with children—or individuals in their family roles—and those that have clear consequences for such families even though the impacts may not have been intended
>
> *(Kamerman, 1996, p. 31)*

Cross-national research has not only established that national policies vary in terms of "family-friendliness" in general, but also in regard to the legal options for families that do not align with traditional assumptions of what constitutes a family. Family policies are made in the context of demographic conditions, priorities of the economy and labor market, and considerations about gender egalitarianism and work-family conflicts. The norms and rights to form a family based on surrogacy or technological assistance, adoption, marital status, cultural background or sexual orientation vary in the selected countries. The consequences of these legal and policy patterns on doing family in non-traditional family forms are of particular interest.

Modern welfare states are legally committed to provide social protection against economic, health, age-related, and other risks for the population. Although the welfare state has a relatively short history, it has experienced tremendous expansion in the 20th century. Gøsta Esping-Andersen (1989) initially distinguished three welfare regimes: the liberal or residual, conservative or corporate, and social democratic or Scandinavian models. This first typology was later supplemented by the "Mediterranean" or "Southern European" and the "post-socialist" models. These classifications are based on the way in which the production and redistribution of social welfare take place in a nation-state. For Esping-Andersen, the key criterion is "de-commodification," which refers to the extent to which social policy reduces citizens' (usually men's) dependence on gainful employment for survival.

Although families and their well-being are key concerns in modern society, the connection between family and state remained invisible in most initial welfare state analysis (Neyer, 2021). It was not until feminist critics of comparative welfare state research developed gender-reflective concepts that liberated the welfare state models from their orientation toward male biographies and employment. It became clear that the models presuppose very different benefits for men in the labor market than for women and families. The welfare state can privilege a particular type of family and gender regime, such as the standard nuclear family with a male breadwinner and female carer, via family policy. While universal monetary benefits for parents can help reduce inequalities among families, tax credits and lengthy paid leave for mothers tend to promote traditional family arrangements. Measures to improve the reconciliation of work and family life for all parents, such as access to an inexpensive range of childcare options, support a broader range of family forms.

As a result, family policy is increasingly regarded as a central component of the welfare state, along with other social policies (Neyer, 2021, p. 25). The extent to which women's gainful employment is constrained by policy prescriptions, women's dependence for social security on (male) breadwinners (familialization), and the degree of social support linked to family have emerged as additional criteria for welfare state classification. Welfare regimes are now viewed "through the analytical lens of the family" (Esping-Andersen, 1999, p. 49). The regimes are also distinguished by how responsibilities for work and family are divided among women, men, the state, and the market (Crompton, 1999), by "cultures of care" (Adler & Brayfield, 2006), i.e., arrangements for child care, which can be organized as a service provided by the family and thus mostly by women, or as a public or private service, and "gender arrangements" (Pfau-Effinger, 2004).

Comparative perspective and selection of countries

The departure from the standard family and the diversification of family forms is observable to differing degrees in all advanced countries. A comparative lens to examine variations among countries is necessary in order to understand the extent to which non-standard families are supported in various welfare states. In this context, our interest is mainly directed at family and gender-related policies and based on a legal and social rights approach. Countries with different cultures, laws, and family policies also vary in their support for parents and children in diverse family forms. That includes variation in countries' recognition of and granting rights to families that do not conform to the heteronormative patterns of the standard, heterosexual, and biological familial relationships. Governments can both enable and promote family diversity, but also impede and inhibit it. We also ask how doing family in non-standard families is justified and accounted for, both externally and internally, in the face of the dominant cultural prescriptions of the biologically based nuclear family, heteronormativity, and the gender binary. The book problematizes the preeminence of data collection, research, and policy that focuses exclusively on standard families.

The selection criteria for the nine OECD countries in this volume included: (1) economic advancement and democratic political order, (2) welfare state classification, (3) geographical coverage, and (4) cultural variety. The countries selected were Canada, France, Germany, Japan, Lithuania, Spain, Sweden, the UK, and the US. Thus, the countries cover three continents, represent different welfare regimes, and reflect differences in family policy, family law, and cultural traditions. All country chapters are written by family researchers from the respective nations.

The US, the UK, and Canada represent different versions of the cluster of "liberal welfare states." In the multicultural US, the dual-earner model and private child care are highly prevalent. There is no public support for family leave, and the welfare system encourages traditional marriage. In contrast, Canada features more generous family policies and public day care, as well as Indigenous, English, and French variations. Although the UK has more generous family policies than the US, its dual-earner gender regime involves fewer full-time-working mothers. Formal child care is widespread but receives little public financial support. France and Germany, by contrast, are considered to be conservative welfare states. However, France is a welfare state with a longer tradition of comprehensive public child care and a high female labor force participation rate. France's policies also have historically been more oriented toward family diversity, gender diversity, and the dual-earner model. This includes support for employed parents, particularly mothers, and the acknowledgment of lifestyles beyond heteronormativity. Germany is a modified conservative welfare state because unification combined two different welfare regimes. West Germany was long considered the prototype of the conservative welfare regime, featuring a traditional breadwinner model and a family policy focused on long leave for mothers. In East Germany, by contrast, the dual-earner system included an expansive affordable childcare system. These differences have not disappeared, even though a one-and-half breadwinner model now dominates and childcare facilities were expanded in the West (Lenz & Adler, 2010).

Japan, as a familialist or "Confucian" welfare state, underwent rapid development after World War II. However, its strong cultural traditions often collide with changes in contemporary family life. Thus, despite higher women's labor force participation, women are expected to care for children and elders in multigenerational households. As a consequence, Japan's fertility rate is one of the lowest in the world. Similarly, Spain's Southern or familialist welfare state has historically provided little state support for families and featured a traditional gender regime. However, Spain recently experienced a rapid transformation in family diversity and very low fertility rates, as well as a shift toward more progressive family policies. Sweden is part of the Social Democratic or Nordic welfare state cluster and is considered to have a very generous family policy regime. In particular, single mothers are supported to the same extent as married mothers. Single, divorced, and gay fathers have the same rights as those in a traditional marriage arrangement. The Eastern European country of Lithuania belongs to the post-socialist cluster of welfare states. As such, Lithuania has undergone major political and economic regime changes while adhering to traditional ideas about the family. At the same time, it features the highest labor force participation rates for women.

The comparative indicators

To facilitate cross-country comparisons, the country chapters have an identical structure. Each chapter begins with an introduction outlining the historically significant developments that contextualize the country's current family diversity. The country-specific definition of family in official statistics will be explained. In the following section, data on the developments in union formation and dissolution, fertility, and living arrangements since 2000 will be presented. The limitations of the data in capturing the extent of family diversity are also highlighted. The third part discusses current research on non-standard family forms and on how they do family. This overview also highlights the impact on family life of political and legal regulations, processes of social change, and technological innovations, particularly in the context of reproductive medicine. The final section identifies the need for research and also addresses the effects of the COVID-19 pandemic on the various family forms.

In order to better compare the nine countries, the contributions present selected indicators for demographic processes and living arrangements in tables. These indicators will be briefly described here.

In terms of union formation, the data include the average age at first marriage and the crude marriage rate (CMR), which is the number of marriages (first and remarriages) in a year per 1,000 inhabitants. These data come from the national official marriage statistics. For union dissolution, the crude divorce rate (CDR), or in some cases, the total divorce rate (TDR) is reported. The CDR is the number of marriages in a year per 1,000 inhabitants. The TDR indicates how many marriages would end in divorce if the divorce frequency of the respective calendar year were to remain constant over a period of 25 years.

The total fertility rate (TFR) indicates how many children a woman would have in the course of her life if her fertility behavior were the same as that of all women between the ages of 15 and 49 in the year under consideration. The final number of children born, or cohort fertility rate, is known only after the completion of the fertile phase and thus is compiled after the relevant cohort of women has reached the age of 45 or 50. Before that, only estimates are possible. It is common practice to report these fertility indicators for women only. In some countries, however, they are now also available for men. In addition, the tables present the average age at birth of the first child or of all children, the percentage of non-marital births, and the proportion of women who never have a child. The non-marital births are measured by the share of non-marital births of the total number of live births a year. The proportion of women who never gave birth to a child out of all women of the respective birth cohort is presented.

For information on living arrangements, different data are available in the selected countries. Family statistics are generally presented as household statistics. As a basic unit, the household is recorded as a residential and economic unit. Official statistics vary in their definition of what is counted as a family. In order to provide comparable information despite the heterogeneity of the data, the country chapters show the proportion of adults living in different living arrangements (e.g., with a spouse, unmarried with a partner, single parent with one or more children, or living alone) and the proportion of household including various family forms.

Our concluding chapter will first present a comparative overview of the observed changes in the demography and living arrangements in the nine countries, including an evaluation of the indicators in relation to OECD averages. In addition, we offer a comparison of current patterns related to the trends regarding "non-standard" family forms in the countries. We then discuss how family diversity is promoted and curtailed in the laws and family policies of the different welfare states. Of interest are those changes in gender regimes and policies that move beyond heteronormativity, biological reductionism, and ethnic homogeneity. Finally, based on the lessons learned from the comparisons of the countries, we make recommendations for new developments in research and family policies addressing the support of diversity.

References

Adler, M. A., & Brayfield, A. (2006). Gender regimes and cultures of care. *Marriage & Family Review, 39*(3–4), 229–253.

Adler, M. A., & Lenz, K. (Eds.). (2016). *Father involvement in the early years. An international comparison of policy and practice.* Policy Press.

Baca Zinn, M., & Wells, B. (2000). Diversity within Latino families: New lessons for family social science. In D. H. Demo, K. R. Allen, & M. A. Fine (Eds.), *Handbook of family diversity* (pp. 252–273). Oxford University Press.

Baykara-Krumme, H. (2015). Migrantenfamilien. In P. B. Hill & J. Kopp (Eds.), *Handbuch Familiensoziologie* (pp. 709–736). Springer VS.

Buschner, A., & Bergold, P. (2017). Regenbogenfamilien in Deutschland. In P. Bergold, A. Buschner, B. Mayer-Lewis, & T. Mühling (Eds.), *Familien mit multipler Elternschaft. Entstehungszusammenhänge, Herausforderungen und Potentiale* (pp. 143–172). Budrich Barbara.

Cherlin, A. J. (2004). The deinstitutionalization of American marriage. *Journal of Marriage and Family, 66*(4), 848–861. Retrieved June 22, 2021, from http://www.jstor.org/stable/3600162

Cherlin, A. J. (2020). Degrees of change. An assessment of the deinstitutionalization of marriage thesis. *Journal of Marriage and Family, 82*(1), 62–80.

Crompton, R. (Eds.). (1999). *Restructuring gender relations and employment. The decline of the male breadwinner.* Oxford Univ. Press.

Eggen, B. (2020). Diversität von Familie und Elternschaft. *Archiv für Wissenschaft und Praxis der sozialen Arbeit, 51*(1), 4–16.

Esping-Andersen, G. (1989). *The three worlds of welfare capitalism.* Wiley, J.

Esping-Andersen, G. (1999). *Social foundations of postindustrial economies.* Oxford University Press.

Finch, J. (2007). Displaying families. *Sociology, 41*(1), 65–81.

Furstenberg, F. F., Harris, L. E., Pesando, L. M., & Reed, M. N. (2020). Kinship practices among alternative family forms in Western industrialized societies. *Journal of Marriage and Family, 82*, 1403–1430. https://doi.org/10.1111/jomf.12712

Harris, S. R. (2008). What is family diversity? Objective and interpretive approaches. *Journal of Family Issues, 29*, 1407–1425.

Jurczyk, K., & Meysen, T. (2020). UnDoing family: Zentrale konzeptuelle Annahmen. Feinjustierungen und Erweiterungen. In K. Jurczyk (Eds.), *Doing und undoing family. Konzeptionelle und empirische Entwicklungen* (pp. 26–54). Beltz: Beltz Juventa.

Kamerman, S. B. (1996). Child and family policies: An international overview. In E. F. Zigler, S. L. Kagan, & N. W. Hall (Eds.), *Children, families, and government: Preparing for the twenty-first century* (2nd ed., pp. 31–48). Cambridge University Press.

Lenz, K. (2013). Was ist eine Familie? Konturen eines universalen Familienbegriffs. In D. Krüger, H. Herma, & A. Schierbaum (Eds.), *Familie(n) heute : Entwicklungen, Kontroversen, Prognosen* (pp. 104–125). Beltz Juventa.

Lenz, K., & Adler, M. A. (2010). *Geschlechterverhältnisse. Einführung in die sozialwissenschaftliche Geschlechterforschung.* Band 1. Juventa.

Moore, M. R., & Stambolis-Ruhstorfer, M. (2013). LGBT sexuality and families at the start of the twenty-first century. *Annual Review of Sociology, 39*, 491–507.

Morgan, D. H. J. (1999). Risk and family practices: Accounting for change and fluidity in family life. In E. B. Silva & C. Smith (Eds.), *The New Family?* (pp. 13–30). SAGE.

Naples, N. A. (2001). A member of the funeral: An introspective ethnography. In M. Berstein & R. Reimann (Eds.), *Queer families, queer politics: Challenging culture and the state* (pp. 21–43). New York: Columbia University Press.

Nelson, M. K. (2006). Single mothers "Do" family. *Journal of Marriage and Family, 68*, 781–795.

Neyer, G. (2021). Welfare state regimes, families policies and family behaviour. In N. F. Schneider & M. I. Kreyenfeld (Eds.), *Research handbook on the sociology of the family* (pp. 22–41). Elgar.

Nordqvist, P. (2021). Telling reproductive stories: Social scripts, relationality and donor conception. *Sociology, 55*(4), 677–695.

Passet-Wittig, J., & Bujard, M. (2021). Medically assisted reproduction in developed countries. Overview and societal challenges. In N. F. Schneider & M. Kreyenfeld (Eds.), *Research handbook on the sociology of the family* (pp. 417–428). Elgar.

Perry-Jenkins, M., & Gerstel, N. (2020). Work and family in the second decade of the 21st century. *Journal of Marriage and Family, 82*(1), 420–453.

Pfau-Effinger, B. (2004). *Development of culture, welfare states and women's employment in Europe*. Ashagate.

Reczek, C. (2020). Sexual- and gender-minority families. A 2010 to 2020 decade in review. *Journal of Marriage and Family, 82*(1), 300–325. https://doi.org/ 10.1111/ jomf.12607

Seltzer, J. A. (2019). Family change and changing family demography. *Demography, 56*(2), 405–426.

Sunderam, S., Kissin, D. M., Zhang, Y., Jewett, A., Boulet, S. L., Warner, L., Kroelinger, C. D., & Barfield, W. D. (2022) Assisted reproductive technology surveillance – United States, 2018. *MMWR Surveillsnce Summary, 71*(4), 1–19. https:// doi.org/10.15585/mmwr.ss7104a1. PMID: 35176012; PMCID: PMC8865855.

Thoma, M. E., Boulet, S., Martin, J. A., & Kissin, D. (2014). Births resulting from assisted reproductive technology: Comparing birth certificate and National ART Surveillance System Data, 2011. *National Vital Statistics Reports, 63*(8), 1–11. https:// www.cdc.gov/nchs/data/nvsr/nvsr63/nvsr63_08.pdf

Van Hook, J., & Glick, J. E. (2020). Spanning borders, cultures, and generations: A decade of research on immigrant families. *Journal of Marriage and Family, 82*, 224–243.

Vaskovics, L. A. (2011). Segmentierung und Multiplikation von Elternschaft. Konzept zur Analyse von Elternschafts- und Elternkonstellationen. In D. Schwab und L. A. Vaskovics (Eds.), *Pluralisierung Von Elternschaft und Kindschaft. Familienrecht, -Soziologie und -psychologie Im Dialog* (pp. 11–40). Barbara Budrich.

Widmer, E. (2021). Family diversity in a configurational perspective. In N. F. Schneider & M. Kreyenfeld (Eds.), *Research handbook on the sociology of the family* (pp. 60–72). Elgar.

Zegers-Hochschild, F., Adamson, G. D., Dyer, S., Racowsky, C., de Mouzon, J., Sokol, R., Rienzi, L., Sunde, A., Schmidt, L., Cooke, I. D., Simpson, J. L., & van der Poel, S. (2017). The international glossary on infertility and fertility care, 2017. *Human Reproduction, 32*(9), 1786–1801.

2

DIVERSITY IN CANADIAN FAMILIES

Choices, constraints, and social policy dimensions

Barbara A. Mitchell and Lun Li

The cultural and policy context of doing family

Canadian family life and its social policy regime have undergone significant transformation since its Confederacy in 1867. After that time, many socio-cultural, technological, and political shifts gradually began to take place. These changes occurred in tandem with the emergence of a social welfare state and most notably after World War II (Statistics Canada, 2014). Roughly occurring between the 1940s and the 1960s, this era celebrated and normalized the most desirable or "ideal" family as family-centric, nuclear, and heteronormative. This North American family model consisted of a suburban stay-at-home wife and breadwinner husband, and many families (especially white middle-class ones) conformed to this Euro-Canadian ideal (Comacchio, 2014).

Yet, as documented by national data sources (e.g., Statistics Canada) and prominent scholars, such as Gee (2000), this brief post-war time period and highly prevalent family type represented a "historical blip." Indeed, Canadian families have almost always been complex and highly diverse, although for a variety of reasons (e.g., Milan, 2000; Mitchell, 2021). Lone-parent families, for instance, were already prevalent in the early decades of the 20th century, representing 12.2% of census families in 1941 (versus 16.1% in 2016; Statistics Canada, 2017a). However, lone parenthood was historically formed through widowhood or desertion of a spouse rather than separation, divorce, or personal choice (Milan, 2000; Mitchell, 2021). While single-parent households tend to be headed by women, more father-headed lone-parent households are emerging (Statistics Canada, 2017a).

Mid-century Canada was characterized by the glorification of the nuclear family, defined by the traditional hierarchies of gender and age (Comacchio, 2014). It was also a time of relative economic prosperity following the war,

DOI: 10.4324/9781003193500-2

whereby many homemaker wives and mothers could rely on a single wage-earning husband. By the end of the 1960s, significant historical shifts included the rise of the feminist, gay, and civil rights movements. The legalization of the birth control pill in the late 1960s also provided women with more choice and agency over their reproductive decisions. Other cultural and socio-demographic events (e.g., immigration, delayed family formation) and economic (e.g., the rise of female labor force participation) and technological advances (e.g., medical and technological advances) were also well underway by 1980 (Mitchell, 2021).

There has also been an overall declining influence of religion, although increased immigration, especially from Asian countries over the past several decades, has contributed to a multi cultural society, especially in large urban areas (Battams, 2018; Mitchell, 2021). According to the Canadian 2016 Census, 21.9% of the total population were first-generation foreign-born immigrants, the highest proportion ever recorded in history (Statistics Canada, 2017a). This rise in immigration has been accompanied by less ethnic/religious homogeneity in partnership formation, with approximately 7% of all common-law or legal marriages in Canada now involving partners of different racial/ethnic backgrounds or "mixed unions" (Aathavan, 2021; Maheux, 2014).

Additionally, the number of multi-generational households has grown recently. However, they represent fewer than 5% of all Canadian households, and most of these multi-generational families include two foreign-born parents and their Canadian-born children (Statistics Canada, 2017a). Cultural and economic factors, such as norms related to extended family living and financial support across the generations, play a role in their formation. For example, multi-generational families are more common among Indigenous groups, and some of these households may be "skipped-generation," meaning that there is no middle generation, or parent, present in the home (Statistics Canada, 2014, 2017a).

Other notable family changes include a rising average age of family formation, including the age at which young adult (permanently) leave the parental home, and the timing of marriage and parenthood, although these ages have fluctuated historically (Mitchell, 2006, 2021, Mitchell & Lennox, 2020). Many of these transformations have occurred in response to changing gender roles and altered economic conditions, such as the high cost of housing and raising children. Delayed family transitions can be traced to people being heavily impacted by feminist movements, particularly during the "Women's Liberation Movement" of the 1970s. Social activists instigated important political pressure groups, such as the National Committee on the Status of Women in 1972, and were instrumental in challenging gender inequality, sexist policies, and prevailing ideologies of "doing gender." These efforts also paved the way for more women entering higher education; full-time employment, including career jobs; and gaining economic independence from men. Changing gender roles and growing gender equity were also accompanied by delayed parenthood and lower fertility levels as family sizes began to shrink (Clarke & Albanese, 2014). State-supported maternity and parental leave legislation in the 1990s were also critical to "new" configurations of families by allowing more involvement of fathers in parenting and more mothers to work as sole breadwinners (Beaupré et al., 2010).

Heterosexual legal marital relationships, while still popular, have also declined and become more fragile, especially with the rise in divorce and cohabiting unions (Statistics Canada, 2014). With the liberalization of divorce laws in 1968 and later in 1985, the grounds for granting divorces were eased (e.g., the minimal separation time was reduced to one year). While cohabitation has become increasingly popular, legally recognized, and less stigmatized, some cultural/ ethnic groups continue to disapprove of any non-traditional marital union (e.g., Mitchell, 2021).

Moreover, the legalization of same-sex marriage in 2005 represented a watershed moment as the law and general public recognized, and became more approving of, a wider array of intimate relationships. In 2016, federal legislation was introduced to protect transgender rights and prevent discrimination based on gender identity. Advances in medically assisted reproduction (MAR) have also expanded choices in family life in important ways.

Another major contextual change is rapid population aging due to the higher life expectancy, resulting in more people over the age of 65 than under the age of 14 (Statistics Canada, 2017a). Indeed, today almost one-third of the Canadian population is part of the baby boom generation (born roughly between 1946 and 1965). Shifts in the population age structure have brought significant implications for women. Caregiving for seniors, for instance, predominantly falls on the shoulders of women who may also be part of the "sandwich generation," simultaneously juggling the demands of caring for children and elders (Mitchell, 2014, 2021).

Additionally, changes in MAR have allowed women experiencing infertility unprecedented opportunities to become parents, especially later in life. It is estimated that approximately 16% (1 in 6) of Canadian couples experience infertility and that this number has doubled since the 1980s (Government of Canada, 2021). Similarly on the rise, albeit relatively less common, is surrogacy (Cattapan et al., 2018). However, the federal government prohibited commercial surrogacy in 2004, making it a criminal act to pay a woman beyond expenditures for serving as a surrogate (Snow, 2016).

Same-sex couples can also become parents through surrogacy or adoption, which was made possible through changes to the Civil Marriage Act of 2005, but adoption rights may vary from province to province. In a similar vein, parenthood via adoption can occur in other contexts (e.g., a stepparent can legally adopt a stepchild), or by fostering. It is also important to note that there has been an over-representation of Indigenous youth in state care. This trend has been attributed to the legacy of Canada's colonial history and racist policies and practices that forcibly separated many Indigenous children from their parents (Jacobs, 2014; Johnson, 1983; see Stote, 2015 for a history of the forced sterilization of Indigenous women within the context of cultural genocide).

Furthermore, while couple relationships have always been the norm, there appears to have been an emergence of consensual non-monogamies (Boyd, 2017a). This term is used to describe romantic relationships that are sexually and/ or emotionally non-exclusive (Grunt-Mejer & Campbell, 2016; Mitchell, 2021). These relationships are legal in Canada, unlike bigamy and polygamy, which prohibit people in more than one dyadic marriage. Yet, there has been growing awareness in some courts that a family can legally include more than two parents and that this situation may be in the best interest of children (Boyd, 2017a). For instance, in 2021, the British Columbian Supreme Court recognized three adults as parents on a child's birth certificate, arguing that the Family Law Act needs to formally recognize polyamorous families (Mulgrew, 2021).

Indeed, within this backdrop of significant and evolving complex social change, family policy has been central to and for Canadians in terms of defining their "acceptable" structures and forms. Policies also determine the eligibility and provisions for state sanctions and support (Krull, 2014). Yet, historically, policies have been premised on a patriarchal and paternalistic heterosexual male as breadwinner model of "the family" (Eichler, 1983; Luxton, 1997). Thus, laws were discriminatory toward women and sexual/ethnic minorities. Moreover, despite lacking a cohesive national policy, Canada's social welfare regime has been labeled a social welfare state, falling between Western European and US models (Béland et al., 2020; Krull, 2014).

Overall, altering structures, forms, and meanings of families have had profound policy implications. Government-based or other official agency-based definitions of families have also varied over time and can vary across domains (e.g., immigration policy, marriage, and divorce laws). These definitions determine who may receive certain formal and informal rights, entitlements, and benefits. For example, an individual may not be able to "legally" immigrate under a family reunification policy if they fall outside certain requirements (Mitchell, 2021).

Statistics Canada, the official census and survey agency for Canada, uses two complementary definitions of family: the census family and the economic family (neither of which would include non-relatives such as "roommates"):

> The census family is the narrower concept, defined by couples living together, with or without children, and lone parents living with their children (biological or adoptive). The economic family is broader, and refers to two or more persons living together who are related to each other by blood, marriage, common-law union, adoption or a foster relationship. All people in a census family are part of one economic family. If there are additional relatives living with them, those people are also in the economic family. The additional relatives, if two or more, may also be in a census family among themselves, provided they are a couple with or without children or a lone parent with children.
>
> *(Statistics Canada, 2017b, p. 1)*

While the government and other agencies have adopted very specific definitions or classifications of family, there is no universally agreed-upon definition of family. Definitions of family are in constant "flux" and judicial uses tend to be "inconsistent, unpredictable...and not always effective" (Albanese, 2014, p. 7). Many pioneering and contemporary feminists have also provided insightful critiques of the over-emphasis on structural or compositional definitions of family (e.g., Eichler, 1983; Gazso, 2009). Smith (1999) has also argued that definitions can operate and serve as "ideological codes," which support traditional and patriarchal views of the family.

Moreover, Clarke and Albanese (2014) note that definitions focused on "Who makes up a family?" often miss questions such as "What makes a family?" (p. 204). Thus, definitions of "the family" must focus on the performative nature of family life. For example, some individuals may creatively turn to their "chosen family" (i.e., non-biological kinship bonds) for mutual support and love, a social practice that has implications for policies that define family as related by blood or marriage.

The Vanier Institute of the Family (est. 1965), a major national independent Canadian organization, adopts a perspective that embraces inclusiveness and the growing diversity of families. This diversity ranges from cultural and socio-demographic characteristics (e.g., ethno-racial group, Indigenous status, age, gender, and sexual orientation) and geographical location, as well as differences in attitudes, values, health, and subjective well-being of family members (Mirabelli, 2018).

Far from being an obscure issue of linguistic and philosophical debate, these varied definitions and legal requirements for families have very real consequences for Canadians. Notably, if certain individuals cannot "legally" claim to be part of a family, they may be ineligible for benefits ranging from housing to health care and sick leave. In addition, those labeled or deemed "non-families" (either subjectively or legally) may be considered illegitimate, inappropriate, or immoral within the community or in other settings. Thus, the term and usage of the word "family" is not simply a matter of definitional concept, but a minefield of contested values and power relationships (Silva & Smart, 1999).

BOX: Same-sex couples: Bill C-38 Civil Marriage Act and adoption rights in Canada

Bill C-38 became federal law which gave same-sex couples the legal right to marry. This made Canada the fourth country in the world to allow same-sex marriage. Official Legislative summary:

This enactment extends the legal capacity for marriage for civil purposes to same-sex couples in order to reflect values of tolerance, respect and equality, consistent with the Canadian Charter of Rights and Freedoms. It also makes consequential amendments to other Acts to ensure equal access for same-sex couples to the civil effects of marriage and divorce.

(Queer Events, n.d.)

While adoption rights for same-sex parents vary from province to province, federally, same-sex parents are allowed to adopt in Canada. Before 1995, same-sex couples were not allowed to apply jointly for adoption, and Ontario became the first province in Canada to legalize adoption. This, along with the passing of the Civil Marriage Act in 2005, gave same-sex parents the same rights as heterosexual parents. After Ontario, other provinces like Alberta, British Columbia, and Nova Scotia have also made it legal for same-sex parents to adopt children in Canada. The only challenge that same-sex couples might face is when they plan to adopt a child overseas. This is because many countries are yet to legalize adoption by same-sex parents.

While adoption has been considered legal since 2005, if the same-sex parents opted for conceiving a child then, only the biological parent had legal parental rights. Birth registration of a child is given to heterosexual parents only, and if a parent dies while giving birth to the child, then the other parent will have no legal rights over the child. To be able to legalize their status as parents, the parent not giving birth will have to legally adopt their own child or get a declaration of parentage with the help of an attorney from Edmonton. This loophole has been identified, and while there are experts working toward rectifying the law, same-sex parents are still legally excluded (Prowse Chowne LLP, n.d.).

Empirical patterns of various family forms

This section presents selected socio–demographic family indicators for Canada, drawing upon existing data between 2000 and 2020. The primary sources for the data are from Statistics Canada, including the 2001 and 2016 National Census Data. The Public Use Microdata File of the General Social Survey (GSS) 2001 and 2017 (with a family focus) was used as supplementary data when relevant data are not available from Statistics Canada. Unfortunately, after 2008, Statistics Canada discontinued collecting and publishing marriage and divorce data, including national marriage and divorce rates due to the prevailing conservative political ideology in the federal government, although relevant data are still collected at the provincial level. Moreover, given that comparable data are not always available, some comparisons should be made with caution (for instance, due to the temporal period of data collection or age ranges provided). These data limitations are noted in this section and/or directly presented in the tables.

Union formation and dissolution

In Canada, although married couples still represent the majority of couples, the popularity of cohabitation in common-law unions increases gradually. As shown in Table 2.1, the crude marriage rate in 2000 was 5.1, and this percentage dropped to 4.4 in 2008. A growing proportion of adults choose to cohabit before marriage: in 2006, about 25% of adults aged between 25 and 64 cohabited with their current spouse before marriage, and this number increased to almost 40% in 2017. Overall, there is a rising tendency for couples to cohabit in common-law unions in recent decades (6.3% in 1981 to 21.3% in 2016) (Statistics Canada, 2019).

Canadians also postpone marriage. The average age at first marriage for women was 27.5 years in 2000, and this rose to 29.6 years in 2008. For men, their average age at first marriage was 29.5 and 31 years in 2000 and 2008,

TABLE 2.1 Selected demographic indicators for Canada, 2000 and latest available data

	2000	Latest available data	
Crude marriage rate[a]	5.1	2008	4.4
Mean age at first marriage[a]			
of women	27.5	2008	29.6
of men	29.5	2008	31.0
Crude divorce rate	2.3	2020	1.1
Remarriage rate[b]			
of women	34.0 (2001)	2017	34.3
of men	48.8 (2001)	2017	50.8
% of adults > 15 never married	27.1	2019	31.4
of women	24.8	2019	28.9
of men	29.6	2019	34.0
Total fertility rate	1.49	2019	1.47
Mean age at first birth			
of women	27.1	2019	29.4
% non-marital births	26.8	2019	29.7
% of women aged 40–44 who had never given birth	13.5 (2001)	2011	16.3
Cohorts	1950		1970
Completed fertility/cohort	1.93		1.77
% of women aged 40–44 who had never given birth[b]	13.9		18.5

a Statistics Canada stops providing these data from 2008.
b Calculated based on General Social Survey 2001 and 2017.
Sources: Statistics Canada: Crude marriage rates, all marriages; number of divorces and divorce indicators; Table 2.3 Marriages and average age at first marriage, 1971 to 2002; Fertility: Fewer children, older moms; Births, 2019; Crude divorce rate, 2020; 2001 Census of Canada; Divorce, 1999 and 2000; Marital Status: Overview, 2011; Human Fertility Data base: Canada.

respectively. National-level data are not available after 2008. In 2016, the average age at the first marriage in the province of Quebec was 33.4 and 31.9 years for men and women, respectively. The proportion of married young Canadians also decreased in the past couple of decades (Statistics Canada, 2021). In 2000, 7.3% of those aged between 20 and 24 years were married, and during the past 5 years, the marriage rate among this age group is stably around 3.5%. The marriage rate of Canadians aged between 25 and 29 years also declined from 31% in 2000 to 20% during the past 5 years.

Turning to union dissolution and remarriage, the crude divorce rate was 2.3 in 2000 and 2.1 in 2008, respectively. According to a recent report (The Vanier Institute of the Family, 2020), the annual divorce rate started to decline since the early 2000s, and there were about six divorces per 1,000 married women in 2016. With regard to remarriage, among those aged 15 years and older, 34% of women and 48.8% of men chose to marry again after their first marriage ended due to divorce or death of spouse before 2001. In 2017, the proportion of people who married again after the end of first marriage was slightly higher for both women and men, at 34.3% and 50.8%, respectively.

There has also been a growing tendency away from "traditional marriage" for both men and women. Notably, in 2000, 27.1% of individuals older than 15 were never married (24.8% of women and 29.6% of men). In 2020, it was estimated that the proportion of individuals who were never married was 31.4%, at 28.9% for women and 34% for men. In 2001, 86.3% of all couples were different-sex spouses. In addition, 30.9% of them had at least 1 child younger than 15 years old in the household, and 52.7% had no children under 15 years old. In 2016, 78.4% of all couples were different-sex spouses. Among these couples, 24.6% lived with at least 1 child younger than 15 years old, and the proportion without a child under 15 years old was 53.8%. The information based on age groups is not available from Statistics Canada. Thus, we provided the age group-specific information based on the Canada General Social Survey 2001 and 2017. In 2001, 30.1% of Canadians aged between 15 and 24 years old were married to a different-sex spouse, and this percentage was 70.2% for 25- to 34-year-olds. In 2017, the proportion of those aged 15–24 years who were married to a different-sex partner rose to 31.1%, while for those aged 25–34 years, the number dropped to 61.7%.

Fertility patterns

The total fertility rate in 2000 was 1.49, and it was 1.47 in 2019, which was lower than the average of OECD countries (1.61). The mean age of women at first birth was 27.1 in 2000, rising to 29.4 in 2019. Also, in 2000, the rate of non-marital births was 26.8%, and this percentage increased to 29.7% in 2019. In 2001, approximately 13.5% of women aged 45–49 had never given birth. By 2017, this rose to 16.3%.

The total fertility rate has been below the cohort replacement level since the 1970s (2.1 children per woman in 1971), and it is now about 1.5 (Statistics Canada,

2018). In addition, the fertility rate for women aged 30–44 years has been gradually increasing since 2000, while a decrease is observed among women aged
15–29 years. The completed fertility rate for the cohort of 1950 was 1.93, and
1.77 for the cohort of 1970. In 2017, 13.9% of women in the 1950 cohort never
had children, and 18.5% of women in the 1970 cohort never gave birth to a child.
These trends reflect a trend toward having fewer children and having them at
older ages, rather than not having children at all.

Changes in household composition and living arrangements

Table 2.2 shows the change in household composition in Canada in the past 20
years. In 2001, 40% of all Canadians were living with their married spouse and
7.8% were cohabiting. In 2016, the proportion living with a spouse or partner was
almost the same as it was in 2001, but a lower proportion was living with a marital spouse (37.6%), and the proportion of those cohabiting was higher (10.2%).
Among Canadians aged 15–24 years, cohabitation is more prevalent than living
with a spouse. Also, about 10% of this age group were living with a partner (3.3%
with a spouse and 7.1% with a cohabiting partner) in 2001. In 2016, a lower proportion of them were living with a partner, with 1.7% living with a spouse and
6.2% cohabiting. For those aged 25–34 years in 2001, approximately 60% were
living with a partner (41.2% with a spouse and 18.9% cohabiting), and roughly
53% of them were living with a partner in 2016 (31% with a spouse and 22.4%
cohabiting). In general, there is a growing propensity for young adults to cohabit,
which correlates with a declining marriage rate over the past two decades.

Intergenerational co-residence households are the fastest growing type of
household in Canada (37.5% increase from 2001 to 2016). Over the past several decades, a growing percentage of young adults live with their parents in

TABLE 2.2 Population in living arrangements in Canada, 2000 and latest available data

% Of persons are living	2000			2020		
	Total	Age 18–24	Age 25–34	Total	Age 18–24	Age 25–34
With spouse	40.0	3.3	41.2	37.6	1.7	31.0
With partner	7.8	7.1	18.9	10.2	6.2	22.4
Child of householder	32.5	75.4	14.5	29.8	76.3	18.4
Alone	10.1	3.4	10.3	11.5	3.8	11.8
Alone with child/ren	4.4	1.9	5.5	4.7	1.2	4.7
With another person(s)	5.2	8.8	9.6	6.2	10.7	11.6

Sources: Statistics Canada: Data tables, 2016 Census; 2001 Census Topic-based tabulations.

the same household. Co-residence statistics include both those who have never left home and those who have returned home as "boomerang kids" (Mitchell, 2006, 2021). Specifically, 32.5% of children over the age of 15 lived with their parents in 2001 (75.4% among those aged 15–24 years and 14.5% among those aged 25–34 years). In 2016, about 29.8% of children over the age of 15 lived in a parental household (76.3% among the age group of 15–24 years old and 18.4% among the age group of 25–34 years). The increasing proportion of young adults aged 25–34 years living at home in the recent decade reflects socio-demographic and economic trends related to later ages of family formation, increased post-secondary education, a rising cost of living, and a more diversified population with more immigrants. Recessionary periods (and the COVID-19 pandemic) have also accelerated this trend, including a tendency for some married couples to live with their parents for housing and economic support (Cherlin et al., 2013; Mitchell, 2021).

With regard to solo living, about 1 in 10 persons was living alone in 2001 (10.1%), and in 2016, this proportion was at 11.5%. In addition, about 4.4% of Canadians were lone parents living with their child/ren in 2001, and this number was similar to 4.7% in 2016. The proportion living with non-core family members was 5.2% in 2001, and this rose to 6.2% in 2016.

Various types of households are presented in Table 2.3. Single-parent families constituted about 15.6% of all households in 2001, including 12.7% for mother-only families and 2.9% for father-only families. In 2016, a slightly higher proportion of families were single-parent families (16.4%), with similar a proportion of mother-only families (12.8%) and a slightly higher proportion

TABLE 2.3 Households in Canada, 2000 and latest available data

% of households consist of	2001	2016
Different-sex spouses[a]	51.0	46.0
with kids <18	30.0	24.4
without kids <18	21.0	21.6
Different-sex partners	10.0	12.5
with kids	4.2	5.5
without kids	5.8	7.0
Mother only with kids	9.2	9.0
Father only with kids	2.1	2.5
Same-sex couple[a,b]	0.6 (2006)	0.9
One person living alone	25.7	28.2

Sources: Statistics Canada: Census Profile, 2016 Census; 2001 Census Topic-based tabulations; Data tables, 2016 Census; Statistics Canada, 2017c: Families, Households and Marital Status Highlight Tables.
a Based on the population aged 15 years and over.
b Same-sex marriage is legal in Canada since 2005, and in 2001, about 0.5% of all Canadians in a couple lived as same-sex common-law partners, and it is about 1.2% among Canadians aged between 15 and 24 years and about 0.7% among Canadians aged between 25 and 34 years.

of father-only families (3.6%). Although the proportion of single-parent families was stable after 2000, the major growth of this type of family occurred between the 1970s and 1990s (Statistics Canada, 2015). Also, most of the growth of mother-only families occurred before the mid-1990s, and most of the growth of father-only families occurred after the mid-1990s.

In 2001, about 0.5% of all couples were same-sex cohabiting partners. In 2006, same-sex couples constituted 0.6% of all couples, and this increased to 0.9% in 2016. Based on the GSS 2017, the proportions of same-sex couples among couples aged 15–24 years (1.0%) and 25–34 years (1.3%) were slightly higher than the general population.

The proportion of unmarried couples among all households was 13.8% in 2001, with 6.3% living as unmarried parent couples and 7.5% as unmarried partner couples without children. In 2016, this type of household increased to 17.8%, composed of 7.9% unmarried parent couples and 9.9% unmarried partner couples. According to General Social Survey 2001 and 2017, the proportion of unmarried parent couples for 15- to 24-year-olds dropped from 2.2% in 2001 to 1.4% in 2017 and the proportion of unmarried partner couples without children from 5.6% in 2001 to 3.4% in 2017.

However, an increasing trend was observed among the age group of 25- to 34-year-olds for both unmarried parent couples (9.2% in 2001 to 10.0% in 2017) and unmarried partner couples without children (9.3% in 2001 to 14.4% in 2017). Also, 25.7% of all households were single-person households in 2001, and this increased to 28.2% in 2016. Based on GSS 2001 and 2017, the proportion of single-person households is stable over the two decades for young Canadians aged 15–24 years (4.4% in 2001 and 4.2% in 2017) and those aged 25–34 years (10.8% in 2001 and 10.7% in 2017).

In summary, families have continued to evolve in recent decades with regard to partnership formation, including changes in marriage, divorce, and fertility. There have also been shifts in household formation, including living arrangements, with increasing numbers of young adults likely to co-reside with their parents, and a rise in single-person, same-sex, and lone-father households. Yet, these trends are fairly broad and mask the diversity that occurs within Canada. There may also be significant regional (e.g., urban/rural) or provincial differences in patterns.

Current empirical research on the various family forms

Reconstituted families (Stepfamilies)

Multiple-partner fertility (MPF), or having children with more than one partner, is a common "family pathway" in Canada, although it is not a new phenomenon (Battams & Novoa, 2020). In the past, widowhood was the primary cause of stepfamilies, whereas current patterns can be attributed to higher rates of conjugal instability and non-martial fertility (Monte, 2019). This family pattern is associated with the rising propensity of cohabiting and married parents to separate relatively early in their lives and then rapidly re-partner and have children in the new union (Fostik & Le Bourdais, 2020). However, despite the rise in reconstituted families, relatively little is known, in part, because of the challenges inherent in trying to identify and document complex family patterns that include coupling, uncoupling, and recoupling (Battams & Novoa, 2020).

Fostik and Le Bourdais (2020) further note that little is known about whether the levels and characteristics of stepfamilies are similar throughout Canada. In order to address this research gap, they drew upon retrospective biographical data from the Canadian 2011 General Social Survey. They find no significant difference across regions in Canada. However, their demographic analysis reveals striking variations in the prevalence and timing of MPF among mothers. Mothers living in the Prairies (Alberta, Saskatchewan, Manitoba) and, to a lesser degree, in British Columbia experience a higher rate of MPF than those living in Ontario and Quebec. Overall, giving birth at a younger age and being in a non-residential partnership is associated with a higher likelihood of MPF. This research has high relevance to our understanding of welfare regimes and family policies (e.g., parental leave and child care) that can influence family behavior across different provinces/territories (Battams & Novoa, 2020).

According to recent data from Statistics Canada, almost 1 in 10 (9.8%) of all children aged 0–14 were living in stepfamilies in 2016, similar to the percentage in 2011 (10.0%). In 2016, 62.8% of children in stepfamilies (6.1% of all children in this age range) were living with one of their biological or adoptive parents and a stepparent by marriage or common-law union. Just over half of them did not have any half-siblings or stepsiblings: any brothers and sisters were the children of the same parent (a simple stepfamily). Slightly fewer than half were living in a more complex situation. This context refers to a situation whereby they had at least one half-brother, half-sister, stepbrother, or stepsister. Over one-third (37.2%) of children in stepfamilies (3.6% of all children aged 0–14) had both their biological or adoptive parents present. These children had at least one brother or sister with whom they had only one parent in common: a half-sibling (Statistics Canada, 2017e).

Canadian stepfamilies experience complicated and variable laws at the federal, provincial, and territorial levels. There are also many biases inherent in policies and institutional processes. While the rights and obligations of stepparents are recognized, they are not the same as biological parents, which can affect issues such as child custody, access, and support (Mitchell, 2021). Qualitative studies on this topic are basically non-existent and/or outdated in Canada.

One-parent and cohabiting families

Single-parent family formation has generally risen over the past several decades (especially father-led households), although historically, this rate and the conditions for it have fluctuated. Most quantitative research has focused on the economic situation of one-parent families, including food insecurity issues (e.g., Sarkar et al., 2020). Some qualitative research has focused on issues of health/well-being and transitions from welfare to work (e.g., Campbell et al., 2016 for a systematic review of Canadian qualitative studies). One innovative qualitative study was done by Gazso and McDaniel (2015), who observed that low-income female-headed families increasingly rely on a wide network of support to supplement the limited, or absent, formal support from the state. Their research explores how lone mothers may actively and opportunistically create "families by choice" (including both kin and non-kin relations) and how economic insecurity gives rise to their family practices.

With regard to cohabiting families, additional statistics reveal that in 2016, approximately 18% of all census families in Canada included a common-law couple, triple the rate in 1981. Quebec has consistently had a relatively high share of cohabiting couples; for instance, in 2016, 40% of people in Quebec were cohabiting, compared with 16% across the rest of Canada (Statistics Canada, 2017d). Moreover, more people are choosing to cohabit before marriage. For instance, according to the 2017 GSS, 39% of married 25- to 64-year-olds cohabited with their current spouse prior to getting legally married, up from 25% in 2006. Moreover, those who had cohabited with their partner had done so for an average of 3.6 years (Statistics Canada, 2019). Some "classical" quantitative research on trends in cohabitation in Canada includes work by Wu (2000), as well as more recent studies on topics, such as how cohabitation affects children's risk of family dissolution (e.g., Pelletier, 2016), first cohabitation and education (e.g., Wright, 2019), and cohabitation and union dissolution in mid-/later life (e.g., Mitchell, 2018; Wright, 2020; Wu & Penning, 2017). Although qualitative studies on this topic are absent, another recent study examined regional differences and the laws and politics of marriage and cohabitation with regard to views on gender equality (e.g., Laplante & Fostik, 2016).

Sex and gender minority

Canada is home to approximately 1 million people who identify themselves as LGBTQA+, comprising 4% of the total population aged 15 and older in 2018. Although the same-sex marriage legislation in 2005 represents a major event, in addition to the protection of gender expression and identity in the *Canadian Human Rights Act and the Criminal Code* in 2017, discrimination remains. For example, there was a spike in hate crimes targeting SGM Canadians in 2019 (Statistics Canada, 2021).

Unlike the overall marriage trends in Canada (which have been declining over time), the number of same-sex marriages has been increasing over the past decade. Recent research also shows that one-quarter of Canada's SGM population were gay men, while 1 in 7 is a lesbian woman (Statistics Canada, 2021). Moreover, half of all same-sex couples in Canada were living in Toronto, Montreal, Vancouver, and Ottawa-Gatineau. In the 2021 Census (data not available yet),

Statistics Canada will be able to help address information gaps about gender diversity by including additional data on trans or non-binary couples.

There remains a lack of studies on many topic areas integral to this diverse SGM family form (e.g., divorce, remarriage for same-sex couples), in addition to data on specific types of other non-gender conforming or non-conventional family forms, which appear to be on the rise such as polyamorous families (see Boyd, 2017b for review). Other examples of some interesting recent Canadian qualitative studies on SGM families include Dyer et al.'s (2020) work on artistic expressions of queer kinship in children's drawings and Travers' (2018) study on transgender children and the day-to-day realities of what it is like to grow up as a non-gender conforming child. Alvi and Zaidi (2021) have also conducted some innovative work on intersectional identities and tensions between family obligations and religious values in Canadian Muslim LGBTQ+ communities.

Adoptive and foster families

One pathway to parenthood is through adoption. The Adoption Council of Ontario (n.d.) defines adoption as "the permanent legal transfer of all parental rights from one person or couple to another person or couple" (para.1). Adoptive parents have the same legal rights and responsibilities as biological parents. In Canada, there are several avenues for adoption (e.g., private, public, international), and laws and policies fall under provincial jurisdiction (Mitchell, 2021). Most adoptions appear to involve adults who are already related to the child, such as a stepparent adopting a stepchild. International adoptions, which are usually arranged through private agencies, are also common (Canada Adopts, 2020). Moreover, with the rise in involuntary childlessness, there also appears to be growing interest in domestic and international adoptions (Albanese, 2020).

National statistics on adoptions and by type are unavailable because Statistics Canada includes adoptive parents with biological parents when counting and measuring different types of families. However, some provinces and regional agencies collect data on adoptions, such as British Columbia. For instance, between 2020 and 2021, 219 children were adopted, with most (71.7%) being adopted from within the province, followed by international adoptions (11.4%) (Adoptive Families Association of BC, 2022).

In 2016, there were more than 28,000 foster children aged 0–14 living in Canada, which was lower than in 2011 at 30,000. According to Statistics Canada data (2017e), more than one-third of these children lived without a biological or adopted parent present in the household (e.g., other living arrangements in this category include skip-generation households and children living with other relatives, such as an aunt or older sibling). There are tens of thousands of children in the child welfare system who are in need of adoptive families, and Indigenous children are vastly over-represented in Canada's child welfare system. Yet, the number of formal adoptions from this source remains relatively low (Albanese, 2020). Many of these children remain in the foster care system. It is also estimated that in 2016, only 0.5% of Canadian private households had at least one foster child aged 14 and under. And although only 7.7% of the Canadian population is Indigenous, they constituted over half (52.2%) of those in foster care (Mitchell, 2021).

Qualitative research on adoption and foster children is sparse in Canada. However, there have been some socio-historical accounts of how cultural genocide, colonization, and discriminatory state policies have created adverse conditions (e.g., generational trauma) for Indigenous parents and their children. These legacies have contributed to their continuing over-representation in the child welfare and judicial systems (e.g., Jacobs, 2014; also see Mitchell, 2021 for review of studies).

Families created by medically assisted reproduction (MAR)

Canadians experiencing infertility as well as single parents and same-sex couples are increasingly turning to MAR procedures to help build their families (Government of Canada, 2022). Although there have been attempts to collect data from medical clinics or organizations in order to provide general estimates, research on these specific trends is lacking. However, data from the *Canadian Assisted Reproduction Technologies Register* reported in 2011 indicate that the use of ART (assisted reproductive technologies) has steadily increased, having tripled in the preceding decade (Gunby, 2017).

Health Canada is responsible for developing policies and regulations under the *Assisted Human Reproduction Act* (for details, see Assisted Human Reproduction Act, 2004). Some provinces/regions and extended health care benefits or tax credits provide financial assistance or programs to support couples who require fertility treatments. For example, on November 15, 2021, Quebec introduced a MAR program, which allows eligible couples treatment services, such as ovarian stimulation and embryo transfers (Quebec Government, 2022).

In Canada, surrogacy is legal, although compensation or commercial surrogacy for fee or profit (including the selling of eggs, sperm, or ovum) is prohibited. As per the *Assisted Human Reproduction Act,* a surrogate mother may only be reimbursed for surrogacy/pregnancy-related expenses, which is called "altruistic surrogacy." Although data are lacking on prevalence and pathways to surrogacy, it is estimated that there are at least 400 surrogacy arrangements made every year. There are seven types of surrogacy arrangements and two types of surrogate mothers: "gestational surrogates" and "traditional surrogates." The most common type of surrogacy arrangement is gestational surrogacy, whereby the mother is unable to carry a baby to full term. Gestational surrogates are known as "gestational carriers" or "host surrogates." Traditional surrogates (involving some form of artificial insemination) are also referred to as "straight surrogates" or "classic surrogates" (Surrogacy in Canada online, 2022). It is expected that surrogacy will continue to rise in the future due to improved reproduction technologies and increased involuntary childlessness and as same-sex partnerships gain more visibility and rights. No known qualitative studies on this topic have been conducted in Canada.

Multicultural and migrant families

Canada is internationally renowned for its embrace of multiculturalism and policies that support immigration and family sponsorship/reunification. Thus, family life has become increasingly ethnically and culturally diverse as a growing number of immigrants and refugees arrive from Asia, Latin America Africa, and the Middle East. The majority of these individuals are officially defined by Statistics Canada as the "visible minority population." As a result of immigration trends, the visible minority population—especially in census metropolitan areas—has grown substantially in the last two decades. The three largest visible minority groups in 2016 were South Asians, Chinese, and Blacks, representing 22.3% of the Canadian population. These groups comprise the top three visible minority groups in the largest urban area (Toronto), while Montreal's top groups include Blacks, Arabs, and Latin Americans. Vancouver's top visible minority groups are Chinese, South Asians, and Filipinos (Statistics Canada, 2017e). With regard to refugees, since 1979, approximately 20,000–25,000 people per year have arrived in Canada as refugees (Mitchell, 2021). In 2016, over one-third (37.5%) of Canadian children had at least one foreign-born parent. It is projected that by 2036, 24–30% of the Canadian population will be immigrants, up from 21% in 2011.

Many Canadian studies have been conducted on immigrant, ethno-cultural, and refugee family life in Canada. Topics range from the effect of state policies on their family life, such as family and spousal sponsorship and reunification (e.g., Satzewich, 2014) to the challenges of assimilation/integration and racism/discrimination for immigrants, refugee, and transnational families (e.g., Kogan et al., 2020; Shik, 2015). Other recent studies (carried out by the primary author) have focused on family relationship dynamics in ethnically diverse Canadian families (e.g., Chinese, Persian/Iranian, South Asian, British), using mixed methods. Some of these topics include parenting and inter-generational conflict (e.g., Mitchell & Lai, 2014) and family stressors/de-stressors (Mitchell et al., 2019, 2021), as well as ethnic diversity and family transitions across the life course (e.g., Mitchell et al., 2020).

Conclusion and recommendations

In this chapter, we have critically evaluated and presented many significant trends in family life, primarily focusing on socio-demographic, cultural, and political changes. Emphasis was placed on historical contexts since the mid-20th century and especially within recent decades, with an emphasis on family change and diversity. We explored changing and varied meanings of families, as well as the institutional and ideological practices involved in defining and measuring them. We have also underscored the importance of situating family life and social change in a relative historical time frame, cultural environment, and socio-political location. Notably, it can be misleading to rely on the prototypical 1950s nuclear family as a benchmark for normative or "traditional" family. Although there has been a general rise in individualization and diversification, Canadian families, in whatever shape or form, have almost always been diverse. Families have also always had to negotiate structural conditions (e.g., policy domains) that have affected their decisions and choices on how to "do" and make family.

Numerous gaps in data availability/accessibility and in research were also highlighted. It was concluded that nationally representative data on family trends have been inconsistently collected, unavailable, incomplete or partial, and not always up to date. Similarly, a review of empirical studies reveals that there is a much greater opportunity for studying areas that have received scant attention in the past or for trends that have emerged more recently.

Consequently, many recommendations can be made for future work. Clearly, there is a need to collect and analyze nationally representative and longitudinal research on a broader array of diverse family structures and forms and their policy implications. Under-represented and emergent groups need to be included in both quantitative and qualitative studies. Moreover, it would be valuable to conduct more cross-national studies using similar indicators and measurements and data collection years. We also need to include and support data collection efforts in countries/nations that have historically been underfunded, ignored, or overlooked. Gaining a better sense of global patterns in family diversity could generate lively policy discussions and debates and ultimately ensure improved policy and service delivery moving forward.

Although it is difficult to forecast how families will look in the future, it is certain that families will continue to change. It is impossible to predict what we will face in our environmental future (e.g., pandemics, climate change, wars, natural disasters), although we will certainly experience many troubled times. Similarly, we do not know what social, economic, political, and technological opportunities and challenges that families will face. However, it does seem likely that families will continue to diversify given projected trends, a trend toward more egalitarianism, and acceptance of non-traditional family forms.

Thus, we know that policies and programs will need to be continually revised or developed in response to the changing life course needs of Canadian families. Notable trends that are expected to persist (or rise) in the near future include delays in family formation and life course transitions, including low fertility and the need for MAR, the growing popularity of non-marital cohabitation, SGM and mixed-race unions, "commuter" or transnational relationships (e.g., due to geographic mobility/dispersion), stable or rising divorce and remarriage, labor force participation of women, population aging, and high rates of immigration.

It is also expected that new technologies (medical, reproductive, electronic/digital) will continue to advance and transform family life. These changes have the potential to dramatically affect not only the structure and forms of families but also the performative nature of "doing" family.

Moreover, in light of the recent COVID-19 pandemic, more research needs to be conducted on how emergent family forms have adapted and reacted to this situation and how they can be better supported. For instance, a recent report found that unique obstacles have been created for SGM Canadians, who already face inequalities in income, financial security, and housing, compared to their non-LGBTQA+ counterparts (Gerasimov, 2021). There is also growing evidence to suggest that many families have experienced high degrees of instability, conflict, and stress (e.g., Fostik, 2020). These types of dire situations are known to constrain many aspects of family life and may contribute to relationship dissolution (e.g., higher rates of divorce and separation), fertility choices (e.g., the postponement of adding children), and changes in household living arrangements (e.g., an increased need for co-residence). While it remains too early to know the full impact of the pandemic on families, future research is crucial to better understand how family life has changed and will continue to change and diversify in the future.

References

Aathavan, K. (2021). *Metrics to meaning: Capturing the diversity of couples in Canada.* Retrieved June 28, 2021, from https://vanierinstitute.ca/metrics-to-meaning-capturing-the-diversity-of-couples-in-canada/

Adoption Council of Ontario. (n.d.). *What is adoption?* Retrieved January 14, 2022, from https://www.adoption.on.ca/what-is-adoption

Adoptive Families Association of BC. (2022). *Adoption stats.* Retrieved January 5, 2022, from https://www.bcadoption.com/statistics

Albanese, P. (2014). Introduction to diversity in Canada's families: Variations in forms, definitions, and theories. In D. Cheal & P. Albanese (Eds.), *Canadian families today: New perspectives* (3rd ed., pp. 2–21). Oxford University Press.

Albanese, P. (2020). *Children in Canada today* (3rd ed.). Oxford University Press.

Alvi, S., & Zaidi, A. (2021). "My existence is not haram": Intersectional lives in LGBTQ Muslims living in Canada. *Journal of Homosexuality, 68*(6), 993–1014. https://doi.org/10.1080/00918369.2019.1695422

Assisted Human Reproduction Act. (2004). Retrieved from https://laws-lois.justice.gc.ca/eng/acts/A-13.4/page-1.html#h-5999

Battams, N. (2018). *A snapshot of family diversity in Canada.* Retrieved May 13, 2021, from https://vanierinstitute.ca/a-snapshot-of-family-diversity-in-canada-february-2018

Battams, N., & Novoa, G. (2020). *Understanding multiple-partner fertility in Canada.* Retrieved January 3, 2022, from https://vanierinstitute.sharepoint.com/sites/PublicWebResources/Documents/Public%20Files/RR_2020-04-14-2_Multiple-Partner-Fertility.pdf

Beaupré, P., Dryburgh, H., & Wendt, M. (2010). Making fathers count. *Canadian Social Trends, 90*, 26–34.

Béland, D., Dinan, S., Rocco, P., & Waddan, A. (2020). Social policy responses to COVID-19 in Canada and the United States: Explaining policy variations between two liberal welfare state regimes. *Policy Administration*, *55*(2), 280–294. https://doi.org/10.1111/spol.12656

Boyd, J. P. (2017a). *Polyamorous relationships and family law in Canada*. Canadian Research Institute for Law and the Family. https://doi.org/10.11575/PRISM/34641

Boyd, J. P. (2017b). *Polyamory in Canada: Research on an emerging family structure*. Retrieved January 11, 2022, from https://vanierinstitute.ca/polyamory-in-canada-research-on-an-emerging-family-structure

Campbell, M., Thomson, H., Fenton, C., & Gibson, M. (2016). Lone parents, health, wellbeing and welfare to work: A systematic review of qualitative studies. *BMC Public Health*, *16*(1), 188. https://doi.org/10.1186/s12889-016-2880-9

Canada Adopts. (2020). *Adopting in Canada FAQs*. Retrieved April 26, 2020, from www.canada adopts.com/adopting-in-canada/adopting-canada-faqs

Cattapan, A., Gruben, V., & Cameron, A. (Eds.). (2018). *Surrogacy in Canada: Critical perspectives in law and policy*. Irwin Law.

Cherlin, A., Cumberworth, E., Morgan, S. P., & Wimer, C. (2013). The effects of the Great Recession on family structure and fertility. *The ANNALS of the American Academy of Political and Social Science*, *650*(1), 214–231. https://doi.org/10.1177/0002716213500643

Clarke, J., & Albanese, P. (2014). Families and health issues. In L. Tepperman & P. Albanese (Eds.), *Principles of sociology: Canadian perspectives* (4th ed., pp. 202–221). Oxford University Press.

Comacchio, C. (2014). Canada's families: Historical and contemporary variations. In D. Cheal & P. Albanese (Eds.), *Canadian families today: New perspectives* (3rd ed., pp. 22–42). Oxford.

Dyer, H., Sinclair-Palm, J., Joynt, C., Yeo, M., & Tait, C. (2020). Aesthetic expressions of queer kinship in children's drawings. *Journal of Canadian Studies*, *54*(2–3), 526–543. https://doi.org/10.3138/jcs-2020-0054

Eichler, M. (1983). *Families in Canada today: Recent changes and their policy implications*. Gage.

Fostik, A. (2020). *Covid-19 impacts: Couple relationships in Canada*. Retrieved January 11, 2022, from https://vanierinstitute.ca/covid-19-impacts-couple-relationships-in-canada

Fostik, A., & Le Bourdais, C. (2020). Regional variations in multiple-partner fertility in Canada. *Canadian Studies in Population*, *47*(1–2), 73–95. https://doi.org/10.1007/s42650-020-00024-w

Gazso, A. (2009). Reinvigorating the debate: Questioning the assumptions about and models of "The Family" in Canada social assistance policy. *Women's Studies International Forum*, *32*(2), 150–162. https://doi.org/10.1016/j.wsif.2009.04.001

Gazso, A., & McDaniel, S. (2015). Families by choice and the management of low income through social supports. *Journal of Family Issues*, *36*(3), 371–395. https://doi.org/10.1177/0192513X13506002

Gee, E. M. (2000). Contemporary diversities. In N. Mandell & A. Duffy (Eds.), *Canadian families: Diversity, conflict, and change* (2nd ed., pp. 78–111). Harcourt Canada.

Gerasimov, D. (2021). *In brief: COVID-19 impacts among LGBTQ2+ Canadians*. The Vanier Institute of the Family. Retrieved January 14, 2022, from https://vanierinstitute.ca/in-brief-covid-19-impacts-among-lgbtq2-canadians/

Government of Canada. (2021). *Fertility*. Retrieved May 18, 2021, from https://www.canada.ca/en/public-health/services/fertility/fertility.html

Government of Canada. (2022). *Assisted human reproduction*. Retrieved January 5, 2022, from https://www.canada.ca/en/health-canada/services/drugs-health-products/biologicsradiopharmaceuticals-genetic-therapies/legislation-guidelines/assisted-human-reproduction.html

Grunt-Mejer, K., & Campbell, C. (2016). Around consensual non-monogamies: Assessing attitudes toward non-exclusive relationships. *The Journal of Sex Research*, *53*(1), 45–53. https://doi.org/10.1080/00224499.2015.1010193

Gunby, J. (2017). Assisted reproductive technologies (ART) in Canada: 2011 results from the Canadian ART Register (CARTR). Retrieved October 25, 2017, from https://cfas.ca/_Library/_documents/ CARTR_2011.pdf

Human Fertility Data base-Canada. (2022). Retrieved January 6, 2022, from https://www.humanfertility.org/cgi-bin/country.php?country=CAN&tab=si

Jacobs, M. D. (2014). *A Generation removed: The fostering and adoption of indigenous children in the postwar world*. University of Nebraska Press.

Johnson, P. (1983). *Native children and the child welfare system*. The Canadian Council on Social Development.

Kogan, I., Fong, E., & Reitz, J. G. (2020). Religion and integration among immigrant and minority youth. *Journal of Ethnic and Migration Studies*, *46*(17), 3543–3558. https://doi.org/10.1080/1369183X.2019.1620408

Krull, C. (2014). Investing in families and children: Family policies in Canada. In D. Cheal & P. Albanese (Eds.), *Canadian families today: New perspectives* (3rd ed., pp. 292–316). Oxford University Press.

Laplante, B., & Fostik, A. L. (2016). Cohabitation and marriage in Canada: The geography, law and politics of competing views on gender equality. In A. Esteve & R. J. Lesthaeghe (Eds.), *Cohabitation and marriage in the Americas: Geo-historical legacies and new trends* (pp. 59–100). Springer.

Luxton, M. (Ed.). (1997). *Feminism and families: Critical policies and changing practices*. Fernwood.

Maheux, H. (2014). *Mixed unions in Canada. NHS in Brief.* 99-010-X

Milan, A. (2000). *One hundred years of families.* Canadian Social Trends no. 56. Catalogue no. 11-008. Statistics Canada.

Mirabelli, A. (2018). *What's in a name? Defining family in a diverse society.* Retrieved May 12, 2021, from https://vanierinstitute.ca/whats-in-a-name-defining-family-in-a-diverse-society

Mitchell, B. A. (2006). *The 'Boomerang Age': Transitions to adulthood in families*. Aldine-Transaction Publishers.

Mitchell, B. A. (2014). Generational juggling acts in midlife families: Gendered and ethno-cultural intersections. *Journal of Women and Aging*, *26*(4), 332–350. https://doi.org/10.1080/08952841.2014.907666

Mitchell, B. A. (2021). *Family matters: An introduction to family sociology in Canada* (4th ed.). Canadian Scholar's Press.

Mitchell, B. A., & Lai, Y. (2014). Intergenerational conflict in ethnically diverse ageing families. *Families, Relationships and Societies*, *3*(1), 79–96. https://doi.org/10.1332/204674313X670151

Mitchell, B. A., & Lennox, R. (2020). 'You gotta be able to pay your own way': Canadian news media discourse and young adults' subjectivities of 'successful' adulting. *The Canadian Journal of Sociology*, *45*(3), 213–237.

Mitchell, B. A., Wister, A. V., & Fyffe, I. (2021). Leisure time satisfaction and activity preferences among ethnically diverse aging parents in Metro Vancouver. *Journal of Cross-Cultural Gerontology*, *36*(4), 387–406. https://doi.org/10.1007/s10823-021-09440-0

Mitchell, B. A., Wister, A. V., Li, G., & Wu, Z. (2020). Linking lives in ethnically diverse families: The interconnectedness of home leaving and retirement transitions. *The International Journal of Aging and Human Development*. Retrieved form https://journals.sagepub.com/doi/10.1177/0091415020943318

Mitchell, B. A., Wister, A. V., & Zdaniek, B. (2019). Are the parents all right? Parental stress, ethnic culture, and intergenerational relations in aging families. *Journal of Comparative Family Studies*, *50*(1), 51–74. https://doi.org/ 10.3138/jcfs.037–2018

Mitchell, P. J. (2018). *Cohabitation among middle-aged Canadians*. Retrieved January 11, 2022, from https://www.cardus.ca/research/family/reports/cohabitation-among-middle-aged-canadians/

Monte, L. M. (2019). Multiple-partner fertility in the United Stats: A demographic portrait. *Demography*, *56*(1), 103–127. https://doi.org/10.1007/s13524-018-0743-y

Mulgrew, I. (2021). Polyamorous parents OK B.C. Supreme court rules. *The Vancouver Sun*, May 26, A4.

Pelletier, D. (2016). The diffusion of cohabitation and children's risks of family dissolution in Canada. *Demographic Research*, *35*, 1317–1342. https://doi.org/10.4054/DemRes.2016.35.45

Prowse Chowne LLP. (n.d.). What are the legal rights for same sex parents in Canada? Retrieved January 3, 2022, from https://www.prowsechowne.com/blog/what-are-the-legal-rights-for-same-sex-parents-in-canada

Quebec Government. (2022). *Medically assisted reproduction program*. Retrieved January 14, 2022, from https://www.quebec.ca/en/family-and-support-for-individuals/pregnancy-and-parenthood/medically-assisted-reproduction/mar-program

Queer Events. (n.d.). Canadian queer history. Retrieved November 23, 2021, from https://www.queerevents.ca/queer-history/rights-freedoms

Sarkar, A., Traverso-Yepez, M., & Gadag, V. (2020). Food insecurity among single parents and seniors: A case study in an urban population in Canada. *Canadian Studies in Population*, *47*(4), 263–277. https://doi.org/10.1007/s42650-020-00037-5

Satzewich, V. (2014). Canadian visa officers and the social construction of 'real' spousal relationships. *Canadian Review of Sociology*, *51*(1), 1–21. https://doi.org/10.1111/cars.12031

Shik, A. W. Y. (2015). Transnational families: Chinese-Canadian youth between worlds. *Journal of Ethnic and Cultural Diversity in Social Work*, *24*(1), 71–86. https://doi.org/10.1080/15313204.2013.838816

Silva, E. B., & Smart, C. (1999). The "New" practices and politics of family life. In E.B. Silva & C. Smart (Eds.), *The new family?* (pp. 1–12). SAGE Publications.

Smith, D. (1999). *Writing the social: Critique, theory, and investigations*. University of Toronto Press.

Snow, D. (2016). Criminalising commercial surrogacy in Canada and Australia: The political construction of 'National Consensus'. *Australian Journal of Political Science*, *51*(1), 1–16. https://doi.org/10.1080/10361146.2015.1108388

Statistics Canada. (2014). *Post-baby boom to the end of the 20th century*. Retrieved May 13, 2021, from https://www150.statcan.gc.ca/n1/pub/91f0015m/2014011/04-eng.htm

Statistics Canada. (2015). *Lone-parent families*. Retrieved January 7, 2022, from https://www150.statcan.gc.ca/n1/pub/75–006-x/2015001/article/14202/parent-eng.htm

Statistics Canada. (2017a). *Families, households and marital status: Key results from the 2016 Census"*. *The Daily* (August 2). Catalogue no. 11-001-X. Ministry of Industry. Retrieved May 12, 2021, from https://www150.statcan.gc.ca/n1/daily-quotidien/170802/dq170802a-eng.htm

Statistics Canada. (2017b). *Families reference guide: Census of population, 2016: Definitions and concepts.* Catalogue no. 98-500-X2016002. Minister of Industry. Retrieved May 12, 2021, from https://www12.statcan.gc.ca/census-recensement/2016/ref/guides/002/98–500-x2016002-eng.cfm

Statistics Canada. (2017c). *Families, households and marital status: Key results from the 2016 Census.* Catalogue no. 11-001-X. Retrieved November 19, 2021, from https://www150.statcan.gc.ca/n1/daily-quotidien/170802/dq170802a-eng.htm

Statistics Canada. (2017d). *Portrait of children's family in Canada in 2016.* Retrieved January 4, 2022, from https://www12.statcan.gc.ca/census-recensement/2016/as-sa/98–200-x/2016006/98–200-x2016006-eng.cfm

Statistics Canada. (2017e). *Immigration and diversity: Population projections for Canada and its regions, 2011 to 2036.* Catalogue no. 91–551. Minister of Industry.

Statistics Canada. (2018). *Fertility: Overview, 2012 to 2016.* Retrieved January 7, 2022, from https://www150.statcan.gc.ca/n1/pub/91–209-x/2018001/article/54956-eng.htm

Statistics Canada. (2019). *Family matters: Being common law, married, separated or divorced in Canada.* Catalogue no. 11-001-X. Retrieved November 22, 2021, from https://www150.statcan.gc.ca/n1/daily-quotidien/190501/dq190501b-eng.htm

Statistics Canada. (2021). *Estimates of population as of July 1st, by marital status or legal marital status, age and sex.* Retrieved January 6, 2022, from https://www150.statcan.gc.ca/t1/tbl1/en/tv.action?pid=1710006001&pickMembers%5B0%5D=1.1&pickMembers%5B1%5D=3.1&pickMembers%5B2%5D=4.1&cubeTimeFrame.startYear=2000&cubeTimeFrame.endYear=2021&referencePeriods=20000101%2C20210101

Statistics Canada. Births, 2019. Retrieved January 6, 2022, from https://www150.statcan.gc.ca/n1/daily-quotidien/200929/dq200929e-eng.htm

Statistics Canada. Census profile, 2016 Census. Retrieved January 6, 2022, from https://www12.statcan.gc.ca/census-recensement/2016/dp-pd/prof/details/page.cfm?Lang=E&Geo1=PR&Code1=01&Geo2=&Code2=&SearchText=Canada&SearchType=Begins&SearchPR=01&B1=All&TABID=1&type=0

Statistics Canada. Crude marriage rates, all marriages. Retrieved January 6, 2022, from https://www150.statcan.gc.ca/t1/tbl1/en/tv.action?pid=3910001101

Statistics Canada. Data. Retrieved January 6, 2022, from https://www150.statcan.gc.ca/n1//en/type/data?MM=1#tables

Statistics Canada. Data tables, 2016 census. Retrieved January 6, 2022, from https://www12.statcan.gc.ca/census-recensement/2016/dp-pd/dt-td/Rp-eng.cfm?LANG=E&APATH=3&DETAIL=0&DIM=0&FL=A&FREE=0&GC=0&GID=0&GK=0&GRP=1&PID=113404&PRID=10&PTYPE=109445&S=0&SHOWALL=0&SUB=0&Temporal=2016&THEME=117&VID=0&VNAMEE=&VNAMEF=

Statistics Canada. Data tables, 2016 census. Retrieved January 6, 2022, from https://www12.statcan.gc.ca/census-recensement/2016/dp-pd/dt-td/Rp-eng.cfm?LANG=E&APATH=3&DETAIL=0&DIM=0&FL=A&FREE=0&GC=0&GID=0&GK=0&GRP=1&PID=113434&PRID=10&PTYPE=109445&S=0&SHOWALL=0&SUB=0&Temporal=2016&THEME=117&VID=0&VNAMEE=&VNAMEF=

Statistics Canada. Divorce, 1999 and 2000. Retrieved January 6, 2022, from https://www150.statcan.gc.ca/n1/daily-quotidien/021202/dq021202f-eng.htm

Statistics Canada. Families, households and marital status highlight tables. Retrieved January 6, 2022, from https://www12.statcan.gc.ca/census-recensement/2016/dp-pd/hlt-fst/fam/Table.cfm?Lang=E&T=11&Geo=00&SP=1&view=1&sex=1&presence=1

Statistics Canada. Fertility: Fewer children, older moms. Retrieved January 6, 2022, from https://www150.statcan.gc.ca/n1/pub/11–630-x/11–630-x2014002-eng.htm

Statistics Canada. Marital status: Overview, 2011. Retrieved January 6, 2022, from https://www150.statcan.gc.ca/n1/pub/91–209-x/2013001/article/11788-eng.htm

Statistics Canada. Number of divorces and divorce indicators. Retrieved January 6, 2022, from https://www150.statcan.gc.ca/t1/tbl1/en/tv.action?pid=3910005101

Statistics Canada. Table 2.3 marriages and average age at first marriage, 1971 to 2002. Retrieved January 6, 2022, from https://www150.statcan.gc.ca/n1/pub/89–503-x/2005001/tab/tab2–3-eng.htm

Statistics Canada. 2001 census of Canada. Retrieved January 6, 2022, from https://www12.statcan.gc.ca/english/census01/home/Index.cfm

Statistics Canada. 2001 census topic-based tabulations. Retrieved January 6, 2022, from https://www12.statcan.gc.ca/english/census01/products/standard/themes/Rp-eng.cfm?LANG=E&APATH=3&DETAIL=1&DIM=0&FL=A&FREE=0&GC=0&GID=0&GK=0&GRP=1&PID=77978&PRID=0&PTYPE=55430,53293,55440,55496,71090&S=0&SHOWALL=0&SUB=0&Temporal=2001&THEME=39&VID=0&VNAMEE=&VNAMEF=

Statistics Canada. 2001 census topic-based tabulations. Retrieved January 6, 2022, from https://www12.statcan.gc.ca/english/census01/products/standard/themes/Rp-eng.cfm?LANG=E&APATH=3&DETAIL=1&DIM=0&FL=A&FREE=0&GC=0&GID=0&GK=0&GRP=1&PID=77979&PRID=0&PTYPE=55430,53293,55440,55496,71090&S=0&SHOWALL=0&SUB=0&Temporal=2001&THEME=39&VID=0&VNAMEE=&VNAMEF=

Statistics Canada. 2001 census topic-based tabulations. Retrieved January 6, 2022, from https://www12.statcan.gc.ca/english/census01/products/standard/themes/Rp-eng.cfm?LANG=E&APATH=3&DETAIL=1&DIM=0&FL=A&FREE=0&GC=0&GID=0&GK=0&GRP=1&PID=57382&PRID=0&PTYPE=55430,53293,55440,55496,71090&S=0&SHOWALL=0&SUB=0&Temporal=2001&THEME=39&VID=0&VNAMEE=&VNAMEF=

Statistics Canada. 2001 census topic-based tabulations. Retrieved January 6, 2022, from https://www12.statcan.gc.ca/English/census01/products/standard/themes/Rp-eng.cfm?LANG=E&APATH=3&DETAIL=0&DIM=0&FL=A&FREE=0&GC=0&GID=0&GK=0&GRP=0&PID=55708&PRID=0&PTYPE=55430,53293,55440,55496,71090&S=0&SHOWALL=0&SUB=0&Temporal=2001&THEME=54&VID=0&VNAMEE=&VNAME

Stote, K. (2015). *An act of genocide: Colonization and the sterilization of Aboriginal women.* Fernwood Publishing.

Surrogacy in Canada Online. (2022). *Surrogacy FAQ.* Retrieved January 5, 2022 from https://surrogacy.ca/surrogacy-in-canada/faq-on-surrogacy.html#how-many-types-of-surrogacy-arrangements-are-there

The Vanier Institute of the Family. (2020). *In conversation: Rachel Margolis on divorce trends in Canada.* Retrieved November 19, 2021, from https://vanierinstitute.sharepoint.com/sites/PublicWebResources/Documents/Public%20Files/AR_2020-02-10_In-Conversation_Margolis.pdf

Travers, A. (2018). *The trans generation: How trans kids (and their parents) are creating a gender revolution*. New York University Press.

Wright, L. (2019). Union transitions and fertility within first premarital cohabitations in Canada: Diverging patterns by education? *Demography, 56*(1), 151–167. http://www.jstor.org/stable/45048070

Wright, M. R. (2020). Relationship quality among older cohabitors: A comparison to remarrieds. *The Journals of Gerontology: Series B Social Sciences, 75*(8), 1808–1817. https://doi.org/10.1093/geronb/gbz069

Wu, Z. (2000). *Cohabitation: An alternative form of living*. Oxford University Press.

Wu, Z., & Penning, M. J. (2017). Marital and cohabiting union dissolution in middle and later life. *Research on Aging, 40*(4), 340–364. https://doi.org/10.1177/0164027517698024

3

THE (IN)VISIBILITY OF FRENCH FAMILY DIVERSITY

Anne-Laure Garcia

The cultural and policy context of doing family

The French governmental interest in families is closely related to a profound and long-reigning fear of population decline. For a long time, France was the country with the largest population in Europe, but beginning in the early 1800s, its demographic growth slowed down. Meanwhile, natality accelerated strongly in neighboring countries. To experience this demographic transition as the first Western country and the crushing defeat in the Franco-Prussian War (1870–1871) legitimated governmental intervention to encourage family building and to nurture the health and well-being of children. Because every single new life was considered precious, the institutionalization of family policy in the Third French Republic (1870–1940) had consolidated around the social duty to protect all children. The collective investment in raising French citizens should be implemented through state institutions. For example, as of 1881, public nursery schools were obligated to provide free care for all children in order to support greater equality of opportunity. For the purpose of protection of unborn children and female fertility, abortion and even the provision of information about methods of contraception were banned between 1920 and 1967.

With the introduction of the Family Code *(Code de la Famille)* in 1938, France's pro-natalist policy was solidified for many decades. It extended family allowances, created in 1932, to all married couples with at least two children to encourage larger families. Allowances were not paid for the first child because starting a family in order to have an heir was considered a matter of course. In addition, financial support to stimulate childbearing is not based on the income of the household but only on the number of dependent children. Regardless of wealth, family allowances were universally increased exponentially for three or more young children. In addition, a fiscal law that was adopted in the postwar

DOI: 10.4324/9781003193500-3

period led to an advantage for households with two married parents and dependent children in order to encourage larger families. Until the end of the 1960s, pro-natalist values dominated French family policy. By the 1970s, demographic considerations were less dominant in family policy intervention. Even though universal familialist values were not completely abandoned and are still existent, social objectives have been introduced in French family policy. New target categories were defined in order to reduce inequalities in conditions of living among households according to the number of children (horizontal solidarity) as well as to redistribute money between high- and low-income households (vertical solidarity). The range of benefits for families has become more extensive and complicated. For example, depending on their income, families can receive allowances for disabled minors since 1971, allowances for childcare costs since 1972, allowances for the beginning of the school year since 1974, single-parent allowances since 1976, or housing allowances since 1977. Through the targeting of low-income families, policy intervention has become a complex system that is "progressively diluting family policy by incorporating it into social policy" (Büttner, 2003, p. 8).

In the 1980s, a new political rhetoric emerged that advocated for an increasing well-being of families based on 'freedom of choice' in the arrangement of their everyday lives. In spite of the gender neutrality of this rhetoric, the focus is primarily on women with young children. In line with notions of social justice and gender equality, the male breadwinner model has eroded and the dual-earner model has become dominant. The ideal of the working mother is supported by childcare by crèches or nannies and by limiting the amount of parental allowance. First, public daycare centers for children under three years were opened mainly in large and middle-sized cities. In rural France, the childcare system is based on independent professional childcare workers who care for the children of employed mothers. In order to limit the employment of non-registered nannies, two new allowances have been introduced. Since 1986, all parents of children under the age of three years can receive in-home childcare allowance, if a nanny takes care of their child or children. Since 1990, parents can obtain another allowance for paying a registered independent childcare worker, who was trained and is supervised by the department of child and maternal protection, if their child or children under the age of six years are cared for. Given that the concept of early and collective socialization of children has a long history and is well received by the French population, many children start attending nursery school by the age of two. As of 2019, compulsory schooling begins in France for all children aged three. The allowance for stay-at-home mothers, which was introduced by the Family Code in 1938, has been abolished since 1978. The French parental allowance, which existed from 1985 until 2021, was initially only granted to parents with three or more children until the third birthday of their youngest child. It was expanded to two-child parents in 1994, and in 2015, this allowance was replaced by a shared benefit for parents. It can be requested by all cohabiting parents for biological children until their third birthday or for adopted children until their twentieth birthday. It was designed to allow both parents to devote themselves entirely to bringing up a child for a period of six months per parent, from the second child onwards for 24 months per parent and in case of a multiple birth with at least three children for 48 months per parent. Regardless of their marital status and their sex category, both parents can take this benefit after maternity or paternity leave. The allowance has to be shared between both parents because the aim of the reform was to promote the involvement of fathers in caring for their young children and to support an early return to employment of mothers. Both parents can receive this parental leave allowance simultaneously or successively. This allowance is not an incentive to labor force withdrawal for well-educated and full-time-working parents because they receive only 389,79 € per month if they completely stop working, 257,80 € if they work part time at most, or 148,72 € if they work between 50% and 80% of a full-time job. Just like the former parental allowance, the shared parental benefit is mainly used by less educated and precariously employed mothers. In 2015, only 13.7% of the mothers and 0.5% of the fathers received the full allowance for their first child, and 13.2% and 0.9% received the part allowance, respectively (Périvier & Verdugo, 2021).

The biggest restructuring of French family policy of the last decades is related to the working time policy. Since 2002, the reconciliation of work and family life has been improved because of the 35-hour workweek. This reduction in working time was expected to improve the work–family balance for parents and to also enhance gender equality. From the age of two or three, all pupils are allowed to be at school all day and in the school care at least four days a week. Most parents can continue to work full-time while having several children, insofar as they share tasks like dropping them off and picking them up from school, they have people who take care of their children on school-free days and vacations, and/or they subscribe their children in a municipal daycare center for pupils. Nevertheless, the time spent by mothers and fathers is still unequal because women continue to perform the majority of parental and domestic tasks.

The dual-earner model has become the norm because of the increase in women's labor force participation, but the two-carer model is still not a commonly accomplished ideal. Hardly any fathers disrupt their employment or reduce their weekly working hours while having children. Helping men to balance work and family responsibilities is a new challenge for French family policy. Based on the model of maternity leave, paternity leave has been introduced in 2002. For all working parents, a leave at the end of pregnancy was introduced in 1946. In the beginning, it lasted 14 weeks, and as of 1980, it was 16 weeks. Its length is increasing with the number of children: 26 weeks for the third child, 34 weeks for twins, and 46 weeks for multiple birth of at least triplets. In 2021, paternity leave was extended from 14 to 28 days and 32 days in case of a multiple birth. In contrast to the mothers, the fathers are entitled to decide if and when they take those days off during the first six months of baby life. In 2013, 7 of 10 fathers used this possibility to focus on caring for 11 days (Antunez & Buisson, 2019).

Transformations of French family policy went hand in hand with legislative reforms of the statutes of the family in the Civil Code. The main guiding principle for these reforms was the removal of inequalities that persisted. The equality between men and women in the preamble of the Constitution of 1946 was facilitated by the abolition of absolute authority of the father over wife and children. In 1970, parental authority was substituted for paternal power, so that both spouses have the same rights. Women are no longer "the eternal minor" (Roussel & Théry, 1988, p. 345) who must first obey their fathers and later their husbands. As spouses and mothers, women are equal to their life partners. The legal hierarchy between children born into a marital or non-marital relationship disappeared in 1972, and all children get equal treatment.

Those reforms facilitate the decoupling of partnership, childbearing, and marriage in France. From the mid-1970s, extramarital cohabitation and parenthood among young people as well as separations and divorces have increased very quickly and have been less and less stigmatized:

> Everyone will be able to choose their own model of coupling: whether to marry or not, whether to precede the marriage with a trial period, whether to set the number of children, and whether to interrupt or forgo the union with their partner.
>
> *(Roussel & Théry, 1988, p. 341)*

Several family forms and living arrangements have become socially acceptable. The formerly dominant standard family model of 'married different-sex couple with children' has lost popularity and is now one among many possible family forms.

Those changes in living arrangements resulted in intensive efforts to adapt and modernize French family law since the late 1990s. The new legal framework structuring couple and family life intends to equalize the rights of partners, parents, and children, who are living in more diversified and complex arrangements. Since 1999, the civil partnership contract *(pacte civil de solidarité—PACS)* allows all unmarried couples to register their partnerships. It gives those living together under a civil partnership, both same-sex and different-sex couples, some social rights similar to those of a married couple. For example, there is no difference between married and PACSed couples in taxation policy. However, in the event of the death of a partner, the surviving PACSed partner is not considered as a widow(er). That is why they are not entitled to the widow(er)'s pension in the amount of 54% of the retirement pension. Furthermore, a PACSed partner is not automatically the heir of the deceased partner. But, if a testament has been drafted, the surviving partner has the same right of exemption from succession tax as a widow(er). PACS relationships are easier to dissolve than marriages. The termination of a civil partnership contract requires only a declaration of one partner. No compensatory allowance can be paid. A divorce takes longer and is more expensive because in the majority of cases, two lawyers and a judgment are needed. Only for divorces proceeding by mutual agreement, it suffices if both lawyers write and send a divorce settlement to a notary after the married partners take a time of reflection of 15 days. The members of a civil partnership still have fewer rights than married couples. They cannot automatically acquire French citizenship after four years, for a long time they were not permitted to adopt a child together, and until 2022 they were not allowed to access medically assisted reproduction (MAR). The recognition of the equality of partnership for same-sex couples led to the 'Marriage for All' act, which replaced the female and male pronouns *husband/wife* and *father/mother* with the gender-neutral terms *spouse/parent* in civil law. Despite "the relative acceptance of homosexuality in French society and the apparent widespread disinterest in the institution of marriage" (Robcis, 2015, p. 447), this draft law provoked vivid discussions and protests questioning the close relationship between marriage and parenthood. Beyond demonstrations with traditionalist Catholic organizations, royalist groups, and neo-fascist associations, heated debates occurred over six months in the medical and parliamentary spheres. In 2013, a law was passed allowing marriage and adoption to same-sex couples. However, same-sex biological parenting still remained impossible because neither same-sex couples nor single persons had the right to access MAR. The universal access to MAR for all persons with a uterus was enacted in 2021. Since the beginning of 2022, MAR treatments are reimbursed by health insurance for all. Embryo donations are only allowed if both parents or women without male partners are infertile with high infertility or likely to transmit a genetic disease. Gestational surrogacy is still illegal in France.

Empirical patterns of various family forms

Two institutions are central for recording and analyzing family statistical data in France: The National Institute of Statistics and Economic Studies (INSEE) and the French Institute for Demographic Studies (INED). Since 1982, a series of surveys on family life based on interviews make it possible to explore fertility patterns in more detail. The last survey *Family and housing* has been conducted in 2011. It contains life histories of around 360, 000 people and integrates new questions about blended families, the PACS, and multiple residences. In addition, a yearly census of the population has been conducted by the Institute since 2004. In 2021, the data for 2018 have been made publicly available. Major changes in family-related trends and patterns are correlated with social transformations in society as well as with legal reforms. Statistics show for example that the decline in stigmatization of births outside of marriage is related to an increase in non-marital fertility; increased labor force participation of women is related to increased divorce rates; and higher education period results in the postponement of first births. However, the statistical definition of family as a household with at least one parent and their child, no matter what age, and the fact that religious and ethnic origins are not registered hide some of the diversification of family in France.

Union formation and dissolution

The mean age at first marriage has increased continuously for the last 50 years, from 22.6 years for women and 24.7 years for men in 1970, to 28.1 years and 30.2 years in 2000, and finally to 31.5 years and 33.1 years in 2018. Since 1976, every year the total number of marriage ceremonies has been lower than the total number of divorces. The proportion of the French population over 15 years of age in the different marital status categories has been stable: In 2017, 40.6% were single, 43.8% were married, 8.3% were divorced, and 7.2% were widowed. It should be noted that since 1999 the category 'single' includes persons who have been registered in a civil union and the PACS is very popular in France. In 2019, there were almost as many PACS agreements as marriages, with 225,000 couples marrying versus 196,000 signing PACS contracts. A large majority among PACSed people are different-sex couples, with 8,400 same-sex unions versus 188,000 different-sex unions in 2016. In the same year, 6,300 same-sex marriages and 218,000 different-sex marriages were celebrated. In other words, despite the trend of a continuous decrease in the number of marriages in recent decades, PACSs contribute to an overall increase in the total number of unions. It is very difficult to interpret the statistics about PACS agreement dissolutions. In 2016, 191,537 new PACS agreements were registered and 84,662 were dissolved. However, a PACS agreement can be dissolved either because of separation from the partner or in order to marry the partner. Indeed, the French civil union is frequently perceived as an official engagement or matrimony on probation, i.e., as an intermediate step for the institutionalization of the partnership. In 2016, 40 972 PACS agreements were dissolved due to separation and 40, 670 because of their marriage.

TABLE 3.1 Selected demographic indicators for (continental) France, 2000 and latest available data

	2000	*Latest available*	
Crude marriage rate	5.0	2018	3.5
Mean age at first marriage			
of women	28.0	2020	31.5
of men	30.2	2018	33.1
Crude divorce rate	1.92	2016	1.93
Total divorce rate	38.2	2017	33.1
Total fertility rate			
of women	1.87	2020	1.79
Mean age at first birth			
of women	27.8	2019	28.9
% non-marital births	43.6	2020	62.2
Cohorts	1950		1979
Completed fertility/cohort	2.12		2.01

Sources: INED; Breton (2022); OECD (2022).

Fertility patterns

In France, the baby boom after the Second World War lasted longer and was more intense than in most European countries. Up until the mid-1970s, birth rates were still high. France had undergone a decline in the number of births, but the total fertility rate (TFR) is higher than in most western countries and has been stable between 1.8 and 2.0 since the mid-1970s. This high fertility used to be explained with a successful public support to alleviate the costs of children for families and the reconciliation between work and family life for all parents. Nowadays, the dominant ideal in France is having two to three children and the percentage of women who remain without children is under 15%, which was lower in comparison with other Western European countries (Köppen et al., 2017, p. 77). One of the largest demographic changes in France concerns the median age of women at first birth: from 27.8 in 2000 it increased to 28.9 in 2020. As shown in Table 3.1, the completed fertility of women at the age of 40 years is relatively stable and childbearing is being postponed. According to Dominguez-Folgueras and Lesnard (2018), postponing parenthood is the consequence of a new parenting norm for women as well as for men. It allows younger generations to complete their degrees, attain their own place of residence, and have financial security before becoming parents (Dominguez-Folgueras & Lesnard,

TABLE 3.2 Population in living arrangements in France, 2006 and latest available data

% of persons living as	2006			2019		
	Total	Age 18–24	Age 25–34	Total	Age 18–24	Age 25–34
Couple with kids	25.2			23.1		
women		5.0	55.2		3.4	50.7
men		2.0	46.7		1.5	42.5
Couple without kids	23.7			24.0		
women		12.4	15.4		9.9	16.6
men		6.8	18.0		6.0	18.9
Child of householder	29.0			28.5		
women		61.6	5.1		64.8	6.1
men		72.7	11.3		73.5	13.1
Alone	14.4			16.9		
women		12.1	11.5		14.2	12.8
men		10.7	17.6		12.7	19.8
Alone with child/ren	3.7			4.6		
women		1.6	9.3		1.6	10.9
men		0.1	1.1		0.2	1.6
With another person(s)	4.0			2.9		
women		7.3	3.5		6.1	2.8
men		7.7	5.3		6.1	4.1

Source: INSEE, MEN7 (2006, 2019).

2018, p. 301). Parents are also less and less associated with marriage: Over 60% of all children born in 2018 had unmarried parents.

Changes in household composition and living arrangements

Table 3.2 shows the distribution of the population across different living arrangements, with the age groups 18–24 and 25–34 shown separately. In Table 3.3, the living arrangements are related to households, and the change from 2006 to 2019 is shown. The proportion of households that are considered to be family households because of living with unmarried 'children' under the age of 25 years has decreased from 26.9% to 23.3%, and the proportion of married couples with children has decreased even from 20.6 to 15.1. At the same time, single households have increased from 33.0% to 36.9%. In most cases, living alone is only a transitory phase after moving out of the parental home, between cohabitations, or before admission into a nursing home. Due to the increase in life expectation and more separations, an increasing proportion of French single households involve senior people who previously lived with a partner and/or children. The basic dichotomy between 'households with a couple with child(ren)' and 'single parent with child(ren)' makes it very difficult to discern an increase in family diversity in French statistics. There are no official data about living arrangements that indicate the sexes of the members of the couples, their religious affiliations, their ethnic background, or blended families. For example, the notion of *familles recomposées* (stepfamilies), that the sociologist Irène Théry (1987)

TABLE 3.3 Households in France, 2006 and latest available data

	2006	2019
Couples (total)		
with kids <25	26.9	23.3
without kids <25	29.3	28.7
Spouses		
with kids <25	20.6	15.4
without kids <25	23.2	21.8
Unmarried Couples		
with kids <25	6.3	7.8
without kids <25	6.0	6.4
Thereof PACS		
with kids <25	NA	2.7
without kids <25	NA	1.5
Mother/fathers only with kids	8.3	9.9
One person living alone	33.0	36.9
Sex-same couples	2013–2017	
Total	39916	
Share of all marriages (%)	3.5	

Source: INSEE, FAM!, Fam2, MEN57 (2006, 2019, Meslay, 2019).

has introduced in French sociological discourse, has been included in political and media vocabulary but not in the categories of official data sources. Remarriages are not a new phenomenon. At the end of the 18th century, 25–30% of marriages that were celebrated were remarriages (Le Gall & Popper, 2013). But since the 1960s, second or third unions are less and less the consequence of widowhood. The stepparents do not take the vacant place of a dead mother or father in a bi-generational family configuration. They are a new additional figure in the families' everyday life. The emergence and the development of their relationship with the stepchildren can happen successively or simultaneously with the bi-parental relationship of the ex-partners who are still co-parenting. Such family configurations pose a challenge for French census statistics because they 'blur' the limits of family and households (Damon, 2013). That is why the same child can be recorded twice in the category 'households with a couple with child(ren)' up until their 25th birthday if they rotate between the housing of their two parents who are at that time each living together with a new partner. Only estimates are possible: In 2018, about 11% of the minor children in France were living in a stepfamily.

Since 2013, same-sex couples have been able to marry in France. In the period from 2013 to 2017, there were approximately 40,000 marriages of same-sex couples. In terms of the total number of marriages, it is a share of 3.5%. According to the available estimates, about one third of all same-sex couples in France are married (Meslay 2019). In French statistics, a complex household is a household with a minimum of two adults who are neither related nor a couple as well as persons who are living in a partnership with more than two adults. It corresponds to a wide range of living situations, such as roommates, cohabitation of single or widowed brothers and sisters in the childhood home, or a polygamous configuration. Nevertheless, many polygamous families are not included in this calculation because only the first marriage is recorded by the French state. The later unions that were celebrated abroad or in religious circles have no legal validity. Moreover, since 1993, foreign citizens who live in a polygamous partnership must choose between a divorce or move out if they want to extend their residence permit or to request French citizenship. That is why many polygamous families are officially registered in different households.

BOX: The metamorphoses of the 'lone parent'

Unmarried women, who gave birth to their child(ren) without living in a partnership with a man, were socially and juridically discriminated against in France for a long time. Labeled as filles-mères (girl-mothers), they were special figures in the French public policies for families since the end of the 19th century (Garcia, 2013). After divorce rates started to increase in the beginning of the 1970s and after the reform of the divorce by mutual consent in 1975, the number of mothers without a husband became higher. Widowed and divorced parents as well as solo women with young children were part of a new category: isolated parents. They were entitled to state aid for isolated parents (1976–2009), had priority for social housing and daycare spaces, and enjoyed fiscal advantages in income tax.

As a consequence of moral liberation and the decrease in stigmatization of lone parents, this category has become less relevant since the beginning of the 21st century. Although one-parent families are still supported in order to reduce the risk of poverty, government intervention no longer focuses on 'mothers without male partners,' but also on single fathers or solo mothers by choice. Since 2022, unmarried women and transgender persons with a uterus, who desire to become solo parents, are allowed to use MAR. No medical reasons are necessary for reimbursement by public health insurance.

Current empirical research on the various family forms

Reconstituted families (stepfamilies)

In France, stepfamilies are defined as households that are formed by a couple, the child(ren) of at least one of the partners from a previous relationship, and possibly common children. In 2019, 800,000 stepparents were living together with the child(ren) of their partners, and about 73% of them were stepfathers. In the same year, the total number of children living with stepparents was 1,699,000. In stepfamilies without common child(ren), the average number of children was 1.9, which is the same number as in traditional families. In stepfamilies with common child(ren), the average number was 2.9.

Stepfamilies are one of the most visible expressions of diversification of family forms in France. A large proportion of stepchildren divide their time between two households. Stepfamilies are defined as "family constellations" (Céline & Bonvalet, 2005, p. 80) that are formed by alternating between several places of residence. In stepfamilies with no common parents and no common family name, the shared residence is a central component for understanding them as a family unit (Céline & Bonvalet, 2005). Moreover, doing family in stepfamilies requires new distinctive rituals that do not conflict with the rituals established in the former and/or other household (Gravillon, 2014). The birth of a new child accelerates the emergence of common family rituals because it provides the feeling of belonging to a stable and sustainable family unit for the stepchildren without biological ties.

One-parent and cohabiting families

Unmarried women, who gave birth to child(ren) without living in a partnership with a man, were socially and legally discriminated against in France for a long time (see Box). Labeled as *filles-mères* (girl-mothers), they were special figures in French family policies (Garcia, 2013). It was thought that births outside of marriage were dangerous to infants because unmarried mothers could abandon or mistreat them without the protection and control of a husband. The perception of lone mothers being disadvantaged victims when compared to married mothers led to the introduction of a specific subsidy measure in 1976, the aid for isolated parents. The isolated parent is a unique French concept that does not exist in other western countries and refers to single pregnant women and parents (generally mothers), who are living alone with their children without receiving any alimony or child support payments. 'Isolation' means the absence of a love relationship that is defined as heterosexual and monogamous. In 2009, the aid for isolated parents and the minimum income benefit were merged so that lone parents no longer wait until the preschool enrollment of their child(ren) before looking for paid employment. For one-parent families with higher incomes, special tax breaks prevent disadvantages resulting from the fiscal support for dual-earner families. In the calculation of the tax deduction (family quotient), their first dependent child counts as much as an adult life partner, and additional children count as much as children of couples.

In France, the category 'one-parent families' is defined as a household with one adult and child(ren). In 2020, 24.7% of the households with minor children were one-parent families; 47.6% included one child, 35.5% two children, 12.0% three children, and 4.9% four or more children. In addition, while 40.5% of those households were below the poverty line, this was the case for only 15.6% of the households with two adults and minor children.

The main focus of the research on one-parent families is the vulnerability of single and separated mothers in disadvantaged working-class areas. They are more likely to live below the poverty line because they are more frequently unemployed, work in part-time jobs, or are employed in unskilled jobs than partnered mothers or lone fathers (Observatoire des inégalités, 2016). In a recent ethnographic study in the disadvantaged areas of a deindustrialized city in Normandy, Deshayes (2018) shows that mothers can positively invest in their maternal identity already during and after separation due to a safety net of family support and social policy. Separated fathers, however, have difficulties maintaining their parental role because they are often unable to play the role of economic provider.

In a qualitative survey with 23 semi-structured interviews, Charpenel and colleagues (2021) describe parenting of single mothers and fathers with minor children in their households. They focus on processes of 'solo parenting' by using the metaphor of a soloist musician who plays alone but who can lean on the orchestra in the background—e.g., grandparents, friends, nannies, teachers—during their performance. Depending on resources, education, and employability, different ways of parenting can be distinguished. Solo mothers with less capital, place more emphasis on their maternal identity and the social marginalization in other social areas, whereas being a solo parent with a lot of capital creates opportunities to diversify social roles. Especially, lone fathers are able to invest in parenting work without negative effects on their career. Besides these differences, a common narrative in the interviews relates to permanently having to prove their parenting abilities.

Sex and gender minority families (SGM)

In France, single and lesbian women were not allowed access to MAR until 2022. Only recently, they gained the same rights as different-sex couples and are now permitted to receive free and anonymous sperm donation. Given that the adoption of children is a very long and difficult process for same-sex couples (Digoix, 2020, pp. 106–108), lesbian couples prefer to carry a child who had been conceived either in a fertility clinic abroad or with a donor from the circle of their acquaintances. Over 90% of lesbian parenting happens in institutionalized relationships, i.e., marriage or PACS (Gratton, 2020a, p. 159), so that the adoption of a child through the partner is a matter of course. According to Emmanuel Gratton (2020b), French male couples who bear children thanks to fertility clinics abroad avoid drawing attention to the medical circumstances of the birth because the use of a surrogate mother is illegal in France. In spite of their right to legally adopt their spouse's children, SGM partners often prefer to remain their stepparent. The possibility of mixed-gender parental dynamics exists for SGM couples inasmuch as they have an agreement to conceive and bring up their child(ren) together (Gratton, 2017). Such co-parenting is based on strategies to find a relationship balance, in which marriage and parenting do not coincide. In those configurations, Gratton shows processes of 'invention of doing family' *("invention du 'faire famille'")* (2017) and observes three models: an exclusive model with two biological parental figures (the biological mothers and fathers) and two stepparental figures; an integrated model with more than two parental figures; and an alternative model with two independent family spaces. From the point of view of the children involved, the different family configurations do not exclude each other: For example, their 'family' can include their solo mother as well as her lesbian ex-girlfriend and their father, his husband, and his stepchildren.

Adoptive and foster families

There are two kinds of adoption in France: a full adoption concerns only children under the age of 15 whose relationship with the original parents does not exist or can be dissolved, and a simple adoption does not sever the link with the birth parents. The adopted minor or major person receives an additional parent.

Since the 1970s, becoming a parent through full adoption generally involves adopting children from abroad, mostly from Africa, Asia, or the Caribbean.

Thus, a pretense of a biological connection between parents and children can rarely be maintained. Those configurations can be considered an archetype of a social, affective, and elective family relationship (Brun, 2021). Ramos and colleagues (2015) show that this kind of adoption also provides a special insight into current parenting norms. Couples and single persons who wish to adopt a child are confronted with the dominant norms concerning proper parenting standards in order to receive accreditation from child welfare services before they can be waitlisted for adoption. This evaluative process reflects public expectations toward all parents, such as constant availability and continuous high investment in or support of the self-fulfillment of their child(ren).

Despite the dominance of the social image of adoptive parents who have fertility issues, the vast majority of adoptions involve stepchildren rather than strangers. In 2018, 9 of 10 legal adoptions were simple adoptions, which serve to formalize long-time emotional bonds between two persons within complex families (Ministère de la Justice, 2020). Since 'Marriage for All' was legalized, full adoptions are also possible for all stepparents. In 2018, 83% of full adoptions of stepchildren happened in same-sex couples, mainly in lesbian couples (Ministère de la Justice, 2020).

Families created by medically assisted reproduction (MAR)

In 2018, one out of 30 children born in France was conceived through MAR and 70% of them were conceived by in vitro fertilization (IVF) (De la Rochebrochard, 2018). About 95% of the children born via MAR were conceived with gametes of a heterosexual couple, almost 4% with a sperm donation, less than 1% with an egg donation, and only 0.01% with an embryo donation. Until 2022, single and lesbian women had to go abroad to access assisted reproductive technologies (ART), and therefore, their children were not included in official statistics. It is expected that the proportion of insemination and sperm donation is going to increase because many single and lesbian women who use MAR do not have infertility problems but need a male donor.

Reforms to the French bioethics law, which regulates the modalities and access to ART, should lead to a reduction in cross-border MAR. Moreover, the heteronormativity and the focus on intra-marital fertilization in French medicine should be reduced. Thus, the new legal framing will facilitate and make more visible the diversification of family forms in France. However, experts expect this biotechnological contribution to the deconstruction of dominant gender and parenthood norms to remain statistically marginal (Rozée, 2019).

Multicultural and migrant families

In France, statistical data distinguish French citizens from non-citizens. In order to get French citizenship, it is necessary to become naturalized on the basis of blood relation, birthright, adoption, or marriage to a French citizen. After acquiring French citizenship, a resident belongs only to the statistical category 'French.' In 2019, among all marriages that have been celebrated in France 80% involved two French residents, 4% two non-citizens, and 15% a French citizen and a non-citizen.

Due to the republican ideal of equality, the use of ethnic and religious categories in statistics is not permitted. Only the INSEE and the INED can request special permission from the National Council for Statistical Information or the National Commission on Computer Technology on Freedom to collect such data for particular studies. Up until now, two surveys *Trajectories and Origins* were conducted. The results for the second survey (2019–2020) have not yet been published. Most results of the first survey concern educational background and labor force participation. The proportion of migrants and the population with French roots that is living together with a partner is similar for all age groups (Lhommeau et al., 2014). The proportion of non-marital cohabitations, marriages, and PACs varies depending on the country of origin. Of all the migrants living with a partner, more than one in four is living with someone who was born in France and 90% with a person with French roots.

Thierry and colleagues (2018) used three surveys to look at the situation of immigrant lone mothers in comparison with French lone mothers and found them to be more vulnerable: 29% of immigrant lone mothers have the responsibility for three or more children as compared to 15% of French lone mothers; 38% are living with a child under the age of six years vs. 31%; 42% have no educational degree vs. 19%; 27% are unemployed vs. 18%; and 10% are living in accommodations without a bathroom vs. 2%. Nevertheless, the immigrant fathers of those children invest more in the relationship to the children: 59% of the immigrant fathers recognize the children vs. 40% of the French fathers; 65% gave their surname to the children vs. 40%; and 40% participate in choosing the child's first name vs. 30%.

Conclusion and recommendations

In France, where family policy has been established on the policy agenda for a long time, people are very much aware of their rights to family benefits, tax advantages, childcare facilities, or public protection in case of absence or death of the second parent. The French accept the intervention of the state. Building on this consensus, reforms and renewals of policies meet changing family ideals and socio-demographic trends quite well.

French public policies have an undeniable impact on the societal recognition of different family arrangements and everyday life of households with children. Among other things, they regulate the balance between family care and employment, encourage a division of labor between parents, and promote gender equality in the private sphere. Since the 1970s, the empowerment of mothers has increasingly been implemented: Women have gained equal rights with the fathers of their children, birth control is covered by health insurance and free until the age of 25, a large proportion of women are unmarried mothers, and maternal employment rates and fertility rates are higher than in most EU countries.

Over the past two decades, demographic developments and various parenthood norms have posed numerous challenges to policies directed toward the elimination of unequal rights among children and between sexes. But the dichotomies 'marital'/'non-marital' and 'man'/'woman' do not reflect the complexity of current family forms anymore. Further reforms are necessary to reduce barriers to father involvement by promoting paternal engagement from the very first day of the child's life rather than by naturalizing maternal competencies in child custody cases or supporting suspicions of pedophilia among single men. In order to account for people transitioning in and out of different family constellations, traditional assumptions about family relationships and the standard family form involving two biological parents should be replaced because they do not reflect the feelings of a large part of the population.

In France, the everyday lives of families and their well-being are topics of research among sociologists and political scientists. Governmental departments, the National Family Insurance Fund (CNAF), or child welfare offices frequently call for studies in order to measure the socioeconomic difficulties in families and to check the effect of redistributive and protective measures. One of the consequences of governmental involvement in emerging research questions, study designs, and methodology is a lack of qualitative and thorough studies about social representations of families, relationships, and siblings.

Due to the universalist republican ideal, it is not possible to measure the plurality of living arrangements. The great barriers to collecting information on ethnic origin, religious beliefs, or sexual orientation prevent the analysis of data that could make family diversity more visible. The increasing variety and complexity of family forms in France are mainly highlighted and analyzed in qualitative studies with quantitative components that are based on questionnaires. This gap in statistics makes it difficult to compare France with other countries.

This chapter has focused on the time before the COVID-19 pandemic disrupted the everyday life of families in France. Owing to the first wave, French President Emmanuel Macron declared a state of war—"Nous sommes en guerre"—in a televised speech on 16 March 2020. French people had less than 16 hours before they were in a near-complete lockdown. This made visible the diversification of family forms as well as the intensity of connection between one or several family units. For example, a lot of students and single adults went back to their parental home, children of medical and nursing staff were sent to their grandparents, or some separated parents lived for a period of two months again together with their young children. It is difficult to estimate whether the pandemic has engendered long-term changes. It has possibly increased separations and led to returns to original homelands or moves from urban centers to villages and small cities. However, there is no doubt that due to the pandemic, an important share of the weddings planned for 2020 were deferred or canceled and that quite a few pregnancies have been postponed (Breton et al., 2021). The magnitude and the persistence of the disruptive impact of the COVID-19 pandemic on French dynamics of unions, separations, births, and relocations of family units remain to be explored.

References

Antunez, A., & Buisson, G. (2019). Les Francais et les congés de maternité et paternité: Opinion et recours. *Études & Résultats*, 1098. Retrieved from https://drees.solidarites-sante.gouv.fr/sites/default/files/er1098.pdf

Breton, D., Belliot, N., Barbieri, M., d'Albis, H., & Mazuy, M. (2021). Recent demographic trends in France. The disruptive impact of COVID-19 on French population dynamics. *Population*, *76*(4), 537–594. Retrieved from https://www.ined.fr/en/publications/editions/Demographic-situation/evolution-demographique-recente-de-la-france-moins-de-naissances-de-mariages-et-de-migrations-plus-de-deces-la-covid-19-bouleverse-la-dynamique-de-la-population-francaise/

Brun, S. (2021). Devenir parent à travers les frontières nationales et raciales. Emparentement et institution du lien parental dans l'adoption internationale. *Revue des politiques sociales et familiales*, *139–140*(2–3), 61–77.

Büttner, O. (2003). France as a family policy exemplar? *Cross-National Research Papers, European Research Centre*, *6*(6), 5–14.

Céline, C., & Bonvalet, C. (2005). Familles recomposées et ancrage résidentiel. *Espaces et sociétés*, *120–121*, 79–97.

Charpenel, M., Garcia, S., Piesen, A., & Pothet, J. (2021). Les effets de la "parentalité solo" sur l'exercice des rôles parentaux et les frontières de l'enfance. *Revue des politiques sociales et familiales*, *138*, 5–25.

Damon, J. (2013). Les familles recomposées. Approche sociologique. *Études*, *418*, 619–630.

De la Rochebrochard, E. (2018). 1 enfant sur 30 conçu par assistance médicale à la procréation en France. *Population & Société*, *556*. Retrieved from https://www.ined.fr/fichier/s_rubrique/28078/556_population.societes.juin.2018.amp.france.fr.fr.pdf

Deshayes, F. (2018). Séparations dans les familles monoparentales précaires. Prise en charge des enfants et soutien familial. *Revue des politiques sociales et familiales*, *127*, 9–21.

Digoix, M. (2020). Introduction – LGBT questions and the family. *European Studies of Population*, *24*, 1–9.

Dominguez-Folgueras, M., & Lesnard, L. (2018). Familles et changement social. *L'année sociologique*, *2*, 297–313.

Garcia, A.-L. (2013). *Mères seules. Action publique et identité maternelle*. Presses universitaires de Rennes.

Gratton, E. (2017). L'invention du "faire famille" du côté de l'enfant en situation de co-homoparentalité. *Dialogue*, *215*(1), 21–35.

Gratton, E. (2020a). La conjugalité gay et lesbienne et ses rapports avec la sexualité et la parentalité. In G. Neyrand (Ed.), *Faire couple, une entreprise incertaine: Tensions et paradoxes du couple moderne* (pp. 145–162). Érès.

Gratton, E. (2020b). The conjugal-parental dynamics of three lesbian couples and the rôle of the outside donor. *International Social Science Journal*, *70*, 25–38.

Gravillon, I. (2014). Beaux-parents, beaux-enfants. Des rituels pour "faire famille". *L'école des parents*, *611*, 21–25.

Ined. *All about population. Data. France*. Retrieved from https://www.ined.fr/en/everything_about_population/data/france/births-fertility/cohort-fertility/

Insee, FAM1. *Nombre de familles selon le type de famille et le nombre d'enfants de moins de 25 ans en 2006.* Retrieved from https://www.insee.fr/fr/statistiques/zones/2028213?debut=0&q=FAM1&sommaire=2130729

Insee, FAM1. *Nombre de familles selon le type de famille et le nombre d'enfants de moins de 25 ans en 2019.* Retrieved from https://www.insee.fr/fr/statistiques/zones/6455807?debut=0&q=FAM1&sommaire=6455840

Insee, FAM2. *Couples selon le statut conjugal des conjoints et le nombre d'enfants de moins de 25 ans en 2006.* Retrieved from https://www.insee.fr/fr/statistiques/zones/2028215?debut=0&q=FAM2&sommaire=2130729

Insee, FAM2. *Couples selon le statut conjugal des conjoints et le nombre d'enfants de moins de 25 ans en 2019.* Retrieved from https://www.insee.fr/fr/statistiques/zones/6455809?debut=0&q=FAM2&sommaire=6455840

Insee, MEN5. *Ménages par type de ménage et âge de la personne de référence en 2006.* Retrieved from https://www.insee.fr/fr/statistiques/zones/2028239?debut=0&q=men5&sommaire=2130729

Insee, MEN5. *Ménages par type de ménage et âge de la personne de référence en 2019.* Retrieved from https://www.insee.fr/fr/statistiques/zones/6455834?debut=0&q=men5&sommaire=6455840

Insee, MEN7. *Population des ménages par sexe, âge et mode de cohabitation en 2006.* Retrieved from https://www.insee.fr/fr/statistiques/zones/2028243?debut=0&q=men7&sommaire=2130729

Insee, MEN7. *Population des ménages par sexe, âge et mode de cohabitation en 2019.* Retrieved from https://www.insee.fr/fr/statistiques/zones/6455838?debut=0&q=men7&sommaire=6455840

Köppen, K., Mazuy, M., & Toulemon, L. (2017). Childlessness in France. In M. Kreyenfeld & D. Konietzka (Eds.), *Childlessness in Europe: Contexts, causes, and consequences* (pp. 77–96). Springer.

Le Gall, D., & Popper, H. (2013). Les familles recomposées à l'heure des parentés plurielles. *Dialogue, 201*, 7–14.

Lhommeau, B., Pailhé, A., Santelli, E., Beauchemin, C., & Hamel, C. (2014). La formation du couple entre ici et là-bas. Trajectoires et origines: enquête sur la diversité des populations en France. *Premiers résultats, Documents de Travail de l'Ined, 168*, 85–94.

Ministère de la Justice Secrétariat général Service de l'Expertise et de la Modernisation Sous-direction de la statistique et des études (2020). *L'adoption en 2018.* Retrieved from http://www.justice.gouv.fr/art_pix/Rapport%20ADOPTION_Version%20finale_sept%202020.pdf" \h

Meslay, G. (2019). Five years of same-sex marriage in France: Differences between male and female couples. *Population, 74*(4), 465–482. Retrieved from https://www.ined.fr/fichier/s_rubrique/178/e_popu_1904_0499.en.pdf

OECD Family Database. (2022i). *SF3.1: Marriage and divorce rates.* Retrieved from https://www.oecd.org/els/family/SF_3_1_Marriage_and_divorce_rates.pdf

Périvier, H., & Verdugo, G. (2021). Cinq ans après la réforme du congé parental (PreParE), les objectifs sont-ils atteints? *OFCE Policy Brief, 88.* Retrieved from https://www.ofce.sciences-po.fr/pdf/pbrief/2021/OFCEpbrief88.pdf

Ramos, E., Kertudo, P., & Brunet, F. (2015). Le contexte adoptif comme observatoire privilégie des modes de réception et de gestion des normes parentales contemporaines. *Recherche sociale, 213*(1), 5–130.

Robcis, C. (2015). Liberté, Égalité, Hétérosexualité: Race and Reproduction in the French Gay Marriage Debates. *Constellations, 22*(3), 447–461.

Roussel, L., & Théry, I. (1988). France. Demographic change and family policy since world war II. *Journal of Family Issues, 9*(3), 336–353.

Rozée, V. (2019). Biotechnologies et procréation: vers un nouveau genre de la famille et de la parentalité? *Neuropsychiatrie de l'Enfance et de l'Adolescence, 67*(4), 194–198. Retrieved from https://www.sciencedirect.com/science/article/pii/S0222961718301661

Théry, I. (1987). Introduction. *Dialogues, 97*, 3–6.

Thierry, X., Prigent, R., Eremenko, T., & Moguérou, L. (2018). Caractéristiques et organisation quotidienne des familles monoparentales immigrées. *Revue des politiques sociales et familiales, 127*, 63–70.

4

GERMAN FAMILIES

East-west differences in diversity

Karl Lenz and Tino Schlinzig

The cultural and policy context of doing family

The (re)unification of two independent states in 1990—the Federal Republic of Germany (FRG) in the West and the German Democratic Republic (GDR) in the East—represents a milestone in German history. However, the different political and economic systems were not merely brought together. Rather, unification was aligned with the Western societal model, resulting in significant pressures on East Germans to adapt. Over 40 years of separation of the capitalist West and the socialist East have resulted in remarkable differences in the realm of families, gender arrangements, and welfare regimes; some of them can still be observed today.

Before unification, marriage and family were constitutionally protected in both German states. However, there were fundamental differences in the relationship between family and state (BMFSFJ, 2022a; Hettlage & Lenz, 2013). While in the West, the autonomy of the family and its private character were strongly emphasized, in the GDR the development of the "socialist personality" was considered a joint task of state and social institutions like family and school. There were also vast differences in the treatment of children born outside of marriage. Unmarried mothers (and fathers) had full parental custody rights in the GDR from the beginning. In the FRG, a public guardian was appointed by the Department of Youth to the children of single mothers, who did not gain parental custody until 1970. Unmarried fathers were not related to their child at all until this reform.

While gender equality was anchored in the constitutions of both states, due to the distinct social systems its legal implementation differed significantly. In the GDR, equal rights for women and men were introduced swiftly and following socialist principles, and gender equality was to be achieved through women's

DOI: 10.4324/9781003193500-4

economic independence from men. The GDR constitution of 1968 elevated the "advancement of women" to a social and state priority. While both spouses were officially assigned the same obligations in terms of childcare and housework, in practice, GDR family law considered mothers as primarily responsible for child and family care.

In the FRG, the inclusion of gender equality in the constitution ("Grundgesetz") met with considerable resistance and its implementation was delayed for a long time. There was widespread concern that equal rights could weaken or even dissolve the family. Consequently, the aim of resulting family policy measures was that married women should not "have to" engage in paid work but should be able to concentrate fully on caring for the family. As a result, a gender division of labor and a male breadwinner model have been codified in West German family law (Adler & Brayfield, 2006).

While the GDR was one of the (few) industrialized countries in which women's employment rates almost converged with men's, rising from 52% in 1950 to 86% in 1980, in the FRG, the rate increased only from 44% to 53% during this period (Lenz & Adler, 2010). The ideal of child-rearing by the mother was propagated in the West as the very core of a private sphere free of state interventions and as the backbone of a free society. Yet, West German women's labor force participation also rose steadily during the postwar period, albeit mainly in the form of part-time employment. Due to the feminist movement of the 1970s, women's increased participation in higher education, and the growth of the service sector, employment became an important part of women's biographies.

In the GDR, women's mainly full-time labor force participation had a significant impact on the provision of public childcare. In order to attract women with young children to the labor market, an extensive public childcare system was established, initially for kindergarten aged children, but soon also for younger children. In West Germany, by contrast, childcare facilities were largely considered as assisting families not able to provide appropriate care. In the 1980s, this attitude changed with respect to kindergarten attendance. These differences vividly show that two fundamentally different gender regimes existed in the two German states. While in the GDR the dual full-time provider model with public childcare became established early, in the FRG the male full-time and female part-time provider model replaced the traditional male breadwinner model.

After unification, a paradigm shift gradually took place in German family policy. The 7th Family Report (BMFSFJ, 2006, p. 6) made a significant contribution with its concept of a "sustainable family policy," emphasizing that "a sustainable family policy must be based on a mix of infrastructure policy, time policy and financial transfer policy." The main political goal was to reconcile family and employment for mothers and increasingly also for fathers. The Child and Youth Welfare Act of 1991 (Bertram & Deuflhard, 2013), which provided a new understanding of kindergarten and daycare centers, had already paved the way for this new family policy. In 1996, the legal entitlement to a kindergarten place for all children over the age of three was introduced. Central to this new family policy is the Federal Parental Allowance and Parental Leave Act ("Bundeselterngeld- und Elternzeitgesetz") introduced in 2007, with an income-based parental allowance ("Elterngeld"). If each of the two parents takes at least two months of parental leave, they are entitled to parental allowance for a total of 14 months; otherwise, they only receive 12 months. The so-called partner months are intended to create a clear incentive for fathers to actively participate in the care of their children. In 2015, with the so-called parental allowance plus, the options of parallel employment while receiving parental allowance were further expanded.

There have also been fundamental changes in the way the state deals with same-sex relationships. The prosecution of male homosexuality was initially continued in the postwar period in the FRG with a version of § 175 German Criminal Code, leading to major prosecution efforts in the 1950s and 1960s resulting in about 45,000 sentences in West Germany (Gammerl, 2010). Despite the retention of criminal liability, the possibility of discontinuing proceedings was used more generously in the East from the 1950s onward. At the end of the 1960s, consensual sexual encounters between adult men were decriminalized. Complete legalization did not occur in the West German states until 1994, six years later than in the GDR (Schäfer, 2006). Major steps toward normalization have been taken in the last two decades. Since 2001, same-sex couples could apply for registered civil partnerships ("eingetragene Lebenspartnerschaft"), and since 2017, they are able to legally marry.

There were also significant differences in the ethnic heterogeneity of the population in the two German states. The GDR had very few immigrants, which meant that the proportion of the foreign-born population was only 1.2% in 1989 (Hettlage & Lenz, 2013), a level that the FRG had already reached in 1961. In the West, the initial postwar immigration of workers from southern and southeastern Europe, later the ethnic German immigration from eastern Europe, and most recently immigration of civil war and poverty refugees have resulted in a high proportion of the population with migration experience.

Empirical patterns of various family forms

In addition to the continuous data collection via registry offices or other state institutions, the German Microcensus provides a central database for the analysis of family forms. The Microcensus is a multi-topic annual survey of households, living arrangements and families, and other topics, which covers 1% of the population. As of 2005, the traditional family concept was replaced by the concept of living arrangements in the official reports (Lengerer et al., 2005). The subunits of households are no longer families, but living arrangements ("Lebensgemeinschaften"), based on the criteria of partnership and parenthood. In the case of couples, the degree of institutionalization (e.g., marriage) and gender are recorded to allow the distinction between married and cohabiting couples of same or different genders. This change parallels a reform of the family concept in official statistics from a marriage-centered concept to a child-centered concept: a family exists when there are unmarried children living in a household, regardless of whether there is a marriage, a non-marital cohabitation, or a single parent. Despite all the improvements, it is necessary to include data from surveys, such as the German Family Panel (pairfam) in order to adequately capture the diversity of living arrangements (Huinink et al., 2011).

For both German states, the early postwar period was dominated by the standard model of the nuclear family, consisting of a married couple and their biological children living in the same household. Marriage and family formation were expected biographical events, firmly anchored in the "normal biography." But as early as the 1960s and even more so in the 1970s, the dominance of this model began to erode, and gradually, different-sex marriage lost popularity as the pluralization of life forms accelerated. The high level of female employment, the strong expansion of extra-familial childcare, and also the consistent promotion of gender equality gave GDR society an edge in advancing family diversity. The unification of the German legal system, economy, and family policy has since brought about convergences in the two regions. Nevertheless, some differences developed during the 40 years of political division still persist.

Union formation and dissolution

Along with a strong liberalization of sexuality, the age of first marriage has been rising since the mid-1970s in the FRG and the early 1980s in the GDR. In unified Germany, this increase has accelerated, and today East German upward trends have overtaken those in the West. East German women married for the first time at an average age of 34.4 years (West: 31.8 years) and East German men at 38.3 years (West: 34.2) (see Table 4.1).

Germans not only postpone marriage; they also increasingly refrain from marrying at all. Marriage data show that among 20-year-old women, only 68% are likely to marry at least once in their lifetime compared to only 62% of men (Dorbritz, 2009). While marriage rates were historically higher in the GDR than in the FRG, today the residents of the West German states show a higher propensity to marry than those in the East. There is also a decline in remarriage among divorced and widowed persons. In the longer term, this trend is even reflected in the crude marriage rate, but not in the period from 2000 to 2020 (Table 4.1). This shows that the decoupling of love and marriage has progressed in both regions, and even more so in the East than in the West. When two people "love" each other, they will no longer necessarily marry. In addition, couples are increasingly postponing the decision to marry. This decline in marriage is accompanied by an increase in non-marital relationships, and in neither region, a tendency away from committed couple relationships can be observed (Lengerer & Klein, 2007).

After a long-term increase in divorce rates in both regions, even after reunification, they are now declining. The total divorce rate (TDR) peaked in 2004

TABLE 4.1 Selected demographic indicators for Germany, 2000 and the latest available data

	2000			Latest available data			
	Total	East	West	Year	Total	East	West
Crude marriage rate	5.1	3.9	5.4	2019	5.1	5.0	5.1
Mean age at first marriage							
of women	28.4	28.0	28.5	2020	32.4	34.4	31.8
of men	31.2	30.7	31.3	2020	34.8	38.3	34.2
Crude divorce rate	2.37	2.11	2.41	2018	1.90	1.58	1.84
Total divorce rate	37.3	35.2	38.1	2018	31.8	29.8	32.2
Remarriage rate							
of women	60.9			2018	53.8		
of men	55.6			2018	52.9		
% of adults > 18 never married							
of women	24.9			2020	33.6		
of men	33.6			2020	39.3		
Total fertility rate							
of women	1.38	1.22	1.41	2020	1.53	1.54	1.55
of men	1.21	1.03	1.26	2019	1.45	1.32	1.48
Mean age at first birth							
of women	29.0			2019	30.1		
of men	NA			2019	33.1		
% non-marital births	23.4	48.6	18.2	2019	33.3	53.3	28.9
% of women aged 40–44 who have born no children	17.2 (2008)	7.3	19.0	2018	21.2	15.3	21.9
Cohorts		**1950**			**1970**		
Completed fertility/cohort	1.72	1.79	1.70		1.51	1.47	1.51
% of women aged 40–44 who have born no children for cohorts	14	7	15	1969	21	12	22

Sources: Statistisches Bundesamt 1919; 2021c; 6.5 Durchschnittliches Heiratsalter nach dem bisherigen Familienstand der Ehepartner (since 2001without Berlin); Zusammengefasste Wiederverheiratungsziffer Geschiedener in Deutschland, 1990 bis 2018; Statistisches Jahrbuch 2019; Endgültige Geburtenziffer der Frauenkohorten, Stand 2020 (since 2001 without Berlin); BIB, Rohe Ehescheidungsziffer für West- und Ostdeutschland (1950–2018); Zusammengefasste Ehescheidungsziffern in Deutschland, West- und Ostdeutschland, 1970 bis 2018; Pötzsch et al. (2020).

at 43.3 in West Germany and 41.0 in East Germany. It indicates how many marriages would be divorced if the divorce frequency of the respective calendar year remained constant over a period of 25 years. In 2018, the TDR was 32.2 and 29.8, respectively. This decline is primarily related to changes in marriage behavior, especially the increase in the age at marriage (BMFSFJ, 2021). Marriages entered in middle age are more stable than unions formed in younger years. Before unification, the divorce rate was higher in the East; after unification, it has been higher in the West, mainly because of a lower propensity to marry in that region. Largely unchanged since the 1990s, about half of divorces involve minor children. Official sources only provide information on divorces, not on separations of unmarried couples. However, German Family Panel data on women from birth cohorts 1971–1973 with one child show that the probability of separation remains higher in the East than in the West. Already at the time of the birth of the child, more East German (11%) than West German (7%) women lived separately from their child's fathers. Once the child is ten years old, this figure had risen to 35% in the East and 26% in the West (BMFSFJ, 2021). The observed reductions in divorce are thus likely due to the increased diversification of family forms.

Fertility patterns

After the baby boom of the early postwar period, birth rates declined in the GDR and the FRG in the mid-1960s. Until the mid-1970s, the similarity in the birth rates of both German states is striking. After a brief increase in births in the GDR due to pronatalist policies, the total fertility rate (TFR) converged again in the 1980s. Due to the collapse of the GDR, which created major biographical uncertainties, birth rates dropped dramatically in the East. The TFR fell from 1.57 (1989) to 0.77 (1994). From the mid-1990s onward, fertility rates in the East rose again, reaching 1.21 in 2000 (West: 1.41). The difference continued to dwindle in the following years, and currently, the TFR for both regions is almost identical (Statistisches Bundesamt, 2021b). Unlike in most other European countries, German birth rates increased in the second decade of the new century. Therefore, Germany is no longer one of the European countries with the lowest birth rates. The higher fertility of foreign-born women and the changes in the origin of immigrants have contributed to this increase in births. However, German women also show a higher birth rate, especially in the fourth decade of life. It is assumed that this is an effect of the new family policy measures (expansion of early childcare and parental allowance) (Pötzsch, 2018). Comparison of the 1950 and 1970 cohorts shows that the cohort fertility rate is declining. Based on current birth trends, this decline is not expected to continue for women born in the 1970s and early 1980s. Data on fertility behavior continue to be reported only for women; some indicators also for men are available only in special analysis (Pötzsch et al., 2020).

Since the mid-1970s—somewhat later in the East—the average age of mothers at first birth has been rising. This trend has continued over the past two decades, increasing from 29.7 years (2000) to 31.5 years (2019). East German first-time mothers and fathers were significantly younger on average than those in the FRG. In 2000, these differences had already been reduced, and now they have largely disappeared. Furthermore, there are differences in the share of non-marital births. In the East, this share has risen dramatically since the end of the 1960s and this trend continued after unification. In West Germany, non-marital births have been rising since the 1990s, albeit at a significantly lower level than in the East. The proportion peaked in 2011 in the East (58.9) and in 2016 in the West (30.4). Since then, the share has declined slightly in both regions. While in West Germany, marriage continues to precede childbirth in the majority of cases, in East Germany, the birth of a child tends to take place before marriage, which may or may not follow.

Germany has one of the highest rates of childlessness in Europe, but there are major regional differences within Germany (Datenreport, 2021). In the 1950 birth cohort, the share of women who never gave birth was 15% in West Germany and 7% in East Germany; for the 1970 cohort, the shares increased to 22% and 12%, respectively. In East Germany, women without children are less common than in the West, and one- and two-child families clearly dominate. The West German fertility pattern shows greater heterogeneity; it includes both considerably more childlessness and more large families.

Changes in household composition and living arrangements

The number of private households (main residence) in Germany has risen since unification—continuing a longer trend: from 34.6 million in 1991 to 40.5 million in 2020 (Statistisches Bundesamt 2021a, p. 23). In addition, households are now smaller on average in the East (1.9) than in the West (2.06).

Changes in the design of the German Microcensus surveys allow a differentiation by living arrangements. In 2020, 42.9% of the population lived with a spouse. Twenty years earlier, the figure was 5% higher (Table 4.2). The percentage of unmarried children living in their parents' households also declined from 26.3% to 23.5%. The share of people living alone increased from 16.2% to 20.1% in the last two decades. In addition, the proportion of the population living with a partner increased from 5.2% to 8.1%. These living arrangements vary by age. Among 18- to 24-year-olds, single children living in the household of their parents clearly dominate (2019: 61%). Dramatic changes can be seen in the age group of 25–34 years, where the proportion living with a spouse declined from 46.4% to 31.5%. The largest increase in this age group has been in non-marital cohabitation.

The data also allow an analysis of living arrangements by certain socio-demographic characteristics. The proportion of different-sex married couples

TABLE 4.2 Population in living arrangements in Germany, 2000 and 2020

% of persons living	2000			2020		
	Total	Age 18–24	Age 25–34	Total	Age 18–24	Age 25–34
With spouse	47.8	7.9	46.4	42.9	3.2	31.5
With partner	5.2	8.6	14.6	8.1	9	21.7
Child of householder	26.3	64.7	12.3	23.5	61	12.2
Alone	16.2	14.5	20.8	20.1	21.3	27.6
Alone with child/ren	3	1.2	3.9	3.1	0.8	3.2
with another person(s)	1.5	3.1	2	2	4.7	3.8

Source: Statistisches Bundesamt (2020), Tab. 4.3. Author's calculation.

was reduced from 50.6% to 42.2% (Table 4.3). This decline has been more pronounced in the East. In 2000, slightly more than half of married couples still lived with children under age 18, while 20 years later married couples without children predominate. In general, living alone is the most common living arrangement in East Germany: 42.9% of households involve only one person. The proportion of one-parent households has not changed much: about 5% of living arrangements consist of a mother with child(ren) and about 1% of a father with child(ren). The number of unmarried cohabiting couples with or without children has increased over these two decades from 5.4% to 7.7%. They are more common in the East, where they also include children more often. The number of same-sex couples living together has increased in both regions—albeit still at a very low level. Since its legal introduction in 2017, 65,600 same-sex couples have married (Statistisches Bundesamt, 2021d).

Even though the concept of living arrangements has brought about a significant improvement in the documentation of family forms other than the standard family, considerable deficits persist because it remains associated with household statistics. Consequently, all relationships and families that extend beyond the household boundary are not captured. For example, couple relationships with two independent households as well as families spanning across households are not included in official statistics. Another deficit concerns the distinction among different types of children. While the fact that children live in a household is recorded, it remains unknown whether they are biological children, stepchildren, adopted children, or foster children. As a result, no information on the prevalence of step, adoptive and foster families can be provided based on these data. In addition, they do not offer information on whether the child resulted from natural or assisted reproduction. Finally, these statistics remain grounded in a cross-sectional logic that systematically underestimates the changes and diversity in relationships and family forms (also Bastin et al., 2013). Only rarely is the first couple relationship a lifelong one. A series of different couple relationships

TABLE 4.3 Households in Germany, 2000 and 2020

Indicator	2000			2020		
% of households consist of	Total	East	West	Total	East	West
Different-sex spouses	50.6	47.5	51.5	42.2	37.1	43.5
with kids <18	25.7	22.9	26.5	19.2	13.2	20.8
without kids <18	24.9	24.7	24.9	23.0	24.0	22.7
Different-sex partners	5.4	7.0	5.0	7.7	9.6	7.2
with kids <18	1.6	3.2	1.2	2.5	4.5	2.0
without kids <18	3.8	3.8	3.8	5.2	5.1	5.2
Mother only with kids	5.4	6.5	5.0	5.0	5.7	4.8
Father only with kids	1.0	1.0	0.9	1.1	1.2	1.0
Same-sex couple	0.1	0.1	0.4	0.7	0.7	0.8
One person living alone	34.4	34.6	34.1	39.4	42.9	38.5

Source: Statistisches Bundesamt (2001, 2021), Table 3.8. Author's calculation.

have become the standard in the German life course. The relationship biography has changed from a "continuity biography" to a "chain biography" (Schmidt et al., 2006). However, these dynamics cannot be made visible with cross-sectional data.

Current empirical research on the various family forms

Reconstituted families (stepfamilies)

Despite some negative connotation, the term "stepfamilies" is still commonly used in Germany. The term "reconstituted families" is not used because a parent with a child is also considered as a family. Conceptually, a stepfamily is created when a new partner is added to a parent-child unit. Stepfamilies are by no means a new phenomenon (Entleitner-Phleps & Rost, 2017; Steinbach, 2015). However, while they were formed almost exclusively after the death of one parent until the mid-20th century, today they are predominantly the result of separation or divorce of a couple. However, stepfamilies do not require a joint household or a new marriage; the stepfamily can also involve a living-apart-together (LAT) relationship. Using German Family Survey data, Bastin (2019) shows that five years after separation, about half of unmarried mothers live with a new partner, and about three-fourths are involved in a new couple relationship after this time. One-third of the mothers included in this sample were in a new couple relationship already after only one year.

While in Germany stepfamilies are not recorded by official statistics, some data are available from surveys (Steinbach, 2015). Findings suggest that 10–14% of all families are stepfamilies. Stepfamilies are more prevalent in East than in West Germany. According to Steinbach's (2008) analysis of Generations and Gender Survey (GGS) data from 2005, 5% of nuclear families and 17% of primary stepfamilies are also secondary stepfamilies, meaning that there is at least another child of one of the partners that is only sporadically present in the family household. Due to high divorce and separation rates, the number of stepfamilies is expected to continue to increase.

On average, stepfamilies include more children than nuclear families and the parents are more likely to be unmarried. Despite their larger size, these families are less likely to involve the classic breadwinner model and a traditional division of labor. Nevertheless, even in this family form, women generally bear the main burden of family care work (Steinbach, 2015).

Stepfamilies are confronted with additional challenges in organizing their everyday life (Heintz-Martin et al., 2015). When a joint household is established, new family members have to be integrated into everyday family life, which involves establishing trust and good relationships with the stepchild(ren). However, because no defined set of role expectations exist for stepparents, their involvement in care work has to be negotiated. As long as stepchildren are not adopted, German stepparents have few rights and duties toward them. If there is continued parental contact and child-rearing is shared, ongoing coordination and communication on how to jointly raise children as post-separation parents are required. The involvement of multiple parents in stepfamilies allows more than the traditional two adults to take on parenting responsibilities (Bergold et al., 2017). While belonging to a nuclear family is largely taken for granted, "boundary ambiguity" can be observed in stepfamilies. The term co-parenting is generally used to describe care arrangements that include a social parent or a parent external to the child's household (Bender, 2021; Entleitner-Phleps et al., 2020). A more restricted definition of the term specifies co-parenting as related to families raising children without a couple relationship (Wimbauer, 2021).

One-parent and cohabiting families

Data from the German Family Survey suggest that one-parent and cohabiting families occur more frequently in the East than in the West (BMFSFJ, 2021). A total of 39% of East German men and 24% of women between 18 and 54 years of age live with children in cohabitation relationships. In less than two decades, the proportion has almost doubled (2000: only 16% and 13%, respectively). This has also occurred in the West—albeit at a lower level (BMFSFJ, 2021). Much of cohabitation is not a permanent arrangement, mainly because the couples get married. According to data from the German Family Survey, every second woman in East Germany who had her first child in a cohabitation is married after ten years. In West Germany, the propensity to marry is somewhat higher (60%).

In the vast majority of cases, one-parent families result from the separation of a parental couple who was married or had a couple relationship with or without a shared household. According to a special report by the Statistisches Bundesamt (2018), 54.4% of single parents in Germany were divorced or living separately in 2017, 40.6% were never married, and only a very small number were widowed.

In East Germany, the proportion of never married parents significantly exceeds that of those divorced and separated. This high proportion of never married parents indicates the high prevalence of non-marital cohabitation and LAT relationships at the time of the birth of the child.

Official statistics overestimate the proportion of single parents because the definition is based on the household, not parental care. Whenever a couple lives separately, the parent with a child in the household becomes a single parent. However, it is quite common that both parents share parental care after they separate and live in separate households. It is also possible that a couple with a child never established a joint household. A large majority of single parents are not alone with their children but are part of two households or a multi-local family (Schlinzig, 2021). Microcensus data do not provide any information on this family form. However, based on a 2016 survey of 1,261 unmarried mothers, Keil & Langmeyer (2020) conclude that only 15% of separated fathers have broken off contact with their children or never had contact. Compared to older studies (e.g., Hartl, 2002), this proportion has decreased and the commitment of separated fathers to remain involved has increased. Joint custody arrangements and a previous marital relationship have positive effects on the continuation of fathers' contact (Köppen et al., 2018). Joint custody as the standard case in divorces was introduced in Germany in 1998.

Despite joint custody, the "residence model" continues to be the predominant living arrangement after divorce and separation. In this model, the children live with one parent (usually the mother), who takes over the main care, while the other parent has visitation rights (Walper et al., 2020). The "shared residence model" ("Wechselmodell"), in which a child is living alternately in each household of the separated parents, has attracted increasing public and academic attention, and social acceptance (Wissenschaftlicher Beirat, 2021). Based on the DJI-Survey AiD: A, Walper and colleagues (2020) concluded that 5% of children under 18 live in a shared residence arrangement, defined as children staying overnight at least 30% of the time in the second household. A qualitative study by Schlinzig (2021) shows that these families respond to pressures to conform with "strategies of normalization": they deconstruct the standard family model and emphasize benefits and strengths of their own multi-local living arrangement.

Single parents face an increased risk of poverty and are more likely to depend on transfer payments from the state. In 2018, their risk of poverty in Germany was four times higher than that of couple households with children (BMFSFJ, 2021). Unmarried mothers are also much more likely to be at risk of poverty than unmarried fathers. Child support payments play an important role in their economic situation. According to data from the DJI Alleinerziehenden-Studie, only 61% of eligible single parents receive full child support, and only in a third of cases when support is not paid in full, the state supplements the income (Hubert et al., 2020). Moreover, single parents with younger children need the ability to reconcile family and work obligations in order to improve their economic situation.

Sex and gender minority families (SGM)

In Germany, it is common to refer to SGM families as "rainbow families" ("Regenbogenfamilien") (Buschner & Bergold, 2017; Vries, 2021), which are defined as "families in which children grow up with at least one LGBTQ parent" (BMBFSJ, Regenbogenportal.de). They can include biological, step, adoptive, or foster children, and also a number of parents. In this context, it is important to mention that since 2018 the gender category "diverse" can be entered in the birth register. In addition, the federal government plans to abolish the Trans-sexual Act ("Transsexuellengesetz") of 1980 and replace it with a broad right to self-determination for trans, intersex, and non-binary people and to change their gender entry and first names (BMFSFJ/BMJ, 2022).

In Microcensus data, only a limited subset of SGM families is counted: same-sex couples in a common household. In 2019, approximately 142,000 same-sex couples were recorded, including 68,000 male couples and 33,000 female couples. About 37% of same-sex couples have taken advantage of the so-called marriage for all introduced in 2017, some of whom already were in registered civil partnerships. About 15,000 same-sex couples lived together with child(ren); 89% of them were women. Of the 22,000 children who lived in SGM families, 18,999 were under the age of 18 (Datenreport, 2021). However, because the raw numbers are small, these estimates are prone to bias and under- or over-estimation (Rupp & Haag, 2016).

According to Microcensus data, these families have been steadily increasing since the 1970s (Lengerer & Bohr, 2019). Higher social acceptance of same-sex relationships has contributed to this increase (Vries, 2021) and has led more couples to publicly communicate and display these living arrangements. However, SGM families continue to be confronted with heteronormative expectations, and discrimination of adults and children is still widespread (Rupp, 2009).

The desire to have children is quite common among SGM couples, even if data on the extent vary greatly (Buschner & Bergold, 2017). However, adding children to their family is often difficult and protracted for SGM couples because it requires at least one external person—either a sperm donor or a surrogate mother abroad. According to a BMJ study (Rupp, 2009), in every second SGM family, the children originated in previous heterosexual relationships, and 43% are born into the current couple relationship. Adoptive or foster SGM families, on the other hand, are rare. Research studies can also be found on the division of labor in this family form (Peukert et al., 2020).

Adoptive and foster families

In adoptive and foster families, the parent–child relationship is not constituted by birth, but by court decision (in the case of adoptive families) or by contract (in the case of foster families) (Gehres & Sauer, 2020). In official statistics, adoptive and foster families—as well as stepfamilies—are counted as couples—predominantly married couples—with children and are not recorded separately. Figures on adoptions and children in full-time care are reported in the child and youth welfare statistics ("Statistiken der Kinder- und Jugendhilfe"). In 2019, there were 3,744 adoptions, and 46% of these children were under three years old (Statistisches Bundesamt, 2020). Stepchild adoption is by far the most common type, accounting for 63%. All cases in which there is no kinship or stepparent relationship are regarded as third-party adoptions. Their share is currently 33%. Since the beginning of the 1990s, adoptions in Germany have been reduced by over 50%. This decline mainly affects third-party adoptions (4,071 to 1,244) and is the result of the availability of medically assisted reproduction (MAR) (Mühling & Franz, 2017). Adoption requires the consent of the parents and of children aged 14 and over. Parental care of the adopted child is transferred to the adopting party, and the relationship to the biological parents and their families ceases permanently.

The path to adoption is time intensive. Currently, the number of adoption applications is five times higher than the number of pre-registered children. Extensive assessments of suitability take place preceding the adoption, including an adoption care trial period. The priority is to establish a secure bond between the adopted child and the new parents (Mühling & Franz, 2017). This is a prerequisite not only for the child but also for the parents. They have to make the child "their own" knowing that it is not biological child. The doing family takes place—as in foster families—on the basis of a "dual parenthood" (Hoffmann-Riem, 1994), biological and social parenthood. How dual parenthood is shaped varies widely—especially in the case of third-party adoption. For a long time, anonymous adoption, in which there is no contact between the relinquishing and receiving parents, was common. Commonly, adoptive families strove to appear as much as possible as a "natural family," what Hoffmann-Riem (1994) has called "as-if-normalization." Because the right of children to know their biological parents has experienced strong support, open adoption is now increasingly practiced. This is also associated with an open context of awareness and a reflexive approach to dual parenthood, a strategy of "own-type-normalization" (Hoffmann-Riem, 1994), which from a socio-educational perspective is perceived as beneficial for the children and family (see Kühn, 2015).

Whereas in adoptive families a parent-child relationship is created that is designed to be permanent, in foster families, it is usually temporary. Except in the special case of kinship care, foster families are constituted by an unrelated adult who takes over parental responsibilities for a specific period of time on behalf of the youth welfare service. Foster care is an alternative to institutional care in a difficult family situation and mainly involves younger children. In 2017, approximately 71,000 adolescent children were in full-time foster care in Germany, including cases where the biological parents lost custody (Köhler et al., 2017). Because the biological parents remain part of the child's life, foster parents have to actively share and coordinate their parenting with them. In addition, the youth welfare office is a relevant actor in this type of family, which means that foster families parent in a triangle between biological parents and the youth welfare office. According to Gehres and Hildenbrand (2008), each case determines whether a foster family is a substitute or a supplement to being family.

Families created by medically assisted reproduction (MAR)

The availability of MAR technologies is of growing importance in Germany. Unlike in other countries, such as Great Britain, there is no legal obligation to officially report the births resulting from MAR (Trappe, 2020; Mayer-Lewis, 2017). However, since 1998, professional organizations are obligated to report data about births through MAR to the German In vitro Fertilization Register. However, these data cover only fertilizations outside the female body; births assisted by IVF are not recorded. In 2019, 21,588 births resulted from ART; this corresponds to a share of 2.8% of all live births. Compared to 2000, the number of such births—after an interim decline—has more than doubled (DIR, 2021).

While ART results in a significantly higher number of multiple births, their overall proportion is declining. The number of live births involving multiple births is now 29% (2000: 39.5%). Indicators for successful MAR treatments are the pregnancy rate (proportion of clinically proven pregnancies per treatment) and the birth rate (proportion of live births per treatment). These vary between treatment modalities; for intracytoplasmic sperm induction (ICSI), now the most common treatment modality, the pregnancy rate is 26.4 and the birth rate is 18.8. Success is shown to be strongly age dependent. The average age of women and men who want to become parents with the help of MAR has increased significantly; it was 35.6 years for women and 38.5 years for men in 2019 (DIR, 2021).

BOX: Legal regulation of medically assisted reproduction (MAR)

In Germany, MAR is regulated primarily by the Embryo Protection Act of 1991. In this context, an embryo is considered to be "the fertilized human egg cell capable of development from the time of nuclear fusion" (§ 8.1). This law focuses on the protection of the embryo, regulated by means of prohibitions under criminal law. The induction of pregnancy and the health interests of the woman and the child are subordinate to this. In Germany, sperm donation is permitted, but egg donation and surrogacy are prohibited. However, they still occur in Germany because of more liberal regulations in other countries (e.g., Denmark, the Netherlands, or for surrogacy: UK, Greece). The reason given for banning egg donation is that it leads to "split motherhood" with negative effects on the identity formation of the child. In contrast, "split paternity" is not seen as a problem. Third-party sperm donation is permitted. The prerequisite is a written declaration of consent between the couple and the donor. Use of anonymous sperm or a mixture of sperm is considered immoral, as it violates the child's right to know their genetic parentage. Under the Sperm Donor Registry Act of 2018, a retention period of 110 years was established for sperm donor personal data. For a long time, the professional law of physicians limited reproductive medicine to heterosexual couples; unmarried couples were permitted only in exceptional cases. It was not until 2018 that this regulation was dropped. The statutory health insurance funds cover 50% of the costs for three treatment cycles. However, this coverage is also subject to conditions (e.g., age); some states provide subsidies, and health insurers cover more of the costs (Schramm, 2018; Trappe, 2020).

Research on MAR families has been very limited (Mayer-Lewis, 2017). Using the process of case reconstructive family research, Funcke (2021) has presented three detailed case studies of lesbian MAR families. One female couple has three children and the other two have one child each, all created through sperm donation. In addition to questions about the desire to have children, the process of becoming a family, and the socialization history of the inseminating mother, the thematic interest is focused on the placement of the lesbian partner in the family and on how she deals with the sperm donor. Using the nuclear family as a key category, Funcke's main concern is to show comparatively the perceived differences and deficits of same-sex insemination families. Beyond this deficit perspective, these activities can also be understood as practiced forms of doing family.

Multicultural and migrant families

In 2005, a new socio-demographic unit "persons with migration background" was introduced into official statistics in Germany. A person has a migration background if they "or at least one parent does not have German citizenship by birth" (Statistisches Bundesamt, 2021c, p. 4). This includes people who were born abroad and immigrated themselves (with their own migration experience) as well as descendants of immigrants born in Germany (for a critique of this definition, see Fachkommission Integrationsfähigkeit, 2021).

In 2019, 21.2 million people "with migration background" lived in Germany and 13.7 million of them had their own migration experience (Datenreport, 2021, p. 31). In 2005, the first year this was recorded, there were 14.4 million. Germany is now the second most important destination country for international migration, after the US. The population share of international migrants is currently 16% in Germany, which is higher than in the US but significantly lower than in Australia (30%), Switzerland (30%), and Canada (21%). About 39% of all families with minor children had a migration background in 2019, about 12% more than in 2005. In West Germany, this share is now 43.2%, while in East Germany, this share is only half as high. Parents with migration background are more likely to be married (77.4% vs 65.1%) and less likely to live in a non-marital cohabitation with children (8.0% vs 13.7%) or as single parents (14.5% vs 21.2%). Traditional gender arrangements are also more widespread. In only 51% of couple families with migration background, both parents are employed (without an immigrant background: 73%; Datenreport, 2021, p. 64).

Although migrants are more likely to live in traditional, often extended, family constellations, migration has greatly increased the ethnic and cultural diversity of family lifestyles in Germany. Nevertheless, migrant families do not constitute an independent family form (Andersson, 2021; Baykara-Krumme, 2015). Rather, these families are characterized by enormous heterogeneity. Considerable differences exist based on the country of origin, individual migration experiences, time in Germany, and social and legal status of the family members.

There are also increasing numbers of transnational families, in which family members are living in different countries. Migration is often associated with a (temporary) separation of family members. The care of the children of a migrant is taken over either by the other parent or other members of the family network. It is also possible that the children are sent to Germany first or that their parents remain in the country of origin. This historic pattern has recently gained increased attention due to the rise in the labor migration of mothers. While labor migration may improve the material situation of families and open new opportunities for children's education, family separation represents a high psychological burden with negative effects on mental health. Today, the maintenance of family relations over spatial distances is facilitated by information and communication technologies (Schier & Schlinzig, 2018). They ensure continuous exchanges about the details of children's life circumstances and serve as substitute forms for togetherness and co-presence (Greschke & Motowidlo, 2020; Shinozaki et al., 2021).

Conclusion and recommendations

In Germany, the diversity of family forms has increased significantly over the last five decades; the nuclear family, long referred to as a standard family, is no longer the dominant family form. In the East German states, this trend is even more pronounced than in the West. This diversity is much greater than conventional measures suggest. In order to understand the full extent of diversity, a longitudinal perspective is necessary.

German family policy has clearly shifted its perspective and now advocates a sustainable family policy, which is oriented toward securing the economic stability and social participation of families, facilitating the reconciliation of family care and employment, promoting the well-being of children, and facilitating the fulfillment of children's wishes as central goals (BMFSFJ, 2021). However, this progress is hindered by various continuing and newly introduced policy measures. For example, spousal splitting ("Ehegattensplitting") in the German tax system continues to reinforce male breadwinner norms. Therefore, the current 9th Family Report recommends "phasing out spousal splitting" (BMFSFJ, 2021) in order to promote the integration of both parents into the labor market. It also recommends to further develop the parental leave allowance policy into a 3 + 8 + 3 months leave model with increased compensation. The allowance should be reserved for three months for each parent, while the other eight months can be used by either parent or shared. In addition, in order to eliminate tax-related differences in state support for children and to reduce social inequalities in the conditions under which children grow up, the child tax benefit should be converted into a child allowance.

The growing diversity of family forms and of the paths to parenthood also requires extensive reforms of family law—as shown in detail in the 9th Family Report (also Dethloff & Timmermann, 2017). Parental responsibility is assumed within and outside of marriage, by different-sex couples and SGM families, by one person, or even more than two. The law must create a framework of conditions that does justice to this diversity of lived and desired parenthood. The best interests of the child rather than biological parenthood should be aligned with the assumption of care responsibilities in the child's daily life. There is an urgent need for a Reproductive Medicine Act because MAR should be available to all regardless of lifestyle, sexual orientation, and income. Egg donation should be a legal option and surrogate motherhood be reconsidered so that it can be organized in an ethical manner.

Official statistics, even supplemented by the Microcensus, are far from sufficient to adequately reflect the existing diversity of family forms. It is essential that family structures across households are recorded. The new Microcensus data collection form, which was used for the first time in 2020, takes the first step toward improving this data gap. There is also a need for differentiated information on child-parent relationships (biological, step, adoptive, or foster children). Also, information on fertility should not only refer to women, but also to men. To adequately describe changes in family forms, cross-sectional studies must be systematically supplemented with longitudinal studies. In this context, family surveys, especially those with a panel design, such as the "Family Research and Demographic Analysis" (FReDA) (Schneider et al., 2021) in conjunction with the German Family Panel (pairfam), are particularly important contributions. However, a problem arises when the number of cases for select family forms, such as those involving SGM or MAR, adoptive or foster families, is too small to draw reliable conclusions about them. This can only be remedied by larger samples for these family forms. Qualitative studies can also make an important contribution in this regard—especially for the study of the ongoing practices of doing family in the different family forms. In contrast to the strong tradition of separating quantitative and qualitative studies in German family research, more interdisciplinary studies with multi-method designs would be highly beneficial.

Migrant families pose a special challenge to research because, as they do not reflect an independent family form, they cannot be studied as a homogenous group. Rather, it is necessary to view migration or geographic origin as a feature that intersects with gender, age, heritage, and social class (Baykara-Krumme, 2015). Migrant families can take on all family forms, and the large number of immigrant families or immigrant family members necessitates that this structural feature is anchored in family research and data collection. It will be important to pay more attention to cultural differences within this group.

Due to the massive impact on everyday life, it is not surprising that the COVID-19 pandemic has also rapidly become a hot topic for family research. Research projects have been expanded or newly initiated, and numerous publications are now available, including special issues of journals (e.g., Journal of Family Research 34,1, 2022). Nevertheless, research has only just begun and the pandemic has not yet ended. Therefore, only preliminary results on the impact on family life and family forms are currently available. The requirement for many workers to work from home while schools and childcare facilities were closed in Germany, placed new demands on work-life balance and increased parental responsibilities. Beyond this, the pandemic also presented numerous challenges for families. Parents had to make children understand the pandemic and explain the measures taken, support them in dealing with emotions, and also compensate for loss of contact with peers. Initial results suggest that the demands were highly stressful for families (Bujard et al., 2021; Zartler, Suwada, & Kreyenfeld, 2022). At the same time, however, it is also clear that parents were very creative and effective in developing coping strategies and also understood how to continuously adapt them to changing demands (Zartler, Dafert, & Dirmberger, 2022). Very clearly, the pandemic demonstrates that a reliable childcare infrastructure is essential for the well-being of parents and children (Vicari et al., 2022). Unmistakably, the pandemic has exacerbated existing social inequalities (Langmeyer et al., 2022). One-parent families and families with low incomes or even with limited space at home were most affected. Highly educated parents were better able to compensate for canceled school classes. The pandemic has enormously increased the demand for digital connectivity and revealed major deficits, such as poor technical equipment in many schools and a lack of connections in households (BMFSFJ, 2021). Contrary to widespread assumptions, the available results show neither a larger reduction in paid working hours among women than men (Knize et al., 2022) nor a re-traditionalization of care work (Naujoks et al., 2022). Mothers have even returned to their pre-pandemic working hours faster than fathers. Reduced work hours seem to have contributed to an increase in paternal involvement in the family. Overall, the division of household labor seems to have remained mostly stable during the pandemic (Hank & Steinbach, 2021). However, gender differences also emerged. Mothers report higher levels of stress, mainly because they performed most of the coping work in the families. The results also reveal that the standard family norm is still dominant in the design of family policy measures. The existing complexity of family structures and the diversity of today's family forms still do not receive enough attention from policy makers (Zartler, Suwada, & Kreyenfeld, 2022).

References

Adler, M.A., & Brayfield, A. (2006). Gender regimes & cultures of care: Public support for maternal employment in Germany and the United States. *Marriage & Family Review*, *39*(3–4), 229–253.

Andersson, G. (2021). Family behaviour of migrants. In N. F. Schneider & M. Kreyenfeld (Eds.), *Research handbook on the sociology of the family* (pp. 253–276). Elger.

Bastin, S. (2019). Single mothers' new partners: Partnership and household formation in Germany. *Journal of Marriage and Family*, *81*(4), 991–1003.

Bastin, S., Kreyenfeld, M., & Schnor, C. (2013). Diversität von Familienformen in Ost- und Westdeutschland. In D. Krüger, H. Herma, & A. Schierbaum (Eds.), *Familie(n) heute: Entwicklungen, Kontroversen, Prognosen* (pp. 126–145). Beltz Juventa.

Baykara-Krumme, H. (2015). Migrantenfamilien. In P. B. Hill & J. Kopp (Eds.), *Handbuch Familiensoziologie* (pp. 709–736). Springer.

Bender, D. (2021). Co-Elternschaften. Familienverhältnisse in Un-Ordnung? In A.-C. Schondelmayer, C. Riegel, & S. Fitz-Klausner (Eds.), *Familie und Normalität: Diskurse, Praxen und Aushandlungsprozesse* (pp. 207–224). Barbara Budrich.

Bergold, P., Buschner, A., Mayer-Lewis, B., & Mühling, T. (Eds.) (2017). *Familien mit multipler Elternschaft*. Barbara Budrich.

Bertram, H., & Deuflhard, C. (2013). Das einkommensabhängige Elterngeld als Element einer nachhaltigen Familienpolitik. *Zeitschrift für Familienforschung*, *25*(2), 154–172.

Bujard, M., Driesch, E, Ruckdeschel, K. Laß, I., Thönnissen, C., Schumann, A., & Schneider, N. F. (2021). *Belastungen von Kindern, Jugendlichen und Eltern in der Corona-Pandemie*. Bundesinstitut für Bevölkerungsforschung.

Bundesministerium für Familie, Senioren, Frauen und Jugend (BMFSFJ). (2006). *Siebter Familienbericht: Familie zwischen Flexibilität und Verlässlichkeit. Perspektiven für eine lebenslaufbezogene Familienpolitik*. Retrieved from https://www.bmfsfj.de/resource/blob/76276/40b5b103e693dacd4c014648d906aa99/7-familienbericht-data.pdf

Bundesministerium für Familie, Senioren, Frauen und Jugend (BMFSFJ). (2021). *Neunter Familienbericht. Eltern sein in Deutschland*. Retrieved from https://www.bmfsfj.de/resource/blob/179392/195baf88f8c3ac7134347d2e19f1cdc0/neunter-familienbericht-bundestagsdrucksache-data.pdf

Bundesministerium für Familie, Senioren, Frauen und Jugend (BMFSFJ). (2022a). *Familienleben und Familienpolitik in Ost- und Westdeutschland*. Monitor Familienforschung – Ausgabe 44. Retrieved from https://www.bmfsfj.de/resource/blob/198756/97c0eb06ddc1d39dbdb145fafad69c97/familienleben-und-familienpolitik-in-ost-und-westdeutschland-data.pdf

Bundesministerium für Familie, Senioren, Frauen und Jugend (BMFSFJ). (2022b) Regenbogenportal: Informationspool der Bundesregierung zu gleichgeschlechtlichen Lebensweisen und geschlechtlicher Vielfalt. Retrieved from https://www.regenbogenportal.de

Bundesministerium für Familie, Senioren, Frauen und Jugend und Bundesministeriums der Justiz (BMFSFJ/BMJ). (2022). Eckpunkte zum Selbstbestimmungsgesetz. Retrieved from https://www.bmfsfj.de/resource/blob/199382/1e751a6b7f366eec396d146b3813eed2/20220630-selbstbestimmungsgesetz-eckpunkte-data.pdf

Buschner, A., & Bergold, P. (2017). Regenbogenfamilien in Deutschland. In P. Bergold, A. Buschner, B. Mayer-Lewis, & T. Mühling (Eds.), *Familien mit multipler Elternschaft* (pp. 143–172). Barbara Budrich.

Datenreport 2021. (2021). *Ein Sozialbericht für die Bundesrepublik Deutschland*. Bundeszentrale für Politische Bildung.

Dethloff, N., & Timmermann, A. (2017). Multiple Elternschaft – Familienrecht und Familienleben im Spannungsverhältnis. In P. Bergold, A. Buschner, B. Mayer-Lewis, & T. Mühling (Eds.), *Familien mit multipler Elternschaft* (pp. 173–194). Barbara Budrich.

Deutsches IVF-Register e.V. (DIR) (2021). Jahrbuch 2020. *Journal für Reproduktionsmedizin und Endokrinologie*. (Sonderheft 3). Retrieved from https://www.deutsches-ivf-register.de/perch/resources/dirjb2020

Dorbritz, J. (2009). Das Heiratsverhalten Lediger, Geschiedener und Verwitweter in Deutschland 2007: Ergebnisse der Berechnung von Heiratstafeln. *Bevölkerungsforschung Aktuell*, *30*(3), 2–6.

Entleitner-Phleps, C., Lux, U., & Walper, S. (2020). Doing Family in komplexen Familienformen: Herausforderungen in der Alltagsgestaltung und im Coparenting in Stieffamilien. In K. Jurczyk (Ed.), *Doing und Undoing Family* (pp. 214–228). Beltz Juventa.

Entleitner-Phleps, C., & Rost, H. (2017). Stieffamilien. In P. Bergold, A. Buschner, B. Mayer-Lewis, & T. Mühling (Eds.), *Familien mit multipler Elternschaft* (pp. 29–56). Barbara Budrich.

Fachkommission Integrationsfähigkeit. (2021). *Gemeinsam die Einwanderungsgesellschaft gestalten.: Bericht der Fachkommission der Bundesregierung zu den Rahmenbedingungen der Integrationsfähigkeit*. Fachkommission der Bundesregierung. Retrieved: https://www. bmi. bund. de/SharedDocs/downloads/DE/veroeffentlichungen/themen/h eimat-integration/integration/bericht-fkintegrationsfaehigkeit. pdf

Funcke, D. (2021). *Die gleichgeschlechtliche Familie: Soziologische Fallstudien*. Springer.

Gammerl, B. (2010). Eine Regenbogengeschichte. *Aus Politik und Zeitgeschichte 15/16*, 7–13.

Gehres, W., & Hildenbrand, B. (2008). *Identitätsbildung und Lebensverläufe bei Pflegekindern*. Springer.

Gehres, W., & Sauer, S. (2020). Adoptiv- und Pflegefamilien. In J. Ecarius & A. Schierbaum (Eds.), *Handbuch Familie* (pp. 1–19). Springer.

Greschke, H., & Motowidlo, J. (2020). Getrennt zusammenleben: Soziotechnische Konstellationen und Praktiken der Fürsorge und Erziehung im Kontext von Transmigration. In S. Maasen & J.-H. Passoth (Eds.), *Soziologie des Digitalen – digitale Soziologie?* (pp. 225–246). Nomos.

Hank, K., & Steinbach, A. (2021). The virus changed everything, didn't it? Couples' division of housework and childcare before and during the Corona crisis. *Journal of Family Research*, *33*(1), 99–114.

Hartl, A. (2002). Die Beziehung des Stiefkindes zu seinem außerhalb lebenden Elternteil. In W. Bien (Ed.), *Stieffamilien in Deutschland: Eltern und Kinder zwischen Normalität und Konflikt* (pp. 177–198). Leske+Budrich.

Heintz-Martin, V., Entleitner-Phleps, C., & Langmeyer, A. N. (2015). Doing (step)family: Family life in (step)families in Germany. In U. Zartler, V. Heintz-Martin, & O. Arranz Becker (Eds.), *Family dynamics after separation: A life course perspective on post-divorce families*. Sonderheft Zeitschrift für Familienforschung, 27 (pp. 65–82). Barbara Budrich.

Hettlage, R., & Lenz, K. (2013). *Projekt Deutschland: Zwischenbilanz nach zwei Jahrzehnten*. Fink.

Hoffmann-Riem, C. (1994). The management of threatened normality in adoption: Structuring the awareness context. In C. Hoffmann-Riem (Ed.), *Elementare Phänomene der Lebenssituation: Ausschnitte aus einem Jahrzehnt soziologischen Arbeitens* (pp. 119–140). Deutscher Studien Verlag.

Hubert, S., Neuburger, F., Sommer, & Maximilian. (2020). Alleinerziehend, alleinbezahlend? Kindesunterhalt, Unterhaltsvorschuss und Gründe für den Unterhaltsausfall. *Zeitschrift für Soziologie der Sozialisation und Erziehung, 40*(1), 19–38.

Huinink, J., Brüderl, J., Nauck, B., Walper, S., Castiglioni, L., & Feldhaus, M. (2011). Panel analysis of intimate relationships and family dynamics (pairfam): Conceptual framework and design. *Zeitschrift für Familienforschung, 23*(1), 77–101.

Keil, J., & Langmeyer, A. N. (2020). Vater-Kind Kontakt nach Trennung und Scheidung: Die Bedeutung struktureller sowie intrafamilialer Faktoren. *Zeitschrift für Soziologie der Sozialisation und Erziehung, 40*(1), 39–61.

Knize, V., Tobler, L., Christoph, B., Fervers, L., & Jacob, M. (2022). Workin' moms ain't doing so bad: Evidence on the gender gap in working hours at the outset of the COVID-19 pandemic. *Journal of Family Research, 34*(1), 161–192.

Köhler, A., Kröper, E., & Gehres, W. (2017). Die Gestaltung geteilter Elternschaft in Pflegefamilien, deren fachliche Begleitung und die Rückkehr von Pflegekindern. In P. Bergold, A. Buschner, B. Mayer-Lewis, & T. Mühling (Eds.), *Familien mit multipler Elternschaft* (pp. 57–84). Barbara Budrich.

Köppen, K., Kreyenfeld, M., & Trappe, H. (2018). Loose ties? Determinants of father–child contact after separation in Germany. *Journal of Marriage and Family, 80*(5), 1163–1175.

Kühn, P. G. (2015). *Zukunft wächst aus Herkunft. Adoptierte suchen ihre Wurzeln – die biografische Aneignung der Adoptionsgeschichte.* Ibidem Verlag.

Langmeyer, A. N, Guglhör-Rudan, A., Winklhofer, U., Chabursky, S., Naab, T., & Pötter, U. (2022). Resources of families adapting the COVID-19 pandemic in Germany: A mixed-method study of coping strategies and family and child outcomes. *Journal of Family Research 34*(1), 333–366.

Lengerer, A., & Bohr, J. (2019). Gibt es eine Zunahme gleichgeschlechtlicher Partnerschaften in Deutschland? Theoretische Überlegungen und empirische Befunde. *Zeitschrift für Soziologie, 48*(2), 136–157. https://doi.org/10.1515/zfsoz-2019-0010

Lengerer, A., Bohr, J., & Janßen, A. (2005). *Haushalte, Familien und Lebensformen im Mikrozensus: Konzepte und Typisierungen.* ZUMA.

Lengerer, A., & Klein, T. (2007). Der langfristige Wandel partnerschaftlicher Lebensformen im Spiegel des Mikrozensus. *Wirtschaft und Statistik, 4*, 433–447.

Lenz, K., & Adler, M. (2010). *Geschlechterverhältnisse: Einführung in die sozialwissenschaftliche Geschlechterforschung Band 1.* Juventa.

Mayer-Lewis, B. (2017). Die Familiengründung mit Gametenspende. In P. Bergold, A. Buschner, B. Mayer-Lewis, & T. Mühling (Eds.), *Familien mit multipler Elternschaft* (113–142). Barbara Budrich.

Mühling, T., & Franz, J. (2017): Adoptivfamilien. In P. Bergold, A. Buschner, B. Mayer-Lewis, & T. Mühling (Eds.), *Familien mit multipler Elternschaf* (pp. 85–112). Barbara Budrich.

Naujoks, T., Kreyenfeld, M., & Dummert, S. (2022). The division of child care during the coronavirus crisis in Germany: How did short-time work affect fathers' engagement? *Journal of Family Research, 34*(1), 67–98.

Peukert, A., Teschlade, J., Wimbauer, C., Motakef, M., & Holzleithner, E. (2020). Elternschaft und Familie jenseits Heteronormativität und Zweigeschlechtlichkeit. Eine Einleitung. *Gender Sonderheft, 5*, 9–27.

Pötzsch, O. (2018). Aktueller Geburtenanstieg und seine Potenziale. *Wirtschaft und Statistik, 3,* 72–89.

Pötzsch, O., Klüsener, S., & Dudel, C. (2020). Wie hoch ist die Kinderzahl von Männern? *Wirtschaft und Statistik, 5,* 59–77.

Rupp, M. (Ed.) (2009). *Die Lebenssituation von Kindern in gleichgeschlechtlichen Lebenspartnerschaften.* Bundesanzeiger-Verl.-Ges.

Rupp, M., & Haag, C. (2016). Gleichgeschlechtliche Partnerschaften: Soziodemographie und Lebenspläne. In Y. Niephaus, M. Kreyenfeld, & R. Sackmann (Eds.), *Handbuch Bevölkerungssoziologie* (pp. 328–345). Springer.

Schäfer, C. (2006). *"Widernatürliche Unzucht" (§§ 175, 175a, 175b, 182 a.F. StGB).* BWV.

Schier, M., & Schlinzig, T. (2018): Familie per Skype, Messenger und Google Docs. Medienvermittelte Eltern-Kind-Beziehungen in der Spätmoderne. In Kapella, O. et al. (eds.), *Familie – Bildung – Migration. Familienforschung im Spannungsfeld zwischen Wissenschaft, Politik und Praxis* (pp. 91–104). Barbara Budrich.

Schlinzig, T. (2021). Zwischen Anlehnung, Zurückweisung und Selbstbehauptung. Positionierungen multilokaler Nachtrennungsfamilien zum Leitbild der "Normalfamilie". In A.-C. Schondelmayer, C. Riegel, & S. Fitz-Klausner (Eds.), *Familie und Normalität: Diskurse, Praxen und Aushandlungsprozesse* (pp. 189–206). Barbara Budrich.

Schmidt, G., Dekker, A., Matthiesen, S., & Starke, K. (2006). *Spätmoderne Beziehungswelten: Report über Partnerschaft und Sexualität in drei Generationen.* VS.

Schneider, N. F., Bujard, M., Wolf, C., Gummer, T., Hank, K., & Neyer, F. J. (2021). Family research and demographic analysis (FReDA): Evolution, framework, objectives, and design of "The German Family-Demographic Panel Study". *Comparative Population Studies, 46,* 149–186.

Schramm, E. (2018). Das verbotene Kind – Zur (straf-)rechtlichen Bewertung der Leihmutterschaft in Deutschland. In E. Schramm & M. Wermke (Eds.), *Leihmutterschaft und Familie. Impulse aus Recht, Theologie und Medizin* (pp. 61–94). Springer.

Shinozaki, K., Abramowski, R., Stöllinger, L., & Winkler, A. (2021). Grenzüberschreitend lebende Familien: Elternschaft im transnationalen Migrationskontext. In Sachverständigenkommission des Neunten Familienberichts (Ed.), *Eltern sein in Deutschland: Materialien zum 9. Familienbericht* (pp. 37–110). DJI-Verlag.

Statistisches Bundesamt. (2001). *Haushalte und Familien. Ergebnisse des Mikrozensus 2000: Bevölkerung und Erwerbstätigkeit Fachserie 1 Reihe 1.* Wiesbaden.

Statistisches Bundesamt. (2018). *Alleinerziehende in Deutschland 2017: Begleitmaterial zur Pressekonferenz am 2. August 2018.* Retrieved from https://www.destatis.de/DE/Presse/Pressekonferenzen/2018/Alleinerziehende/pressebroschuere-alleinerziehende.pdf?__blob=publicationFile

Statistisches Bundesamt. (2020). *Statistiken der Kinder- und Jugendhilfe: Adoption 2019.* Retrieved from https://www.destatis.de/DE/Themen/Gesellschaft-Umwelt/Soziales/Adoptionen/Publikationen/Downloads/adoptionen-5225201197004.pdf;jsessionid=E3ECAF7ED165B1F5059D205516747C3A.live732?__blob=publicationFile

Statistisches Bundesamt. (2021a). *Haushalte und Familien. Ergebnisse des Mikrozensus 2020: Bevölkerung und Erwerbstätigkeit Fachserie 1 Reihe 1.* Wiesbaden. Retrieved from https://www.destatis.de/DE/Themen/Gesellschaft-Umwelt/Bevoelkerung/Haushalte-Familien/Publikationen/Downloads-Haushalte/haushalte-familien-2010300207004.pdf?__blob=publicationFile

Statistisches Bundesamt. (2021b). *Zusammenfassende Übersichten Eheschließungen, Geborene und Gestorbene 1946–2020.* Wiesbaden.

Statistisches Bundesamt. (2021c). *Bevölkerung mit Migrationshintergrund – Ergebnisse des Mikrozensus 2020.* Bevölkerung und Erwerbstätigkeit. Fachserie 1 Reihe 2.2. Wiesbaden.

Statistisches Bundesamt. (2021d). *Eheschließungen nach der Konstellation der Ehe.* Retrieved from https://www.destatis.de/DE/Themen/Gesellschaft-Umwelt/Bevoelkerung/ Eheschliessungen-Ehescheidungen-Lebenspartnerschaften/Tabellen/ eheschliessungen-paarkonstellation.html?nn=208760

Steinbach, A. (2008). Stieffamilien in Deutschland. *Zeitschrift für Bevölkerungswissenschaft, 33*(2), 153–180.

Steinbach, A. (2015). Stieffamilien. In P. B. Hill & J. Kopp (Eds.), *Handbuch Familiensoziologie* (pp. 563–610). Springer VS.

Trappe, H. (2020). Reproduktionsmedizin und Familie. In J. Ecarius & A. Schierbaum (Eds.), *Handbuch Familie.* Springer Fachmedien Wiesbaden.

Vicari, B., Zoch, G., & Bächmann, A. C. (2022). Childcare, work or worries? What explains the decline in parents' well-being at the beginning of the COVID-19 pandemic in Germany? *Journal of Family Research, 34*(1), 310–332.

Vries, L. D. (2021). Regenbogenfamilien in Deutschland. Ein Überblick über die Lebenssituation von homo- und bisexuellen Eltern und deren Kindern. In Sachverständigenkommission des Neunten Familienberichts (Ed.), *Eltern sein in Deutschland: Materialien zum 9. Familienbericht* (pp. 1–35). DJI-Verlag.

Walper, S., Entleitner-Phleps, C., & Langmeyer, A. N. (2020). Betreuungsmodelle in Trennungsfamilien: Ein Fokus auf das Wechselmodell. *Zeitschrift für Soziologie der Sozialisation und Erziehung, 40*(1), 62–80.

Wimbauer, C. (2021). *Co-Parenting und die Zukunft der Liebe: Über post-romantische Elternschaft.* Transcript.

Wissenschaftlicher Beirat für Familienfragen. (2021). *Gemeinsam getrennt erziehen. Gutachten.* BMBSFJ. Retrieved from https://www.bmfsfj.de/resource/ blob/186694/14f09ddddab459a2e2cefaab6b45c630/gemeinsam-getrennt-erziehenwissenschaftlicher-beirat-data.pdf

Zartler, U., Dafert, V., & Dirnberger, P. (2022). What will the coronavirus do to our kids? Parents in Austria dealing with the effects of the COVID-19 pandemic on their children. *Journal of Family Research, 34*(1), 333–366.

Zartler, U., Suwada, K., & Kreyenfeld, M. (2022). Family lives during the COVID-19 pandemic in European societies: Introduction to the special issue. *Journal of Family Research, 34*(1), 1–15.

5

LIMITED FAMILY DIVERSITY IN JAPAN

A legacy of traditional familism

Takashi Yamashita

The cultural and social context of doing family

Japanese society reflects some aspects of the concept of "compressed modernity" (Chang, 1999), i.e., the condensed socio-economic and cultural developments experienced in other East Asian nations, as well as signs of re-traditionalization (Ochiai, 2014). Social and economic changes that took centuries to develop in Western nations occurred much more rapidly in East Asia—in the decades since World War II (WWII). The lack of family diversity observed in contemporary Japan hints at the coexistence of contradictory historical and new societal features that both reinforce and challenge the relatively homogenous Japanese life course. Ochiai (2014) identifies the mid-1970s as turning point in the rapid "Westernization" of Japan and observes that rather than embracing individualism and gender equality, a familialist welfare state regime was put in place and public attitudes began to reflect "familialistic individualization." Despite economic prosperity and comparatively high labor force participation rates of women, Japan's government did not enact more generous provisions for families at the time. Instead, by invoking Japanese traditions, the neo-liberal "Japanese-type welfare" state centers on the traditional obligations of families and the care work women perform in families (Ochiai, 2014). However, the family form being promoted in policies since then is the Western male breadwinner model rather than the multigenerational family based on economic exchange relationships. Although the Basic Law for a Gender-equal Society was passed in 1999 and the Long-term Care Insurance Act in 2000, the traditional institution of marriage and the deeply entrenched gender-based division of labor remain dominant in Japanese families (Ochiai, 2014).

Japan has a long history of patriarchal family traditions rooted in Confucian familism, such as hierarchical relationships based on seniority and

DOI: 10.4324/9781003193500-5

cross-generational wealth transfer, and a gendered division of household labor. Simply put, traditionally each generation is expected to play specific gendered roles—men are the breadwinners and women take care of the household and child/ren, while also caring for older parents—and eventually, they inherit the family assets. However, this traditional model is no longer considered the standard family form in modern Japanese society. Demographically, the most salient changes regarding family formation and family policy were initially observed after WWII. Although there was the first wave of the baby boom (1947–1949) after the war, a national birth control policy resulted in a rapid decline in the fertility rate and started a 70-year-long low fertility trend in the early 1950s (Sasaki, 2015).

After WWII, the Japanese government mainly focused on economic development, and family-related policy has been somewhat supplemental to economic and labor policy. Thus, until recently, the emerging diversity in family forms and family formation, and the necessity of related family policies have not been extensively discussed (Taki, 2013). In general, the most noteworthy post-WWII changes in the family forms in Japan are the decrease in three-generation households from 12% to 6% between 1970 and 2005 and the simultaneous increase in single-person households from 20% to 30% during that time period (Cabinet Office of Japan, 2006). Other important family-related trends in Japanese society are its rapidly aging population and women's increased labor force participation. As of 2015, approximately 30% of the population was aged 65 years and older, and this has impacted every aspect of individual lives, families, communities, and society in general (Otsu & Shibayama, 2022). Finally, the labor force participation rates of Japanese women grew from less than 50% in the early 1970s to 76% by 2016 (Shambaugh et al., 2017). This combination of changes in family tradition, demographic trends, population aging, and women's labor force participation has created unprecedented challenges to families and state policies in Japan.

Despite these changes and decades of below-replacement level fertility, the Japanese state only recently started implementing pro-natalist policies (Jones, 2019). The policy measures to stave off rapid population decline usually target marriage, fertility, and immigration. In Japan, policies to increase immigration are not popular so that only means-tested child allowance policies and public childcare expansion as well as marriage incentives that increase access to housing and employment have been introduced (Jones, 2019). The effect of these policies remains limited because any "flight from marriage" is not necessarily only related to avoiding childbirth. The demand for child care remains larger than the supply, and the economic burden of child-rearing is not reduced significantly with existing policies. The challenge is to expand welfare state policy to include more generous family transfers, parental leave, widely available childcare, and more family-friendly workplaces within the context of an aging society that resists the move away from Confucian familism (Jones, 2019).

Japanese culture has traditionally defined family strictly in terms of blood relatives. The primary reason for the importance of blood lineage is the continuation of the family name and the transfer of wealth across generations. Due to increasing westernization and demographic changes, such as rapid population aging and extremely low fertility rates in the last several decades, family is now more broadly defined as a small group consisting mainly of blood relatives that aim to ensure each other's direct welfare (Takemura, 2019). Thus, the members of a family are expected to be related by blood or marriage and to provide care to each other. Traditionally, a typical Japanese family involved a multigenerational household that includes older parents, their married children, and their grandchildren. Such multigenerational households are conventionally based on a mutual understanding of delayed social exchanges, which means that the older parents will transfer their wealth to the younger generation in exchange for the provision of family care in old age. However, in view of the social and cultural transformations, this traditional family has undergone changes in form and function.

In general, Japanese families are viewed through the lens of social obligations and provision of a safety net. They are expected to maintain the legacy of ancestors (the transmission of wealth and the good reputation of the family) and provide care and financial resource to vulnerable family members, such as older adults and children (Tabuchi, 2021). Indeed, the familist Japanese welfare state heavily relies on families, and especially on women, to provide care to their older parents and children. For example, until the current long-term care insurance program was established in 2000, caregiving to older family members was provided predominantly by family members (Yamada & Arai, 2020). Families have also been socially expected to produce and re-produce the labor force across generations. Nevertheless, due to the major demographic and socio-economic changes observed in recent decades, the functions of families have changed (Garon, 2010). Families have gradually expanded their responsibilities to providing and/or fulfilling basic need security (residence, food), labor force production, social support, emotional well-being, initial human development to become a member of society, and meeting sexual needs (Watanabe, 2008). In short, the family as a social unit, rather than the state, is a multipurpose group that addresses the needs of individuals and society.

Relatedly, the Japanese government's definition of family forms may not clearly reflect the current living arrangements of families. From the government statistics perspective, family forms generally focus on blood/legal relationships, the existence of two different-sex parents (as opposed to one-parent or same-sex families) in households with child/ren, multiple generations (i.e., grandparents, parents, and child/ren), and age (e.g., age 65 years and older). However, traditional family functions, such as caregiving across generations, cannot be captured in the available government statistics. For example, the percentage of older adults who live with their children has been declining since the 1970s and reached less than 50% around 2000 (Yasuda et al., 2011). Yet, the reasons for the declining intergenerational coresidence are complex and related to the observed demographic changes (e.g., increasing older population, lower fertility, and fewer children), economy, and attitudes toward coresidence (Yasuda et al., 2011). That is to say, the existing family statistics may not capture the actual meaning and structure of families and living arrangements in Japan.

Japanese families have several unique socio-cultural features. The culturally dominant family form is a nuclear heteronormative patriarchal family with one wage-earning husband, one wife, and two children. This "standard" family has been used as the reference or comparison group in Japanese official statistics and family sociology. Although this family form is still relatively common, it only describes approximately 30% of all families in the 21st century, and using it as the normative reference group has been criticized as families have become more diverse in recent years (Iwai, 2011). Furthermore, in Japan, relatively strict gender norms in terms of the division of labor prevail within families and society. Specifically, the male breadwinner/female homemaker model (sengyou shuhu) is the social norm (Lewis, 1992). Thus, men are expected to be workers and providers, whereas women are in charge of household maintenance and caregiving, for both children and older parents. Interestingly, while the oldest son is expected to provide care for his older parents in exchange for the inheritance of wealth from his parents, it is usually his wife who provides most of the direct care for the activities of daily living (e.g., eating, bathing, and toileting) of her parents-in-law (Slote & De Vos, 1998). Bumpass and colleagues (2009) refer to this as the "marriage package," which includes a heavy care burden for women, and thus, anecdotally, women joke about asking potential male partners before marriage whether they are the oldest sons to avoid future caregiving responsibilities. In fact, this may be a reason for the reduced popularity of marriage.

These traditional perceptions of family and the gender division of labor are rooted in the cultural ideology of Confucianism. Confucian familism, which originated in China, places particular importance on the centrality of the family as the fundamental social unit (Keller, 2012). Japan belongs to the so-called Confucian culture zone, which also includes China and Korea, and is guided by Confucian cultural principles and practices. One of the most salient ideas is filial piety or familial obligation to parents and ancestors. That is, family members are expected to take care of each other and worship their ancestors in their everyday lives and through seasonal events. Traditionally, filial piety guides the responsibilities of adult children to provide care for their parents. However, grandparenting and other support from older parents to their adult children have been growing (Nakazawa et al., 2017).

Another key aspect of Confucian familism is the gender division of household labor. Specifically, women's primary role is to bear and raise children who will carry family traditions and resources to future generations (Keller, 2012). The Confucian-informed gender division of labor within families has spread across different domains of life, including labor force participation and civic engagement (Fleckenstein & Lee, 2017). Indicators of gender equality show that Japan ranks very low among developed nations: in fact, it is 121st among 153 countries (World Economic Forum, 2019). Women tend to earn significantly lower wages than men, have fewer opportunities to advance in employment and political

TABLE 5.1 Selected demographic indicators for Japan, 2000 and latest available data

	2000	*Latest available data*	
Crude marriage rate	6.4	2019	4.8
Mean age at first marriage			
of women	27.0	2019	29.6
of men	28.8	2019	31.2
Crude divorce rate	2.1	2019	1.70
Remarriage rate			
of women	13.4	2019	16.9
of men	15.0	2019	19.7
% of adults > 15 never married			
of women	23.7	2020	24.8
men	31.8	2020	34.6
Total fertility rate	1.36	2019	1.36
Mean age at first birth			
of women	28.0	2019	30.7
% non-marital births	1.6	2015	2.3
% of women who have born no children	10.1 (2002)	2015	21.8
Cohorts	**1950**		**1970**
Completed fertility/cohort	N.A.		N.A.
% of women aged 40–44 who have born no children for cohorts	N.A.		N.A.

Sources: Moriizumi (2019b); Statistics Bureau of Japan (2021); The World Bank (2021); OECD (2022).

positions than men, and spend about four times more time on unpaid domestic work than men (World Economic Forum, 2019). While the gender gap in health and education has narrowed in the past decades, men still remain the head of their households due to their advantages in economic and political positions.

Compared to Western developed nations, ethnic and racial diversity in Japanese society as a whole is limited in several ways. The vast majority of the population is ethnic Japanese, and out of a total population of about 126 million, only 2.3% are foreign-born (Statistics Bureau of Japan, 2021). Three in four immigrants come from other Asian countries, such as China, South Korea, Vietnam, the Philippines, and Nepal (Immigration Services Agency of Japan, 2021). In this context, Japan's relatively homogenous life course and cultural composition, in addition to the group-oriented culture, may serve to resist the development of diverse family forms. Overall, Japan has not seen some of the value changes underlying the observed family diversification in Western nations, such as the embrace of individualism, emphasis on women's empowerment, and societal acceptance of non-marital cohabitation and childbearing outside of marriage.

Empirical patterns of various family forms

Union formation and dissolution

Table 5.1 presents marriage-related data for the year 2000 and the most recent year for which data are available. Overall, since 2000, the number of marriages and divorces has decreased, while the average age at first marriage and the proportion of remarriage have increased. The annual marriage rate decreased from 6.4 (per 1,000 population) in 2000 to about 4.8 in 2019 (Statistics Bureau of Japan, 2021). The number of marriages reduced from approximately 800,000 to 635,000 between 2000 and 2015 (Ministry of Health Labour and Welfare, 2015). In 2000, the average age at first marriage was around 29 for men and 27 years for women. This increased to 31 and 30 in 2019, respectively. Consistent with this change, two in five people got married after the age of 30 in 2015, while in 2000, it was one in five people. Among the factors explaining this delay in marriage are extended higher education, women avoiding the disadvantages associated with the "marriage package" (Bumpass et al., 2009), diversification of life course alternatives, increasingly demanding workplaces, and concerns over work–family conflicts (Jones, 2019). The proportion of remarriages among all marriages rose from 15% for men and 13% for women in 2000 to about 20% and 17% in 2015. In the same time period, the number of divorces decreased from 264,246 to 226,198, and the crude divorce rate decreased from 2.1 to 1.7 (per 1,000 population). Although these numbers reflect recent trends in family formation, the interpretation and explanation require caution. For example, the decrease in marriage rates may reflect historical trends, such as the marriage boom in the 1970s as well as the size of the cohort (i.e., sub-populations born in a specific time period, such as baby boomers). Also, the decrease in the divorce rate may be due to economic hardships experienced by married couples. For example, married women tend to be responsible for household work, and therefore, leaving the labor market causes a gap in their career trajectories (Ono & Sanders, 2009). Thus, some women who want to end their marriage may not have sufficient economic resources to sustain an independent life and may need to remain in the current marriage rather than divorce. Further data exploration is beyond the scope of this chapter but is necessary to fully understand the family formation and dissolution trends in future research. The percentage of never-married adults (24.8% of women and 34.6% of men) in 2015 has increased somewhat since 2002 (23.7% of women and 31.8% of men), which continues a trend observed since the 1990s. In the absence of official statistics on cohabitation, estimates based on the National Survey on Population, Family, and Generations in Japan (SPFG) show that although cohabitation is quite rare in Japan compared to other advanced nations, it may be increasing more rapidly than expected in the new millennium (Iwasawa, 2004; Raymo et al., 2009).

Fertility patterns

The total fertility rate in Japan has been one of the lowest in the world since the late 1970s (The World Bank, 2021). The rate has been about 1.36 for the last two decades (OECD, 2021). Thus, on average, upon completion of her childbearing years, a woman had only 1.4 children. Given that marriage is generally a key life event that precedes having children in Japan and given that the non-marital birthrate is extremely low, part of the reason for this lower fertility could be due to the lower marriage rate and the delay of marriage (Jones, 2019). Because a fertility rate of 2.1 is needed for population replacement without immigration and because immigration to Japan is quite low, the population size has shrunk by 1 million: from 126,843,000 to 125,836,021 between 2000 and 2020 (The World Bank, 2021). Interestingly, the median age at first birth has increased from 30.1 to 32.8 between 2000 and 2019, reflecting a trend toward postponing childbirth. The percentage of births to unmarried women is quite low, but it has increased from 1.6 to 2.3 since 2000. However, recent vital statistics data show that about one in four first marriages is preceded by pregnancy, referred to as "bridal pregnancy" (Raymo & Iwasawa, 2008). The percentage of women who have born no children has doubled to 21.8% in 2015, compared to 10.1% in 2002.

Changes in household composition and living arrangements

Tables 5.2 and 5.3 show the changes in living arrangements and household structure between 2000 and 2020. There are a few interesting trends. There was a slight increase from 14.2% to 17.1% in households with married couples only. Also, among those aged 85 and over, there was an increase from 10.7% to 18.0% in the households of married couples. Presumably, the older age at the first marriage, the longer life expectancy, and resulting increased care needs jointly explained these trends. Notably, the proportion of those living alone has increased between 2000 and 2020. More adults aged 85 years and older are living alone, an increase from 14.7% to 25.2%. Although the utilization of long-term care facilities has grown in accordance with population aging, three in four older

TABLE 5.2 Population in living arrangements in Japan, 2000 and latest available data

% of adults are living	2000			2020		
	Total	Age 20–24	Age 25–29	Total	Age 20–24	Age 25–29
With spouse	NA	NA	NA	NA	NA	NA
With partner	NA	NA	NA	NA	NA	NA
Child of householder	NA	NA	NA	NA	NA	NA
Alone	10.4	23.6	17.9	14.7	26.3	24.9
With other relatives	4.8	3.8	4.6	3.7	3.5	3.7
With non-relatives	1.4	1.9	1.5	1	1.9	2.5

Source: Statistics Bureau of Japan (2022).

TABLE 5.3 Households in Japan, 2005 and latest available data

% of households consist of	2005	2015
Different-sex spouses		
with kids <18	29.8	26.9
without kids <18	19.6	20.1
Different-sex partners	NA	NA
with kids <18		
without kids <18		
Mother only with kids	7.1	7.6
Father only with kids	1.2	1.3
Same-sex couple	NA	NA
One person living alone	29.5	34.6
Other households	12.8	9.4

Source: Statistics Bureau of Japan (2022).

adults want to receive care at their own homes if needed in later life (Cabinet Office of Japan, 2018). Also, among the 25–29 age group, the proportion of those living with non-relatives has slightly increased (1.5–2.5%). This may partially reflect the economic hardship among younger workers (e.g., sharing a room to save the housing cost).

Current empirical research on the various family forms

Reconstituted families (Stepfamilies)

Despite the absence of national statistics, researchers point out that due to rising divorce and remarriage rates, there has been an increase in the proportion of Japanese stepfamilies in the last decades. One study of over 3,000 mothers with infants suggests that only about 2% of their households involved a stepfamily (Sugimoto & Yokoyama, 2017). Interestingly, there is no commonly used term for "stepfamily" in the Japanese language so that "suteppufamiri" had to be imported from English into the Japanese dictionary (Nozawa, 2020). Because this term is not commonly used in public discourse, stepfamilies remain socially invisible and the development of legal frameworks, social service provision, and comparative research on stepfamilies is hampered (Nozawa, 2008). In addition, rather than referring to "stepfather" and "stepmother," the terms "new father" and "new mother" are used in an effort to replicate the original nuclear family. In fact, Japanese law considers divorce a matter of private agreement between partners and does not treat stepfamilies differently than the standard family (Nozawa, 2020). This also relates to the fact that family law only allows one legal parent after divorce, supporting the "scrap and build" or "substitute family" household model, in which one of the initial parents is replaced by the stepparent to maintain the same family size and structure (Nozawa, 2020). While until the 1960s legal custody for children after divorce typically went to fathers, in the vast majority of cases, mothers gain sole custody today. Due to these pressures against extended stepfamilies, many children lose contact with their non-custodial parent after divorce. However, survey results show that in 2016 about 29% of divorced mothers and 48% of divorced fathers coreside with their own parents (Ministry of Health Labour and Welfare, 2017).

More recently, family policy began focusing on the Western notion of "the best interests of the child" through long-term parent–child relationships after divorce, and in 2011, the Civil Code was reformed to include child support payments and visitation rights of the non-custodial parent (Minamikata, 2014). This is also reflected in the recent increase of stepfamilies in which children are simultaneously members of and move between both their mother's and father's households. Nozawa (2020) refers to this as the "expanded and interconnected network" or "enduring family" household model, which adds stepparents to biological parents rather than substituting stepparents for biological parents. However, the trend toward post-divorce coparenting is only slowly increasing. In addition to the two stepfamily models, coresiding grandparents also diversify relationships in stepfamilies due to the reciprocal caregiving responsibilities (e.g., grandparenting and caregiving to old parents).

These different variations of stepfamilies in Japan can also lead to conflicts among the members of the stepfamilies and various disadvantages. Studies show that the stepparent-stepchild relationship is often strained by the "substitution" arrangements and stepchildren may exhibit behavioral problems as a result (Nozawa, 2020). The new custodial/residential parent may assume the identity of an "older sister" or "uncle" rather than as new mother or father in order to de-emphasize parental authority (Nozawa, 2020). While more research is needed to identify specific dynamics, Sugimoto and Yokoyama (2017) also reported that the mothers in stepfamily households were more likely to face economic disadvantages, lack of support (e.g., childbirth education), risky behaviors (e.g., smoking when pregnant), and mental health issues compared to mothers in non-stepfamily households. Given the culturally negative views on divorce and remarriage, particularly toward divorced women, as well as the invisibility of stepfamilies in Japanese society, members of stepfamilies may need additional public and social support in Japan (Ono & Sanders, 2009).

One-parent and cohabiting families

Cohabitation is an uncommon but rapidly emerging family form among the young cohorts in Japan, who tend to have more progressive attitudes, and it often leads to marriage and "bridal pregnancy" (Raymo et al., 2009). Neither cohabitation nor childbirth outside of marriage are normatively approved family forms in Japan. It is also generally challenging to meaningfully distinguish between common-law marriages and unmarried cohabitation (Fukuda, 2020).

For example, less than 2% of adults aged between 18 and 34 years old form a non-marital union (Statistics Bureau of Japan, 2021), but the Japanese Census may or may not count a couple as members of the same household, depending on whether they jointly file tax returns. In other words, given the Japanese Census's household definition, which includes sharing the living expenses, unmarried couples may not be counted as household members when filing their tax returns separately.

The low rate of cohabitation is a key difference between Japan and Western nations, where cohabitation is significantly more common and generally accepted. One of the few large data sets on cohabitation in Japan showed that approximately 15% of women cohabit before marriage in 2004, and the percentages seem to be higher among adults in their 20s and 30s (Raymo et al., 2009). Research has shown that cohabitation is becoming more popular as an alternative or preliminary family form to marriage that enables young unmarried couples to manage limited economic resources and develop stability (e.g., career) (Raymo et al., 2009). Also, when a cohabiting couple has a baby, this child is considered an "illegitimate" child in Japan. While the biological mother of a child is automatically recognized as a legal parent regardless of her marital status, the father of a child may require a certificate to obtain legal custody or parental rights when he is not married to the mother. In Japan, more national data and empirical studies on cohabitation would shed light on how family is done when Japanese people cohabit (Moriizumi, 2019a).

In 2019, there were 1,419,000 one-parent households in Japan (Gender Equality Bureau Cabinet Office, 2019). About 87% of them were single-mother households. Historically, the top two reasons for one-parent households were divorce and spouse's death (Ministry of Health Labour and Welfare, 2016a). For example, in the early 1980s, 49% and 36% of one-parent households resulted from divorce and spouse's death, respectively. However, in 2016, in 80% of cases, divorce was the main reason for one-parent households, and being an unmarried mother (8.7%) became a more common reason than the death of spouse (8.0%). Single mothers' social and socio-economic disadvantages have been widely researched. Not only are women increasingly likely to become single mothers, they also face financial difficulties. In 2016, the average income of single-mother households was 3,480,000 yen (roughly equivalent to US$32,000), while that of single-father households was 5,730,000 yen (US$53,000) (Ministry of Health Labour and Welfare, 2016a). Shirahase and Raymo (2014) explain that the reason for the income gap by gender among one-parent households is that women lack access to high-paying jobs. In fact, recent statistics show that approximately 60% of one-parent households reported financial difficulties and 36% experienced food insecurity, compared to 48% and 26% of two-parent households in Japan, respectively (The Japan Institute for Labour Policy and Training, 2020). One of the common coping strategies for one-parent families in poverty, especially single-mother families, is to coreside with their parents to share the living expenses (Shirahase & Raymo, 2014).

Sex and gender minority families (SGM)

Except for several local policies, same-sex marriage is not legally recognized in Japan (Tamagawa, 2018). Indeed, Japan is the only G7 country without the legalization of same-sex marriage, and Taiwan is the only place where same-sex unions are legal in Asia (Pew Research Center, 2019). One survey of Japanese adults aged 40 years and older showed that about 73% of them support same-sex marriage (Ishida et al., 2020). Additionally, the capital of Japan Tokyo made a recent announcement that a new policy that recognizes same-sex partnership may be implemented in 2022. The public attitudes as well as policy directions appear to be supportive of legalizing same-sex marriage in Japan in the near future.

However, there are several socio-cultural issues that have been discussed. The legal definitions of family and marriage refer to different-sex couples and reproduction, and therefore, the idea of same-sex families does not align with the legal system, despite increasing public support (Komatsu, 2016). Also, the existing definition of legal parent-child relationships does not recognize children born outside of traditional marriage, which makes it more difficult to include same-sex parenting in national family policy. In addition, religiosity seems to be linked to negative attitudes toward same-sex marriage. A study by Ishida and colleagues (2020) showed that 20% of religious adults oppose same-sex marriage, compared to 6% of non-religious adults, although there is variability across different religions, with Christians and Shintoists more likely to oppose. Moreover, in terms of political affiliation, conservatives are more likely to have negative attitudes (43%) toward same-sex marriage, compared to 19% of liberals in Japan (Ishida et al., 2020). Another relevant phenomenon is the so-called marital squeeze, which describes the increasingly shrinking pool of eligible male partners, given the greater number of highly educated and economically independent women (Fukuda, 2009). According to existing data of nationally representative surveys, political views and public attitudes seem to generally support same-sex marriage in Japan. In terms of marriage equality, Japan is behind Western nations. At the same time, it should also be recognized that the long history of family and marriage traditions and lack of existing policies may require additional work to legalize same-sex marriage in Japan.

National data related to same-sex marriage are limited. However, an increasing number of local governments allow same-sex partnerships, which provides similar legal recognitions and social benefits to different-sex marriage. For example, two of the districts—Sibuya-ku and Setagaya-ku in the City of Tokyo—approved same-sex partnership in 2015, although the number of approved partnerships was only 133 at the end of 2017 (Shibuya Ku, 2017). However, as of the mid-year of 2021, 110 local governments approved 2,018 same-sex partnership certificates (Niji Bridge, 2021). Also, same-sex couples may request to be legally recognized as households with child/ren (e.g., legally acknowledged kinship and legal rights) (Tamagawa, 2016). The Japanese Census is considering the collection of additional information to capture details on various household forms and family formation in the near future.

Only a handful of recent Japanese studies address LGBTQA+ issues, which are highly relevant to SGM families and public perceptions toward them. Tamagawa (2018) studied a convenient sample of 136 LGBTQA+ adults and found that "coming out of the closet" in Japan was more difficult for parents than for friends and coworkers. Also, Tamagawa reported that coming out to mothers resulted in more negative experiences compared to fathers. These intersections of social network (family and friends) and gender seem to reflect persistent homophobia, and heteronormativity or conventional gender roles in Japanese society (Sano & Yasumoto, 2014). Previous surveys show that more than half of the LGBTQA+ adults supported the legally acknowledged same-sex marriage in Japan (Kamano et al., 2016; Tang et al., 2019). Clearly, the voices and living arrangements of sex and gender minorities are not yet adequately reflected in statistics, laws, and public attitudes in Japan.

Adoptive and foster families

In Japan, there are two types of adoption systems in place—ordinary adoption and special adoption. Here, special adoption and relevant studies are briefly described; for ordinary or adult adoption, see Box 1. Similar to the common adoption system in Western nations, adults who are 25 years and older may adopt a child who is not related by blood. However, only married couples are currently allowed to legally adopt a child aged 15 years and younger through the special adoption program, and same-sex couples or couples who cannot agree on the adoption are not eligible for adoption (Ministry of Justice, 2019). Since 2020, the updated policy allows the adoption of children aged 15 years or younger; previously, the policy referred to children six years old or younger. When a child is adopted, the relationship with the biological parents legally ends. The biological parents may retract their permission for adoption within two weeks. A government agency monitors the first six months of the adoption and may revoke the adoption if the new parents are found to be unfit to provide for the child's needs and well-being. It should be noted that special adoption in Japan is less common compared to Western nations. In 2015, only 544 children were approved for special adoption in Japan (Ministry of Health Labour and Welfare, 2021), making the rate of adoption in Japan comparatively quite low. Relatedly, fostering children is also not as common as in other economically advanced nations. There were 9,949 registered foster families, and 4,731 children were temporarily living with foster families in 2015 (Ministry of Health Labour and Welfare, 2016b). Experience as a foster parent can be an important evaluation criterion when a special adoption is considered. As such, the foster care system may promote adoption. Overall, while adoption is one of the family formation mechanisms, the number of cases is still relatively small, and it is unlikely that adoption has a significant impact on national family diversity statistics in Japan.

There are several issues surrounding adoption in Japan. First, legal experts and non-profit organizations that support individual adoptions are limited, and thus, adults who consider adoption are faced with a complex legal process for adoptions (Hayes, 2008). Also, the feasibility of adoption may be heavily influenced by individual socio-economic status. For example, one of the primary functions of adoption in Japan is to fulfill the cultural norm of maintaining the family line, which implies the need for high social status or wealth of adoption candidates. Also, families may use adoption to avoid inheritance taxes (Buchanan, 2017); for instance, parents may adopt, even only on paper, their adult child's spouse to save inheritance taxes. International adoption is also rare in Japan. However, if the Japanese court approves, intercountry adoption of orphans and of children whose parents are unable to provide for their care is feasible (U.S. Department of State, n.d.). Although there are about 45,000 children who need adoptive or foster parents for a variety of reasons, such as loss of parents or abuse, public attitudes toward adoption are still somewhat negative in Japan (Ministry of Health Labour and Welfare, 2021).

BOX: Adult adoption in Japan (Muko Youshi)

Adult adoption is a centuries-old Japanese tradition that is still practiced today. Adult adoption (ordinary adoption) is allowed for adults aged 20 years and older, but the adopted individual needs to be younger than the adopting parents. Adoptions of adult men (Muko Youshi—adopted son-in-law or bridegroom) are based on the need for male heirs in this patrilineal society to fulfill the Confucian tradition of continuing the family name and ancestor worship. As women conventionally change their family name to their husbands' when getting married, having sons guarantees the continuation of family names and traditions. It should be noted that in recent years, it has become more common that women are keeping their own family names after marriage.

In the Muko Youshi or son-in-law (Ministry of Health Labour and Welfare, 2021) system, an adult man is first adopted by his future wife's parents, takes the last name of these parents, and then, marries their daughter. This way, a family that may only have one or more daughters can ensure that their family name continues to exist in the next generation. The rights of Muko Youshi are different from legally married sons-in-law. One of the main differences between Muko Youshi and Muko (a man married to a woman without adoption) is the right of inheritance. Muko Yoshi is eligible to receive an equal portion of the inheritance from his biological parents as well as his parents-in-law. Muko may not be eligible to receive his parents-in-law's inheritance at the same rate as his wife, who is biologically/legally related to them. In case Muko Youshi's biological father passes away, the biological/legal mother inherits half of the deceased father's wealth, and the two children receive equal amounts. In addition, Muko Youshi is eligible to receive an equal amount of the inheritance when his adoptive father passes away.

Families created by medically assisted reproduction (MAR)

Given the historically low birth rates, along with the postponement of marriage and economic hardship among parents, an increasing number of Japanese adults face possible infertility issues and rely on medically assisted reproduction (MAR) to become parents. While some of the non-scientific approaches, such as natural treatments and traditional Chinese herbal medicine are still popular, public health, medical, and policy experts increasingly advocate for biomedical interventions, such as artificial insemination and in vitro fertilization (IVF) in Japan (Castro-Vázquez, 2015). Assisted reproductive technology (ART) is not only associated with family planning but also with family formation in the late thirties to forties. For example, a single person may want to start a family, and fertility considerations may be very relevant in choosing a potential partner (Van Bavel, 2012). In 2019, 458,101 treatment cycles and 60,598 neonates were recorded at 619 registered MAR facilities in Japan (Katagiri et al., 2022).

There are still a number of MAR-related issues that need to be addressed at the policy level, although the use of ART has become more common in Japan in recent years. One of the primary concerns is economic access. For example, the average cost of an IVF treatment is JPN¥550,000 (roughly US$ 4,600 based on the 2021 currency exchange rate) (Nomura Research Institute, 2021). Although there has been occasional financial assistance from the government in the past, as of April 2022, most of the costs associated with infertility treatments are partially covered by universal health insurance in Japan (Ministry of Health Labour and Welfare, 2022). The high costs of infertility treatments may result in unequal access by socio-economic status. Also, the general population shows a mixture of positive and negative attitudes toward MAR: only about 36% approve of embryo donation and 46% of gestational surrogacy, respectively (Yamamoto et al., 2018). In addition, the legality of sperm or egg donation and the child's right to know how they were conceived are critical issues to be resolved in the context of Japanese society (Yamamoto et al., 2018). Currently, there is no specific policy that regulates children's right to know about sperm or egg donors in Japan. In addition, there have been incidences of sperm or egg donors' false information, and current policies do not regulate use of false information and rely on agreements between the donors and recipients.

From the family formation standpoint, one critical issue regarding MAR is the legal relationship between a parent and child. For example, in 2020, a new national policy states that when a woman gives birth using ART and a donated egg, she will be considered the legal mother of the child, and if a woman gives birth using ART with donated sperm, her husband cannot deny the legitimacy of the child under the law (Ministry of Justice, 2020). In addition, the Japan Society for Reproductive Medicine generally advocates that MAR should be limited to married couples, but they also acknowledge the need to expand ART availability to sex and gender minority couples, unmarried couples, and cohabiting couples (e.g., common-law marriage) (Japan Society for Reproductive Medicine, 2020).

Multicultural and migrant families

As mentioned earlier, Japan is not a multicultural society—it remains very ethnically homogenous with limited immigration, and national data are clear on the limited extent of ethnic, cultural, and racial diversity in Japan. Compared to economically advanced Western nations, Japanese immigration policy is significantly stricter and therefore results in a small proportion of immigrant families (Peng, 2016). Consequently, there are limited statistics and no research studies on multicultural families available.

Only about 143,000 of the few foreign-born immigrants have either spouses or children who are Japanese citizens (Statistics Bureau of Japan, 2021). The citizenship eligibility at birth differs for men and women. When a child is born to a Japanese mother and a non-Japanese father, the child receives Japanese citizenship as the blood relationship is clear. However, when a child is born to a Japanese father and a non-Japanese mother, the father needs to be legally married to the mother or to officially acknowledge that the child is his before the birth of the child to establish its citizenship. Simply being born in Japan does not result in Japanese citizenship, although birthright citizenship is given in other nations, such as the US and Canada.

In addition, there is also very little diversity of religion in Japan. Approximately 92% of the Japanese population consider themselves as Shintoists or Buddhists, and of those with a different religion, only about 1.5% are Christians (Central Intelligence Agency, 2021). These are important points to note in terms of the formation of multicultural households. For example, each religion may offer different perspectives on the forms and functions of marriage and family. As Japan may become more open to immigrants to combat population reduction, there will be an increased need for research on migrant and multicultural families.

Conclusions and recommendations

Based on the review of available national data and research literature on Japanese family forms, two overall themes emerge. First, the meanings of family in Japan need to be updated, reflecting global trends in family diversity. That is, more diverse forms of families should be recognized in statistics, public policy, and social research. While Japan places particular importance on tradition and culture when it comes to families, given the recent demographic changes and projections (e.g., expected future changes in the family forms), describing the various forms families can take in Japan is necessary. Indeed, families as social units are more important than ever in a society characterized by decreasing population due to low fertility rates and population aging. However, due to both the legacy of Confucian familism and simultaneous modernization trends, there is confusion about what constitutes families and how to best support them. For example, the legal and biological definitions of family are still different and not fully aligned in Japan (Mackie, 2013). That is, even though mothers and fathers may be considered biologically a child's parents, they may not automatically be considered legal parents under the current law, depending on their nationality, sexuality, and marital status. In other words, one may say that the current policy only guarantees legal parental status when parents are married heterosexual Japanese citizens.

Second, Japanese society may need to rethink its national identity and cultural diversity in general. The vast majority of the Japanese population is ethnically Japanese. Moreover, even the small number of immigrants is of Asian origin. One of the growing issues in Japan is discrimination against racial and ethnic minorities, and some argue that this partially stems from the lack of diversity throughout Japanese history (Iwabuchi & Takezawa, 2015). Related to the first point, revisiting the role of family diversity in the context of low fertility and population aging, social issues like racism and sexism must be addressed in social policies. By the same token, discrimination against gender minorities also is an important policy issue in Japan (Tamagawa, 2016). In the global community where SGM and multicultural families are rapidly growing, Japan may be left behind unless it embraces diversity.

There are two preliminary recommendations that may help move the discussions and practices in terms of family policies forward in Japan. Expanding the scope of national data collection as well as more research on doing family in non-standard families will contribute to understanding the growing family diversity better. Japanese family sociologists tend to focus on the functions of families rather than family dynamics (Tabuchi, 2021). The examination of other advanced nations' data collection on various family forms as well as successful family policies is necessary to support the development of family diversity in Japan. In this context, making national family data more comparable with existing international data sets would be beneficial. Currently, national data with detailed family classifications that are comparable to other nations are limited. However, rigorous comparisons of welfare state types and family policies across nations may help guide Japan's future family policy agenda as it relates to family diversity (Seeleib-Kaiser & Toivonen, 2011). And scholarship in Japanese family sociology that is accessible in English is still scarce, and finding cross-national studies is challenging. Adapting national data collection strategies and disseminating data and relevant documentation in English may open new possibilities and encourage international researchers to study emerging patterns of family diversity in Japan.

Finally, removing the siloed policy structure across different government agencies may lead to more comprehensive support for diverse families in Japan. Currently, family support policies seem to be compartmentalized in a way so that they address only specific pressing issues. For example, the recent labor shortage partially promoted women's labor force participation, and public opinion and social policies on childcare were forced to change (Seeleib-Kaiser & Toivonen, 2011). Instead of only facilitating reactive policies to support new types of families, identifying existing underlying intersecting issues, including social, political, cultural, and demographic changes, is a reasonable next step. Presumably, opening up borders to international research communities and promoting national data dissemination in English and Japanese may lead to more innovative ideas and cultural acceptance of new forms of family.

Although there are only a few studies on doing family in Japan during the COVID-19 pandemic, several studies provide preliminary insights. Due to the COVID-19 pandemic-related restrictions, family members started spending more time together, often in relatively small dwellings typical for Japan. In addition, increased financial insecurities and the gendered division of labor within households may have increasingly strained the relationships among family members (Kim & Zulueta, 2020). Also, mental health issues of family members in general, and that of mothers, in particular, increased during the pandemic (Shibusawa et al., 2021). Finally, the pandemic highlighted the importance of multigenerational family social networks in order to receive public health and medical information among older adults (Ohta & Yata, 2021). Research on how the pandemic impacted family formation and dissolution, as well as other family dynamics, is yet to become available. The homogenous traditional notion of family form and function over the life course, group-oriented cultural expectations, and current family welfare policy seem to resist change toward nontraditional values (e.g., individualism) and accepting family diversity in Japan.

References

Buchanan, K. (2017). *Many adoptions in Japan are not about raising children.* Retrieved from https://blogs.loc.gov/law/2017/04/many-adoptions-in-japan-are-not-about-raising-children/

Bumpass, L. L., Rindfuss, R. R., Choe, M. K., & Tsuya, N. O. (2009). The institutional context of low fertility: The case of Japan. *Asian Population Studies, 5*(3), 215–235.

Cabinet Office of Japan. (2006). *Shoushika shakai hakusho.* Retrieved form https://www8.cao.go.jp/shoushi/shoushika/whitepaper/measures/w-2006/18webhonpen/index.html

Cabinet Office of Japan. (2018). *Annual report on the ageing society.* Retrieved October 11 from https://www8.cao.go.jp/kourei/english/annualreport/2018/2018pdf_e.html

Castro-Vázquez, G. (2015). Assisted reproductive technologies in contemporary Japan: Experiences and perceptions of some Japanese mothers. *Gender, Technology and Development, 19*(3), 271–291. https://doi.org/10.1177/0971852415596862

Central Intelligence Agency. (2021). *The world factbook: Japan.* Retrieved from https://www.cia.gov/the-world-factbook/countries/japan/

Chang, K.-S. (1999). Compressed modernity and its discontent: South Korean society in transition. *Economy and Society, 28*(1), 30–55.

Fleckenstein, T., & Lee, S. C. (2017). Democratization, post-industrialization, and East Asian welfare capitalism: The politics of welfare state reform in Japan, South Korea, and Taiwan. *Journal of International and Comparative Social Policy, 33*(1), 36–54. https://doi.org/10.1080/21699763.2017.1288158

Fukuda, S. (2009). *Shifting economic foundation of marriage in Japan: The erosion of traditional marriage* (MPIDR Working Paper, Issue). https://www.demogr.mpg.de/papers/working/wp-2009-033.pdf

Fukuda, S. (2020). Marriage will (continue to) be the key to the future of fertility in Japan and East Asia. *Vienna Yearbook of Population Research, 18*(1), TBA-OLF.

Garon, S. (2010). State and family in modern Japan: a historical perspective. *Economy and Society, 39*(3), 317–336. https://doi.org/10.1080/03085147.2010.486214

Gender Equality Bureau Cabinet Office. (2019). *Danjo Kyoudou Sanga Hakusho.* Retrieved March 10, 2019, from https://www.gender.go.jp/about_danjo/whitepaper/r01/zentai/index.html#pdf

Hayes, P. (2008). Special adoption in Japan: Its problems and prospects. *Adoption Quarterly, 11*(2), 81–100. https://doi.org/10.1080/10926750802370775

Immigration Services Agency of Japan. (2021). *Zairyu gaikokujin toukei [Statistics of the Immigrants].* Retrieved from https://www.moj.go.jp/isa/policies/statistics/toukei_ichiran_touroku.html

Ishida, H., Iwamoto, T., & Kamano, S. (2020). *Douseikonni kansuru ishikichousa houkokusho.* Retrieved from https://www.marriageforall.jp/research/

Iwabuchi, K., & Takezawa, Y. (2015). Rethinking race and racism in and from Japan. *Japanese Studies, 35*(1), 1–3. https://doi.org/10.1080/10371397.2015.1044153

Iwai, N. (2011). JGSS-2000~2010 kara mita kazokuno genjou to henka [The current picture and overall trends of the Japanese family based on JGSS cumulative data 2000–2010]. *Kasoku Shakaigaku Kenkyu, 23*(1), 30–42.

Iwasawa, M. (2004). Partnership transition in contemporary Japan: Prevalence of childless non-cohabiting couples. *The Japanese Journal of Population, 2*(1), 76–92.

Japan Society for Reproductive Medicine. (2020). *Guideline.* Retrieved from http://www.jsrm.or.jp/guideline-statem/guideline_2020_09.html

Jones, G. W. (2019). Ultra-low fertility in East Asia: Policy responses and challenges. *Asian Population Studies, 15*(2), 131–149.

Kamano, S., Ishida, H., Kazama, T., Yoshinaka, T., & Kawaguchi, K. (2016). *Attitudes toward sexual minorities in Japan: Report of 2015 national survey.* Retrieved from http://alpha.shudo-u.ac.jp/~kawaguch/chousa2015.pdf

Katagiri, Y., Jwa, S. C., Kuwahara, A., Iwasa, T., Ono, M., Kato, K., Kishi, H., Kuwabara, Y., Harada, M., Hamatani, T., & Osuga, Y. (2022). Assisted reproductive technology in Japan: A summary report for 2019 by the Ethics Committee of the Japan Society of Obstetrics and Gynecology. *Reproductive Medicine and Biology, 21*(1), e12434. https://doi.org/https://doi.org/10.1002/rmb2.12434

Keller, R. R. (2012). *Light and truth: A latter-day saint guide to world religions.* Deseret Book.

Kim, A. J., & Zulueta, J. O. (2020). Japanese families and COVID-19: "Self-Restraint", confined living spaces, and enhanced interactions. *Journal of Comparative Family Studies, 51*(3–4), 360–368. https://doi.org/10.3138/jcfs.51.3-4.011

Komatsu, H. (2016). Douseikon hihan. *Sougou Bunnka Kenkyuu, 1*, 1–34.

Lewis, J. (1992). Gender and the development of welfare regimes. *Journal of European Social Policy, 2*(3), 159–173. https://doi.org/10.1177/095892879200200301

Mackie, V. (2013). Genders and genetics: The legal and medical regulation of family forms in contemporary Japan. *Australian Journal of Asian Law, 14*(1), 1–18. Retrieved from https://search.informit.org/doi/10.3316/agispt.20152765

Minamikata, S. (2014). Dissolution of marriage in Japan. In J. Eekelaar & R. George (Eds.), *Routledge handbook of family law and policy* (pp. 122–132). London, UK: Routledge.

Ministry of Health Labour and Welfare. (2015). *Heisei 27nen jinkoudoutaitoukei geppounenn-kei (gaisu) no gaikyo [heisei year of 27" Population statistics monthly report].* Retrieved from https://www.mhlw.go.jp/toukei/saikin/hw/jinkou/geppo/nengai15/index.html

Ministry of Health Labour and Welfare. (2016a). *Heisei 28 nendo zenkoku hitorioyasetaitou tyousa kekka houkoku.* Retrieved from https://www.mhlw.go.jp/stf/seisakunitsuite/bunya/0000188147.html

Ministry of Health Labour and Welfare. (2016b). *Satooya oyobi tokubetu youshi eng-umi no genjou ni tsuite [Current status of the foster parents and special adaption system].* Retrieved from https://www.mhlw.go.jp/file/05-Shingikai-11901000-Koyoukintoujidoukateikyoku-Soumuka/0000147429.pdf

Ministry of Health Labour and Welfare. (2017). Heisei 28 Nendo Zenkoku Hitorioya-setaitoutyousakekkanogaiyounitsuite. Retrieved from https://www.mhlw.go.jp/file/05-Shingikai-12601000-Seisakutoukatsukan-Sanjikanshitsu_Shakaihoshoutantou/0000190571.pdf

Ministry of Health Labour and Welfare. (2021). *Kousei roudou.* Retrieved from https://www.mhlw.go.jp/stf/houdou_kouhou/kouhou_shuppan/magazine/202105.html

Ministry of Health Labour and Welfare. (2021). *Tokubetsu Youshi Engumi Seido ni Tsuite [About the adoption policy].* Retrieved from https://www.mhlw.go.jp/stf/seisakunitsuite/bunya/0000169158.html

Ministry of Health Labour and Welfare. (2022). *Hunin Chityou ni kansuru torikumi.* Retrieved from https://www.mhlw.go.jp/index.html

Ministry of Justice. (2019). *hutsuu youshi engumi to tokubetsu youshi engumi nitsuite.* Retrieved from https://www.moj.go.jp

Ministry of Justice. (2020). *Seisyokuhojoiryou no teikyoutou oyobi koreniyori syusseishitakono oyakokannkeinikansuru minpounotokureini kansuru houritsunoseiritsuni tsuite.* Retrieved from https://www.moj.go.jp/MINJI/minji07_00172.html

Moriizumi, R. (2019a). An analysis of childlessness in Japan [In Japanese]. *Journal of Population Problems, 75*(1), 26–54.

Moriizumi, R. (2019b). Nihon ni okeru mushi ni kansuru kenkyu [A study of Childless-ness in Japan] *Journal of Population Problems, 75*(1), 26–54.

Nakazawa, J., Hyun, J.-H., Ko, P.-C., & Shwalb, D. W. (2017). Grandparents in Japan, Korea, and China: From filial piety to grandparenthood. In *Grandparents in cultural context* (pp. 187–219). Routledge.

Niji Bridge. (2021). *Shibuya city office, NPS Nijiiro Diversity collaborative study of LGBT partnership coverage in Japan.* Retrieved from https://nijibridge.jp/wp-content/uploads/2021/07/20210630_infographic_ND.pdf

Nomura Research Institute. (2021). *Hunintiryou no jittaini kansuru tyousa kenkyu.* Retrieved from https://www.mhlw.go.jp/content/000766912.pdf

Nozawa, S. (2008). The social context of emerging stepfamilies in Japan. In J. Pryor (Ed.), *The international handbook of stepfamilies: Policy and practice in legal, research, and clinical environments* (pp. 79–99). Wiley & Sons.

Nozawa, S. (2020). Similarities and variations in stepfamily dynamics among selected Asian societies. *Journal of Family Issues, 41*(7), 913–936. https://doi.org/10.1177/0192513X20917766

Ochiai, E. (2014). Leaving the West, rejoining the East? Gender and family in Japan's semi-compressed modernity. *International Sociology, 29*(3), 209–228. Retrieved from https://doi-org.proxy-bc.researchport.umd.edu/10.1177/0268580914530415

OECD. (2021). *Data.* Retrieved from https://data.oecd.org/

OECD. (2022). *Family Database.* Retrieved from https://www.oecd.org/els/family/database.htm

Ohta, R., & Yata, A. (2021). The revitalization of "Osekkai": How the COVID-19 pandemic has emphasized the importance of Japanese voluntary social work. *Qualitative Social Work*, *20*(1–2), 423–432. https://doi.org/10.1177/1473325020973343

Ono, H., & Sanders, J. (2009). Divorce in contemporary Japan and its gendered patterns. *International Journal of Sociology of the Family*, *35*(2), 169–188. http://www.jstor.org/stable/23070722

Otsu, K., & Shibayama, K. (2022). Population aging, government policy and the postwar Japanese economy. *Journal of the Japanese and International Economies*, *64*, 101191. https://doi.org/https://doi.org/10.1016/j.jjie.2022.101191

Peng, I. (2016). Testing the limits of welfare state changes: The slow-moving immigration policy reform in Japan. *Social Policy & Administration*, *50*(2), 278–295. https://doi.org/https://doi.org/10.1111/spol.12215

Pew Research Center. (2019). *Same-sex marriage around the world*. Retrieved from, https://www.pewforum.org/fact-sheet/gay-marriage-around-the-world/

Raymo, J. M., & Iwasawa, M. (2008). Bridal pregnancy and spouse pairing patterns in Japan. *Journal of Marriage and Family*, *70*, 847–60.

Raymo, J. M., Iwasawa, M., & Bumpass, L. (2009). Cohabitation and family formation in Japan. *Demography*, *46*(4), 785–803. https://doi.org/10.1353/dem.0.0075

Sano, Y., & Yasumoto, S. (2014). Policy responses to population-declining society: Development and challenges of family policies in Japan. In M. Robila (Ed.), *Handbook of family policies across the globe* (pp. 319–331). Springer.

Sasaki, M. (2015). Sengono shoushikaseisakuto kazokuno shousankasikou. *Social Analysis*, *42*, 81–100. Retrieved from http://jsasa.org/paper/42_6.pdf

Seeleib-Kaiser, M., & Toivonen, T. (2011). Between reforms and birth rates: Germany, Japan, and family policy discourse. *Social Politics: International Studies in Gender, State & Society*, *18*(3), 331–360. https://doi.org/10.1093/sp/jxr016

Shambaugh, J., Nunn, R., & Portman, B. (2017). *Lessons from the rise of women's labor force participation in Japan*. Brookings. Retrieved from https://www.brookings.edu/wp-content/uploads/2017/10/es_110117_lessons_from_rise_womens_labor_force_participation_japan_economic_analysis.pdf

Shibusawa, T., Ishii, C., Nakamura, S., Tamura, T., & Watanabe, T. (2021). The COVID-19 Pandemic and Families in Japan. *Australian and New Zealand Journal of Family Therapy*, *42*(1), 58–69. https://doi.org/https://doi.org/10.1002/anzf.1438

Shibuya Ku. (2017). *Shibuya-Ku, partnership shoumei jittai chousa houkokusyo [Shibuya District, partnership certificate report]*. Retrieved from https://www.city.shibuya.tokyo.jp/assets/com/partnership_hokoku29b.pdf

Shirahase, S., & Raymo, J. M. (2014). Single mothers and poverty in Japan: The role of intergenerational coresidence. *Social Forces*, *93*(2), 545–569. https://doi.org/10.1093/sf/sou077

Slote, W. H., & De Vos, G. A. (1998). *Confucianism and the family*. Suny Press.

Statistics Bureau of Japan. (2021). *Seihu toukei no souhou madoguchi [The Portal Site of Official Statistics of Japan]*. Retrieved from https://www.e-stat.go.jp/

Sugimoto, M., & Yokoyama, Y. (2017). Characteristics of stepfamilies and maternal mental health compared with non-stepfamilies in Japan. *Environmental Health and Preventive Medicine*, *22*(1), 48. https://doi.org/10.1186/s12199-017-0658-z

Tabuchi, R. (2021). Family sociology in Japan: Recent developments and the current state of the field. *International Sociology*, *36*(2), 231–242. https://doi.org/10.1177/02685809211005354

Takemura, Y. (2019). Sengonihonnokazokuhendou Aratanakazokushisutemunoteian [Postwar Japanese Family Change: Proposal of a New Family System]. *Kochi University of Technology Journal*, *16*(1), 177–182. http://hdl.handle.net/10173/00002120

Taki, A. (2013). Japan's family policy. *The Hiroshima Economic Review, 37*(2), 69–76. Retrieved from https://ir.lib.hiroshima-u.ac.jp/files/public/3/36142/20141104003001543775/HER_37-2_69.pdf

Tamagawa, M. (2016). Same-sex marriage in Japan. *Journal of GLBT Family Studies, 12*(2), 160–187. https://doi.org/10.1080/1550428X.2015.1016252

Tamagawa, M. (2018). Coming out of the closet in Japan: An exploratory sociological study. *Journal of GLBT Family Studies, 14*(5), 488–518. https://doi.org/10.1080/1550428X.2017.1338172

Tang, D. T.-S., Khor, D., & Chen, Y.-C. (2019). Legal recognition of same-sex partnerships: A comparative study of Hong Kong, Taiwan and Japan. *The Sociological Review, 68*(1), 192–208. https://doi.org/10.1177/0038026119858222

The Japan Institute for Labour Policy and Training. (2020). *Singata Corona uirusu kansenshou no hitorioyakateih eno eikyou ni kansuru kinkyuu tyousa kekka.* Retrieved from https://www.jil.go.jp/press/documents/20201210.pdf

The World Bank. (2021). *World Bank open data.* Retrieved from https://data.worldbank.org/

U.S. Department of State. (n.d.). *Japan intercountry adoption information.* Retrieved from https://travel.state.gov/content/travel/en/Intercountry-Adoption/Intercountry-Adoption-Country-Information/Japan.html

Van Bavel, J. (2012). The reversal of gender inequality in education, union formation and fertility in Europe. *Vienna Yearbook of Population Research, 10,* 127–154.

Watanabe, A. (2008). Nihon no kazoku seisaku [Japanese Family Policies]. *The Journal of the Study of Modern Society and Culture, 43,* 55–72.

World Economic Forum. (2019). *Global gender gap report 2020.* Retrieved from http://www3.weforum.org/docs/WEF_GGGR_2020.pdf

Yamada, M., & Arai, H. (2020). Long-Term Care System in Japan. *Annals of Geriatric Medicine and Research, 24*(3), 174–180. https://doi.org/10.4235/agmr.20.0037

Yamamoto, N., Hirata, T., Izumi, G., Nakazawa, A., Fukuda, S., Neriishi, K., Arakawa, T., Takamura, M., Harada, M., Hirota, Y., Koga, K., Wada-Hiraike, O., Fujii, T., Irahara, M., & Osuga, Y. (2018). A survey of public attitudes towards third-party reproduction in Japan in 2014. *PLOS ONE, 13*(10), e0198499. https://doi.org/10.1371/journal.pone.0198499

Yasuda, T., Iwai, N., Chin-chun, Y., & Guihua, X. (2011). Intergenerational Coresidence in China, Japan, South Korea and Taiwan: Comparative analyses based on the East Asian social survey 2006. *Journal of Comparative Family Studies, 42*(5), 703–722. https://doi.org/10.3138/jcfs.42.5.703

6

LITHUANIAN FAMILIES

Living diversity in times of outdated policies

Aušra Maslauskaitė

The cultural and policy context of doing family

The development of the Lithuanian family in the 20th century until today can be analytically partitioned into several segments. Each of them overlaps with sweeping historical changes and the establishment of a fundamentally new political and economic order, and the new institutional contexts in which family life was/is embedded and transformed. Though each period is characterized by a distinct political and economic regime, the trajectory of family developments shows some continuities. Despite the fundamental shifts in the institutional settings, the collective understanding of family and gender persists to shape the current social organization of families.

Between the two world wars in the first half of the 20th century, Lithuania succeeded in building a system of state-supported cooperative capitalism (Norkus, 2014). Family-based agricultural or economic trade units were consolidated into large cooperatives of production and/or trade, and these institutions were the backbones of the interwar economic system. The authoritarian political regime, which grew in momentum after the coup of 1926, favored a strong state and relied heavily on ethnic nationalist ideology, which saw the traditional family as a cradle of the nation.

The interwar period brought modern ideas about family, which centered around the emotional ideals of romantic love, closeness, and mutual understanding, but also included mothering as the essential part of women's identity (Maslauskaitė, 2004). These ideas were seeded into the culture, but only the small urban middle class embraced and lived them.

At the beginning of the 20th century, Lithuanian families demographically followed the so-called northwestern European marriage pattern with late marriages and a large share of never-married persons (Puur et al., 2012). This trend

DOI: 10.4324/9781003193500-6

was sustained through the interwar period. In 1939, the share of married women aged 16 and over was 43.3% and for men, it was 50%; the mean age of women at the first marriage was around 26 years (Stankūnienė, 2016). The social and economic bar for marriage was high due to restrictive agricultural policies, limited demand for the industrial workforce, and social rules related to marriage. Even though many did not marry because of these structural constraints, singles were stigmatized as outliers for not fitting into the social fabric of the nation (Černiauskas & Klumbys, 2019). Unmarried mothers were vulnerable and experienced harsh moral judgment. Divorce was rare because marriage was regulated by Catholic Canon Law.

The first welfare initiatives by the state were introduced in the interwar period. The measures involved social insurance and social care, and increased funding for social issues (Aidukaitė et al., 2012; Černiauskas, 2016). Although the demand for childcare was growing, provision of institutionalized childcare (creches and kindergartens) was marginal, and services were mainly delivered by charity or religious institutions. In the second half of the 1930s, the state began to take a more active role in regulating childcare. However, the care was provided primarily by the family, and state interventions were marginal. The ideological agenda of the state echoed the patriarchal gender order, familialism, and a limited role of the state in securing welfare, which fit well with authoritarian nationalism and an economic system that relies on family-based agricultural units.

The Soviet occupation substantially reshaped the institutional context of the family. The totalitarian political system and socialist planned economy were introduced, and the private ownership of property and land was abolished. From the late 1950s to the mid-1970s, the country experienced massive restructuring of the economy and rapid industrial expansion (Vaskela, 2012). Families formerly relying on their land and agricultural production became units supplying labor to industry or collective farms (*kolhoz*). Employment outside of the family rapidly and completely transformed the family-economy nexus characteristic of the interwar period.

Due to the rising demand for industrial labor, women were drawn *en masse* into the labor market, and this was accompanied by Soviet propaganda on gender equality. By the end of the 1960s, 80% of women were employed (Kanopiene, 1983). The share of university-educated men and women was very similar, and by the end of the 1980s, women outnumbered men in university education (Gruzevskis & Kanopiene, 2016). Through liberalization of divorce laws in 1965, divorce became simplified and more accessible (Maslauskaitė & Baublytė, 2012).

However, the sweeping structural changes and official Soviet ideology on gender equality did not dramatically alter the cultural ideas about family and gender. The pre-war universe of cultural meanings about family and gender was preserved and continued to shape everyday life (Maslauskaitė, 2010). Several factors contributed to this situation. First, Soviet structural modernization was not followed by cultural modernization. The totalitarian political system prevented the pluralization of worldviews and individualization of society. Thus, there were limited opportunities to realize the new ideas and scripts of family life, gender, and personal identities. Second, Soviet family ideology reiterated the patriarchal gender regime, despite the official ideological dedication to gender equality. Women remained the main family care providers, motherhood was still naturalized, and femininity was connected to subordination. Third, under the totalitarian regime families became the 'pocket of silent resistance,' where one could exercise freedom from totalitarian control (Havelkova, 1993). This deepened the public-private divide and helped to preserve the pre-Soviet cultural ideas about families. Moreover, family was also a place to foster national identity, which clashed with the official ideology of the Soviet nation (*sovietskij narod*). The family became the battlefield where the nation was symbolically defended against the hostile state, which was imposed from outside, oppressive, and aggressive. Ideas about 'being the Lithuanian family' were also indirectly supported by the form of the political economy—national communism. The central communist party tolerated the nationalistic sentiments in exchange for the general political passivity of society (Norkus, 2008). All this contributed to the continuity of the pre-war cultural inertia related to the ideas on nation, gender, and family. Yet, the Soviet period brought slow changes in sexual norms and marriage (Leinarte, 2021).

During the Soviet period, families experienced major demographic shifts. The share of the married population increased substantially. Marriage became universal and easily accessible and was entered at early ages. Eighty percent of women and 75% of men older than 16 years were ever married in 1979 (Stankūnienė, 2016). The mean age at first marriage gradually decreased and reached 22 years for women and 24 years for men at the end of the 1980s (Demographic Yearbook 2017, 2018). Since 1965, the divorce rates started to increase, the crude divorce rate (CDR) reached 3.1 in 1977 and afterward stagnated with marginal fluctuations for the Soviet period (Maslauskaitė & Baublytė, 2012). Non-marital fertility fluctuated at around 7% and was similar to interwar decades (Maslauskaitė, 2014a). Cohabitation as the family formation strategy did not exist and was not condoned. The late Soviet period witnessed the slow liberalization of sexual norms, and around one third of women of the 1950–1960s birth cohorts became pregnant before entering marriage (Maslauskaitė, 2009). However, the sexual revolution with explicit discussions on sex and sexuality only began at the end of the 1980s with *Glastnost* (Healey, 2014). Homosexuality remained criminalized in the entire Soviet Union (Alexander, 2018).

In 1982, family policy became more comprehensive as the range and coverage of the measures were substantially expanded (Stankūnienė et al., 2013). This reform was the pronatalist reaction to the declining birth rates since the 1970s. Maternity leave for employed mothers was introduced at the beginning of the Soviet period, but in 1982, it became longer and partially paid (Stankūnienė et al., 2013). While childcare services for preschool children were expanding, they never met the demand (Leinarte, 2021). Forty percent of children under the age of 3 years and 53% of 3–6-year-olds attended nurseries in 1980 (Stankūnienė

& Jasilionienė, 2008). Thus, the Soviet period was marked by multiple contradictions in relation to gender and family policies. The official ideology of gender equality was opposed by the pervasive patriarchal sentiments shared by society. On the other hand, the state was incapable of meeting the demands of the dual-earner families despite the official ideological dedication to gender equality.

The year 1990 marked the restoration of independence, the establishment of democratic institutions, and the transition to a capitalist economy. The economic reforms were quite radical because the country had to build 'capitalism from scratch' and this involved the extreme form of neoliberal capitalism (Bohle & Greskovits, 2007). The early 1990s witnessed the collapse of the socialist economy, de-industrialization, a dramatic decline in GDP (by around 50%), and hyper-inflation (Šimėnas, 1996). The economic transformation led to enormous economic growth in the 2000s, but that was accompanied by very high social costs. The country experienced increasing inequalities, growing number of families at risk of poverty, and high rates of emigration, which placed Lithuania among the countries with the highest negative net migration rate in the EU (Statistics Lithuania, 2021c). The social costs of the transition were also exacerbated by austerity policies in response to the 2008–2009 crisis (Sommers et al., 2014).

The early transitional period was marked by a re-traditionalization of family policies, and overall, Lithuania replicated the trend observed in other post-communist countries (Glass & Fodor, 2007). In the early 1990s, pushing women out of the labor market and cutting back formal childcare infrastructures became part of a new political agenda that aimed to distance itself from the socialist regime and, thus, intentionally rejected policies providing for women's emancipation (Gal & Kligman, 2000). In the subsequent decades, female employment recovered, and the provision of care services also expanded. However, Central Eastern Europe (CEE) Lithuania clusters with more conservative countries in relation to gender values alongside Hungary, Poland, Bulgaria, and Russia (Buber-Ennser & Panova, 2014; Fodor & Balogh, 2010).

The 1990s and early 2000s witnessed a 'sexual revolution,' and information on sex and sexuality became more accessible. While homosexuality was decriminalized in 1993, this change "went hand in hand with an increasing patriarchalism, the lack of basic civil rights for LGBTQ+ people and state-sponsored homophobia" (Tereškinas, 2019, p. 14). However, in 2019, the Constitutional Court decided that foreign, same-sex spouses must be granted residence permits by the country's migration department, despite same-sex unions not being recognized (Tereškinas, 2019).

The field of family and gender policy substantially altered and expanded post-1990. Accession to the EU in 2004 resulted in a major advancement of the gender equality legislation; however, the subsequent advancement was lethargic. Family policy became more comprehensive though the developments were contradictory and inconsistent. Currently, the design of parental leave policies is similar to the Nordic model as is the women's and mothers' employment rates (Aidukaitė et al., 2021). Yet, the paid leave policies are not accompanied by the advancement of the service infrastructure. In addition, Lithuania along with the other two Baltic States is among the least generous welfare states in the EU, which results in a high level of commodification (Aidukaitė et al., 2021).

Empirical patterns of various family forms

Union formation and dissolution

The demographic development of families in Lithuania in the first two decades of the 2000s should be viewed in light of the fundamental changes of the 1990s, which marks the seminal turn in the retreat from the 'golden age of marriage.' At the beginning of the 1990s, marriage rates substantially declined from 9.8 (crude marriage rate—CMR) in 1990 to 4.8 in 2000 (Statistics Lithuania, 2021a). In the subsequent decade, marriage rates fluctuated at around 7, with a decrease in 2020 to 5.5, which was an effect of the COVID-19 pandemic (see Table 6.1).

TABLE 6.1 Selected demographic indicators for Lithuania, 2000 and latest available data

	2000	*Latest available data*	
Crude marriage rate	4.8	2020	5.5
Mean age at first marriage			
of women	23.6	2020	28.2
of men	25.7	2020	30.3
Crude divorce rate	3.1	2020	2.7
Remarriage rate			
of women	28 (est. 2009)		NA
of men	46 (est. 2008)		NA
% of adults > 15 never married			
of women	21.1	2021	26.3
of men	28.2	2021	32.0
Total fertility rate	1.30	2020	1.48
Mean age at first birth			
of women	23.9	2020	28.2
% non-marital births	22.6	2020	27.0
% of women aged 40–44 who have born no children	8.8	birth cohort 1975–1979	14.0
Cohorts	**1950**		**1970**
Completed fertility/cohort	2.01		1.7
% of women aged 40–44 who have born no children for cohorts	5.6 (1955)		12.3

Sources: Statistics Lithuania, www.stat.gov.lt; Cohort Fertility Rates—Human Fertility Database, 2021

Marriages were also delayed: the mean age at marriage grew from 23 to 28 for women and from 25 to 30 for men.

The decline in marriage rates signaled a shift in matrimonial behavior and the establishment of a new pattern of family formation, which in turn increased family diversity. Prior to the 1990s, cohabitation already was part of the demographic landscape, but it was stigmatized and mostly practiced as a way to reconstitute a family after divorce or the death of a partner (Maslauskaitė, 2009). In the last decade of the 20th century, cohabitation became increasingly popular among young couples as they started their family life in non-marital unions and postponed marriage. Thus, at the beginning of the 1990s, the share of all first partnerships starting as cohabitations was 32%, while a decade later (2000–2004) it rose to 67% (Puur et al., 2012). However, over the past two decades, the trend remained more or less stable (Dirsytė & Maslauskaitė, 2020). The proliferation of cohabitation increased the mean age at the first marriage. In 2000, the mean age at first marriage was 23.6 for women and 25.7 for men, and in 2020—28.2 and 30.3.

Changes in the way families are formed resulted in a decrease of the ever-married population. At the beginning of the 21st century, the share of never-married women was 21.1% and two decades later, it reached 26.3%. For men, the growth is from 28.2% to 32%. The retreat from marriage is more common among the socio-economically disadvantaged groups, and while it is observed for men and women, it is stronger for men. The risk to end up not being married is almost twice as high for lower-educated men compared to those who are university-educated (Maslauskaitė & Jasilionis, 2015).

In the past two decades, CDR was almost stable and fluctuated at around 2.7–3 divorces per 1,000 population. This is a long-term trend, which started in the Soviet period in the late 1970s. Divorce adds to family diversity, yet the partnership dynamics after divorce is gender specific. Twenty-eight percent of divorced women re-partner (remarry or cohabit) within ten years after the divorce, while for men the rate is 46%, according to some estimates from surveys (Maslauskaitė & Baublytė, 2015). However, the data on re-partnering and remarriage are very inconsistent. Official statistics provide information only on the share of higher-order marriages among all annually registered marriages, which is app. 23–25% and has been stable for several decades. The only other data source is the Generation and Gender Survey, which recorded the detailed partnership histories and had a sufficiently large sample size. However, it was administered in the late 2000s, which leaves the dynamics of past two decade remains not documented.

Fertility patterns

Lithuania experienced a sharp decrease in fertility after 1990. The total fertility rate (TFR) was 1.3 in 2000, reduced from 2.3 in 1990 (Demographic Yearbook 2017, 2018). While the TFR started to recover somewhat in the 2000s to around 1.6, in 2020 it was at only 1.4 (Statistics Lithuania, 2021b).

The slight recovery of fertility observed in the second half of the first decade of the 21st century reflects the change in the childbearing model caused by cohabitation, postponement of first marriage, and first and higher-order births. A similar process was observed in other CEE countries (Stankūnienė & Baublytė, 2016). The mean age at first birth for women increased from 24 to 28 years. The completed cohort fertility indicator, which is less sensitive to the changes in the fertility model or other short-term effects of the exogenous factors, shows that the average number of children born by women of the 1960 cohort was 1.88, for the 1965 cohort it was 1.7, and it plateaued for the younger cohorts who already completed their reproductive stage (Human Fertility Database, 2021).

Non-marital fertility, which had stagnated at around 6–7% for most of the 20th century, started to increase after 1993. In 2000, it was 22.6%, and it reached 27% in 2020. Childbearing in cohabitation is more pronounced among members of the less socio-economically privileged groups and the non-marital fertility level is higher among the rural population, which is also less educated and more socio-economically vulnerable (Maslauskaitė, 2014a). Consequently, while cohabitation has diversified the family formation path and delayed marriage and first births, it did not profoundly increase single-parent or cohabiting-parent families, because childbearing mainly occurs in marriage.

Previous research reveals that for the 1930–1954 birth cohorts, the percentage of women who have born no children was low and leveled at about 9% (Sobotka, 2017; Stankūnienė & Baublytė, 2016). However, the percentage of women without children peaked at 13–15% for the 1962–1975 birth cohorts (Human Fertility Database, 2021). This rate is similar to the one observed in Sweden and Denmark and challenges the assumption (Sobotka, 2017) that Lithuania has relatively lower rates.

Changes in household composition and living arrangements

Table 6.2 shows the changes in the household patterns in Lithuanian society in the first decade of the 21st century based on the information from the Censuses of 2001 and 2011. Though the Census 2021 was conducted, at the time of the preparation of this chapter the data were not released yet and there are no other data sources, which could document the detailed household patterns among the different age groups.

Since the beginning of the 21st century, the share of persons living with a spouse has decreased from 42.7% in 2000 to 38.9% a decade later, while the share of those cohabiting increased (see Table 6.2). This pattern is even more evident among younger age groups. In 2001, half of the population aged 25–34 years was living with a spouse, which was reduced to 34.6%. The share of persons of this age group cohabiting increased from 6.1 to 10.5% during the same time period. Table 6.2 also shows that there was a slight increase in persons living alone (from 11.2% to 13.3%) overall. Among the 25–34 age group, the share of living single increased from 8.9 or 11.1%, and this reflects the trend of postponement of marriage. During the discussed period, the share of single parents also grew from 2.9% to 3.6% among all household types.

Table 6.3 provides information on the distribution of different types of households. Based on the 2001 and 2011 Censuses information, the married and non-married different-sex-couple households decreased from 37.8% to 34.5%. In addition, there is a substantial reduction in households with children under 18 years of age and an increase of couple households without children. This trend is the outcome of the dramatic decline in fertility and population aging.

Overall, the share of single-parent households remained stable over the first decade of the 21st century and comprises approximately 4.5%. The majority of these families are led by mothers, but the share of families led by fathers is also slightly growing.

TABLE 6.2 Population in living arrangements in Lithuania, 2000 and latest available data

% of persons living	2000			2011		
	Total	Age 18–24	Age 25–34	Total	Age 18–24	Age 25–34
With spouse	42.7	20.9	52.0	38.9	7.4	34.6
With partner	3.1	4.8	6.1	5.0	6.5	10.5
Child of householder	23.7	NA	NA	18.4	NA	NA
Alone	11.2	14.4	8.9	13.3	12.1	11.1
Alone with child/ren	2.9	4.0	7.5	3.6	3.3	7.9
With another person(s)	16.2	55.7	25.4	20.1	70.0	35.6

Note: No current data available.
Sources: Statistics Lithuania, www.stat.gov.lt.

TABLE 6.3 Households in Lithuania, 2000 and latest available data

% of households consist of	2000	2011
Different-sex spouses	37.8	34.5
with kids <18	21.5	14.3
without kids <18	16.3	20.2
Different-sex partners	3.0	4.6
with kids <18	1.5	2.3
without kids <18	1.5	2.3
Mother only with kids	4.5	3.8
Father only with kids	0.3	0.6
Same-sex couple	n.a.	n.a.
One person living alone	29.1	31.6
Other families (incl. two families household)	31.1	31.0

Note: No current data available.
Sources: Statistics Lithuania, www.stat.gov.lt.

In addition, the share of households of cohabiting couples with children and the share of non-married couples without children also increased. However, in discussing the distribution of the household types, one has to consider that other than one-family households are prevalent in Lithuania and account for approximately 1/3 of all households. Usually, these are multigenerational households, where parents (or one of the parents) co-reside with the family of their children. In the majority of these households, there are underage children (2011 Visuotinio, 2013).

Current empirical research on the various family forms

Reconstituted families (stepfamilies)

Although divorce is rather common in Lithuania, research on reconstituted families and on life in stepfamilies is rather limited. Stepfamilies and their structural and demographic diversity are not covered by official statistics. Evidence from a large-scale survey shows gender-specific patterns of re-partnering after divorce, with substantially lower rates of entry into a new partnership for women (Maslauskaitė & Baublytė, 2015). The presence of children (disregarding their age) diminishes the chances of re-partnering for women but not for men (Maslauskaitė & Baublytė, 2015). Lower re-partnering rates for women might be related to demographic factors, such as high out-migration rates for working-age men and high mortality rates for middle-aged men (in the age group of 35–54). Cohabitation is more common after divorce, and fewer women than men intend to move from cohabitation into marriage (Maslauskaitė, 2009). Comparative evidence from the early 2000s shows that 33% of children lived in a stepparent family after parental union dissolution, and this rate is relatively low compared to Estonia or Sweden (Andersson et al., 2017). One small-scale qualitative study on the subjective motives of re-partnering after divorce shows that individuals experience less social pressure to enter a new union as compared to their first marriage and feel that their choices are more guided by expectations of forming higher-quality relationships (Platūkytė, 2020).

The research on post-divorce family life has mostly focused on non-resident father–child relationships. A large majority of children stay with their mothers after parental break-ups. Lithuania does not have shared custody arrangements, and after divorce, the child resides with one of the parents (usually the mother), while the other parent receives visitation rights. Legally, parents' rights and obligations to the child are the same for previously married and cohabiting parents. However, the differences in the legal procedures involved in the termination of marriage and cohabitation result in unequal outcomes. Marriage is dissolved only by the court, which includes legal resolutions of all issues related to child custody, alimony payments, and non-resident parent-child contacts. In contrast, the separation of the cohabiting couple does not entail compulsory legal procedures related to the regulation of parental rights and duties, because there are no laws related to unregistered partnerships. This results in disadvantages for formerly non-married fathers, and their parenting rights are more dependent on the mother's goodwill and cooperation. Socio-economically disadvantaged fathers are even more vulnerable because their limited capacities to provide can be used by mothers to block access to the children (Maslauskaitė & Tereškinas, 2017).

Culturally and legally, Lithuania prioritizes the economic provider role of divorced fathers rather than their nurturing role. Qualitative studies reveal three post-divorce fathering models: undoing fatherhood, adhering to normative expectations, and absenting (Tereškinas & Maslauskaitė, 2019). Undoing fatherhood involves the struggle to create new scripts for fathering and rebelling against normative expectations and traditional identities. Some of these fathers succeed in negotiating shared residence arrangements for the children, which is uncommon because it is legally not an option in Lithuania. Men adhering to normative expectations follow the script of traditional masculinity and limit their fathering to the provider role, which is an important part of their masculine identity. The absent fatherhood model is a constraint rather than a choice and is part of divorced or separated unemployed and low-income men's lives. The inability to provide for their children, which is the main characteristic of this group of men, brings feelings of shame and guilt (Tereškinas & Maslauskaitė, 2019).

One-parent and cohabiting families

While single-parent families are very common in Lithuanian society, they are also the most financially vulnerable households, and existing social policy measures are not effective in reducing their poverty. Nevertheless, single motherhood has only recently entered the arena of social research. Research based on 2011 Census data revealed that one in four children grows up in a single-parent family (Stankūnienė et al., 2016). About 42% of these families result from divorce, one third are married mothers who do not live with the father of the children, and about 20% are formed after the dissolution of cohabitation or because the mother remained unpartnered (Stankūnienė et al., 2016). Family change related to cohabitation and family dissolution due to migration also contribute to single motherhood. In addition, research reveals the poor living conditions of never-married single mothers in rural areas; for almost half of them (46%), the main source of income is various family allowances (Stankūnienė et al., 2016).

Research based on qualitative biographical interviews shows that single mothers' consumption patterns of goods and services reflect social exclusion from the normative image of the 'good life' (Maslauskaitė, 2014b). Depending on their social status, these mothers experience different degrees of dissonance between their way of life and the 'good life,' which is subjectively experienced as hopelessness and helplessness. Some mothers develop a strategy of fantasizing about the future and having unrealistically high expectations, others live with a general hope for a better future. Single mothers develop a cognitive matrix of consumption, which is strictly followed in everyday life and includes such principles as prioritization of children's interests, strict planning, and saving. A representative survey of single mothers also shows a positive association between economic deprivation and low personal well-being (Maslauskaitė, 2015; Maslauskaitė & Platūkytė, 2019). Yet, the survey also documents the heterogeneity of single mothers and that education is the main factor determining economic and overall well-being. Although research confirms that divorce has a negative effect on the financial stability of single mothers, almost half of Lithuanian single mothers perceived their financial situation as either the same or better after divorce (Maslauskaitė, 2015). Kuconytė-Būdelienė (2017) documented the intergenerational support received by single mothers and how the various types of support help mothers manage employment and childcare tasks.

Although cohabitation has become the preliminary stage of marriage, it does not replace marriage. Marriage generally sustains its relevance as the desired and socially acceptable arrangement for families with children. The socially dominant life trajectory experienced by 65% of men and women of the 1970–1984 birth cohort in the years after entering a partnership involves first cohabitation, then a transition to marriage, and the birth of the first child within marriage (Dirsytė & Maslauskaitė, 2020). The chances of converting cohabitation into marriage are very high (about 80% within three years from the start of cohabitation), while the risk of dissolution of cohabitation is low (Dirsytė & Maslauskaitė, 2020). Thus, most couples enter into cohabitation with the expectation of eventual marriage. Younger cohorts spend more time living in cohabitation compared to those who formed their families in the 1990s or 2000s. However, cohabitation mainly serves as a testing ground for family relationships and ends in marriage when couples start to consider to have or are already expecting children. Cohabiting men have more pronounced intentions to marry than women, as do those who are more highly educated (Dirsytė, 2021).

Earlier research shows that there is no significant difference in the dynamics of the partnership relationships in cohabiting and married couples. There is gender asymmetry in household task sharing, yet women have more power in decision-making in both types of family arrangements. However, the conflict level is higher in cohabiting couples compared to married couples if all other structural characteristics are equal (Maslauskaitė, 2009).

Sex and gender minority families (SGM)

Sex and gender minority (SGM) families and their everyday life are not reflected in Lithuanian family scholarship. As discussed previously, same-sex couples do not have rights to register partnerships or marry, and there is no legislation governing this type of family relationship. There is no information based on surveys or demographic statistics available, which could reveal the prevalence of these families, their structure, and the socio-economic conditions of these partnerships. Qualitative studies are also rare, and they do discuss the family relationships of non-heterosexuals (Radžiūnienė, 2012; Šumskaitė, 2014). In her research on fatherhood, Šumskaite (2014) included several non-heterosexual men and revealed the complex interconnections between sexuality, hegemonic masculinity, and fatherhood. In order to fulfill their fatherhood obligations, men negotiate different-sex and same-sex family relationships and live with the resulting inner contradictions and conflict (Šumskaitė, 2014). For some of the men, fatherhood represents a superior status within the LGBTQA+ community, where men are often restricted to becoming fathers via adoption or assisted reproductive technology (ART). Other qualitative research that analyzed the childrearing intentions of gay men revealed that they employ three main strategies (Šumskaitė, 2014). Some adapt to the negative public opinions and restrictive policies and plan to either realize their fatherhood intentions by entering a heterosexual relationship or they completely reject the idea of fatherhood. Others employ the 'waiting and hoping for better' strategy, expecting a positive turn in family policy and the possibility of adoption in the near future.

Tereškinas (2019) critically examined the restrictive policies and public discourse on SMF and concluded that

> LGBTQ+ people remain clearly dispossessed by regimes of gender and sexual normativity and their intimacies are rendered precarious in the country. Intimacies of people with so-called 'nontraditional sexual orientation' are qualified, in the public discourse, as a threat, danger, and harm to both an individual and the nation.
>
> *(p. 24)*

BOX: The Battle surrounding Registered Partnership Law

Although demographically, families have diversified during the last decades, the legal discourse on families remains centered around the standard heteronormative marriage-based family model. No legislation supporting non-marital unions (same- or different-sex) existed, adoption is restricted to married couples, the execution of parenting rights after union dissolution is different for previously married and cohabiting couples, and some state support programs prioritize married couples.

While the Lithuanian Constitution declares that the family unit is the foundation of society and the state (Lietuvos Respublikos Konstitucija, 1992), it does not explicitly define family relationships. However, it does state that marriage is between men and women (Lietuvos Respublikos Konstitucija, 1992). The spread of cohabitation in the late 1990s motivated discussions on necessary changes in the legal system, and the legal institute of the registered partnership was introduced in the Civil Code Third Book on Family Law in 2000 (Lietuvos Respublikos civilinis kodeksas, 2000). The implementation of legal policy related to registered partnerships required the passage of accompanying laws, which would define the content and regulation of registered partnerships and also harmonize it with the legal norms of Family Law. In the last 20 years, more than 10 attempts to accomplish this failed, despite the different political constellations and balances at the Parliament. In one of the last attempts, in the Spring of 2021, the bill failed to pass the first reading, lacking just two votes in favor, and it was returned for revision. A year after, the revised version passed the first vote in the parliament and will return for the second plenary vote in the summer of 2022. The bill defines partnership in a gender-neutral way, but excludes the option of adoption in same-sex unions.

Each attempt to pass the law was accompanied by general tensions in politics and society, and social protests backed by the political forces with the national populist sentiment. New to the trend is the social mobilization and institutionalization of the supporters of the 'traditional family.' Organizations with large numbers of supporters have been established that succeeded in staging several massive protests. The partnership law is discursively portrayed as a threat to the constitutional order, the traditional family, and the nation. The opponents of the law rely on essentialist gender arguments and use anti-gender and anti-gay discourse.

Yet, these discussions on registered partnership law mark only the most recent episode in the discursive and legal encounter in the intersecting fields of gender, sexuality, and family. There were numerous legal attempts to define the content of family relationships and to introduce a normative, exclusionary definition of the family. For example, in 2008, the Parliament approved the State Family Policy Concept, which would limit family to spousal relationships or relationships emerging from the marital bond (i.e., divorced single-mother family). The Constitutional Court ruled against this law and considered it unconstitutional (Ambrazevičiūtė et al., 2012). Any new initiatives to define the family and/or reduce it to marital relationships surface periodically, usually after parliamentary elections.

Adoptive and foster families

The right to adopt is restricted to married couples, while non-married couples or single individuals are eligible only in exceptional cases. In contrast, provision of foster care is not limited to married couples. In the period of 2016–2020, the annual average share of adopted children (out of all available for adoption) fluctuated at around 20–27% (Statistics Lithuania, 2021d). Absolute numbers are very small with 50–90 adopted children annually. The majority of foster families take care of the children of relatives (VTKTA, 2020).

The research on adoptive and foster families mostly occurs in the field of social work, and this is related to changes in institutional context. For almost two decades, Lithuania has been implementing reforms aimed at transforming the system that cares for children whose parents have lost their parenting rights, who have limited parenting rights, or who are orphans. The aim of the reform is to provide family or community-based care instead of care in boarding institutions. The reform includes wide legal and institutional changes, and it is still ongoing. Scientifically, the reform was mostly evaluated by examining the institutional capacities and their development, care workers' qualifications, various forms of support for adoptive and foster parents, and the outcomes of the reform for children (see the most recent overview in Pivorienė, 2018).

However, the adoptive or foster family dynamics remain less documented by research. Some scattered evidence is provided by small-scale qualitative studies. One of them explores the foster families' experiences in self-help groups and reveals that group participation enhanced personal growth in foster parents, improved their parenting skills, increased reflexivity regarding their roles as parents and spouses, and helped to solve tensions between the biological and foster children (Gvaldaitė, 2018). Interviews with foster parents reveal the motivations, challenges, and strategies used when including a foster child into their family (Gvaldaitė, 2017). The author concludes that "the main task of foster parents is to rebuild the lost relationship, unconditionally giving themselves, but not replacing and devaluing the families of origin, which remains for a child as a fact, the aspect of truth about him" (Gvaldaitė, 2017, p. 63). Another qualitative study reveals that some adoptive parents encounter social disapproval or hostility from society (Raščiuvienė, 2016). Earlier research based on a media discourse analysis shows that adoption is frequently portrayed in the media in a negative light, focusing on the problematic sides of the adoptive parent–child relationships (Povilaitytė, 2015).

Families created by medically assisted reproduction (MAR)

In Lithuania, MAR is not available to single women or SGM families, and surrogacy is prohibited. A law on ART or MAR, enacted in 2017, restricts the eligibility to receive MAR to married different-sex couples or those living in registered partnerships, and only two cycles of the ART are partially covered by the state. Moreover, women have to be 43 years old or younger to receive ART. Although this law marks a significant change in the biopolitics of the state, public discussions on the moral issues related to ART or the different aspects of its regulation (for example the age limit of women) remain.

Multicultural and migrant families

Lithuanian society is ethnically and religiously homogenous. The majority of the population is ethnically Lithuanian (84% in 2021) and Roman Catholic (74%) (Statistics Lithuania, 2021e). The share of the foreign-born population is only 4.5% (Stankūnienė, Ambrozaitienė, Baublytė 2019). While marriages involving foreign-born residents comprise around 15–17% of all marriages annually (Statistics Lithuania, 2021f), only 6% of all partnerships (marriage and cohabitation) in the country involve one foreign-born and one Lithuanian partner (Lanzieri, 2012). Regretfully, no comprehensive data on minority or immigrant families in Lithuania are collected. Small-scale qualitative research on immigrant families from non-EU countries reveals how women are disadvantaged in the process of social adaptation. Traditional gender norms and values shared by immigrant family members often result in the marginalization of women in social and professional life (Blažytė, 2017).

Research on migrant families has recently increased due to high rates of out-migration in the last three decades and increasing numbers of transnational families. The research predominantly focuses on Lithuanian families with members living in different nation-states. Multiple methodologies are used to examine various family configurations and family membership, the re-distribution of family commitments, the re-shaping of family identities, and the sense of belonging (see Juozeliūnienė & Budginaitė, 2018; Juozeliūnienė & Seymour, 2015, 2020). Recently, Juozeliūnienė and Seymour (2020) used an innovative conceptual framework to analyze the legal, policy, and academic discourse on transnational families and revealed that transnational families are portrayed as problematic and that the migration of family members is discursively constructed as a threat to family stability rather than as a family life stage which may pose some challenges. A lot of research also explores transnational families' everyday practices in the migratory context (Butėnaitė, 2015; Česnuitytė, 2015; Juozeliūnienė, 2015) by applying theoretical concepts, such as 'family display' and 'family practices.' According to Finch (2007) family "display is the process by which individuals, and groups of individuals, convey to each other and to relevant audiences that certain of their actions do constitute 'doing family things' and thereby confirm that these relationships are 'family' relationships" (p. 67). Using the 'family display' concept, Juozeliūnienė et al. (2020) document how care for children and elders in Lithuanian transnational families is provided, and how it helps families to assign meanings to the family relationships and to present themselves as the family to significant others. Some studies also examine the role of everyday practices in creating and recreating family identity ("we" as a family) and family memory. Thus, Žilinskienė (2020) shows that migration encourages family members living in the host country to take an active part in family memory building and maintenance. In addition, Česnuitytė (2020) revealed how participation in family feasts and religious festivities reflects the boundaries of the family, to create a sense of belonging and to maintain family identity of those family members living abroad.

Conclusion and recommendations

Lithuanian family life and policies are shaped by ideas of the 'traditional family,' which is culturally recognized as the foundation for securing the current and future welfare of society. The 'traditional family' ideology has a strong connection to nationalist sentiments, which remain a powerful instrument in defining the collective identity of Lithuanian society. The turbulent historical legacy, contradictions under Soviet rule, and the high social costs of the transition to capitalism have preserved and encouraged a public discourse on the nation-state, which is linked to the 'traditional family.' The establishment of political democratic institutions and EU membership, which resulted in the synchronization of national and EU laws, have not catalyzed a fundamental change in Lithuanian collective identities and perceptions of the relationships among family, gender, and society. The political, legal, and public discourse remains restrictive toward what constitutes a family and considers the increasing complexities of family life to a very limited extent.

Lithuania stepped into the paths of family diversity rather late. The process slowly began during the Soviet era with the liberalization of divorce laws and the proliferation of divorce, single-mother families, and stepfamilies. However, family diversification was stalled, accelerating only after the 1990s with the dramatic changes brought about by the transition to capitalism. The 1990s marked the proliferation of cohabitation, non-marital fertility, and transnational families. The sexual revolution, which engulfed society in the last decade of the 20 th century, liberated and made more visible diverse sexual identities and SGM families. However, despite this growing diversity of family forms, the existing legal system prioritizes the heteronormative family and is not adapted to the everyday realities of diverse families.

Family diversity and complexity are still rarely addressed in Lithuanian research. There are no solid empirical sources covering SGM families, stepfamilies, families created by ART, and other non-standard family forms. This relates to the state of Lithuanian sociology in general. Only in the 1990s did sociology begin to develop more actively and systematically and become institutionalized as the academic field of studies, and social scientists started to collaborate on an international scale to create datasets of higher methodological standards. However, the general underfunding of research, limited research capacities, and inconsistent science policy continue to constrain the advancement of family research and the production of socially and politically relevant studies. This situation particularly affects scientific knowledge of Lithuanian family diversity. The future of family research is first and foremost dependent on the development of methodologically advanced longitudinal datasets, which so far are missing, as well as on the consolidation and growth of the research capacities and more generous research funding.

Overall, the main challenges for politics and policies involve acknowledging that family diversity is an inescapable reality of contemporary society. The political and social discourse should perceive family diversity not as a threat to the community, but as the outcome and the reflection of the complexities of current social life. There is a long way to go in order to achieve this goal and to re-define family policies, which would more adequately consider the lived realities of contemporary families. A relevant role in this process lies with non-governmental organizations that support diverse families and with the research community. The widespread communication of scientific knowledge and the mobilization of interest groups could raise public awareness and lead to changes in the political and social discourse and reforms.

The COVID-19 pandemic and its effects on family life pose opportunities and challenges for the social acceptance of family diversity. The current data on family demography show how partnership formation and dissolution and fertility behaviors were affected by the COVID-19 pandemic. On the one hand, the pandemic revealed the interdependence of family life and wider contextual factors in society. On the other hand, the collective experience of the pandemic as a societal threat might trigger a more paternalistic role of the state and increase right-wing nationalist sentiments. Against this backdrop, the engagement of civic society and the scientific community becomes even more crucial in supporting diverse family forms and shifting the perspectives of the family policy discourse accordingly.

Funding

This project received funding from the European Social Fund (project No. 09.3.3-LMT-K-712-01-0020) under grant agreement with the Research Council of Lithuania (LMTLT).

References

Aidukaitė, J., Bogdanova, N., & Guogis, A. (2012). *Gerovės valstybės kūrimas Lietuvoje: mitas ar realybė?* Lietuvos socialinių tyrimų centras.

Aidukaitė, J., Hort, S., & Kuhnle, S. (2021). Baltic and Nordic countries from a comparative perspective – family policies and pensions in the era of ageing. In J. Aidukaitė, S. Hort, & S. Kuhnle (Eds.), *Challenges to the welfare state. Family and pensions policies in Baltic and Nordic States* (pp. 1–11). Edward Elgar Publishing.

Alexander, R. (2018). Soviet legal and criminological debates on the decriminalization of homosexuality (1965–75). *Slavic Review*, 77(1), 30–52. https://doi.org/10.1017/slr.2018.9

Ambrazevičiūtė, K., Kavoliūnaitė, E., & Mizaras, V. (2012). Šeimos kaip teisės kategorijos turinys Lietuvos Respublikos įstatymuose. *Teisės problemos*, 4(78), 74–107.

Andersson, G., Thomson, E., & Duntava, A. (2017). Life-table representations of family dynamics in the 21st century. *Demographic Research*, 37, 1081–1230. https://doi.org/10.4054/DemRes.2017.37.35

Blažytė, G. (2017). *Imigracija dėl šeimos susijungimo Lietuvoje: lytis ir etniškumas socialinės adaptacijos procese* (Doctoral dissertation, Lietuvos socialinių tyrimų centras).

Bohle, D., & Greskovits, B. (2007). Neoliberalism, embedded neoliberalism and neocorporatism: Towards transnational capitalism in Central-Eastern Europe. *West European Politics, 30* (3), 443–466. https://doi.org/10.1080/01402380701276287

Buber-Ennser, I., & Panova, R. (2014). *Attitudes towards parental employment across Europe, in Australia and in Japan* (No. 5/2014). Vienna Institute of Demography Working Papers. Retrieved from http://hdl.handle.net/10419/106646

Butėnaitė, R. (2015). Asmeniniai tinklai. In I. Juozeliūnienė & J. Seymour (Eds.), *Šeiminiai pokyčiai atvirų Europos sienų ir globalaus mobilumo akivaizdoje: resursai, procesai ir praktikos* (pp. 81–92). Vilniaus universitetas.

Černiauskas, N. (2016). Urbanizacija kaip modernėjančios visuomenės fenomenas In D. Bukelevičiūtė, Z. Butkus, N. Černiauskas, A. Grodis, A.P. Kasperavičius, & G. Polkaitė-Petkevičienė (Eds.), *Socialiniai pokyčiai Lietuvos valstybėje 1918–1940 metais* (pp. 154–178). Vilniaus universiteto leidykla.

Černiauskas, N., & Klumbys, V. (2019). Seksualumo karai ir revoliucijos XX a. Lietuvoje. Naujasis Židinys-Aidai, 6. Retrieved from https://nzidinys.lt/seksualumo-karai-ir-revoliucijos-xx-a-lietuvoje-norberta-cerniauska-ir-valdemara-klumbi-kalbina-antanas-terleckas-nz-a-nr-6/

Česnuitytė, V. (2015). "Mes" daryba: šeimos tradicijos ir laisvalaikis. In I. Juozeliūnienė & J. Seymour (Eds.), *Šeiminiai pokyčiai atvirų Europos sienų ir globalaus mobilumo akivaizdoje: resursai, procesai ir praktikos* (pp. 114–129). Vilniaus universitetas.

Česnuitytė, V. (2020). Doing Family across borders: the role of routine practices, traditions and festivities in Lithuania. In I. Juozeliūnienė & J. Seymour (Eds.), *Making Lithuanian families across borders* (pp. 99–126). Vilnius University Open Series.

Demographic Yearbook 2017. (2018). Lietuvos statistikos departamentas.

Dirsytė, I. (2021). Marriage intentions among cohabiters in Lithuania. *Socialinė teorija, empirija, politika ir praktika, 23*, 26–40. https://doi.org/10.15388/STEPP.2021.35

Dirsytė, I., & Maslauskaitė, A. (2020). Šeiminio gyvenimo kelio trajektorijos: sekų analizės rezultatai. *Filosofija. Sociologija, 31*(2), 139–147.

Finch, J. (2007). Displaying families. *Sociology, 41*(1), 65–81. https://doi.org/10.1177/0038038507072284

Fodor, É., & Balogh, A. (2010). Back to the kitchen? Gender role attitudes in 13 East European countries. *Zeitschrift für Familienforschung, 22*(3), 289–307. Retrieved from https://nbn-resolving.org/urn:nbn:de:0168-ssoar-354956

Gal, G., & Kligman, G. (2000). Introducion. In G. Gal & G. Kligman (Eds.), *Reproducing gender: Politics, publics, and everyday life after socialism* (pp. 3–20). Princeton University Press.

Glass, C., & Fodor, E. (2007). From public to private maternalism? Gender and welfare in Poland and Hungary after 1989. *Social Politics, 14*(3), 323–350. https://doi.org/10.1093/sp/jxm013

Gruzevskis, B., & Kanopiene, V. (2016). Lithuania. In G. Razzu (Ed.), *Gender inequality in the Eastern European labour market* (pp. 151–168). Routledge.

Gvaldaitė, L. (2017). Priėmimas globojant vaiką: patirtis, kurianti naują kultūrą. *Socialinė teorija, empirija, politika ir praktika, 14*, 48–63.

Gvaldaitė, L. (2018). Promoting foster families' self-help groups in Lithuania. *Relational Social Work, 2*, 34–49.

Havelkova, H. (1993). A few prefeminist thoughts. In N. Funk & M. Mueller (Eds.), *Gender politics and post-communism: Reflections from Eastern Europe and the former soviet union* (pp. 13–36). Routledge.

Healey, D. (2014). From Stalinist Pariahs to subjects of 'Managed Democracy': Queers in Moscow 1945 to the Present. In M. Cook & J. V. Evans (Eds.), *Queer cities, Queer cultures Europe since 1945* (pp. 95–117). Bloomsbury.

Human Fertility Database. (2021). Max Planck institute for demographic research (Germany) and Vienna institute of demography (Austria). Retrieved from www. humanfertility.org

Juozeliūnienė, I. (2015). Šeima abipus sienų: pokyčiai, šeimos sampratos ir vaidmens elgsena. In I. Juozeliūnienė & J. Seymour (Eds.), *Šeiminiai pokyčiai atvirų Europos sienų ir globalaus mobilumo akivaizdoje: resursai, procesai ir praktikos* (pp. 161–183). Vilniaus universitetas.

Juozeliūnienė, I., & Budginaitė, I. (2018). How transnational mothering is seen to be 'Troubling': Contesting and reframing mothering. *Sociological Research Online, 23*(1), 262–281. https://doi.org/10.1177/1360780417749464

Juozeliūnienė, I., & Seymour, J. (Eds.) (2015). Šeiminiai pokyčiai atvirų Europos sienų ir globalaus mobilumo akivaizdoje: resursai, procesai ir praktikos. Vilniaus universitetas.

Juozeliūnienė, I., & Seymour, J. (2020). *Making Lithuanian families across borders*. Vilnius University Open Series.

Juozeliūnienė, I. E., Bielevičiūtė, I., & Budginaitė-Mačkinė, I. (2020). Portraying migrant families in academic publications: naming and framing. In I. Juozeliūnienė & J. Seymour (Eds), *Making Lithuanian families across borders* (pp. 64–75). Vilnius University Open Series.

Kanopiene, V. (1983). *Trud zhenschin v Litovskoj SSR*. Vilnius.

Kuconytė-Būdelienė, D. (2017). Vienos vaikus auginančios motinos ir tarpgeneracinės paramos modeliai Lietuvoje. *Kultūra ir visuomenė: socialinių tyrimų žurnalas, 8*(1), 35–53. http://dx.doi.org/10.7220/2335-8777.8.1.2

Lanzieri, G. (2012). Merging populations a look at marriages with foreign-born persons in European countries. *Statistics in focus* 29/2012.

Leinarte, D. (2021). *Family and the state in Soviet Lithuania: Gender, law and society*. Bloomsbury Publishing.

Lietuvos Respubikos Konstitucija (1992). Lietuvos aidas, Nov 10, 1992, No. 220-0.

Lietuvos Respublikos civilnis kodeksas. Trečioji knyga. Šeimos teisė (2000). Žin., Nr. 74–2262.

Maslauskaitė, A. (2004). *Meilė ir santuoka pokyčių Lietuvoje*. Vilnius Socialinių tyrimų institutas.

Maslauskaitė, A. (2009). Kohabitacija Lietuvoje: šeimos formavimo etapas ar nauja šeima? In A. Maslauskaitė & V. Stankūnienė (Eds.), *Lietuvos šeima, tarp tradicijos ir naujos realybės* (pp. 69–123). Socialinių tyrimų institutas.

Maslauskaitė, A. (2010). Lietuvos šeima ir modernybės projektas: prieštaros bei teorizavimo galimybės. *Filosofija. Sociologija, 4*, 310–319.

Maslauskaitė, A. (2014a). Nesantuokinis gimstamumas Lietuvoje: raida ir erdvinė diferenciacija. *Lietuvos socialinė raida, 3*, 54–65.

Maslauskaitė, A. (2014b). Vienišos motinos, vartojimas ir socialinė atskirtis. *Kultūra ir visuomenė: socialinių tyrimų žurnalas, 2*, 13–36. http://dx.doi.org/10.7220/2335-8777.5.2.1

Maslauskaitė, A. (2015). Vieniškos motinos, materialinė deprivacija ir gyvenimo kokybė. In A.Tereškinas & J. Bučaitė-Vilkė (Eds.), *Socialinė atskirtis ir geras gyvenimas Lietuvoje* (pp. 72–120). Vytauto Didžiojo universitetas.

Maslauskaitė, A., & Baublytė, M. (2012). *Skyrybų visuomenė: ištuokų raida, veiksniai, pasekmės: mokslo studija*. Lietuvos socialinių tyrimų centras.

Maslauskaitė, A., & Baublytė, M. (2015). Gender and re-partnering after divorce in four central European and Baltic countries. *Sociologický časopis/Czech Sociological Review, 51*(6), 1023–1046. http://dx.doi.org/10.13060/00380288.2015.51.6.227

Maslauskaitė, A., & Jasilionis, D. (2015). Vyrų išsilavinimas ir pirmoji santuoka. Ar universitetas suteikia privalumų? *Kultūra ir visuomenė. Socialinių tyrimų žurnalas, 5*, 11–26. http://dx.doi.org/10.7220/2335-8777.6.1.1

Maslauskaitė, A., & Platūkytė, E. (2019). Material deprivation and personal wellbeing of single mothers in Lithuania. In V. Cesnuityte & G. Meil (Eds.), *Families in Economically Hard Times: Experiences and Coping Strategies in Europe* (pp. 73–98). Emerald Publishing Limited.

Maslauskaitė, A., & Tereškinas, A. (2017). Involving nonresident Lithuanian fathers in child-rearing: The negative impact of income inequalities and sociolegal policies. *Men and Masculinities, 20*(5), 609–629.

Norkus, Z. (2008). *Kokia demokratija, koks kapitalizmas? Pokomunistinė transformacija Lietuvoje lyginamosios istorinės sociologijos požiūriu.* Vilnaus universitetas.

Norkus, Z. (2014). *Du nepriklausomybės dvidešimtmečiai. Kapitalizmas, klasės ir demokratija Pirmojoje ir Antrojoje Lietuvos Respublikoje lyginamosios istorinės sociologijos požiūriu.* Aukso žuvys.

Pivorienė, J. (2018). Deinstitutionalization of long term social care system in Lithuania in the context of EU data. *Sociológia a spoločnosť, 3*(1), 37–45.

Platūkytė, E. (2020). *Partnerystės kūrimas po skyrybų: sociologinių veiksnių analizė.PhD thesis.* Vytautas Magnus University Press.

Povilaitytė, K. (2015). Įvaikinimo ir globos diskursas Lietuvoje, deinstitucionalizacijos kontekste: delfi. lt ir lrytas. lt atvejai.MA thesis. Vytautas Magnus university.

Puur, A., Rahnu, L., Maslauskaite, A., Stankuniene, V., & Zakharov, S. (2012). Transformation of partnership formation in Eastern Europe: The legacy of the past demographic divide. *Journal of Comparative Family Studies, 43*(3), 389–417. https://doi.org/10.3138/jcfs.43.3.389

Raščiuvienė, I. (2016). *Neužmiršti, bet palikti sau: vaiką globojančių šeimų patirtis. MA thesis.* Vytautas Magnus University.

Radžiūnienė, L. (2012). Netradicinis' tėvas šiuolaikinėje Lietuvoje. *STEPP: Socialinė teorija, empirija, politika ir praktika 6*, 112–124. https://doi.org/10.15388/STEPP.2012.0.1854

Sobotka, T. (2017). Childlessness in Europe: Reconstructing long-term trends among women born in 1900–1972. In M. Kreyenfeld & D. Konietzka (Eds.), *Childlessness in Europe: Contexts, causes, and consequences* (pp. 17–53). Springer.

Sommers, J., Woolfson, C., & Juska, A. (2014). Austerity as a global prescription and lessons from the neoliberal Baltic experiment. *The Economic and Labour Relations Review, 25*(3), 397–416. https://doi.org/10.1177/1035304614544091

Stankūnienė, V. (2016). Santuokinio statuso kitimas: ilgalaikė trajektorija ir šiuolaikinė situacija. In V. Stankūnienė, M. Baublytė, K. Žibas, & D. Stumbrys. *Lietuvos demografinė kaita: ką atskleidžia gyventojų surašymai: mokslo studija* (pp. 137–174). Vytauto Didžiojo universitetas.

Stankūnienė, V., Ambrozaitienė, D., & Baublytė, M. (2019). Lietuvos imigracinė subpopuliacija: užsienyje gimusios kartos. *Lietuvos statistikos darbai, 58*(1), 4–15. Retrieved from https://www.journals.vu.lt/statisticsjournal/article/view/16665/15794

Stankūnienė, V., & Baublytė, M. (2016). Gimstamumas: ilgalaikė kohortinė perspektyva ir diferenciacija. In V. Stankūnienė, M. Baublytė, K. Žibas, & D. Stumbrys (Eds.), *Lietuvos demografinė kaita: ką atskleidžia gyventojų surašymai: mokslo studija* (pp. 175–244). Vytauto Didžiojo universitetas.

Stankūnienė, V., Baublytė, M., & Maslauskaitė, A. (2016). Vienų motinų su vaikais šeimos Lietuvoje: demografinės ir socioekonominės charakteristikos. *Sociologija. Mintis ir veiksmas, 1*, 64–85. http://dx.doi.org/10.15388/SocMintVei.2015.2.9867

Stankūnienė, V., Maslauskaitė, A., & Baublytė, M. (2013). *Ar Lietuvos šeimos bus gausesnės?* Lietuvos socialinių tyrimų centras.

Stankūnienė, V., & Jasilionienė, A. (2008). Lithuania: Fertility decline and its determinants. *Demographic Research*, *19*(20), 705–742.

Statistics Lithuania. (2021a). Crude marriage rate. Retrieved from https://osp.stat.gov.lt/statistiniu-rodikliu-analize#/

Statistics Lithuania. (2021b). Total fertility rate. Retrieved from https://osp.stat.gov.lt/statistiniu-rodikliu-analize#/-totalfertilityrate

Statistics Lithuania. (2021c). Crude divorce rate. Retrieved from https://osp.stat.gov.lt/statistiniu-rodikliu-analize#/

Statistics Lithuania. (2021d). Adopted children. Retrieved from https://osp.stat.gov.lt/statistiniu-rodikliu-analize?indicator=S3R0110#/

Statistics Lithuania. (2021e). 2021 m. gyventojų ir būstų surašymas: etnokultūrinės chrakeristikos. Retrieved from https://osp.stat.gov.lt/informaciniai-pranesimai?articleId=9792051

Statistics Lithuania. (2021f). Marriages. Retrieved from https://osp.stat.gov.lt/lietuvos-gyventojai-2020/santuokos-ir-istuokos/santuokos

Šimėnas, A. (1996). *Ekonomikos reforma Lietuvoje*. Pradai.

Šumskaitė, L. (2014). Norminis vyriškumas tėvystės praktikose. *STEPP: socialinė teorija, empirija, politika ir praktika*, *8*, 33–50. https://doi.org/10.15388/STEPP/2014.0.2663

Tereškinas, A. (2019). Precarious sexualities, alternative intimacies in postsocialist Lithuania. *Kultūra ir visuomenė: socialinių tyrimų žurnalas*, *10*(1), 11–28. https://doi.org/10.7220/2335-8777.10.1.1

Tereškinas, A., & Maslauskaitė, A. (2019). Undoing fatherhood: Postdivorce fathering practices in Lithuania. *NORMA*, *14*(1), 18–34. https://doi.org/10.1080/18902138.2018.1494401

Vaskela, G. (2012). Lietuvos ūkio raidos specifika XX a. 5–6 dešimtmečiais. *Lietuvos istorijos metraštis*, *2*, 109–124.

VTKTA. (2020). *Vaiko teisių apsaugos kontrolieriaus tarnybos ataskaita*. Vilnius.

Žilinskienė, L. (2020). Doing family memory in the case of emigration experience. In I. Juozeliūnienė & J. Seymour (Eds.), *Making Lithuanian families across borders* (pp. 155–180). Vilnius University Open Series.

2011 m. *Visuotinio gyventojų ir būstų surašymo Lietuvoje rezultatai (2013)*. Lietuvos statistikos departamentas.

7

FAMILY DIVERSITY IN SPAIN

A portrait of rapid transformation

Gerardo Meil, Jesús Rogero-García and Vicente
Díaz-Gandasegui

The cultural and social context of doing family

Family life in Spain, as in all developed countries, underwent drastic change in the 20th century as the heteronormative male-breadwinner family model gave way to a pluralization of lifestyles. That transformation took place later than in neighboring countries, however, due to the nearly 40-year (1939–1976) military rule that considered the patriarchal nuclear family as one of the mainstays of society and the political regime. The traditionalist dictatorship instituted at the end of a traumatic civil war (1936–1939) abolished all the measures geared to liberalizing family structures that had been previously adopted and restored the patriarchal family model in its entirety, reinforced by a very active family policy that encouraged marriage, marital fertility, and traditional gender roles (Meil, 2006).

Franco's death in 1975 gave way to the establishment of democracy that included changes in family legislation, increased gender equality, and the institution of a welfare state as a mechanism for integration and social legitimation of the new order. Beginning in 1976, profound legal reforms based on the principles of individual freedoms, equality, and non-discrimination, led to decriminalizing consensual extra-marital unions, same-sex relations, and the sale and use of contraceptives and also establishing specific family planning and sex education facilities. Furthermore, spousal rights and obligations were equalized, marriage licenses disappeared, and married women regained full legal status. Parental rights and obligations of marital, extra-marital, and adopted children were also equalized. Lastly, the right to dissolve a marriage, religious or civil, at the spouses' will was also reintroduced, albeit under fairly restrictive conditions because of the opposition of the Catholic Church and conservative groups. The system adopted consisted of two stages, first a legal separation (decreed by the

DOI: 10.4324/9781003193500-7

court), with divorce only allowed after a full year of de facto separation. The outcome was that many legal separations were never carried through to divorce.

These transformations, undertaken by a center-right party (1976–1982), inspired scant conflict, thanks among others to the social changes that had been underway since the 1960s (Iglesias de Ussel, 1990). Family policy disappeared from the political agenda due to its association with Francoism and the patriarchal family model, while unemployment insurance and pension benefits became increasingly relevant during the severe economic crisis (Meil, 2006).

The election of a socialist government (1982–1995) brought greater freedom of choice in pathways to parenthood and also increased support for gender equality. Legislation approving the voluntary interruption of pregnancy and regulating medically assisted reproduction (MAR) was enacted and contested by the Catholic Church as well as by the conservative opposition party. While the abortion law was restrictive, the act on MAR, a pioneer in that domain, gave all women, in case of sterility, the right to use MAR, irrespective of their marital status or sexual orientation. That same period also witnessed far-reaching reform of the provisions for legal adoption, regarded from 1988 onward as a mechanism to protect children and their well-being through integration into a family (Castón & Ocón, 2002). In a similar vein, foster parenting was introduced as an alternative to the institutionalization of children.

Social policy, fueled by Spain's entrance into the European Union in 1985, explicitly addressed gender equality. The newly created Women's Institute was entrusted, among other issues, with proposing and assessing periodic intervention plans. Gender equality was also pursued regionally, irrespective of the party in power, instituting an administration characteristic of a public gender regime (Lombardo & Alonso, 2020). The plans formulated in that initial and in subsequent periods focused primarily on fostering women's access to the labor market and removing any obstacles to such entrance, as a response to social preferences (Moreno-Mínguez et al., 2019).

The conservative government in power from 1996 to 2003 accepted the measures instituted under the preceding administration, with the exception of adopting a new and more restrictive act on MAR in 2003. However, significant initiatives were approved in social policy. The periodic formulation of gender equality plans continued while a comprehensive family support plan was established. Conservative regional governments instituted comprehensive plans along similar lines (Ayuso & Bascón, 2021). The nationwide plan translated into enhanced tax treatment initially intended to aid families with the heaviest burdens (members with disabilities, families with more than three children, solo parents, mothers of children under three working outside the home), although they ultimately benefited mostly high-income groups. Harmonization of work and family life was also fostered through improvements in parental leave policy which, while qualifying fathers for such leave, adopted a gender-neutral stance that in the end reinforced traditional gender roles (Meil, 2006). Although early schooling was encouraged, care for children under three continued to be provided primarily by families (Meil et al., 2021). The plan also laid the grounds for an act to protect large families, including a variety of benefits for families with three or more children (whether or not from the same or prior relationships) or fewer if any family member had a disability. Another outcome was the enactment of legislation guaranteeing grandparents' rights to continue their relationship with their grandchildren after separation or divorce or to assume tutorship where required.

The return to power of a socialist government (2004–2011) increased individual rights in family formation and development. The new act on divorce acknowledged the right to divorce by any party, without cause or prior separation. Also, equal marriage rights were instituted in 2005, regulating same-sex marriage under the same provisions as heterosexual marriage, which were contested by the Catholic Church as well as by the conservative opposition party. As public opinion was generally in favor of or indifferent to same-sex marriage in proportions similar to those found in countries where it had already been instituted (Meil, 2003), its declaration as a constitutional right generated no significant opposition.

In contrast, the more ambiguous support for greater liberalization of the voluntary interruption of pregnancy has underpinned the acute political confrontation prompted by the respective measures, such as the amendment of abortion (2010). The new term-based (14 weeks) criterion and its extension on therapeutic or embryopathic grounds increase women's freedom of choice. Moreover, the amendments also established shared custody for minor children as a possible solution. The provisions on MAR were extended to cover cases of genetic disease, broaden the types of MAR allowed, and include MAR in public health coverage.

The gender equality policy implemented by the administration in that eight-year period included two innovations with a significant impact on family dynamics. In 2004, a comprehensive law was enacted to tackle gender violence, and in 2007, a gender equality act was adopted in pursuit of 'effective equality between men and women' which, among others, introduced two-week paid paternity leave (Meil et al., 2019). Public compensation for family burdens was also provided in the form of a generous Birth allowance (*"cheque bebe"*), also with a view to encouraging natality, although criticized by conservatives as a waste of public resources.

The conservative government (2011–2018) elected in the wake of the severe economic crisis initiated in 2007 upheld nearly all the reforms introduced by the preceding administration, including the act on egalitarian marriage. However, the government attempted to retroactively apply a law that sought to protect the life of the unborn and rights of pregnant women. The strategic pillars of the second comprehensive family support plan (2015–2017) instituted by the national conservative government included aid for mothers and the creation of an environment favorable to family life. One of the lines of action of that second (as in the first) edition of that plan and of the gender equality plans was the furtherance of work-life balance (although with no explicit support for parental co-responsibility) and protection for the most vulnerable families (large, one-parent or those caring for members with disabilities). Despite that protection, one-parent and large families continued to be the ones at greatest risk of poverty, and in the same line as child poverty the rates are higher than in other European Union countries.

The return to power of a socialist government in 2018 brought strong support for parental co-responsibility, particularly in terms of work and family life balance. That objective led to the gradual equalization of paid maternity and paternity leaves (see box). An act adopted in 2021 on protection of childhood and adolescence against violence broadens the definition of such violence, requires any attack to be reported, persecutes internet-mediated offenses, creates specialized units and a welfare coordinator in schools, and lengthens the term of the statute of limitation for sex offenses. A bill is presently being drafted to reinforce transexual rights, which is highly controversial and strongly opposed by feminist movements. The discussion revolves around the existing requirement for a diagnosis of gender dysphoria and the existence of medical (but not necessarily surgical) treatment to publicly record a change of sex and name. Under the new provisions, free self-determination of sex would be a right acknowledged to anyone over the age of 16 (lowered from 18) with no need for a medical diagnosis.

Overall, social control over families has declined in Spain as democracy allowed greater individual freedom to express sexual identity and live out family arrangements according to personal aspirations and desires. The romantic conception of love, in contrast with its fluid expressions, remains, however, predominant in Spanish society (Roche Cárcel, 2020). Related to that process is the acknowledgment of the individual rights of socially vulnerable members of families (primarily women and children), now regarded as subjects with inalienable social rights. That in turn has translated into growing pluralization of family arrangements. This process has been facilitated by the absence of a formal definition of the family in the Constitution and in Civil Law (Iglesias de Ussel, 1990; Salar Sotillos, 2018).

Empirical patterns of various family forms

Union formation and dissolution

Demographic indicators for the last two decades reveal the depth of change experienced by Spanish families. First, the types of unions have changed significantly. The percentage of cohabiting households has spiked, as reflected in the decline in the crude marriage rate from 5.4 in 2000 to 1.9 in 2020 and in the rise of the crude divorce rate from 0.9 to 1.6 (Table 7.1). Significantly, the divorce rate among 35- to 39-year-olds grew from 8.67% in 2005 to 14.33% in 2006. In divorces involving different-sex couples, child custody was awarded to mothers in 2020 in 54.5% of cases, with custody awarded to fathers in only 3.9%. Shared

TABLE 7.1 Selected demographic indicators for Spain, 2000 and latest available data

	2000	latest available data	
Crude marriage rate	5.4	2020	1.9
Mean age at first marriage			
of women	28.1	2020	34.9
of men	30.2	2020	37.2
Crude divorce rate	0.9	2020	1.6
Remarriage rate			
of women	5.4	2020	22.9
of men	6.6	2020	24.5
% of adults >15 never married			
of women	40.1	2020	42.2
of men	47.2	2020	49.4
Total fertility rate	1.23	2020	1.36
Mean age at first birth			
of women	29.1	2020	31.2
of men			
% non-marital births[a]	17.7	2018	47.3
% of women aged 40–44 who have born no children	9.2 (1999)	2018	19.4
Cohorts	1950		1970
Completed fertility/cohort	2.15		1.45
% of women aged 40–44 who have born no children for cohorts	9.0 (1999)		18.4

a   Share of extramarital births: proportion (%) of all live births where the mother's legal marital status at the time of birth was other than married.
Sources: INE: 2001 census; 1999 and 2018 fertility surveys, 2020 Continuous Household Survey, 2019 marriage statistics; OECD: Family Database.

custody, the fastest growing model in recent years, accounted for 41.4% and was awarded to other family members or institutions for the remaining 0.4% (INE, 2021).

At the same time, the number of blended or multiple partner families (MPF), i.e., households with children from one or both parents' previous relationships, has grown. In 2020, 5.7% of all families with children under 25 were blended compared to 3.1% in 2001 (INE, 2004). The nearly four-fold rise in marriages involving divorced persons provides further evidence of that trend (Table 7.1).

The Spanish demographic profile is also characterized by a fairly late transition to adult life, rather than by the traditional independence-through-marriage pattern. In 2020, 39.7% of persons between the ages of 25 and 34 and 85.9% of emergent adults (those between 20 and 24 years of age) still lived with their parents (Table 7.2). These values are much higher than those observed in other European countries. This later transition to adult life also means a delay in other significant life events, such as first marriage. The mean age at first marriage rose between 2000 and 2020 from 28.1 to 34.9 among women and from 30.2 to 37.2

among men (Table 7.1). In addition, the percentage of persons over age 15 who remain unmarried rose from 43.6 to 45.7, and this 2% increase is similar for women and men.

Fertility patterns

The mean age at first birth of women reached 31.2 in 2020, 2.1 years older than in 2000, and also non-marital births rose from 17.7% to 47.6%. These delays in some crucial demographic and socioeconomic events, in combination with increasing job insecurity, have affected the fertility rate, which remains extremely low, although it grew slightly from 1.23 in 2000 to 1.36 in 2020. Moreover, completed cohort fertility declined from 2.15 children per woman for the 1950 cohort to 1.46 per woman for the 1970 cohort, while the percentage of childless women between the ages of 40 and 44 doubled in these cohorts and also from 1999 to 2018 (Table 7.1).

Changes in household composition and living arrangements

The growing pluralization of family arrangements can be explained in part by these changes in demographics. Although a substantial share of the population continues to live with a partner, the percentage of households consisting of couples with children living at home declined by over half, from 43.4% in 2001 to 20.9% in 2020 (Table 7.2). In line with those values, the proportion of people living with their parents decreased from 37.5% to 31.4%. The percentage of households comprising couples with no children at home rose from 19.5% to 33.1%. Those changes are largely attributable to variations in the age structure of Spain's population, in which the percentage of under 30-year-olds (most of whom are still living with their families of origin) dropped from 37.2% in 2001 to 29.9% in 2020 and the percentage of over 60 years old rose from 23.2% to 29.2% (2011 census and 2020 Continuous Household Survey, INE). That explains the larger percentage of people who live alone (10.4% of the overall population in 2020, up from 7.1% in 2001) and the fairly high proportion (26.1%) of Spanish households with one member in 2020 (Table 7.3). That prevalence of one-person households is related to rising life expectancies and greater economic and functional independence among elderly householders, who most frequently are woman over age 64 (Rogero-García, 2015). In Spain, as in other European countries, intergenerational relations have been patterned after what Rosenmayr (1970) called the 'intimacy – but at-a-distance' model.

   The proportion of one-parent households has also increased, an outcome of the rise in the number of dissolved unions and non-marital childbearing. The percentage of such households has tripled over the last 20 years, from 1.7% to 5.2% (Table 7.2). Approximately 8 in every 10 one-parent families are headed by women, 40% by separated or divorced persons, 37.2% by widows/ers, 14.8% by unmarried, and 8.1% by married persons.

TABLE 7.2 Population in living arrangements in Spain, 2000 and latest available data

% of persons are living	2000			2020		
	Total	Age 20–24	Age 25–34	Total	Age 20–24	Age 25–34
With spouse	44.3			40.5		
women		7.0	43.8		2.7	23.0
men		2.5	31.4		0.8	15.1
With partner	2.5			7.8		
women		4.1	6.3		2.9	23.4
men		2.3	5.9		2.9	19.0
Child of householder	37.5			31.4		
women		80.0	37.8		82.4	32.8
men		84.6	47.4		89.3	46.2
Alone	7.1			10.4		
women		2.5	5.2		2.2	8.0
men		3.2	7.7		1.2	10.5
Alone with child/ren	1.7			5.2		
women		0.4	2.3		1.6	5.2
men		0.1	0.4		0.1	0.5
with another person(s)	6.8			4.7		
women		5.9	4.6		6.0	7.7
men		7.4	7.2		5.8	8.4

Source: INE (2020) Continuous Household Survey and 2001 census.

TABLE 7.3 Households in Spain, 2000 and latest available data

% of households[1] consist of	2001	2020
Different-sex spouses	62.6	54.0
with kids <18	43.4	20.9
w/out kids <18	19.5	33.1
Different-sex partners	4.0	9.7
with kids <18	1.9	5.0
w/out kids <18	2.1	4.8
Mother only with kids	8.0	8.4
Father only with kids	1.9	1.9
Same-sex couple	0.1	0.6
One person living alone	20.3	26.1

Source: INE (2020) Continuous Household Survey and 2001 census.

Recent decades have witnessed an increase in the diversity of the types of unions. First, cohabitation has eclipsed marriage as a pathway for forming a family, either as a prelude to marriage or as an alternative to marriage. Cohabitation is particularly prevalent among the young: in 2020 21.2% of 25 to 34 years old lived in such unions, compared to 6.1% in 2001. The percentage of persons in that age-group living with a spouse declined from 37.5% in 2001 to 19% in 2020 (Table 7.2). Secondly, family arrangements have also diversified with respect to sexual orientation. The number of same-sex couples has grown six-fold since being legally possible in 2005, accounting for 0.6% of all households (Table 7.3).

BOX: De-gendering parental leave-taking

Motherhood is still a source of discrimination in the labor market and as such one of the causes of the decline in fertility. Since 1986, a number of policy measures to address this problem have been part of the gender equality plans, focused primarily on enhancing the harmonization of family and work life for both parents. Nonetheless, as these measures have been primarily used by women, they have ultimately reinforced gender discrimination. In order to change that, a 2019 policy was adopted to gradually raise the duration of paternity leave to equal that of maternity leave, from 5 to 16 weeks (Meil et al., 2019; Flaquer & Escobedo, 2020). Since 2021, both parents (employed, self-employed, or on unemployment) have been entitled to 16 weeks of paid 'leave for birth and childcare' at 100% of their previous salary, which is non-transferable to the other parent. Six of those weeks are compulsory after birth and the rest are optional and subject to flexible use (either part- or full-time) during the child's first year of life. Same-sex and adoptive parents are entitled to the same rights as biological parents, although single mothers are entitled to maternity leave only. The primary aims of the policy are to de-gender parental leave-taking, reduce gender discrimination, and raise fathers' involvement in family responsibilities. However, because the policy is not designed to foster fathers' leave-taking to care for the baby alone while the mother returns to paid work, its potential for changing intra-couple gender relations is limited. According to microdata from the 2021 edition of the Young Spanish Families survey (QUIDAN survey), most eligible fathers take this leave for nearly the full legal duration: 90% who had a child in 2020 took it for an average of 11 of the 12 weeks to which they were entitled. Nonetheless, only 43% of qualifying fathers took it on a part-time basis to spread it out over the first year.

Current empirical research on the various family forms

Demographic and sociological research on families has revealed significant changes in their composition as well as the increasing co-existence of diverse families. Such changes mirror Spanish society's adaptation to new economic, social, and demographic circumstances (Del Campo & Tezanos, 2008). Some authors (Meil, 1999) have called this the 'postmodern family' in an allusion to two of the common elements of the new models of families: greater freedom of choice and instability.

Reconstituted families (stepfamilies)

Stepfamilies tend to form 'family constellations' (Beck-Gernsheim, 2003) consisting of household networking around childcare. Such networks often generate complex relationships and roles involving biological, legal, and social factors (Rivas, 2012).

Childcare continues to be associated with women rather than men. One illustration of the persistence of that image is found in blended families, where children from previous relationships are more frequently brought to the new couple by the woman. Rivas (2012), drawing from the 2001 census, found that in blended families with no common children, the number of cases in which the children from a previous relationship were brought into the family by their mother was nearly double compared to the number of those who came with their father. In a more recent study, Treviño, Gumà, and Permañer (2013) observed that in 87% of blended families with no common offspring, the children were from the mother's and in just 10% from the father's previous relationships. In only 3%, both adults brought children to the new household. Moncó (2014) observed that in families with children from the father's prior relationship the role of the 'stepmother' was a substitute for or complement to the biological mother. That circumstance placed her in a conundrum of relative affective intimacy with or distance from her partner's children, contributing to the complexity of her relationship with the mother of the offspring.

While custody was traditionally awarded to mothers, shared custody arrangements are now increasingly common, driven by regional legislation subsequently endorsed by a Supreme Court ruling (López-Narbona et al., 2021). The goal is for the two parents to alternate full-time care on a regular basis to ensure the children benefit from co-responsibility and retain their ties to both parents (Jiménez & Becerril, 2020). As Jiménez, Becerril, and García (2020) observed, amendments to the legislation and the growing social acceptance of shared custody constitute an acknowledgment of separated fathers' role in raising their children while decentering mothers as being solely responsible for children's care and well-being. The same authors also observed, however, that sole custody is awarded more often to women aged 35–39 than to older women, probably because they have younger children, an indication that the association between motherhood and childcare has not disappeared yet and traditional attitudes toward maternity and paternity are prevalent when deciding the custody.

One-parent and cohabiting families

The rise in the proportion of one-parent households, increasing from 1.7 in 2000 to 5.2 in 2020, results from the frequent dissolution of marriages and consensual unions and the higher frequency of motherhood by choice. It is the effect, then, of fluctuating, or what Bauman (2009) termed more 'fluid' circumstances. The related changes often lead to precarious life situations characterized by fragility and vulnerability, from which one-parent households are not exempt. Sociological research on such families, headed primarily by women, has recently focused on one of the challenges they confront: the difficulty of reconciling employment and childcare. A number of studies show that social exclusion is more common when a woman raises her children alone, and around half of one-parent families are in that situation (Flaquer et al., 2006; Santibáñez et al., 2018). Many lone mothers lack occupational qualifications, and therefore hold insecure jobs with low salaries, are part of the temporary workforce or face unemployment. Such mothers often depend on family support, normally from grandparents and especially maternal grandmothers (Tobío & Fernández, 1999). As a consequence, despite being included in the different family policy plans at national and regional levels as subjects of special social protection, many of these families are highly dependent on the employment conjuncture and a majority are at risk of poverty or social exclusion as cash benefits for dependent children continue to be extremely low (EAPN-Spain, 2021).

Although marriage is still the preferable option for Spanish couples, its social value has declined steadily in favor of cohabitation as a way of initiating a common live project, based on an almost universal legitimization of this arrangement (Cea d'Ancona, 2007; Ayuso, 2019). Cohabiting unions account for 9.7% of the total in 2020, compared to 4% in 2001, and also public attitudes seem to reinforce this modification of the practices: according to the 2012 wave of the International Social Survey Program (Family and Changing Gender Roles IV), 83% of the Spanish population agreed with the statement 'it is all right for a couple to live together without intending to get married'.

Although cohabitation has been primarily an option among the younger cohorts and is understood as 'trial marriage' (Meil, 2003), it has also been observed among more mature age-groups. In 53.4% of the couples that cohabit, one of the members is 40 years old or over, and in 8% of the cases, both are over 60 (Continuous Household Survey 2020, INE). Moreover, 52.9% of these unions have children, 40.8% are common, and in 12.1% of the couples, the children are not from both (at least one). Cohabiting couples are also more frequent among mixed couples considering the national origin: in 14.4% of cohabiting couples, at least one of their members is not Spanish, compared to 3.2% of all marriages. Additionally, Domínguez-Folgueras and Castro-Martín (2013) observed that the socio-demographic profile of cohabiting partners is characterized by high levels of education, high employment rates, low levels of religiosity, and progressive values. Moreover, these couples were more egalitarian in the distribution of family work but also were more prone to separation than married couples (Meil, 2003).

In recent years, couples living apart together (LAT), a type of relationship not envisaged in the distinction between cohabitation and marriage, have attracted the attention of social researchers. Although these arrangements are fairly infrequent, with just 6% of women from age 30 to 39 defining their relationship in those terms (Ayuso, 2012), their number has been growing since the turn of the century. Moreover, the ambiguous definition of LAT could also explain why the decline in the number of marriages has not been offset by a proportional rise in the number of cohabiting unions. LAT couples attest to the trend toward individuality in postmodern households and women's increasing power in partnerships, as they devote more time to domestic chores when living with a partner (Ayuso, 2019). As Castro-Martín, Domínguez-Folgueras, and Martín-García (2008) note, in Spain, LAT couples are found primarily in younger segments of the population, for whom they constitute a strategy for accommodating adverse labor market conditions and the scant opportunities for emancipation. Such arrangements enable young adults to balance their needs for intimacy with the inter-generational solidarity afforded by their families of origin, as 60% of partners in such couples live with their parents (Ayuso, 2012). In other words, a significant proportion of LAT couples are in transitory family arrangements that serve as a bridge until they land in a sufficiently stable employment to afford emancipation with the couple. Nonetheless, the heterogeneity of LAT relationships reflects a preference among the other 40% for different strategies, such as independence in their relationship with a partner, reflecting the aforementioned inclination toward individuality instead of collective living arrangements (Castro-Martín et al., 2008). In this sense, the new models of family not based on traditional provisions represent the illustration of the confrontation of the 'me' and the 'network' (Castells, 2001) and the demand for individuality that coexists with the desire to share their lives with others, with new bonds, flexible and adaptive to the circumstances.

Sex gender minority families (SGM)

As mentioned in the introduction, the 2005 family law reform introduced the right for same-sex couples to get married with the same rights and obligations as different-sex couples, including joint adoption of children. The rise in the proportion of same-sex marriages also mirrors the change in Spanish societal behavior and values with respect to family matters. As Montes et al. (2016) showed in a study of 66 same-sex couples with children, the legal approval of same-sex marriage had a significant impact on the acceptance in the diverse social contexts of which they form part.

Although initially such couples were mostly composed of men, the proportion of male unions (marital or consensual) has declined in recent years to 61.2% of the total. In 2020, nearly half (48.5%) of same-sex couples were married; more men couples (52.5%) were married than women couples (42.1%) (Continuous Household Survey 2020, INE). Also, according to the 2011 census, 21.3% of women couples lived with children, compared to only 7.3% of men couples (Castro-Martín & Seiz Puyuelo, 2014). The analysis of microdata from the *Continuous*

Household Survey shows that in 2020 the percentage of couples living with children rose to 25% in the case of lesbian couples and decreased to 4.9% among gay couples. The mean number of children is similar to different-sex couples (1.64 in gay couples and 1.34 in lesbian couples compared to 1.63 in different-sex couples) and generally, those children are common to both parents (74.5% in lesbian couples and 91% in gay couples).

Recent studies on same-sex couples have focused on the distribution of domestic tasks and the time spent on them under the assumption that in couples where gender roles are absent, the domestic division of labor should be more equal. Meil (2003) and Domínguez Folgueras (2012) found that domestic chores were distributed more equally in same-sex than in different-sex couples, with time availability and intra-couple negotiation, along with the employment-related contributions made to the family by each adult, being the key factors in the decision-making.

Another line of research around same-sex parent households broached in recent years focuses on their children. After interviewing 71 same-sex couples with children, Agustín Ruíz (2013) reported that 5.6% had children from prior heterosexual relationships, 73.2% had children as a result of MAR, even though surrogate pregnancy is currently illegal as mentioned above, 15.5% had adopted, 4.2% were fostering and 1.2% had children as a result of an agreement with a heterosexual person.

Foster and adoptive families

Foster parenting and adoption have also undergone significant change in recent years. As mentioned in the introduction, adoption law was deeply reformed in 1988, introducing for the first time the principle of the best interest of the child and the institution of foster care. From then on, courts were obliged to ascertain children's preference and their consent when the children are over 12. The criteria for approval no longer included the adopters' marital status, sex, or sexual orientation. This realignment of the adoption law implied that the adoptees had to break their legal and social ties with their family of origin, but their right to investigate their origins is recognized. However, the 2015 act on the protection of minors instituted 'open adoption' (maintenance of some contact with the biological family). While charting a course for more complex family formulations, those provisions met considerable resistance from adopting families and some public agencies (Díez Riaza, 2018).

In the context of the sharp drop in fertility and the change in values, adoption ceased to be stigmatized and was conceived as a manifestation of solidarity and altruistic action to connect the needs of children with the desires of care of families and was also conceived as an alternative to MAR (Berástegui Pedro-Viejo, 2010). In 2019, 996 children were adopted (12 per 100,000 of the total population under 18), down from a peak of 6,369 in 2004. Also, in 2019, 19,320 children (232.1 per 100,000 of all minors) were foster-parented, 65.2% of whom were fostered by the extended family and the remaining 34.8% by other families (Ministry of Social Rights and Agenda 2030, 2020). A further 23,209 minors were fostered in institutions (278.8 per 100,000), which is a sharp increase since 2015, when the number was 13,596. In 2019, 59.5% were foreign-born children.

In 2007, an international adoption lawsuit was approved. Certainly, international adoptions rose significantly in the first decade of the 21st century, positioning Spain at the forefront of countries with a higher proportion of international adoptions (Selman, 2012). However, the number of international adoptions has dropped drastically in recent years, while the number of domestic adoptions rose. In 2004, 5,541 international and 828 domestic adoptions were recorded, while in 2019 the figures turned to 370 international and 626 national adoptions. Particularly striking is the near disappearance of adoptions from African countries, from 139 in 2015 to just 4 in 2019, accounting for 1.8% of the total, while 66.4% of international adoptions were of children from Asia, 19.5% from Europe, and 14% from America.

Families created by medically assisted reproduction (MAR)

Spanish women are among those with the lowest number of children in low-fertility Europe, contributing to what is known as 'lowest low' fertility (Billari & Kohler, 2004). Social, economic, and institutional constraints have been shown to reinforce the individualization of western society, leading to low fertility rates (Bueno & García Román, 2020). In addition to job instability, lack of affordable housing, and the difficulty in achieving a satisfactory work-life balance, the absence of government support raises the economic cost of having children and explains Spain's low fertility rate (Castro-Martín & Martín García, 2013).

In this line, according to recent sociological studies, in Spain low fertility, voluntary childlessness, and the desire to have children co-exist (Seiz, 2013), as reflected by the large number of children born as a result of MAR. MAR was first regulated in 1988, acknowledging all women the right to benefit from such techniques to offset sterility irrespective of their marital status or sexual orientation, although subject to their husband's consent where married. Surrogate pregnancy was nonetheless explicitly prohibited, as was sex selection. In 2006, the provisions on MAR have been extended, including MAR in public health coverage in cases of genetic disease, also increasing the types of medical technologies allowed.

The significant rise in the percentage of children born with the help of MAR also reflects more flexibility in forming families in recent decades, which are related to the postponement of motherhood and various legal changes referred to earlier. According to the 2018 Fertility survey (INE, 2018), 8.6% of women in reproductive age resorted to MAR to become mothers, which positions Spain among the leading European countries where such treatments are used (Rivas et al., 2018). As a result, the proportion of multiple births also rose from 2.5% in

1996 (Castro Martín & Seiz Puyuelo, 2014) to 4.5% in 2014, although it fell back to 3.6% in 2019 (population data and birth statistics, INE).

Although surrogate pregnancy continues to be illegal, the births of children born via surrogacy in countries where it is permitted are since then registered. Registration is subject, however, to the existence of a court sentence or resolution issued in the country of birth accrediting parenthood and the assurance of the rights of the surrogate mother (Crespo, 2019). Surrogate pregnancy has received considerable attention lately in social research because of the issues raised in conjunction with third-party involvement and the resulting ethical and legal considerations. A number of qualitative studies (Jociles et al., 2017; Rivas et al., 2018; Álvarez et al., 2019) have explored the accounts of intended families and surrogate mothers to understand their decision to participate in this type of MAR and what kinds of narratives are conveyed to children about how they were conceived and carried.

Multicultural and migrant families

Spanish families are also increasingly transnational and multicultural. The steep rise in immigration beginning in 1995 has led to growth in the proportion of couples with different nationalities, although in most cases the spouses (Europeans or Latin Americans) have similar cultural backgrounds. Such unions reflect the growing visibility and acceptance of globalization and contribute in diversifying the traditional perception of the Spanish family.

In 2020, 4.3% of all unions involved one foreign-born person and 4.4% of the unions were formed by two foreign-born residents (2020 Continuous Household Survey, INE). In that year, 74% of the couples in which at least one of the members was not born in Spain were married. In 43.3% of such marriages, the woman was foreign-born, in 26.2% the man was foreign-born, and in 27% both were immigrants. Also, in 12.4% of same-sex unions, at least one of the members was not born in Spain. According to the 2019 data on spousal nationality, 41.6% of Spanish women were in inter-marriages with (Latin or other) Americans, 32.8% with other Europeans, 22.2% with Africans, and 3.1% with Asians. On the other hand, 55.1% of Spanish men were married to (Latin or other) Americans, 32.2% to Europeans, 9.2% to Africans, and 3.3% to Asians (marriage statistics, INE). In 2019, the crude divorce rate involving immigrants was significantly higher than among Spanish-only couples: 4.53 compared to 3.81 (divorce indicators, INE).

Conclusion and recommendations

In Spain, as in other developed countries, family life has grown more diverse in recent decades. The types of families, their social acceptance, and their legal regulation have changed, leading to a greater freedom of choice when planning a family. These changes have come later and have been more intense in a number of respects than in other European societies because the military dictatorship in power for the better part of the 20th century was built around the patriarchal family model.

Although the Catholic Church and conservative sectors opposed many of the new measures, nearly all have been endorsed by the Constitutional Court and, with the exception of the voluntary interruption of pregnancy, accepted by subsequent conservative administrations. Pioneering legislation has been adopted to protect LGBTQA+ rights and freedoms, thanks in part to the power and influence acquired by these organizations. Provisions are now in effect on their right to change sex and to adopt, marry, and access assisted reproduction under the same conditions as heterosexuals.

These changes in types of household in contrast to the inertia of tradition as well as social and economic constraints have obstructed the fulfillment of individual and family aspirations. Low fertility rates have therefore become a social problem of considerable magnitude in Spain, mirrored in the difference between families' preferred size and the number of children they ultimately have (Castro-Martín et al., 2020). This gap between reality and aspiration or ideal shows the existence of a welfare deficit for Spanish couples that affects their family planning. Recent research findings on public, universally available pre-school institutions demonstrate their potential for raising fertility rates. Sharing childcare between the state and families facilitates women to enter the labor market and reduces the opportunity cost of having children when they work outside the home (Baizán et al., 2016; Díaz Gandasegui et al., 2021; Ibáñez & León, 2014).

Although harmonization of work and family life has been a priority in public policy and many measures have been adopted in its pursuit, the percentage of workers claiming to encounter difficulties in that regard is substantially higher than in the rest of the European Union. Recent initiatives, such as de-gendering leave-taking, may contribute to reaching that goal by fostering greater father involvement in childcare and household tasks. Parents also demand new legislation, similar to other European countries, to enable them to take leaves when their children are ill.

Socioeconomic constraints also affect the living strategies of Spanish young adults, who live with their families of origin much longer than young adults in most other European countries. Their late independence, associated with the obstacles they encounter in the labor and housing markets, reflects the ongoing importance of family ties and inter-generational solidarity. In Spain, young adults prefer cohabitation as the option to partner up. While marriage continues to be a highly valued option for forming a family, it is no longer considered a permanent institution. Spain's crude divorce rate is as high as the mean across the EU, even though the right to divorce was recognized later than in other European countries. The rise in divorce also leads to an increase in the number of one-parent and blended families, a clear indication of the de-institutionalization of families because relationships are more frequently built, dissolved, and rebuilt based on individual aspirations and desires.

Spanish family policies are largely geared toward protecting the most vulnerable families (large, one-parent, those affected by gender violence, or caring for a disabled member). Those families' poverty and social exclusion rates are among the highest in the EU and reflect the failure of recent policies to ensure minimum-level welfare for all children or prevent their social exclusion. In this sense, it would be convenient to substantially increase direct money transfers to families with dependent children and low-income levels, as suggested among others by the OECD (2022). Likewise, it is necessary to further develop public services for the care of dependent persons to ease the burden of informal care for their relatives, especially in those families with lower economic resources.

Social research on Spanish families, conducted primarily from the 1980s onward, has created nationally and internationally connected research teams. Those researchers have described and rigorously analyzed the main changes in Spanish families, along with the causes and social and economic effects of such transformations. Nonetheless, knowledge gaps in this domain remain, especially in connection with emergent family arrangements. Very few studies shed light, for instance, on same-sex parent households or the origin of their descendants, the composition of blended families, or the de-institutionalization of marriage, and more specifically on how partnering arrangements affect the various dimensions of union- and family-building (intra-union violence, distribution of family obligations, and similar).

More recently, social research has been focused largely on the effects of the socio-health crisis triggered by COVID and its impact on families. During the weeks of strict confinement, families have been exposed to a social laboratory in which work and domestic spaces have merged and practices such as teleworking and teleeducation have been implemented, transforming family routines and dynamics. The time dedicated to care has increased, but structural gender inequalities have not been transformed, with women being the ones who have cared the most and increased their time of care the most (Ayuso et al., 2020). The weeks of confinement and subsequent opening with limitations have faced Spanish families with a series of changes and challenges. Relationships with the elderly have been reduced to telephone or video calls, making visible the importance of the extended family, especially when approximately half of the citizens expressed their frustration for not being able to see their relatives during the lockdown period. Grandparents were unable to take care of their grandchildren and had to use technological devices to be in contact with them, as more than half of the grandparents did (CIS, 2021). In this time of forced and abrupt change, the vulnerability of families with fewer resources, such as one-parent families, has also increased (EAPN-Spain, 2021). The need to care for and work in the same space and time has been an obstacle for many one-parent families in their professional activities and also their children, who in many cases required the aid of parents, for school activities. Likewise, these families, a large proportion in a situation of exclusion, have experienced difficulties in being able to teleeducate or telework, when the available technological resources were not sufficient (Bonal & González, 2020).

Funding

This work was supported by the Agencia Estatal de Investigación under Grant CSO2017–84634-R.

Note

1 The conceptualization of households in the statistics of the INE and Eurostat produce a confusion which is reflected in the academic literature. Eurostat considers only 'one-parent households with dependent children'; therefore, it does not include one-parent families living with grandparents as a survival strategy, nor those cases in which the parent lives with non-dependent children. However, INE does not consider the former but does consider the latter.

References

Agustín Ruiz, S. (2013). *Familias homoparentales en España: integración social, necesidades y derechos*. Universidad Autónoma de Madrid.

Álvarez, C., Rivas, A. M., & Jociles, M. I. (2019). Vínculos y contactos socioafectivos de las familias españolas con gestantes por sustitución de Estados Unidos, Canadá y Ucrania. In F. Lledó, P. Ferrer, I. Benítez, C. Ochoa, C. y O. Monje (Eds.), *Gestación subrogada. Principales cuestiones civiles, penales, registrales y médicas. Su evolución y consideración (1988–2019)* (pp. 779–792). Dykinson.

Ayuso Sánchez, L. (2012). Living apart together en España. ¿Noviazgos o parejas independientes? *Revista Internacional de Sociología, 70*(3), 587–613.

Ayuso Sánchez, L. (2019). Nuevas imágenes del cambio familiar en España. *RES. Revista Española de Sociología, 28*(2), 269–287.

Ayuso Sánchez, L., & Bascón Jiménez, M. (2021). The discovery of family policies in Spain: Between ideology and pragmatism. *Revista Española de Investigaciones Sociológicas, 174*, 3–22. http://dx.doi.org/10.5477/cis/reis.174.3

Ayuso Sánchez, L., Requena, F., Jiménez-Rodriguez, O., & Khamis, N. (2020). The effects of COVID-19 confinement on the Spanish family: Adaptation or change? *Journal of Comparative Family Studies, 51*(3–4), 274–287.

Baizán, P., Arpino, B., & Delclós, C. E. (2016). The effect of gender policies on fertility: The moderating role of education and normative context. *European Journal of Population, 32*(1), 1–30.

Bauman, Z. (2009). *Modernidad líquida*. Fondo de Cultura Económica.

Beck-Gernsheim, E. (2003). *La reinvención de la familia. En busca de nuevas formas de convivencia*. Paidós.

Berástegui Pedro-Viejo, A. (2010). Adopción internacional: ¿solidaridad con la infancia o reproducción asistida? *Aloma, Revista de Psicologia, Ciències de l'Educació i de l'Esport, 27*, 15–38.

Billari, F., & Kohler, H. P. (2004). Patterns of low and lowest-low fertility in Europe. *Population Studies, 58*(2), 161–176.

Bonal, X., & González, S. (2020). The impact of lockdown on the learning gap: Family and school divisions in times of crisis. *International Review of Education, 66*(5), 635–655.

Bueno, X., & García Román, J. (2020). La fecundidad según la diferencia educativa y laboral entre cónyuges: ¿Tanto monta, monta tanto? *Perspectives Demogràphiques, 21,* 1–4.

Castells, M. (2001). *La era de la información: La sociedad red.* Alianza Editorial.

Castón Boyer, P., & Ocón Domingo, J. (2002). Historia y Sociología de la adopción. *Revista Internacional de Sociología, 33,* 173–209.

Castro-Martín, T., Domínguez-Folgueras, M., & Martín-García, T. (2008). Not truly partnerless: Non-residential partnerships and retreat from marriage in Spain. *Demographic Research, 18,* 443–468.

Castro-Martín, T., & Martín García, T. (2013). Fecundidad bajo mínimos en España: pocos hijos, a edades tardías y por debajo de las aspiraciones reproductivas. In G. Esping-Andersen (Ed.), *El déficit de natalidad en Europa. La singularidad del caso español* (pp. 48–88).Obra Social La Caixa.

Castro-Martín, T., Martín-García, T., Cordero, J., & Seiz, M. (2020). La muy baja fecundidad en España: la brecha entre deseos y realidades reproductivas. *Dossier Economistas sin Fronteras, 36,* 8–13.

Castro-Martín, T., & Seiz Puyuelo, M. (2014). *La transformación de las familias en España desde una perspectiva socio-demográfica.* Informe FOESSA.

Cea d'Ancona, M.A. (2007). La deriva del cambio familiar. *Centro de Investigaciones Sociológicas, colección monografías, 306.850946 C4,* 241 pp.

CIS. (2021). *Efectos y consecuencias del Coronavirus: Estudio III.* Diciembre de 2020.

Crespo, E. (2019), Gestación subrogada: enfoque legal y estado actual en España. Retrieved from https://www.elenacrespolorenzo.com

Del Campo, S., & Tezanos, J. F. (2008). *España siglo XXI: La sociedad.* Biblioteca Nueva.

Díaz Gandasegui, V., Elizalde-San Miguel, B., & Sanz, M. T. (2021). Back to the future: A sensitivity analysis to predict future fertility rates considering the influence of family policies—The cases of Spain and Norway. *Social Indicators Research,* 154(3), 943–968.

Díez Riaza, S. (2018). La aplicación de la adopción abierta en España. Una visión en cifras y algo más. *Revista de Derecho UNED, 22,* 159–182.

Domínguez Folgueras, M. (2012). La división del trabajo doméstico en las parejas españolas. Un análisis de uso del tiempo. *Revista internacional de sociología, 70*(1), 153–179.

Domínguez-Folgueras, M., & Castro-Martín, T. (2013). Cohabitation in Spain: No longer a marginal path to family formation. *Journal of Marriage and Family, 75*(2), 422–437.

EAPN-Spain. (2021). *El Estado de la Pobreza. Seguimiento del indicador de Pobreza y Exclusión Social en España 2008–2019.* Madrid: EAPN-ES. Retrieved from https://www.eapn.es/estadodepobreza/ARCHIVO/documentos/informe-AROPE-2021-contexto-nacional.pdf

Flaquer, L., Almeda, E., & Navarro, L. (2006). Monoparentalidad e infancia. *Obra social Fundación "la Caixa", colección estudios sociales, 20.*

Flaquer, L., & Escobedo, A. (2020). Las licencias parentales y la política social a la paternidad en España. In L. Flaquer, T. Cano, & M. Barbeta (Eds.), *La paternidad en España: La implicación paterna en el cuidado de los hijos* (pp. 161–190). CSIC.

Ibáñez, Z., & León, M. (2014). Early childhood education and care provision in Spain. In M. León (ed.), *The transformation of care in European societies* (pp. 276–300). Palgrave Macmillan.

Iglesias de Ussel, J. (1990), La familia y el cambio político en España. *Revista de Estudios Políticos (Nueva Época), 67,* 236–259.

INE. (2001). *Censo de Población y Viviendas, 2001.* Instituto Nacional de Estadística. Retrieved from https://ine.es/dyngs/INEbase/es/categoria.htm?c=Estadistica_P&cid=1254734710984

INE. (2004). *Cifras INE.* Boletín Informativo del Instituto Nacional de Estadística. ISSN: 1579-2277.

INE. (2018). *Encuesta de fecundidad, 1999 y 2018.* Instituto Nacional de Estadística. Retrieved from https://ine.es/dyngs/INEbase/es/categoria.htm?c=Estadistica_P&cid=1254735572981

INE. (2019). *Estadísticas de matrimonios y nacimientos. Movimiento Natural de la Población.* Instituto Nacional de Estadística. Retrieved from https://ine.es/dyngs/INEbase/es/categoria.htm?c=Estadistica_P&cid=1254735572981

INE. (2020). *Encuesta continua de hogares.* Instituto Nacional de Estadística. Retrieved from https://ine.es/dyngs/INEbase/es/categoria.htm?c=Estadistica_P&cid=1254734710984

INE. (2021). *Nota de prensa de la Estadística de Nulidades, Separaciones y Divorcios 2020.* Instituto Nacional de Estadística. Retrieved from https://www.ine.es/dyngs/Prensa/notasPrensa.htm

Jiménez Cabello, J., & Becerril Ruiz, D. (2020). Main characteristics associated with the assignment of Custodies after the divorce. *Journal of Divorce & Remarriage, 61*(8), 615–635.

Jiménez Cabello, J., Becerril Ruiz, D., & García Moreno, J. M. (2020). La relación entre reformas legales y la asignación de la custodia compartida en España (2007–2017). *Revista Española de Ciencia Política, 53,* 119–142.

Jociles Rubio, M. I., Rivas, A. M., & Álvarez Plaza, C. (2017). Strategies to personalize and to depersonalize donors in parental narratives of children's genetic/gestational origins (Spain). *Suomen antropologi, 42*(7), 25–50.

Lombardo, E., & Alonso, A. (2020). Gender regime change in decentralized states: The case of Spain. *Social Politics, Fall 2020,* 449–466. https://doi.org/10.1093/sp/jxaa016

López-Narbona, A. M., Moreno-Mínguez, A., & Ortega-Gaspar, M. (2021). Family structure, parental practices, and child wellbeing in post- divorce situations: The case of shared parenting. In J. M.de Torres Perea, E. Kruk, & M. Ortiz-Tallo (Eds.), *The Routledge international handbook of shared parenting and best interest of the child* (pp. 170–182). Routledge.

Meil, G., Diaz Gandasegui, V., Rogero-García, J., & Romero-Balsas, P. (2021). Non-parental childcare in France, Norway and Spain. In A. M. Castrén et al. (Eds.), *The Palgrave handbook of family sociology in Europe* (pp. 345–360). Palgrave Macmillan. https://doi.org/10.1007/978-3-030-73306-3_17

Meil Landwerlin, G. (1999). *La postmodernización de la familia española.* Editorial Acento.

Meil Landwerlin, G. (2003). *Las uniones de hecho en España.* Centro de Investigaciones Sociológicas, colección monografías 201.

Meil Landwerlin, G. (2006). The evolution of family policy in Spain. *Marriage and Family Review, 39*(3–4), 359–380.

Meil Landwerlin, G., Romero-Balsas, P., & Rogero-García, J. (2019). Spain: Leave policy in times of economic crisis, 2007–2017. In P. Moss, A. Z. Duvander and A. Koslowski (Eds.), *Parental leave and beyond: Recent developments, current issues, future directions* (pp. 21–38). Policy Press.

Ministerio de derechos sociales y Agenda 2030. (2020). *Boletín de datos estadísticos de medidas de protección a la infancia. Datos 2019.* Boletín número 22. Informes, Estudio e Investigación 2020.

Moncó, B. (2014). Madres y madrastras: modelos de género, heterodesignación y familias reconstituidas. *Feminismo-s, 23*, 113.

Montes, A., Gonzalez, M., López-Gaviño, F., & Angulo, A. (2016). Familias homoparentales, más visibles y mejor aceptadas: efectos del matrimonio en España. *Apuntes de Psicología, 34*(2–3), 151–159.

Moreno-Mínguez, A., Ortega-Gaspar, M., & Gamero-Burón, C. A. (2019). Sociostructural perspective on family model preferences, gender roles and work–family attitudes in Spain. *Social Sciences, 8*(1), 4. https://doi.org/10.3390/socsci8010004

OECD. (2022). *Evolving family models in Spain: A new national framework for improved support and protection for families.* OECD Publishing. https://doi.org/10.1787/c27e63ab-en

OECD. (2022a). *Family database.* https://www.oecd.org/els/family/database.htm

Rivas, A. M. (2012). El ejercicio de la parentalidad en las familias reconstituidas. *Portularia, 12*(2), 29–41.

Rivas, A. M., Jociles Rubio, M. I., & Álvarez Plaza, C. (2018). La intervención de "terceros" en la producción de parentesco: perspectiva de los/as donantes, las familias y la descendencia. Un estado de la cuestión. *Revista de Antropología Social, 27*(2), 221–245.

Roche Cárcel, J. (2020). La coexistence de l'amour romantique et du confluent en Espagne. *Sociétés, 149*, 87–102. https://doi.org/10.3917/soc.149.0087

Rogero-García, J. (2015). *Personas mayores y familia.* In C. Torres-Albero (Ed.), *España 2015: situación social* (pp. 374–381). Centro de Investigaciones Sociológicas (CIS).

Rosenmayr, L. (1970). Family relations of the elderly. In C. C. Harris (Ed.), *Readings in Kinship in Urban society* (pp. 367–386). Elsevier. https://doi.org/10.1016/B978-0-08-016038-2.50023-3

Salar Sotillos, M. J. (2018). La familia en la jurisprudencia del Tribunal Constitucional español. *Actualidad Jurídica Iberoamericana, 8*(bis), 196–225.

Santibáñez, R., Flores, N., & Martín, A. (2018). Familia monomarental y riesgo de exclusión social. *Iqual. Revista de género e igualdad, 1*, 123–144.

Seiz, M. (2013). Voluntary childlessness in Southern Europe: The case of Spain. *Population Review, 52*(1), 110–128.

Selman, P. (2012). The rise and fall of intercountry adoption in the 21st century: Global trends from 2001 to 2010. In J. Gibbons y K. Rotabi (Eds.), *Intercountry Adoption: Policies, Practices, and Outcomes* (pp. 7–27). Ashgate.

Tobío, C., & Fernández Cordón, J. A. (1999). Monoparentalidad, trabajo y familia. *Revista Internacional de Sociología, 22*, 67–97.

Treviño, R., Gumà, J., & Permañer, I. (2013). Las parejas de familias reconstituidas. Una caracterización desde la perspectiva de género. *Papers de Demografía, 419*, 1–41.

8

CHANGES IN FAMILY DIVERSITY IN SWEDEN

Opportunities, constraints and challenges

Barbara Hobson, Livia Sz. Oláh and Glenn Sandström[1]

The cultural and policy context of doing family

Swedish family policy has been celebrated as a paradigm of gender equality and the gold standard for policies enabling father's involvement in care. It has also been criticized for denying families agency and choice. We present a more nuanced account by engaging with the legal barriers in recognizing diversity in families and the challenges that remain.

Historically, three distinctive features of the Swedish welfare state have been central in shaping laws, discourses and policy practices related to family diversity: (1) the framing of gender equality; (2) the construction of fatherhood; and (3) the mother/father binary in heteronormative parenthood.

Beginning in 1917, Swedish family law formalized the paternity of fathers of children born outside of marriage by denying them the right to remain anonymous, in contrast to other countries. This legal change, which sought to reduce the financial burden on municipalities, had little effect. Nevertheless, having a known biological father became a central tenet in Swedish family law and continues to be salient in the context of increasingly diverse family forms. Another principle established in the marriage code of 1920s was that both parents have economic responsibility for the care of their children. This principle was reverberated in the specific policies and practices in the Swedish dual-earner model that took shape in the 1970s.

The 1970s was a transformative decade with 74 government commissions addressing marriage and family law and policy. Sweeping changes were recommended to recognize diversity in families and gender equality (Florin & Nilsson, 1999). Increasing number of couples forming cohabitant unions was reflected in legal changes removing distinctions between married and cohabitant couples and children born to married and unmarried parents. There is no formal definition

DOI: 10.4324/9781003193500-8

of what constitutes a family in legal documents. Nonetheless, the above legal changes constituted, in fact, a recasting of the notion of what is a family, framed in a new discursive and policy landscape that assumed: (1) that policy should be neutral in relation to family forms and (2) that how parents organize their relationship should not affect their rights and duties to their children (SOU, 1972:41).

This blurring of boundaries between marriage and cohabitation paved the way for greater diversity in family forms in an era of rising divorce, re-partnering, stepfamilies, and increasingly complex family constellations, although the privileged position of the biological father remained.

From the 1970s onwards, doing family became intertwined with doing gender. The laws, policies and discourses that emerged in this decade became the foundation for the Swedish model of the dual-earner, dual-carer family (Hobson, 2004; Korpi, 2000). Policies to promote this model extended into multiple domains, including individualized taxation, the end of marriage subsidies for a dependent spouse, generous publicly supported daycare provision, and the world's first gender-neutral parental leave policy that allowed fathers to participate in the care of their children during the first years (Ferrarini & Duvander, 2010). The parental leave policy, one of the most flexible and generous, did not specify which parent should take leave or whether some of this leave should be reserved for the father. It took more than 20 years to enact a law that mandated non-transferable months of leave to each parent, now at three months.

Fathers' increasingly active role in daily care of their children, reflected in their share of the leave (since 2018 about 30%), has also had an effect on fathering practices after separation and divorce. Joint custody became the norm during the 1990s. The courts enforced this principle in rare cases when parents disagreed over custody. The joint custody default re-enforces the position of the biological father. Even if he has played no role in the child's upbringing and had little contact with his child, he can at any time make claims for joint custody (Bergman & Hobson, 2002). This stipulation placed the stepfather in legal and social limbo. He had no financial obligations to support non-biological children in the family nor did he have any right to have contact with them after divorce, no matter how many years he had been the caring father in everyday life. This has remained unchanged in Swedish family law.

Shared physical (residential) custody has increased dramatically in the last decade, reaching 35–40% (Fransson et al., 2018), the highest among European countries. This has also led to a significant recent policy change beyond the law on parental leave (SFS, 1995:584[2]) that allowed the transfer of leave to spouses after remarriage or if the biological parent and his/her new partner had a joint child together. Since July 2019, biological parents can transfer portions of their share of the leave to cohabiting partners and spouses without a birth child requirement. Embedded in this change is the recognition that there can be four persons parenting in a family. Still, these entitlements given to social parents are derived from their relationship with the biological parents and do not enable them to have rights to contact with children after divorce or separation.

Recognizing sex-gender minority (SGM) families under Swedish law has not been straightforward; sometimes Sweden appeared as a trailblazer; other times as a laggard. Full recognition of the diversity in LGBTQA+ families is a goal not yet achieved. Homosexuality was de-criminalized in 1944; however, it was listed as a mental disorder until 1979 when the National Board of Health and Welfare ceased to classify it as an illness. Same-sex couples were not included in laws regulating property during cohabitation until 1987 (SFS, 1987:813[3]).

Sweden was among the first countries in Europe to recognize same-sex partnerships (1995) and allowed parents in same-sex couples to adopt children (2003). However, the Marriage Code was not amended to include same-sex marriages until 2009. Soon thereafter, the non-birth mother in a lesbian couple could be registered as a legal parent (Malmquist, 2015). This legal change involved two foundational principles: the presumption of paternity (that the father who conceived the child is the parent) and the primacy of biological fatherhood. Under Swedish law, a child can only have two legal parents so that recognizing the non-birth lesbian parent is an example of how the marriage law had to become gender-neutral (Ryan-Flood, 2009).

Sweden has the longest legal timeline with respect to transgender law and parenthood. It was the first country in the world to allow persons to legally change their gender (SFS, 1972:119[4]). However, this required the person to be a Swedish citizen, unmarried, and infertile, and consequently, to divorce if married and to undergo sterilization. This model was later adopted in many other countries. The sterilization requirement remained until 2013 when the Swedish high court ruled that forced sterilization violated human rights. Five years later, the Swedish government recognized this infringement of basic human rights in the law by compensating transgender individuals who had undergone mandatory sterilization in order to have their sex legally reassigned (SFS, 2018:162[5]).

Recognizing diversity in transgender families has stretched the limits of the binary framework of gender and parenthood in family law (Johnson & Mägi, 2021). Transgender families challenge how paternity is established in diverse family forms and who is assigned to be the father or the mother before and after birth. Moreover, adapting the Swedish parental code to comply with a recent European Court of Human rights decision poses other challenges (Zadeh, 2016). This requires that gender reassignment include the right to keep one's previous gender identity private, which until recently was not possible for transgender parents.

Empirical patterns of various family forms

To study partnership trends in Sweden, we can rely on vital statistics providing precise information on marriages and divorces but not on non-marital cohabitation because there is no legal requirement to register such relationships. The latter can be traced in population registers for couples having children together, but the Census and large-scale surveys are the only sources that provide reliable information on cohabiting relationships without joint children until 2011. Vital statistics on registered partnerships are available at Statistics Sweden from 1995 onwards. Since 2009 when marriage became gender-neutral, registered partnerships cannot be formed anymore in Sweden. However, information on same-sex marriages (including those ending due to the death of a partner or divorce or separation) is available in relevant vital statistics.

Union formation and dissolution

Between the late 1960s and early 2000s, Sweden continually had the lowest marriage rates in Europe, even in comparison to other Scandinavian nations. The only exception was a temporary boom in 1989 due to changes in the widow's pension rules, which prompted many couples to marry. A 'marriage revival' during the first decades of the 2000s resulted in higher crude marriage rates in 2018 than at the turn of the century (Table 8.1), even exceeding the EU average.

Despite these trends, the decision to enter into marriage has been increasingly postponed in Sweden, reaching the ages well into the thirties in the 2000s, the highest in Europe. Comparing these figures with the mean age at first birth along with the proportion of non-marital births (Table 8.1) reveals that the traditional

TABLE 8.1 Selected demographic indicators for Sweden, 2000 and latest available data

	2000	*Latest available data*	
Crude marriage rate	4.5	2019	4.7
Mean age at first marriage			
of women	30.5	2019	33.9
of men	33.1	2019	36.3
Crude divorce rate	2.4	2019	2.5
Remarriage rate			
of women	5.7	2018	7.5
of men	5.7	2018	6.9
% of adults >15 never married			
of women	26.8	2019	31.2
of men	33.7	2019	37.5
Total fertility rate	1.54	2019	1.70
Mean age at first birth			
of women	28.2	2019	29.6
of men			
% non-marital births	55.3	2019	54.5
% of women aged 40 who have born no children	14	2019	13
% of women aged 45 who have born no children	12	2019	13
Cohorts	**1950**		**1970**
Completed fertility/cohort	1.99		1.88

Sources: Eurostat; Statistics Sweden.

family formation patterns have been increasingly replaced from the mid-/late 1970s onwards, with young adults cohabiting first and having their first and sometimes second child before marriage. The proportion of persons being never married is not negligible in Sweden (Ohlsson-Wijk et al., 2020).

Along with the growing prevalence of non-marital unions, the instability of marriages has become an increasingly important aspect in the emerging family diversity. The risk of divorce rose considerably in Sweden in 1974 as a consequence of one of the most liberal divorce laws in the world, which grants immediate divorce without cause if the couple agrees and has no minor children. Otherwise, there is a six-month waiting period (Ohlsson-Wijk et al., 2020). In the 1980s and 1990s, the rising trends to divorce applied particularly to parents, but no further increase has been noted in the 2000s. Looking at both marriages and cohabiting unions reveals an overall levelling-off in partnership instability, with slightly more than one-half of all couples breaking up within 15 years from the 1980s onwards (Ohlsson-Wijk et al., 2020). The share of children whose parents separated before the child turned 15 remained at about 30%. As for remarriages, the increasing trends of the 1970s reversed in the late 20th century, followed by a slight increase only among women with children. The propensity to form a higher-order marriage for divorced persons and widows/widowers remained low in the 2000s.

In the mid-/late 1990s, the prevalence of registered same-sex unions was about 5 new registered partnerships to every 1,000 new different-sex marriages (Andersson et al., 2006), and male couples vastly outnumbered female couples. Female same-sex union formation has, however, increased about six-fold a year between 1996 and 2012, compared to male couples, which have doubled (Kolk & Andersson, 2020). In any event, same-sex partnerships, especially female couples, have been considerably less stable than traditional marriages. Among childless couples, male same-sex unions are the least likely to end in divorce, even less so than different-sex marriages without children (Kolk & Andersson, 2020).

Fertility patterns

Total fertility rates fluctuated greatly in Sweden since the 1960s. This relates to higher female labour force participation, business cycle changes and the success of family policies in mitigating the opportunity cost of childbearing while parenthood has been increasingly delayed (Oláh & Bernhardt, 2008). In the 1990s, fertility declined rapidly from the replacement level to the lowest levels ever measured in the country. After fertility started to climb in the 2000s (Table 8.1), it decreased again slowly since 2010. The proportion of women who had no children by age 50 remained rather stable (13–14%), accompanied by cohort fertility levels at about two children per woman on average. There is a strong two-child norm in Sweden, and one-fourth of women have three or more children (Oláh & Bernhardt, 2008; Statistics Sweden, 2020a). Childbearing in same-sex partnerships was rather uncommon prior to the legal changes of the early 2000s but has become comparable in female couples and in different-sex partnerships in recent years. The contribution to fertility levels due to ART is nearly 4% of all newborns annually in more recent years (Statistics Sweden, 2021a).

Changes in household composition and living arrangements

With respect to living arrangements, the share of married couples decreased somewhat in the 2000s, from 45% to around 40%, while the proportion of cohabiting remained stable, close to 20% in the adult population (Table 8.2). Marriage is a living arrangement for more mature ages, seen in the low proportions of married couples even at ages 25–34. The proportion of adults still living in the parental home nearly doubled over the first decades of the 2000s, reaching almost 8%. Below age 25, this is the most common living arrangement. We see a slight decline in people living alone among all adults, especially at ages 18–24.

The share of one-parent families remained quite stable in the early 21st century. This living arrangement is very rare in the youngest age group, around 1%, and three times as large at ages 25–34. Indeed, the path to single motherhood via teenage childbearing is negligible in Sweden. Couples become parents in their later 20s or later, and they are less likely to dissolve their union when their children are very young (Oláh & Bernhardt, 2008). Partnership breakups in turn contribute to the slight increase in complex multi-person living arrangements (to 6.3% among adults), while multi-generational families remain uncommon.

Regarding households, we have no information for the first years of the 2000s. The dwelling register, established in 2011, allows us to address the composition of households in the late 2010s (Table 8.3). The largest category, comprising nearly 40% of all households, is living alone, which is especially common at older ages. One-person households also include a not-insignificant proportion of individuals in living-apart-together relationships (Oláh et al., 2021). Different-sex married couples (12% with minor children and 19.4% without) comprise nearly

TABLE 8.2 Population in living arrangements in Sweden, 2002/2003 and latest available data

% of persons are living	2002/2003			2018		
	Total	Age 18–24	Age 25–34	Total	Age 18–24	Age 25–34
With spouse	45.0	2.4	24.6	39.7	2.1	21.7
With partner	19.3	19.0	40.9	18.4	13.9	32.5
Child of householder	4.3	46.3	2.8	7.8	54.6	9.5
Alone	25.1	26.5	25.4	22.8	17.6	21.7
Alone with child/ren	5.0	1.2	4.4	4.9	0.8	3.7
with another person(s)	1.2	4.6	1.8	6.3	10.9	10.7
Unknown	0.0	0.0	0.0	0.2	0.1	0.2

Source: For living arrangements in 2002/2003: EU–SILC/ULF, whereas SCB dwelling register is the source for all information in 2018

TABLE 8.3 Households in Sweden, latest available data

% of households consist of	2018
Different-sex spouses	
with kids <18	11.9
w/out Kids <18	19.4
Different-sex partners	
with kids <18	7.1
w/out kids <18	7.8
Mother only with kids	5.1
Father only with kids	1.8
Same-sex couple	0.1
One person living alone	39.5
Other multiperson households	7.4

Note: No data for 2000.
Source: SCB dwelling register.

one-third of all households, whereas the joint share of unmarried couples with and without children is 15% (their proportions are nearly equal, slightly above 7%). Same-sex couples represent 0.1% of all households. The shares of one-parent households and other multi-person households are nearly equally large (around 7%). Mother-only households vastly outnumber father-only households (5.1% versus 1.8%).

Current empirical research on the various family forms

Reconstituted families (stepfamilies)

The vast majority of parents raise only their biological or adopted children in Sweden. However, about 2% of mothers and 4.5% of fathers also have stepchildren or foster children, and 1% and 2.5% respectively have only stepchildren or foster children (Statistics Sweden, 2020b). Such family complexity is usually linked to union dissolution: around one-fifth of first-born children experience the separation of their parents before they enter school (Duvander & Korsell, 2020). Nevertheless, three of four minor children live with both their biological parents. Among those who do not, about 40% have shared residential custody (Statistics Sweden, 2021b), in which the child spends nearly equal amounts of time in either parent's home. Regarding the children who live with one biological parent, 40% have a stepparent and nearly one-tenth have two stepparents (Statistics Sweden, 2021c), as both the mother and the father entered new co-residential unions.

Research shows that the doing of family does not change crucially for separated parents in Sweden; rather, they continue to share care responsibilities (Duvander & Korsell, 2020). Although parents take fewer parental leave days after separation than parents who live together, this is mainly due to economic constraints, given that the amount of the parental benefit is somewhat less than 80% of a full salary and separated parents are usually worse off financially than co-resident parents. Separated fathers are, however, as likely to use longer leave over two months, as non-separated fathers (Duvander & Korsell, 2020).

Parental engagement with a child after union dissolution is further reinforced through shared residential custody. Scholars demonstrate in numerous studies the positive impact of such arrangements on child well-being in contrast to living full time with one parent, often the mother (Fransson et al, 2018; Turunen, 2017). Such beneficial outcomes are found also with a stepparent present in one or both homes (Fransson et al., 2018). As highlighted by Thomson and Turunen (2021), shared residential custody should be considered a new family form as it provides a unique context for fulfilling gender-equal parental obligations sequentially rather than simultaneously. When the child resides with one parent at a time, family members across multiple households are involved in a constant negotiation to optimize the arrangement.

One-parent and cohabiting families

As in most countries and noted above, single-parent mother households comprise the majority of one-parent families. Hobson and Takahashi (1997) and Hobson (2004) have highlighted the disadvantage of single mothers within Sweden's dual-earner/dual-carer model. Using Luxembourg Income Study data for the 1990s, they showed that single mothers tended to be in full-time employment, although they would have fallen into poverty without the social transfers for low-income families. Current research shows that single mothers' situation has worsened in the last decades: they work less than married mothers, are more likely to be unemployed and have a poverty rate three times higher than couples with children (Nieuwenhuis, 2021). Alm et al. (2020), controlling for a range of individual-level variables, maintain that continuous declines in income replacement for unemployment and stricter entitlements have affected one-parent households adversely.

The universalist framework of the Swedish welfare state does not permit targeting specific groups for specific benefits. That single mothers as a group have not been stigmatized is a positive effect of this principle. Nieuwenhuis (2021) underscores the need for specific benefits for single mothers, who, even when employed, do not have adequate earnings. Single mothers can vary by education and income, although in Nordic countries the low educated women are more likely to become and remain single parents (Härkönen & Dronkers, 2006). Single mothers can also differ in terms of time poverty and care responsibilities with the shared residential custody a salient factor.

Unlike many other countries, cohabiting families differ little from married families in Sweden where cohabitation has become the first step of the family career and marriage comes after the birth of the first or second child

(Oláh & Bernhardt, 2008). Thus, in recent research on families in Sweden, married and cohabiting couples are often analysed together. Although consensual unions have remained more fragile, parenting practices are very similar to those in marriages, for example, married and cohabiting fathers devote the same amount of time to childcare in Sweden (Ono & Yeilding, 2009).

Sex gender minority families (SGM)

Beyond legal achievements regarding SGM families, Sweden is considered a society that is highly tolerant of diverse family forms and supports LGBTQA+ rights. These values are mirrored in social institutions, in ruling political parties, and in social media. Attitudinal surveys at the European level and in the World Values Survey place Sweden either first or second compared to other nations with respect to measures of tolerance. For instance, there is strong agreement with the statements: 'gay men and lesbians should be free to live their own life as they wish' and 'a same-sex couple can bring up a child as well as a male-female couple' (Takács et al., 2016).

There is a dearth of quantitative data on same-sex marriages. In Nordic countries, demographers using excellent register data have been able to trace family dynamics, family formation, and divorce over time. Swedish demographers have been at the forefront of this research. Kolk and Andersson (2020) focus on how different policy changes with regard to same-sex marriage, divorce, and childbearing have affected same-sex families over two decades. Same-sex registered couples did not tend to switch to marriage after the marriage code became gender-neutral. This is not surprising given the weak normative pressures for couples to marry in Sweden. The dramatic rise in lesbian marriages that they find reflects policy changes recognizing legal parenthood, access to medically assisted reproduction (MAR), and adoption rights. What they refer to as the feminization of same-sex marriage dynamics represents a pattern in LGBTQA+ research: women are much more prone than men to both enter and dissolve same-sex marriages. Qualitative studies also have engaged with similar policy changes that have influenced same-sex couples' choices in family formation.

Ryan-Flood's pathbreaking comparative qualitative study of lesbian mothers in Sweden and Ireland (2009, p. 20) takes as its point of departure that institutional contexts shape reproductive choices available to lesbian women. In the Swedish case, she found that lesbian mother families reflected the cultural coding of biological fatherhood in law and discourses on participatory fathering. These were mirrored in their preferences for a father donor (most often a gay man) who would be involved throughout the child's upbringing. She refers to this as a three-way shared parenting model with the birth mother, non-birth mother, and father donor.

This lesbian shared parenting model has waned with the expansion of choices for family formation through MAR and recognition of lesbian parenthood in a changing sociopolitical landscape. Nevertheless, Flood's theoretical insights on

LGBTQA+ and diverse family forms have influenced research on lesbian families, specifically her emphasis on how institutional cultural context can enable and hinder same-sex couples' choice in family and parenting. This has been the focus of much of Swedish research on lesbian parents' family formation and gay male couples' pursuit of fatherhood.

Anna Malmquist and colleagues have taken the lead in this research with respect to policy changes giving lesbian couples access to IVF in public health clinics. Based upon qualitative interviews, Malmquist et al. (2016) find that many lesbians did not avail themselves of public services but rather chose private services in clinics abroad where the donor's identity can remain anonymous. However, there are consequences to this choice: the non-birth mother in the couple cannot obtain legal parenthood without a known donor and she risks losing contact with the child after divorce.

For gay couples, the pursuit of fatherhood is impeded by legal constraints and discrimination by social agencies and adoption agencies (Andreasson & Johansson, 2017). The laws on same-sex couples' right to adopt included male same-sex couples; however, this is not a route that male couples often pursue given that adoption agencies maintain that adoption-sending countries do not approve of gay couples (Malmquist & Spånberg Ekholm, 2020). Although surrogacy is illegal in Sweden, the government does not prevent gay couples from going abroad for surrogacy. To do this demands economic resources and entails uncertainties involving lawyers, clinics abroad, mothers and their families. Few couples take the risk of embarking on this path (Malmquist & Spånberg Ekholm, 2020).

Malmquist and Spånberg Ekholm (2020) offer a unique qualitative study of the experiences of 30 gay fathers who were able to navigate the difficult path of becoming parents, overcoming the lack of legal certainty and discretion of social agencies. Those who sought adoption abandoned this strategy after they were advised by the adoption centre not to apply since their application would not be prioritized. With respect to foster fathers, one couple waited for two years before their application was accepted. They have no guarantees that the child will stay with them throughout its childhood nor do they have a legal right to parental leave. Most chose a surrogate mother from abroad. Obtaining legal parenthood status for these men was arduous. For the birth father, it could take months and often much longer. For the non-birth father, it was not a possibility; the delay in recognition of legal parenthood resulted in loss of their parental leave rights because the birth mother, who nearly always is a non-citizen, could not register in the Swedish system to transfer the leave to the birth father (Malmquist & Spånberg Ekholm, 2020). Because there is no legal framework for incorporating male parenthood through surrogacy into family law on parenthood, this is decided case by case (Malmquist & Spånberg Ekholm, 2020).

Evertsson and colleagues (2020) provide a framework for rethinking the conceptual challenges that diverse families pose to welfare regime research. Previous research on welfare and gender regimes assumes a heteronormative framework of the family in which defamilization has been the standard measure of gender quality (Hobson, 2021). Arguing for a queering of welfare regimes, Evertsson et al. (2020) introduce the concept of parentalization, which encompasses two core dimensions that are enabling for same-sex couples doing family: (1) their ability to become parents (fertility treatments) (2) and the recognition of the non-birthing parent. Mapping the differences in parentalization and parental leave rights in Sweden, Norway, Denmark, Finland and the Netherlands, the authors conclude that who can become a parent and whether their ideals of parenting can be realized challenges the heteronormativity in these Nordic legal frameworks, considered family diversity friendly.

Several scholars in Sweden have engaged with the implications of the heteronormative foundation of Swedish family law (Mägi & Zimmerman, 2015; Stoll, 2008). They argue that LGBTQA+ rights for same-sex couples, although they appear gender-neutral, are exceptions grafted onto the binary division of maternity and paternity (Mägi & Zimmerman, 2015). For instance, the parenthood status of a transgender man (W to M) was registered to be the legal mother, and a transgender woman (M to W) was registered to be the father. In tax and civil registers and tax law, transgender individuals were able to choose their legal identity. The potential for discrimination and stigmatizing effects was inherent in these complex legal statuses of assigning maternity and paternity to transgender parents that differ from their legally chosen identity (Jonsson & Mägi, 2021). In 2019, in response to new European guidelines, Sweden enacted legislation that removes these distinctions so that transparents are entitled to have their gender legal identity on all documents. A transgender man who gives birth is thus registered as the father and a transgender woman who gives sperm is the mother (Jonsson & Mägi, 2021).

Adoptive and foster families

National adoptions are mostly stepchild adoptions in Sweden (Statistics Sweden, 2018). Neither economic nor social reasons push parents to give up a child for adoption in Sweden because high female employment rates and sufficient support from the Swedish welfare state in forms of cash provision and services enable parents to raise their children themselves. Since 2013, national adoptions have exceeded intercountry adoptions as the latter decreased worldwide in the early 21st century (Statistics Sweden, 2018).

Transnational adoption has long dominated the formation of adoptive families in Sweden. Indeed, Swedes were among the top adopters in the world in the late 1990s-early 2000s, well ahead of the United States and other affluent English-speaking countries. Compared to adoption ratios (that is, the number of transnational adoptions per 1,000 live births) in the range of 0.4–6.5 in these nations, the figures for Sweden reached 10.8–11.7 (Selman, 2006). Adoptees most often came from Korea, India, China and Columbia. Transnational adoption, however, is less of an option for same-sex couples, gay men in particular, who have major difficulties in adopting because they often are not considered suitable for parenthood by international adoption agencies. It thus took nearly 15 years for the first transnational adoption to a male same-sex couple to happen in Sweden (Malmquist & Spånberg Ekholm, 2020).

Relatively little is known with respect to the division of care among adoptive parents. Research has found, however, that in heterosexual couples, adoptive fathers take more days of parental leave in the first year after adoption than biological fathers do in the first year of their child's life (Duvander & Viklund, 2013). The explanation offered was the higher age of the child at adoption, as fathers are more likely to engage with older children even regarding their biological offspring. Moreover, research has shown that the parents' education matters for fathers' leave uptake, as highly educated parents share the care for their children to a greater extent. Adoptive parents are more likely to be highly educated; hence, they also share the care for their children more equally than biological parents on average. However, adoptive mothers still use a much larger part of the parental leave than adoptive fathers, mirroring the persistent gendered pattern of doing family in Sweden (Duvander & Viklund, 2013).

Foster families represent another research gap with respect to the doing of family in Sweden. If conditions for safe child development are lacking in the home environment, municipal social services can place a child in foster care, in line with the Social Services Act (SFS, 2001: 453[6]), although in cases of grave risk to the child, they are obligated to do so (SFS, 1990: 52[7]). In both cases, the placement in foster care is considered temporary and the biological parents' capabilities are reassessed every six months (Wissö et al., 2022). Foster parents are not eligible for parental benefits, except when caring for a sick foster child, or in rare cases, when they are given custody of the young foster child (Blomé & Espvall, 2021).

Families created by medically assisted reproduction (MAR)

MAR treatments in Sweden have increased from around 3,000 in 1992 to over 22,000 (Q-IVF, 2020). Although different- sex couples could avail themselves of ART for decades, lesbian couples and single women were denied access to IVF in publicly supported clinics. Both of these cases reveal the over-reach of the state in regulating family choice.

Single women seeking to become mothers through IVF are not a vulnerable group; they tend to have high education and well-paid employment (Volgsten & Schmidt, 2021). Yet, they were discriminated against as single mothers to be. They were the last group to be granted rights to assisted reproduction in Swedish clinics in 2016, 11 years after lesbian parents. As Lind (2019) has revealed in her study of debates surrounding single women's right to ART, the two-parent norm is embedded in the definition of the best interests of the child. In the policy debates before and after passage of the law allowing single women for equal access to assisted reproduction, she found that conflicting interpretations of the best interests of the child came into play: the need for child to have two parents and the child's right to have access to information on the biological father and genetic origins (Lind, 2019). Given that single mothers had been using ART services abroad, the latter prevailed. Despite the change in the law, they still face discrimination in public health care clinics in which assessments of the best interests of the child prioritize two-couple families. This is evident in data showing the high proportions of single women using private clinics (Q-IFV, 2020).

Lesbian mothers could not be treated for ART at clinics covered by national health insurance until 2005. As discussed above, most often, they choose donor fathers' – men (often gay) who played an active parental role. Having access to public health services required that they agree to have a known sperm donor and inform their children of their genetic origins and biological father's identity, codified in the Genetic Integrity Act (GIA). Lesbian couples who prefer an anonymous donor continue to use private clinics abroad and argue that the GIA denies them their rights to determine their family structure or family relationships, forcing them to adapt to the normative father/mother binary (Malmquist et al., 2016). Furthermore, they maintain that having a known father would weaken the position of the non-birth mother in the family.

BOX: Sperm donor anonymity, biological fatherhood and the best interests of the child

In 1985, Sweden became the first country to recognize the right of a child created by artificial insemination to know the identity of the sperm donor (SFS, 1984: 1140[8]). The law stated that a donor must sign an agreement that his identity could be disclosed. In practice, it only applied to heterosexual families because until 2005, only they could obtain ART in Swedish clinics. The GIA (SFS, 2006: 351[9]) codified the procedures of sperm donor identity: medical records had to be stored for 70 years, and counselling services were to be provided for children and families. The 'duty' of parents to inform children who are the offspring of sperm donors is more a moral than a legal obligation (Stoll, 2017) because it is not formally enforced. Heterosexual couples can ignore this pressure because the legal father of the child is known. However, when the child becomes aware that they are the offspring of a sperm donor, the parents must help a child over 18 to access relevant information. The GIA brings into focus the conflicting interests of various parties: the rights of parents to define the relationships within the family, the rights of children to know their biological fathers and the rights of Swedish sperm donors who donate sperm outside of Sweden to remain anonymous.

In Swedish law, the rights of children to know their genetic origins and biological father's identity supersede other rights. Although lesbian couples are not prosecuted for violating GIA rules, the non-birth parent in lesbian couples does not have legal parenthood if the donor is anonymous. Whereas donors who follow GIA rules are protected from the presumption of paternity, donors who do not register their identity are not. The GIA provided scope for the presumption of paternity, seen in one recent case in which the parties involved were living in Sweden, a single mother was inseminated by a Swedish donor's sperm from a Danish clinic allowing donor anonymity, and the presumption of paternity was applied after social services learned of the donor's identity (Stoll, 2017).

Multicultural and migrant families

Transnational migration has been an important force in changing the ethnic composition of Sweden. The foreign-born population increased from 11% to 19% between 2002 and 2018; those of non–European origin comprise the vast majority of newcomers (Statistics Sweden, 2022). The share of children born in Sweden to two foreign-born parents increased from 13% to 24% over this period, while the share with one Swedish and one foreign-born parent remained at 12–13% (Statistics Sweden, 2020a). This is in line with a vast amount of research that shows intermarriages between natives and immigrants being relatively rare (Elwert, 2020; Irastorza & Elwert, 2021), reflecting the processes of segregation in Sweden, including housing, neighbourhood, schools and the labor market (Bursell et al., 2021; Malmberg et al., 2018).

The size of families including Swedish- or foreign-born parents differs. The two-child family is predominant among those with Swedish-born parents. Individuals with two foreign-born parents are more likely either to have no children or more than three children (Statistics Sweden, 2020a). Considering families with children, Andersson et al. (2017) found that daughters with African and Asian parents are 50% more likely to have three or more children than those with Swedish-born parents.

Care for children is divided differently in the group with foreign-born parents than in the majority population. For example, after separation, only one-tenth of children of foreign-born parents have shared residential custody arrangements compared to four of ten children born to two Swedish-born parents (Statistics Sweden, 2014). Parental leave share is another example of how foreign-born parents differ from the majority population. Duvander and colleagues studied the use of parental leave in native and migrant families (Ma et al., 2020; Mussino et al., 2018). They found that low use of the leave was most common among foreign-born fathers with a foreign-born partner, especially fathers from Asian and African societies. This difference has been explained by their weak position in the labor market and lack of information on Swedish policies, although low acceptance of the policy promoting gender-equal parenting may also contribute.

However, the latter nuance is missing in the policy discourse in which immigrant fathers are singled out as a group who do not take the advantage of their parental leave rights.

Conclusion and recommendations

In this chapter, we have highlighted the distinctive features of the Swedish welfare state that have shaped the doing of family among diverse groups and for individuals at different life phases in family formation, marriage, divorce and re-partnering. Gender equality policy and discourses that formed the Swedish dual-earner, dual-carer model gave rise to participatory fatherhood, which continues after separation and divorce. Residential custody can be seen as creating a new family form and gender equality in parenting in a complex web of multiple stepfamilies. While the gender equality discourse has been enabling divorced women to be single parents without stigma, it has not taken into account the amount of their previous unpaid care before divorce. For same-sex couples, gender equality has been at the core of framing rights for access to the same rights as different-sex couples.

We have explored the formidable challenges diverse families have faced in the longstanding Swedish legal coding of the heteronormative family. Throughout we have sought to reveal the complexities, contradictions and ambivalent positions in the policy frameworks for recognizing diversities among families, tracing the barriers that had to be overcome and the challenges that remain. Although we have revealed weaknesses and discriminatory treatment toward individuals and groups, we have not downplayed the achievements in the laws and policies including enabling family formation and recognition of SGM families; the pathbreaking law on children's rights to know genetic origins and father donors; the recent parental leave legislation addressing the complexity in multiple stepfamilies with shared parenting and residential custody; new laws facilitating non-birth parent legal status in same-sex couples; and finally legal recognition of transgender parents.

The European Region of the International Lesbian, Gay, Bisexual, Trans and Intersex Association's evaluation of 28 countries in 2021 gave Sweden one of the highest scores *on recognition of family diversity (93%)* (ILGA, 2022). Legal gender recognition and bodily integrity, evaluative criteria in ILGA, have been improved with two recent policies. A legal change made in 2022 allows digital automatic registration of the non-birth parent that includes different- and same-sex parents with known donors. The Swedish law that allows trans people to be registered as parents according to their gender identity rather than their biological functions is the first to implement transgender parenthood guidelines formulated by the Parliamentary Assembly of the Council of Europe (Prop. 2017/2018: 155[10]). However, trans men are still discriminated against compared to other fathers in that the presumption of fatherhood is not applied to them. They must still prove a biological connection to the child of their partner. A true gender-neutral policy remains to be achieved.

Self-determination and choice in doing of family is an important dimension for policy assessments of diverse family forms (ILGA, 2022). We have examined the overreach of the state in steering choice in family relationships. For example, although IVF is available to lesbian couples and single women, other family constellations do not have access (SFS, 2006: 351[11]), so that male couples resort to fake marriages with female friends (Mägi & Zimmerman, 2015). The issue of self-determination in the doing of family is also relevant when considering the imposition of joint custody in divorce even when both couples agree to single custody. Finally, the legal overreach of courts was apparent in the presumption of paternity involving donor anonymity from a sperm bank in another country.

In particular, the need to address the legal and social barriers impeding male couples from parenthood through adoption, foster parenting and ART need to be addressed. The question of surrogacy has been the subject of multiple investigations, where the pros and cons of pending legislation have been discussed (Statens medicinsk-etiska råd 2013; SOU, 2016:11), and legislation made to ease establishment of legal fatherhood for the genetic father of a surrogate child born abroad (Prop 2017/2018, 155). However, the non-genetic parent in shared parenting arrangements has no clear routes to formal parenthood. In this context, Evertsson's concept of parentalization, encompassing the ability to become parents (fertility treatments) and the recognition of non-birth parents, applies and should be a measure of family-friendly diversity comparing welfare states.

Considering the projections for diverse families in the future, we have emphasized that full recognition of diverse families cannot be achieved unless the foundations in the Swedish legal framework are altered. This would imply the abandonment of the two-parent constellation, the dislodging of the primacy of biological fatherhood and the replacement of the binary of maternity and paternity with the gender-neutral category of parenthood.

Although there is a vast literature on the effects of policy on parenting and the doing of family in Sweden, recent policy changes and practices necessitate further research. The recognition of social mothers and fathers in the formal parental leave system is documented in formal registers. What effect this change has had on actual practices in the everyday organization of care responsibilities needs to be explored.

Research has shown that single mothers are not a unified category. With the dramatic increase in residential custody, scholars need to address one-parent families.

Over the last decade, Swedish studies of doing family of same-sex couples have provided rich insights into the processes shaping recognition of rights to parenthood. However, the burgeoning literature on lesbian couples in Sweden, which focuses on family formation and practices, has yet to encompass the doing of family after separation and divorce.

Transgender legal recognition has been the subject of much research; however; little research exists on the everyday experiences of individual parents and their children in schools, health and social services.

The extensive register data in Sweden allow for studies of diverse family forms, including same-sex couples. However, only two legal parents can be registered and children may have three, four or more 'parents' involved in children's upbringing. Mix method approaches using multiple data sources could shed light on the complex constellations in parenthood and parenting.

Finally, the effects of the COVID-19 pandemic need to be more thoroughly explored. Sweden approached the pandemic differently than other Western countries. Lockdowns were limited and not enforced; masks were not mandated or even recommended until a late stage. Shops and restaurants remained open and children from pre-school to age 15 continued to attend school.

The Swedish Health Authority assumed that with their pronounced trust in governmental institutions, Swedes would follow recommendations. In effect, each individual was made responsible for taking care of themselves. Those over 70 were viewed as exceptions. Regardless of their health or family situation, they were treated as 'vulnerables', and unlike the rest of society, were expected to isolate totally. In the doing of intergeneration family care, grandparents, nevertheless, used innovative digital strategies, socially distanced meetings, and in some instances, took risks in order to provide support for their children and grandchildren (Eldén et al., 2022).

At the same time, the high rates of COVID infection and deaths among immigrant families were attributed to their lack of language skills and institutional awareness. However, Aradhya et al. (2021) did not find any significant difference in COVID mortality between families with two migrant parents and those with one migrant and one Swedish parent. It was not a lack of integration but their high likelihood of exposure to infection as frontline workers in homes for elders or precarious employment in restaurants and other sectors that could explain their high mortality (Aradhya et al., 2021).

As research has shown in many countries, the pandemic is not the great leveller with respect to COVID deaths, loss of jobs and well-being. In Sweden, during the pandemic, families with two parents, with secure employment who could work from home while their kids were in school, may also have been able to organize a better work-life balance than other families.

Notes

1 We thank to Björn Halleröd and Mikael Stattin for providing access to the ULF dataset "Panel Survey of Ageing and the Elderly" (Dnr: FAS 2009:1989. PI: Björn Halleröd) to calculate estimates regarding living arrangements in Sweden in 2002/2003. We are grateful to Laura Carlsson for her insights and interpretations of Swedish law.
2 SFS 1995:584 is The Parental Leave Act, Sweden (Föräldraledighetslagen).
3 SFS 1987:813 is The Homosexual Cohabitees Act (Lag om homosexuella sambor).

4 SFS 1972:119 is The Gender Recognition Act (Lag om fastställande av könstillhörighet i vissa fall).
5 SFS 2018:162 is The Act on State Compensation in Certain Cases to Persons Who
   Have Had Their Changed Gender Verified (Lag om statlig ersättning till personer
   som har fått ändrad könstillhörighet fastställd i vissa fall).
6 SFS 2001:453 is the Social Services Act (Socialtjänstlag).
7 SFS 1990:52 is The Care of Young Persons Act (Lagen med särskilda bestämmelser
   om vård av unga).
8 SFS 1984:1140 is The Insemination Act (Lag om insemination).
9 SFS 2006:351 is The Genetic Integrity Act (Lag om genetisk integritet).
10 Prop. 2017/2018:155 is The Swedish Government proposition on new rules regarding
   assisted reproduction and parentage (Proposition om modernare regler om assisterad
   befruktning och föräldraskap).
11 SFS 2006:351 The Genetic Integrity Act (Lag om genetisk integritet).

References

Alm, S., Nelson, K., & Nieuwenhuis, R. (2020). The diminishing power of one? Welfare
state retrenchment and rising poverty of single-adult households in Sweden in 1988–
2011. *European Sociological Review, 36*(2), 198–217. https://doi.org/10.1093/esr/jcz053

Andersson, G., Noack, T., Seierstad, A., & Weedon-Fekjaer, H. (2006). The demographics of same-sex marriages in Norway and Sweden. *Demography, 43*(1), 79–98. https://
doi.org/10.1353/dem.2006.0001

Andersson, G., Persson, L., & Obućina, O. (2017). Depressed fertility among descendants of immigrants in Sweden. *Demographic Research, 36*(39), 1149–1184. https://doi.
org/10.1353/dem.2006.0001

Andreasson, J., & Johansson, T. (2017). *It All Starts Now!* Gay Men and Fatherhood in Sweden. *Journal of GLBT Family Studies, 13*(5), 478–497. https://doi.
org/10.1080/1550428X.2017.13088

Aradhya, S., Brandén, M., Drefahl, S., Obućina, O., Andersson, G., Rostila, M., Mussino, E., & Juárez, S. P. (2021). Intermarriage and COVID-19 mortality among immigrants. A population-based cohort study from Sweden. *BMJ Open, 11*, e048952.
https://doi.org/10.1136/bmjopen-2021–048952

Bergman, H., & Hobson, B. (2002). Compulsory fatherhood: The coding of fatherhood
in the Swedish welfare state. In B. Hobson (Ed.), *Making men into fathers: Men, masculinities and the social politics of fatherhood* (pp. 92–124). Cambridge University Press.

Blomé, H., & Espvall, M. (2021). Custody transfers of children and young adults in foster
care. *Genealogy, 5*(3), 80. https:// doi.org/10.3390/genealogy5030080

Bursell, M., Bygren, M., & Gähler, M. (2021). Does employer discrimination contribute
to the subordinate labor market inclusion of individuals of a foreign background?
Social Science Research, 98, 102582. https://doi.org/10.1016/j.ssresearch.2021.102582

Duvander, A-Z., & Korsell, N. (2020). Will separations lead to more or less gender-equal
parenthood? Mothers' and fathers' parental leave use in Sweden. In M. Kreyenfeld &
H. Trappe (Eds.), *Parental life courses after separation and divorce in Europe. Life course research
and social policies*, vol. 12. Springer. https://doi.org/10.1007/978-3-030-44575-1_6

Duvander, A-Z., & Viklund, I. (2013). Adoptivföräldrar delar föräldrapenning jämnare
(Adoptive parents share the parental leave more equally). *Välfärd, 3*, 28–29.

Eldén, S., Anving, T., & Alenius Wallin, L. (2022). Intergenerational care in corona
times: Practices of care in Swedish families during the pandemic. *Journal of Family
Research, 34*(1), 538–562. https://doi.org/10.20377/jfr-702

Elwert, A. (2020). Opposites attract: Assortative mating and immigrant–native intermarriage in nontemporary Sweden. *European Journal of Population*, *36*, 675–709. https://doi.org/10.1007/s10680-019-09546-9

Evertsson, M., Jaspers, E., & Moberg, Y. (2020). Parentalization of same-sex couples: Family formation and leave rights in five Northern European countries. In R. Nieuwenhuis & W. Van Lancker (Eds.), *The Palgrave handbook of family policy*. Palgrave Macmillan. https://doi.org/10.1007/978-3-030-54618-2_16

Ferrarini, T., & Duvander, A-Z. (2010). Earner-carer model at the cross-roads: Reforms and outcomes of Sweden's family policy in comparative perspective. *International Journal of Health Services*, *40*(3), 373–398. https://doi.org/10.2190/HS.40.3.a

Florin, C., & Nilsson, B. (1999). "Something in the nature of a bloodless revolution . . ." Gender equality policies in Sweden In the 1960's and 70's. In R. Torstendal (Ed.), *Social Policy and Gender System in two German states and Sweden, 1945–1989* (pp. 11–77). Uppsala University, Historica.

Fransson E., Brolin Låftman, S., Östberg, V., & Bergström, M. (2018). Wellbeing among children with single parents in Sweden: focusing on shared residence. In R. Nieuwenhuis & L. C. Maldonado (Eds.), *The triple bind of single-parent families. Resources, employment and policies to improve wellbeing* (pp. 145–167). Policy Press.

Fransson E., Hjern, A., & Bergström, M. (2018). What can we say regarding shared parenting arrangements for Swedish children? *Journal of Divorce & Remarriage*, *59*(5), 349–358. https://doi.org/10.1080/10502556.2018.1454198

Härkönen, J., & Dronkers, J. (2006). Stability and change in the educational gradient of divorce. A comparison of seventeen countries. *European Sociological Review*, *22*(5), 501–517. https://doi.org/10.1093/esr/jcl011

Hobson, B. (2004). The individualised worker, the gender participatory and the gender equity models in Sweden. *Social Policy and Society*, *3*(1), 75–83. https://doi.org/10.1017/S1474746403001519

Hobson, B. (2021). Stretching the canvas: Beyond welfare state typologies to capability and agency. In J. Aidukaite, S. E. O. Hort, & S. Kuhnle (Eds.), *Challenges to the welfare state. Family and pension policies in the Baltic and Nordic countries*. Edward Elgar. https://doi.org/10.4337/9781839106118.00022

Hobson, B., & Takahashi, M. (1997). The parent-worker model: Lone mothers in Sweden. In J. Lewis (Eds.), *Lone mothers in European welfare regimes: Shifting policy logics* (pp. 121–139). Jessica Kingsley Publishers.

ILGA (International Human Rights Situation of Lesbian, Gay, Bisexual, Trans, and Intersex Association). (2022). Annual review of the human rights situation of Lesbian, Gay, bisexual, trans, and intersex, people in Sweden covering the period of January to December 2021, Accessed January 2022.

Irastorza, N., & Elwert, A. (2021). Like parents, like children? The impact of parental endogamy and exogamy on their children's partner choices in Sweden, *Journal of Ethnic and Migration Studies*, *47*(4), 895–915. https://doi.org/10.1080/1369183X.2019.1654160

Jonsson, E., & Mägi, E. (2021). Ändrad könstillhörighet och rättsligt förädraskap (Gender Reassignment and Legal Parenthood), *Juridisk Publikation*, *2*, 273–305.

Kolk, M., & Andersson, G. (2020). Two decades of same-sex marriage in Sweden: A demographic account of developments in marriage, childbearing, and divorce. *Demography*, *57*, 147–169. https://doi.org/10.1007/s13524-019-00847-6

Korpi, W. (2000). Faces of inequality: Gender, class, and patterns of inequalities in different types of welfare states. *Social Politics: International Studies in Gender, State & Society*, *7*(2), 127–191. https://doi.org/10.1093/sp/7.2.127

Lind, J. (2019). The rights of intended children. The best interests of the child argument in assisted reproduction policy, *Childhood*, *26*(3), 352–368. https://doi.org/10.1177/0907568219853331

Ma, L., Andersson, G., Duvander, A-Z., & Evertsson, M. (2020). Fathers' uptake of parental leave: Forerunners and laggards in Sweden, 1993–2010. *Journal of Social Policy*, *49*(2), 361–381. https://doi.org/10.1017/S0047279419000230

Mägi, E., & Zimmerman, L-L. (2015). Stjärnfamiljejuridik: svensk familjelagstiftning ur ett normkritiskt perspektiv. (Star family law: Swedish family law from a norm-critical perspective) Gleerups.

Malmberg, B., Andersson, E.K., Nielsen, M.M., & Haandrikman, K. (2018). Residential segregation of European and non-European migrants in Sweden: 1990–2012. *European Journal of Population*, *34*, 169–193. https://doi.org/10.1007/s10680-018-9478-0

Malmquist, A. (2015). Pride and prejudice: Lesbian families in contemporary Sweden. PhD. thesis, Linköping University, Department of Behavioural Sciences and Learning, Psychology. Linköping University, Faculty of Arts and Sciences.

Malmquist, A., Polski, A., & Zetterqvist Nelson, K. (2016). No one of importance: Lesbian mothers' constructions of permanently anonymous sperm donors. In A. Sparrman, A. Westerling, J. Lind, & K. Dannesboe (Eds.), *Doing good parenthood. Palgrave Macmillan studies in family and intimate life*. Palgrave Macmillan. https://doi.org/10.1007/978-3-319-46774-0_3

Malmquist, A., & Spånberg Ekholm, A. (2020). Swedish Gay men's pursuit of fatherhood: Legal obstacles and strategies for coping with them. *Lambda Nordica*, *24*(2–3), 53–80. https://doi.org/10.34041/ln.v24.580

Mussino, E., Duvander, A.-Z., & Ma, L. (2018). Does time count? Immigrant fathers' use of parental leave for a first child in Sweden. *Population*, *73*, 363–382. Retrieved from https://www.cairn-int.info/journal--2018-2-page-363.htm

Nieuwenhuis, R. (2021). Directions of thought for single parents in the EU. *Community, Work & Family*, *24*(5), 559–566. https://doi.org/10.1080/13668803.2020.1745756

Ohlsson-Wijk, S., Turunen, J., & Andersson, G. (2020). Family forerunners? An overview of family demographic change in Sweden. In D. Farris & A. Bourque (Eds.), *International handbook on the demography of marriage and the family. International handbooks of population*, vol. 7. Springer. https://doi.org/10.1007/978-3-030-35079-6_5

Oláh, L. Sz., & Bernhardt, E.M. (2008). Sweden: Combining childbearing and gender equality. *Demographic Research*, *19*(28), 1105–1144. https://dx.doi.org/10.4054/DemRes.2008.19.28

Oláh, L. Sz., Karlsson, L., & Sandström, G. (2021). Living-apart-together (LAT) in contemporary Sweden: (How) Does it relate to vulnerability? *Journal of Family Issues*, online first. Retrieved from https://journals.sagepub.com/doi/abs/10.1177%2F0192513X211041988

Ono, H., & Yeilding, R. (2009). Marriage, cohabitation and childcare: The US and Sweden. *Social Indicators Research*, *93*, 137–140. https://doi.org/10.1007/s11205-008-9417-2

Q-IVF. (2020). Fertility treatments in Sweden. National Report for 2020: Refers to treatments in 2018. Results – trends – comparisons. Retrieved from https://www.medscinet.com/qivf/uploads/hemsida/Fertility%20treatments%20in%20Sweden.%20National%20report%202020.pdf

Ryan-Flood, R. (2009). *Lesbian motherhood: Gender, families and sexual citizenship*. Palgrave Macmillan.

Selman, P. (2006). Trends in intercountry adoption: Analysis of data from 20 receiving countries, 1998–2004. *Journal of Population Research*, *23*(2), 183–204. https://doi.org/10.1007/BF03031815

SOU 1972:41. Familj och äktenskap. Betänkande avgivet av Familjelagssakkunniga. Retrieved from https://weburn.kb.se/metadata/390/SOU_621390.htm

SOU 2016:11. Olika vägar till föräldraskap. Retrieved from https://www.regeringen.se/rattsliga-dokument/statens-offentliga-utredningar/2016/02/sou-201611/

Statens medicinsk-etiska råd. (2013). Assisterad befruktning – etiska aspekter. Smer rapport 2013:1. (The Swedish National Council on Medical Ethics: Assisted reproduction – ethical aspects). Retrieved from https://smer.se/en/2013/02/28/assisted-reproduction-ethical-aspects/

Statistics Sweden. (2014). Olika familjer lever på olika sätt – om barns boende och försörjning efter en separation. Demografiska rapporter 2014:1 (Demographic reports 2014:1 Different families live in different ways – a survey on residence and support of children after a separation). Statistics Sweden.

Statistics Sweden. (2018). Två av tre adoptioner 2017 var styvbarnsadoptioner. (Two of three adoptions in 2017 were stepchild-adoptions). Retrieved March 1, 2022 from https://www.scb.se/hitta-statistik/artiklar/2018/allt-fler-adopterar-styvbarn/

Statistics Sweden. (2020a). *Migration, barnafödande och dödlighet — Födda 1970–2018 efter föräldrarnas födelseland. Demografiska rapporter 2020:2* (Migration, childbearing, and mortality among persons born 1970–2018 based on parents' country of birth. Demographic reports 2020:2). Statistics Sweden.

Statistics Sweden. (2020b). Kort analys: Fler biologiska mammor än pappor. (Short note: More biological mothers than fathers). Retrieved March 5, 2022 from https://www.scb.se/hitta-statistik/artiklar/2020/fler-biologiska-mammor-an-pappor/

Statistics Sweden. (2021a). Sveriges framtida befolkning 2021–2070. Demografiska rapporter 2021:1 (The future population of Sweden 2021–2070. Demographic reports 2021:1). Statistics Sweden.

Statistics Sweden. (2021b). Statistiknyhet: 66 000 barn var med om en separation år 2020 (Statistics news: 66,000 children experienced parental break-up in 2020). Retrieved March 5, 2022 from https://www.scb.se/hitta-statistik/statistik-efter-amne/levnadsforhallanden/levnadsforhallanden/barn-och-familjestatistik/pong/statistiknyhet/barn--och-familjestatistik-2020/

Statistics Sweden. (2021c). Kort analys: 215 000 barn har en bonusförälder (Short note: 215,000 children have a stepparent). Retrieved March 4, 2022 from https://www.scb.se/hitta-statistik/artiklar/2021/215-000-barn-har-en-bonusforalder/

Statistics Sweden. (2022). Statistical database – Number of persons with foreign or Swedish background (detailed division), by region, age and sex. Year 2002–2020. Retrieved February 28, 2022 from https://www.statistikdatabasen.scb.se/pxweb/en/ssd/START__BE__BE0101__BE0101Q/UtlSvBakgFin/

Stoll, J. (2008). Swedish donor offspring and their legal right to information Ph.D. Dissertation, Department of Law, Uppsala University.

Stoll, J. (2017). Establishing paternity by court judgment following sperm donation: Some reflections on two judgments rendered by the Svea Court of Appeal. In M. Brattström & M. Jänterä-Jareborg, (red.) För barns bästa: vänbok till Anna Singer, Iustus förlag, pp. 317–341.

Takács, J., Szalma, I., & Bartus, T. (2016). Social attitudes toward adoption by same-sex couples in Europe. *Archives of Sexual Behavior, 45*, 1787–1798. https://doi.org/10.1007/s10508-016-0691-9

Thomson, E., & Turunen, J. (2021). Alternating homes – A new family form – The family sociology perspective. In L. Bernardi & D. Mortelmans (Eds.), *Shared physical custody. European studies of population*, vol. 25. Springer. https://doi.org/10.1007/978-3-030-68479-2_2

Turunen, J. (2017). Shared physical custody and children's experience of stress. *Journal of Divorce & Remarriage, 58*(5), 371–392. https://doi.org/10.1080/10502556.2017.132 5648

Volgsten, H., & Schmidt, L. (2021). Motherhood through medically assisted reproduction – Characteristics and motivations of Swedish single mothers by choice. *Human Fertility, 24*(3), 219–225. https://doi.org/10.1080/14647273.2019.1606457

Wissö, T., Melke, A., & Josephson, I. (2022). Social workers' constructions of parents to children in foster care. *Qualitative Social Work, 21*(4), 748–764. https://doi.org/10.1177/14733250211019455

Zadeh, S. (2016). Disclosure of donor conception in the era of non-anonymity: Safeguarding and promoting the interests of donor-conceived individuals? https://doi.org/10.17863/CAM.594

9

DIVERSITY IN UK FAMILIES

Liberalization of public attitudes and policies

Ursula Henz

The cultural and policy context of doing family

During the second half of the 20th century, the once dominant male bread-winner family has given way to a diverse set of family forms in the UK. In the majority of couples with children, both parents are now in paid work (Roantree & Vira, 2018). In the 1970s, the proportion of married couple families with children started to decrease, whereas divorce and re-partnering rates increased as well as one-parent families and non-marital cohabitation. At the end of the 20th century, Britain had one of the highest divorce rates in Europe, and the highest rate of one-parent families in Western Europe (Allan et al., 2001). Britain also featured a high rate of births outside marriage and high rates of unmarried teenage motherhood (Allan et al., 2001). During the last 20 years, some of these trends continued—like the declining rate of marriage and increasing numbers of non-marital cohabiting relationships—whereas others halted or reversed, most notably the proportion of one-parent families and the rate of divorce. At the same time, new family types have become recognized. These changes went hand-in-hand with changes in policies and public attitudes.

The UK has a liberal welfare regime according to Esping-Andersen's (1990) typology. The state has traditionally limited its interference in family life to a minimum. After the Second World War, the Beveridge Report led to the intro-duction of limited social security provisions for all families, assuming a male breadwinner model (Wasoff & Dey, 2000). The Conservative governments of the 1980s and 1990s upheld traditional family values. The "New Right" ideol-ogy pursued more reliance on private and family provision, with the state being considered a safety net if the family and market provision failed. Family policies became means tested and more targeted at "problem families" (Wasoff & Dey, 2000). The Labour governments from 1997 to 2010 were more tolerant of family

DOI: 10.4324/9781003193500-9

diversity. They emphasized parenthood, rather than partnership, which led to enhanced rights and responsibilities for fathers. In addition, a strong ethics of paid work bore policies that helped families to reconcile work and family life, including parental leave, subsidized formal childcare, and parents' right to flexible employment. The years after 2010 were marked by "austerity," including cuts to many welfare benefits and services, and increased work requirements for receiving benefits.

During the last few decades, attitudes in the British population toward sexuality, gender, and the standard family have liberalized remarkably. The earlier decline in the support for traditional gender roles continued in the new millennium. Whereas 17% of the population agreed in 2002 that it is a man's job to earn money and a woman's job to look after the home and family, only 8% did so in 2017 (Phillips et al., 2018). Between 2002 and 2012, a genuine moral shift occurred in the attitudes toward mothers' work, followed by relative stability in the following years (Phillips et al., 2018). It is now generally accepted that paid work is the norm for mothers, unless they have young children. Even in this situation, only one in five adults supported the male breadwinner model in 2018 (Curtice et al., 2019).

British people have also become more accepting of sex outside marriage. Three-quarters of respondents regard premarital sex "not wrong at all" in 2018 compared to 63% in 2000 (Curtice et al., 2019). Acceptance of cohabitation has also grown further. A comparison of data from 2006/2007 to 2018/2019 shows a drop in disapproval of non-marital cohabitation—from 14% to 8%—and of having children in non-marital unions—from 21% to 12% (Curtice et al., 2020). The same surveys also report a decline in disapproval of divorce when children are younger than 12 years from 28% to 16% (Curtice et al., 2020).

Another striking change in public attitudes regards the further rise in the approval of same-sex relationships. The percentage of respondents who thought that same-sex relationships were "not wrong at all" rose from 34% in 2000 to 66% in 2018 (Curtice et al., 2019).

Finally, there is a strong indication that racial prejudice has decreased in the family context. The proportion of the population that minded if a close relative were to marry a person of Black or West Indian/Asian background declined from 35% (Black) and 32% (Asian) in 1996 to 22% (Black) and 21% (Asian) in 2013 (Kelley et al., 2017). Similarly, in a 2020 survey, 89% of British adults agreed or strongly agreed that they were "happy for [their] child to marry someone from another ethnic group," and up from 75% in 2008 (Ipsos Mori, 2020).

These changes in public attitudes toward diversification of family life are also reflected in several legal reforms. The 1967 Divorce Reform Act made a no-fault divorce possible on the grounds of irreconcilable differences. It indicated a new understanding of marriage and divorce as "issues of a couple's own making and unmaking, rather than subject to the 'higher' moral code of the church and state" (Williams, 2004, p. 26). This view also bore on the Children Act of 1989, which separated marriage from parenting by stipulating mothers' and fathers' responsibilities for their children after the breakdown of their marriage.

Welfare policies continued to move away from the "male breadwinner family" to an "adult worker" model, where both men and women are active in the labor market (Lewis, 2001). Since the late 1990s, successive UK governments have implemented welfare policies that aim to move benefit recipients into paid work and provide financial support for working parents on low incomes. Under more recent governments, parents' benefits became increasingly conditional on their employment.

The Equality Acts of 2007 and 2010 protect people against discrimination based on sexual orientation. They led to further legal changes, for example, the extension of legal parentage following assisted conception to unmarried couples in 2008. Gay and lesbian couples could be recognized first through civil partnerships in 2004 and then through marriage in 2014. In contrast to these liberalization trends, more restrictive immigration policies and the UK's withdrawal from the European Union have raised barriers to family life in migrant and transnational families.

The liberalization of many public attitudes and laws regarding family behavior occurred together with an increasing cultural diversity of British society. Britain has become a more secular society. Between 2000 and 2018, the proportion of British people identifying as Christians declined from 55% to 38%; the proportion of non-Christians increased from 5% to 9%; and the proportion of people who do not regard themselves as belonging to any religion increased from 40% to 52% (Curtice et al., 2019). Britain's cultural diversity is partly due to successive waves of migration—from the former colonies in the period after the Second World War and since 2004 increasingly from the EU, when eight Central and Eastern European countries joined the EU (Matheson, 2009). The proportion of the UK population born abroad increased from 7.3% in 1991 to 8.8% in 2001 and further to 14.2% in 2018 (Migration Watch, 2020).

The cultural diversity of the UK is enhanced through its four constituent nations of England, Scotland, Wales, and Northern Ireland. Because of the devolved government, some official figures about family and population statistics are not available for the whole of the UK. In this situation, the chapter will often draw on publications about England and Wales (E&W), which together comprise 89% of the population of the UK, or report my own analyses from the UK Labour Force Surveys (LFS)(ONS, 2022b). Laws and policies can also differ among the four nations, and the chapter will flag some major differences.

Empirical patterns of various family forms

Union formation and dissolution

Like in many other European countries, in UK, marriage rates have fallen since their peak in the early 1970s when 8.5 marriages were contracted per 1,000 members of the population. In 2000, the marriage rate was down to 5.2, and in 2019, it reached 3.7 (see Table 9.1). Only 67% of women above age 15 had ever been married in 2020 and 62% of men. This long-term decline does not indicate a retreat from partnerships in principle, but rather reflects the delayed entry into marriage and the rise in non-marital cohabitation (Beaujouan & Bhrolchain, 2011). From 2000 to 2019, the mean age at first marriage has increased by nearly four years for women from 28.2 to 32.1 years and for men from 30.5 to 33.9 years. The figures for 2019 include same-sex marriages, which are entered, on average, at higher ages than different-sex marriages (ONS, 2017a). Premarital cohabitation has become a normative life event as about four in five people who married at 50 years or younger report having lived together with their partner prior to marriage (Beaujouan & Bhrolchain, 2011).

The 1967 Divorce Reform Act and the changing social climate facilitated a strong rise in divorce rates in the subsequent years. In 1985, the UK had the highest divorce rate of Western European countries, and in 2000, it was second

TABLE 9.1 Selected demographic indicators for UK 2000 and latest available data

	2000	*Latest available data*	
Crude marriage rate	5.2	2019	3.7
Mean age at first marriage			
Women	28.2	2019	32.1
Men	30.5	2019	33.9
Crude divorce rate	2.6	2020	1.7
Remarriage rate[a]			
Women	17.1	2019	10.6
Men	17.4	2019	20.9
% of adults > 15 never married	28.3	2020	35.3
Women	25.3	2020	32.9
Men	31.5	2020	37.7
Total fertility rate	1.64	2020	1.56
Mean age at first birth[a]			
Women	26.5	2020	29.1
% non-marital births	39.5	2017	48.2
% of women aged 40–44 who have born no children[a]	18.5	2020	17.2
Cohorts	**1950**		**1970**
Completed fertility/cohort[a]	2.07		1.91
% of women aged 40–44 who have born no children for cohorts (only)[a]	14		17

a   The statistic refers to England and Wales.
Sources: OECD (2022); ONS Dataset "Marriages in England and Wales; ONS 2022b, Labour Force Survey, Individual files, own calculations; ONS (2021); ONS Dataset 'Births by parents' characteristics"; ONS Dataset "Fertility rates by parity" 1934 to 2020, England and Wales; ONS Dataset "Childbearing for women born in different years."

only to Belgium (Lappegård, 2014). However, in the mid-1990, the trend started to reverse (ONS, 2019a). The crude divorce rate fell between 2000 and 2020 from 2.6 to 1.7. In addition, the remarriage rate dropped from 37.4 to 20.9 for men and from 17.1 to 10.6 for women between 2000 and 2019.

Fertility patterns

The UK total fertility rate (TFR) had been declining at the end of the past century (Berrington et al., 2021) and was 1.64 in 2000. In the following years, it increased to 1.91 in 2008, stayed at about this level until 2012, and then decreased to 1.56 in 2020.[1] Analyses for England and Wales have suggested that the main factors that led to rising levels of fertility were a catching up at higher ages by women who had previously postponed childbirth, and an increase in the number of births by foreign-born women (Tromans et al., 2009). The decline of fertility rates after 2012 has been related to real and perceived higher uncertainty about employment and lower career opportunities as well as cuts to benefits (ONS, 2015).

The rise and fall of the TFR in the past two decades happened despite a very persistent increase of the mean age at first birth from 26.5 to 29.1. The proportion of women aged 40 to 44 years who had born no children increased in all years since the early 1990s to reach a plateau at about 20% in 2002. Since 2010, the proportion has declined. Women born in 1950 had, on average, 2.07 children, whereas women born 20 years later had on average 1.91 children. The proportion of women who have born no children was 14% for women born in 1950, increased to 20% for women born in 1961 to 1966, and declined to 17% for women born in 1970.

The proportion of children born out of wedlock had started to rise rapidly in the 1980s. By 1990, it had reached 27.9%, 39.5% in 2000, and 46.9% in 2010. During the last ten years, the increase slowed down markedly, attaining 48.2% in 2017. About two-thirds of children born outside marriage or civil partnership were born to cohabiting parents (ONS, 2017b).

Changes in household composition and living arrangements

Table 9.2 presents information about the living arrangements of the adult population for the two selected time points and different age groups. Whereas 55.5% of adults lived with a spouse in 2000, fewer than half of all UK adults did so in 2019/2020. The older the individual, the more likely they were to live with a spouse. In each age group, the proportions are lower in 2019/2020 than in 2000, which may be because more people are postponing or forgoing marriage.

Most of the drop in living with a spouse is made up by an increase in the proportion of individuals living with a partner, which was particularly strong for individuals aged 25–34. Among the 25-to-34-year-olds in 2019/2020, about equal numbers lived with a spouse as with a partner. Individuals younger than

TABLE 9.2 Population in living arrangements in UK 2000 and latest available data

	2000			*2019/20*		
% of adults are living	*Total*	*Age 18–24*	*Age 25–34*	*Total*	*Age 18–24*	*Age 25–34*
With spouse	55.5	5.4	43	49.3	2.0	32.4
With partner	9.1	15.2	20.8	14.2	17.7	31.1
Child of householder	9.5	56	12.2	10.8	62.5	17
Alone	15.6	4.8	10.6	15.8	3.5	7.3
With other relatives[a]	3.1	18.1	2.7	4	23.7	5.2
With non-relatives	2.6	12.6	4.3	3	13.1	6.3

a "Other relatives" comprise any relatives except spouses, partners and own children unless the child is married, divorced, separated or has a child.
Source: Labour Force Survey (LFS) Household files, own calculations. For the second time point, the pre-pandemic surveys from the last three quarters of 2019 and the first quarter of 2020 were analyzed.

35 years increasingly lived with their parents and relatively fewer lived alone in 2019/2020 compared to 2000. In the UK, this trend reflects economic uncertainty in young adulthood and pressure on the housing market, which makes it unaffordable for many young people to buy their own home (Berrington et al., 2017). In addition, young people returned to the parental home in connection with unemployment or partnership breakdown (Stone et al., 2014).

Table 9.3 presents the distribution of different household types in the UK in the years 2000 and 2019/2020, giving the distribution in the total population and for four ethnic groups. According to the Office for National Statistics (ONS), a household is

> one person living alone, or a group of people living at the same address who share cooking facilities and share a living room, sitting room or dining area. A household can consist of a single family, more than one family or no families in the case of a group of unrelated people
>
> *(ONS, 2022c, p. 2)*

The ONS defines a family as "a married, civil partnered or cohabiting couple with or without children, or a lone parent with at least one child, who lives at the same address" (ONS, 2022c, p. 2). Children can be "dependent"—under the age of 16 years, or 16 to 18 years and in full-time education—or "non-dependent"—aged 19 years or older or 16 to 18 years and not in full-time education (ONS, 2022c). Children who are married, partnered, or divorced, or have a child are excluded from both categories.

In Table 9.3, the first eight rows of data refer to single-family households. Looking at the distribution for the UK overall, at both points in time, the most common type of household was formed by different-sex married couples. The proportion of these households dropped by nearly 6 percentage points between

TABLE 9.3 Households in UK 2000 and latest available data

Indicator	2000					2019/20				
% of households[b] consist of	Total[a]	White	Black/British Black	Indian	Pakistani/Bangladeshi	Total	White	Black/British Black	Indian	Pakistani/Bangladeshi
Different-sex spouses	48.6	49	28	59	60	42.9	42	29	62	61
with dep. kids[c]	19.2	19	17	36	50	16.8	15	19	39	49
w/out dep. Kids	29.4	30	11	23	10	26.1	27	10	23	12
Different-sex partners	7.7	8	8	2	1	11.2	12	7	3	2
with dep. Kids	3	3	4	1	1	4.4	5	4	1	1
w/out dep. Kids	4.7	5	4	1	1	6.8	7	3	2	1
Mother only with dep. kids	5.8	5	21	4	9	5.1	5	20	4	7
Father only with dep. kids	0.6					0.6				
Same-sex couple[d]	0.2					0.8				
One person living alone	28.6	29	27	14	7	29.5	30	27	15	9
Other	8.5	8	16	21	22	9.9	9	17	15	20

a The results for "Mixed ethnic group" and "Other ethnic group" are not shown.
b Households are classified according to the ethnic group of the household reference person.
c Dependent children are children under the age of 18.
d This indicator counts all households with a same-sex couple, irrespective of the household composition.
Data source: Labour Force Survey (LFS) Household files, own calculations. For the second time point, the pre-pandemic surveys from the last three quarters of 2019 and the first quarter of 2020 were analyzed.

2020 and 2019/2020, affecting couples with dependent children and those without. More than half of the decline was balanced by an increase in different-sex partnerships with and without dependent children.

After 2001, the proportion of one-parent households increased in the UK until 2012 and decreased thereafter (ONS, 2022a). A possible explanation for the decline is the stabilization of marriages (Berrington, 2014). The proportion of one-parent households in 2019/2020 was very similar to their proportion in 2000, but there has been a shift toward one-parent households with only non-dependent children. The proportion of mother-only households with dependent children has declined from 5.8% in 2000 to 5.1% in 2019/2020. At the same time, the proportion of mother-only households with only non-dependent children has increased from 2.2% to 2.8%. Father-only households contributed about 1.3% of all households at both points in time, consisting of 0.6% of father-only households with dependent children and 0.7% of father-only households with only non-dependent children at both points in time. It is important to note that some one-parent families live with other family members and might count toward "Other" households.

Table 9.3 shows an increase in the proportion of same-sex couple households from 0.2% in 2000 to 0.8% in 2019/2020. In 2019/2020, but not in 2000, they include civil partnerships and married same-sex couples. After a strong increase in the proportion of one-person households in Britain from 12% in 1961 to 29% in 2001 (Macrory, 2012), the proportion of one-person households fluctuated between 28.5% and 29.5% in the UK in the first two decades of the new millennium (ONS, 2022a).

In 2019/2020, the proportion of "Other" households was somewhat higher than that in 2000. Other households comprise multi-generation family households, which account for about 1% of households (LFS, own calculations). Other households include households where a grandparent is the household reference person. In the UK, there were about 250,000 such grandparent households in 2017, constituting 3.2% of all households with dependent children (ONS, 2019b). About 0.4% of all households with dependent children consisted of a grandparent as household reference person and their grandchild(ren) only.

Table 9.3 also reports the distribution of the different types of households separately for four ethnic groups. Households are classified according to the ethnic group of the household reference person, using a six-category classification of ethnicity. The samples are too small to present separate statistics for the Black Caribbean and Black African ethnic groups, which is why they are combined into the category "Black or Black British." Two further categories of ethnicity ("Mixed ethnic group," "Other ethnic group") are not shown. Because of changes to the ethnicity questions in the UK LFS, the ethnicity categories are not fully comparable over time (Smith, 2002).

Past research has highlighted the high marriage rates and low divorce rates of Indians, Pakistanis, and Bangladeshis (Berrington, 1994; Platt, 2009). Correspondingly, the proportion of different-sex married couple households is highest among these households (about 60%) and lowest in Black or Black British households (about 28%).

In 2000, the proportion of different-sex partner households was about the same in White households as in Black or Black British households, but it was less common in South Asian households. Only in the White population, the proportion of these households has markedly increased in 2019/2020 compared to 2000. Compared to White and South-Asian ethnic groups, it was far less common to live with a spouse or partner among people of a Black or Black-British origin, which confirms earlier findings (Berrington, 1994; Platt, 2009).

Mother-only households with dependent children were far more common in Black or Black-British households than in the other groups. Interestingly, the prevalence of mother-only households was similar in Indian and White populations. With 9% in 2000 and 7% in 2019/2020, the proportion of only mothers with dependent children was higher in Pakistani/Bangladeshi households than in White households. This corresponds to earlier observations that the Muslim population had higher than average proportions of lone parenthood (The Muslim Council of Britain, 2015). The raised levels of marital instability in British-Pakistani families have been related to transnational spouse selection and the tradition of arranged marriages (Qureshi et al., 2014).

It is also noteworthy that Other households are more common in ethnic minority groups than among Whites, especially among families from a South-Asian origin, where multi-generation households are more prevalent. The drop from 21% to 15% of Other households with Indian heritage from 2000 to 2019/2020 might indicate a trend away from multi-generational households in this group, in contrast to Pakistani or Bangladeshi groups. There are also large differences among ethnic groups in the likelihood of living alone. It is most common among the Black or Black British and Whites, where 27 to 30% of households were one-person households, compared to only about 15% among Indians and 7 to 9% among Pakistanis/Bangladeshis.

Current empirical research on the various family forms

Reconstituted families (stepfamilies)

About 13% of couple families with dependent children in England and Wales were stepfamilies in 2001, dropping to 11% in 2011 (ONS, 2014a). The decline might be related to women's rising age at first birth (ONS, 2014a). It is also possible that divorced or separated parents increasingly prefer living apart together (LAT) relationships—intimate relationships where the partners live at separate addresses. LAT relationships allow individuals to experience couple intimacy and at the same time maintain personal autonomy and pre-existing commitments, for example, to children from their previous relationship (Duncan & Phillips, 2011). Especially women favor a LAT relationship after the experience of a divorce

(Lampard & Peggs, 2007). The majority of stepfamilies include children from the woman's previous relationship. Only 4% of stepfamilies included children from both partners' previous relationships (ONS, 2014a).

Stepparents have no legal rights regarding their stepchildren. The 1989 Children Act introduced the option of a parental responsibility agreement or a parental responsibility order in England and Wales, which give the stepparent the right to make decisions about the care and upbringing of the child.[2] As a result, a stepchild can have legal relationships with three adults (or even more) at one time. The parental responsibility agreement/order has been designed as an easier option than adoption. Adoptions have further consequences, like a removal of parental responsibility from the birth parent who is not living with the child and an end of legal relationships to the child's other parent's birth family, including rights of inheritance.

The 1989 Children Act has been centrally important for the situation of post-divorce families in Britain. The act separates the marital relationship from the parent–child relationship; a divorce no longer means the end of a parent's responsibility as mother or father (Williams, 2004). As a consequence, divorce also "no longer means emotional or financial freedom from a former spouse" (Smart, 2004, p. 403). Smart and Neale's (1999) analysis of post-divorce parenting found that many parents were not ready to take on their full parenting (father) and economic (mother) roles, raising issues of fairness of the new legal framework. For example, by insisting on joint custody, fathers devalued mothers' earlier "sacrifice" of giving up their career for the sake of the children and left the mother struggling economically. Other fathers demanded joint custody but did not rise to the demands associated with the shared responsibility for the child.

Analyses of stepfamily relationships often draw on the concept of negotiation (Allan et al., 2011). Two interview-based UK studies demonstrate some limitations to this approach. Ribbens McCarthy and colleagues (2003) noted that parents and stepparents agreed that children took priority; romantic love was subordinated to the needs of the children. Allan, Crow, and Hawker (2011) observed instances of "token negotiations," where more powerful people exercised their advantage. Some family tensions could not be solved by negotiations but by avoiding conflict, for example by keeping parts of the stepfamily networks apart.

The same research also highlights class-based understandings of parenting within and across households (Ribbens McCarthy et al., 2003). Middle-class families emphasized the biological parenthood across households, while working-class interviewees were more concerned with parenting as a practice in the (step)family. Working-class fathers were more likely than middle-class fathers to cut back contact with their child when the mother of their children re-partnered. These differences are important because recent legal and policy reform favors the middle-class emphasis on biological ties.

One-parent and cohabiting families

Compared to other European countries, except Ireland, lone mothers are, on average, rather young in the UK because of a high proportion of young unpartnered mothers (Letablier & Wall, 2018). In the 1970s, the teenage birth rate in the UK was similar to that in other Western European countries (SEU, 1999). However, whereas the rates fell in the other countries, they remained high in the UK. In 1995, the UK recorded 28 births per 1,000 women aged 15–19 years, falling to 12 births in 2019 (OECD, 2022). The decline has been partly attributed to the comprehensive "Teenage Pregnancy Strategy for England" launched in 1999, which combined measures for a better prevention of teenage pregnancy with more support for teenage mothers to enter education, training, and employment. Despite the decrease, adolescent fertility rates in the UK remain among the highest in developed countries (OECD, 2022). Research shows the many challenges experienced by lone mothers when striving to sustain work and care (Millar, 2019) (see Box).

Non-marital cohabitation presents another alternative to married-couple families. The increase in non-marital cohabitation should not belie the continuing legal differences between cohabitation and marriage (Perelli-Harris & Gassen, 2012). These differences are relatively small in England when it comes to taxation, even after the introduction of a new tax allowance for married couples in 2015 to privilege marriage. The differences are also small in access to health care and parenting rights. However, major legal differences between marriage and cohabitation persist in inheritance and the division of property after separation or divorce. In addition, marriage and civil partnership, but not non-marital cohabitation, with a UK citizen gives immigrants privileged access to citizenship (Perelli-Harris & Gassen, 2012).

It is an open question whether growing up in married-couple families is advantageous for children compared to cohabiting-couple families. Children whose parents were married, instead of cohabiting, at birth show some advantages in cognitive and emotional development and physical health (Crawford et al., 2012; Jarvis et al., 2021; Panico et al., 2019). Some studies find that these advantages reflect differential selection rather than causal effects of marriage (Crawford et al., 2012; Panico et al., 2019) but in other studies, part of the differences persists even when controlling for a large range of factors (Jarvis et al. 2021).

BOX: One-parent families

Before 1997, the UK had a maternalist policy, supporting mothers as full-time carers (Millar, 2019). One-parent families were entitled to state benefits without condition if they had a child up to age 16 (Millar, 2019). The high poverty rates of one-parent families in the mid-1990s in the UK (Nieuwenhuis & Maldonado, 2018) made these families a target for government intervention.

From 1998 onward, New Labour's "New Deal for Lone Parents" offered lone parents support to enter paid work by providing advice, information, and training opportunities. At the same time, New Labour launched the National Childcare Strategy that increased affordable childcare and early education places for three and four-year-olds, initially in marginalized communities. Although these policy changes were welcomed by many lone mothers, they often failed to provide financial security (Millar, 2010).

Since 2009, lone parents have been required to be available for work from when their youngest child reaches the age of 10 (Klett-Davies, 2016). In the following years, the work requirements for lone parents were extended and benefits were cut (Millar, 2019). In parallel to these policy changes, lone mothers' employment rate has increased from 42% in 1993 to 70% in 2017 (Roantree & Vira, 2018). However, many fail to earn enough income to stay above the poverty line (Klett-Davies, 2016; Millar, 2010; Zagel et al., 2021).

To understand family life under conditions of poverty, Daly and Kelly (2015) interviewed 51 low-income families in Northern Ireland, including 21 lone-parent families. These families expended a lot of energy on money and its management, which Daly and Kelly termed "poverty work." Budgeting decisions did not only follow a rational economy that prioritized essential items for the family as a whole but also a moral economy that prioritized expenditure for children over those for adults and comprised selfless giving of parents to children. Managing in circumstances of poverty and low income is "not just about keeping a household functioning" but also about "maintaining a sense of family integrity and loyalty to family" (Daly & Kelly, 2015, p. 77).

Sex gender minority families (SGM)

Although homosexual acts were legalized in England and Wales in 1967[3] and the age of consent reduced stepwise to 18 years in 1994 and 16 years in 2001, non-heterosexuals arguably did not enjoy full citizenship at the end of the 20th century in the UK because legislation and policies were too often based on the traditional family model (Donovan et al., 1999). However, gay and lesbian campaigning for partnership recognition and parenting rights and the vulnerability of the LGBTQA+ community apparent in the HIV/AIDS epidemic prepared the ground for major legal changes. In 2005, the Civil Partnership Act came into effect in the UK, which allowed same-sex couples aged 16 and older to obtain a legal recognition of their relationship. Civil partners rights include taxes and benefits, financial orders available at the dissolution of a civil partnership, and the right to apply for parental responsibility for their civil partner's child. After a peak of the number of civil partnership formations at 14,943 in 2006, the numbers stabilized around 6,000 civil-partnership formations in the following years

(ONS, 2020). From 2013 onward, the number of civil partnership formations in England and Wales declined because the Marriage (Same Sex Couples) Act 2013 came into effect in 2014.[4] About 68,000 same-sex marriages have been recorded by 2018 (ONS, 2019c). In 2019, there were 212,000 same-sex families in the UK (ONS, 2019d), of which 57,000 were married-couple families (including 10,000 with dependent children), 46,000 civil partnerships (of which 5,000 had dependent children), and 109,000 same-sex cohabiting families (including 3,000 with dependent children) (ONS, 2022a).

The Adoption and Children Act from 2002, which came into force in England in 2005, allowed same-sex couples to jointly adopt children and to adopt the child of their partner.[5] The British Social Attitudes Survey shows, however, that only a minority of British people approve of same-sex couples adopting children (Ross et al., 2011). Nevertheless, same-sex couples have embraced the opportunity to adopt. As many as one in six adoptions of children looked after by a local authority in England were by same-sex couples (Department for Education, 2021a). Other milestones toward the equal treatment of SGM families were the Equality Acts from 2007 and 2010, which include sexual orientation as a protected category and prohibit direct and indirect discrimination.

SGM families have to invent their identities and lifestyles because the narratives of traditional families do not fit their situation (Weeks et al., 2004). Dunne's studies on lesbian motherhood (2000) and gay fatherhood (2001) demonstrate how these groups challenge heteronormativity norms and extend the boundaries of what would normally be motherhood or fatherhood. Dunne's (2001) exploratory study on the experiences of married and divorced non-heterosexual fathers also draws attention to the bonds of affection between gay men and the mothers of their children with whom they continued to raise their children after coming out.

Almack (2011) describes how having a child in a lesbian parent family requires the mothers to work out the new kin relationships between the newborn child and the mothers' families of origin and the extent to which these relationships are recognized and validated. Display work was central in these processes. The lesbian mothers saw themselves as rejecting convention and seeking legitimacy at the same time.

Adoptive and foster families

During the last three decades of the 20th century, the number of children adopted in England and Wales dropped strongly because of new abortion laws and changed attitudes to single motherhood. Since the Adoption and Children Act from 2002, adoption orders could be made in favor of civil partners, same-sex couples, and unmarried couples, as well as single people and married couples (ONS, 2013).

An increasing proportion of adoptions concern older children who are looked after by local authorities, that is, local government (Jones & Hackett, 2011).

In 2000, 2,710 of these "looked-after" children were adopted. The number increased until 2015 but then declined in response to court rulings, according to which adoption orders should only be the last resort when alternatives, such as placing a child with birth relatives, were not available. In 2021, 2,870 looked-after children were adopted (Department for Education, 2021a). The numbers of intercountry adoptions into England have been falling during the last decade, reaching 53 adoptions in 2020 (WhatDoTheyKnow, 2021).

Among the children adopted from local authority care, more than three quarters were one to four years old. Only 6% of the children were less than one year old (Department for Education, 2021b). Compared to the English population under 18 years of age, fewer White children are in local authority care, and more are adopted from local authority care. Asian or Asian British children are underrepresented both among children under local authority care and among those adopted. Children of mixed heritage form 5% of the under-18 population but 10% of children in local authority care and 10% of children in local authority care who were adopted.

Instead of adopting a child, people with a close relationship to the child can obtain a special guardianship order (SGO), which gives them parental responsibility until the child grew up. It does not remove parental responsibility from the child's birth parents. In 2021, 3,800 children left local authority care as the subject of an SGO (Department of Education, 2021a). Most of these were granted to relatives or friends, and about 10% to foster carers.

Jones and Hackett (2011) have studied family practices and displays of family in the creation of adoptive kinship, drawing on 23 qualitative interviews with adoptive white mothers and fathers. Adoption practice has moved away from a model of substituting one family with another to one of an extended kinship network of adopted children, birth relatives, and adopters (Jones & Hackett, 2011, 2012). Adoptive parents retain significant relationships with the child's birth relatives through direct contact or indirect contact via adoption agencies. Maintaining relationships with the birth parents requires active efforts from adoptive parents and sometimes includes negotiations of the boundaries of kinship.

After a dramatic decline of using children's homes in the 1980s, about three-quarters of children looked after by local authorities in England tend to be in foster care (Narey & Owers, 2018). Since 1994, the number of looked-after children and the number of children in foster care have continuously increased, the latter reaching 55,990 children in 2017 (Narey & Owers, 2018; Ofsted, 2021). Most children in foster care have suffered abuse or neglect. For a smaller proportion, parental illness or disability had led to chronically inadequate parenting (Narey & Owers, 2018).

Families created by medically assisted reproduction (MAR)

The Human Fertilisation and Embryology Act of 1990 created the Human Fertilisation and Embryology Authority (HFEA), which regulates assisted conception treatments in the UK. Surrogacy is legal in the UK. In order to become the legal parents of a child after surrogacy, the mother and father have to apply to the court for a parental order (PO) (Bindmans, 2019). The eligibility criteria for a PO include that the intended parents were married, aged 18 or over, domiciled in the UK, that one parent was genetically related to the child, the surrogate mother gave consent, and only "reasonable expenses had been paid" (Crawshaw et al., 2012, p. 268). The Human Fertilisation and Embryology Act of 2008 extended the right to legal parentage following assisted conception to unmarried couples living in an enduring family relationship, including same-sex relationships. More recently, the Act was amended to make it possible for single people to apply for a PO instead of having to adopt the child to become a legal parent. Parents who are eligible for a PO are entitled to adoption leave and pay.

The legal rights and obligations of sperm donors depend on whether sperm donation happened through a HFEA-licensed clinic or not. The donor has no legal rights or obligations toward the child if a licensed clinic was used. Otherwise, the donor will be the legal father.

About 2.7% of children born in the UK in 2019 were conceived with the use of IVF, up from 1.3% in 2000 (own calculation using ONS (2021) and HFEA (2021)). In both years, about 0.1% of all births were conceived through donor insemination (own calculation). Most IVF treatments use patient eggs and partner sperm—86% of IVF cycles in 2019—, followed by the use of patient eggs and donor sperm (HFEA, 2021). Since 2004, IVF treatment has been possible through the National Health Service under certain conditions.

Cases of surrogacy are also rising in the UK. In 2008, there were only 67 PO applications (Brilliant Beginnings, 2022), rising to 280 applications in 2018. Thirty-eight single parents applied for a PO when it became available in 2019. A major obstacle to surrogacy in Britain can be the prohibition of paying the surrogate mother more than her expenses. Many gay couples turn to the USA, where surrogacy is available and easier to navigate in legal terms, but also comes at high financial costs (Dermott, 2008). High costs can be a reason to have a surrogate in a country other than the USA, but such couples often experienced some difficulties in obtaining legal parenthood on their return to the UK (Jadva et al., 2021). People who travel abroad for fertility treatment use a number of strategies for accommodating the foreign donor within their family life (Hudson, 2017). Their practices included concealing and minimizing the donation with the aim of "normalizing" their family relationships. Surrogate parents formed networks to help them deal with the stresses of assisted fertility and manage their own ambivalences.

Multicultural and migrant families

Until June 2021, EU citizens faced no obstacle in joining their partners or family members in the UK. For non-EU nationals, family migration was more restricted. British citizens or non-British settled residents can apply for family unification, which permits entry and legal residence in the UK of spouses or civil partners; fiancé(e)s or proposed civil partners; unmarried partners (including same-sex partners); or children of the British citizens or settled residents (Walsh, 2021).

The UK had abolished the "primary purpose rule" in 1997, which required foreign nationals to prove that immigration to the UK was not the primary purpose of their marriage. After a few years, the rules for family unification of spouses were tightened again by extending the probationary period, introducing a language requirement and increasing the minimum income requirement of the sponsor to at least £18,600 (Charsley et al., 2012). Before obtaining permanent settlement in the UK, the migrant partners have no recourse to public funds.

The policy changes form part of a move from justifying restrictive conditions for marriage migrants on cultural grounds to economic grounds, which has led to increasing class differences in the access to family/marriage migration (Kofman, 2018) as well as differences by gender and ethnic background (Sumption & Vargas-Silva, 2019). Qualitative research suggests that the measures have forced couples to marry earlier than they otherwise would have and have led to the involuntary separation of couples (Nehring & Sealey, 2020).

With the increasing ethnic diversity of the UK population, interethnic couple relationships have become more common. The proportion of interethnic relationships of all couple relationships has increased from 7% in 2001 to 9% in 2011 (ONS, 2014b). They are more common in non-marital cohabiting relationships than in marriages. A high proportion of married men and women with a Caribbean background are married to a partner from the native UK population, which differs from the other main minority groups from South Asia (Kulu & Hannemann, 2019; Lucassen & Laarman, 2009; Muttarak, 2010). The decline of endogamous marriage in the second generation is rather slow for South Asians (Kulu & Hannemann, 2019), which contradicts expectations of increasing exogamy in the second generation (Muttarak & Heath, 2010).

The increasing prevalence of interethnic relationships resulted in growing numbers of mixed ethnicity children in the UK. Interestingly, mixed ethnicity has been associated with a socio-economic advantage for some groups of children in the UK (Panico & Nazroo, 2011). However, children of intermarriage might experience stigmatization and social isolation (Kalmijn & Rodríguez-García, 2015). Interviews with mixed race, ethnicity, or faith families in Britain identify a variety of everyday approaches adopted by parents to negotiate difference and create a sense of belonging for their children (Caballero et al., 2008): some parents promote a sense of belonging based on a "single" aspect of their children's heritage; others stress the "mix"; and even others see their children's identity as "individual", that is, not rooted in their particular racial, ethnic, or faith backgrounds. The authors report that each of the approaches worked for the families concerned. The "individual" approach was more common among middle-class parents. Analyzing English survey data, Kalmijn and Rodríguez-García (2015) found that mixed children's social, cultural, and economic integration was in between the outcomes for children from immigrants and natives, often being closer to the outcomes for immigrants than for natives.

Conclusion and recommendations

In today's UK, romantic relationships are even more regarded as a private matter than at the start of the century. New family forms, especially SGM families and families created by MAR, have been recognized in UK family laws and policies. A lot of the diversification of families in the second half of the 20th century was driven by marital instability. In the 21st century, marriages have become some-what more stable, but they have also become less prominent in adults' lives. At the same time, non-marital cohabitation has become more common, especially in the younger population. More research is needed to fully understand the sig-nificance of these changes for young adults' lives and well-being.

Research into diverse families faces many challenges. Some new family forms are too rare for survey-based research and others are exceedingly complex. The latter applies to step- and patchwork families. There is little quantitative research in the UK about family relationships in complex step- or patchwork families partly because of a lack of data. New large-scale surveys are necessary that collect detailed information about family relationships across different households.

Furthermore, research into stepfamilies directs attention to the dynamic nature of modern family life. Being an only parent or being in a partnership is increasingly transient states. Instead of addressing single types of families, it is becoming increasingly important for family researchers to understand the development of family life courses and the legacies of individuals' previous families.

The discussions in this chapter have not systematically addressed differences in family forms in different socio-economic groups. Diversity is not just a matter of choice. Diversity can also be a matter of constraints, for example, when partner-ships receive too little support and break down under the pressures of daily life. For developing policies that support diverse families, we need to consider more fully the intersection of their cultural and material contexts.

Most UK policies are inclusive of diverse family types. However, the condi-tioning of benefits on employment is a way of treating families formally equally, but it neglects the diversity of families' needs and constraints. The research reviewed in this chapter has highlighted some of the efforts involved in creating and maintaining family relationships, especially in some "new" types of families. Making sure that all families are able to build strong and caring relationships remains a task for future policy development.

This chapter has addressed trends in UK families up to 2020. Since then, the COVID-19 pandemic has brought about further changes. For example, young adults who were living independently before the pandemic, especially students, often moved back into the parental home (Zilanawala et al., 2020). One-parent families suffered particularly strong declines in earnings because of the need to cut down working hours during the pandemic (Crossley et al., 2020). In addition, families were affected by the reduced capacity of public services. For example, the COVID-19 lockdowns made the adoption process more difficult and limited the capability of social services to identify vulnerable cases (Dafydd & Taylor, 2021).

Notes

1 The TFR for Scotland was lower and the TFR for Northern Ireland was higher than the TFR for England and Wales (Berrington et al., 2021).
2 Similar rules were introduced in Northern Ireland. Stepparents in Scotland can apply for a Residence Order.
3 Same-sex sexual acts were de-criminalised in Scotland in 1981 and in Northern Ireland in 1982.
4 Same-sex marriage became legal in Scotland in 2014 and in Northern Ireland in 2020.
5 Corresponding laws were passed in Scotland in 2009 and in Northern Ireland in 2013.

References

Allan, G., Crow, G., & Hawker, S. (2011). *Stepfamilies*. Palgrave Macmillan.

Allan, G., Hawker, S., & Crow, G. (2001). Family diversity and change in Britain and Western Europe. *Journal of Family Issues, 22*(7), 819–837. https://doi.org/10.1177/019251301022007002

Almack, K. (2011). Display work: Lesbian parent couples and their families of origin negotiating new kin relationships. In E. Dermott & J. Seymour (Eds.), *Displaying families: A new concept for the sociology of family life* (pp. 106–118). Palgrave.

Beaujouan, E., & Bhrolchain, M. N. (2011). Cohabitation and marriage in Britain since the 1970s. *Population Trends, 145*, 1–25. https://doi.org/10.1057/pt.2011.16

Berrington, A. (1994). Marriage and family formation among the white and ethnic minority populations in Britain. *Ethnic and Racial Studies 17*(3), 517–546. https://doi.org/10.1080/01419870.1994.9993837

Berrington, A. (2014). *The changing demography of lone parenthood in the UK* (Working Paper 48). ESRC Centre for Population Change, University of Southampton, UK. Retrieved from https://eprints.soton.ac.uk/364230/

Berrington, A., Duta, A., & Wakeling, P. (2017). Youth social citizenship and class inequalities in transitions to adulthood in the UK (Working Paper 81). ESRC Centre for Population Change, University of Southampton, UK. Retrieved from https://eprints.soton.ac.uk/405269/

Berrington, A., Ellison, J., Kuang, B., Vasireddy, S., & Kulu, H. (2021). Recent trends in UK fertility and potential impacts of COVID-19 (Working Paper 95). ESRC Centre for Population Change, University of Southampton, UK. Retrieved from https://eprints.soton.ac.uk/448062/

Bindmans. (2019). *UK surrogacy law embraces single parents*. Retrieved from https://www.bindmans.com/insight/blog/uk-surrogacy-law-embraces-single-parents

Brilliant Beginnings. (2022). *New data from English family court shows 350% growth in UK and international surrogacy over the last 12 years*. Retrieved from https://brilliantbeginnings.co.uk/new-data-family-court-350-percent-growth-surrogacy/

Caballero, C., Edwards, R., & Puthussery, S. (2008). *Parenting 'mixed' children: Negotiating difference and belonging in mixed race, ethnicity and faith families.* Joseph Rowntree Foundation. Retrieved from https://www.jrf.org.uk/sites/default/files/jrf/migrated/files/2231-parenting-children-difference.pdf

Charsley, K., Storer-Church, B., Benson, M., & Van Hear, N. (2012). Marriage-related migration to the UK. *International Migration Review, 46*(4), 861–890. https://doi.org/10.1111/imre.12003

Crawford, C., Goodman, A., Greaves, E., & Joyce, R. (2012). Cohabitation, marriage and child outcomes: An empirical analysis of the relationship between marital status and child outcomes in the UK using the Millennium Cohort Study. *Child and Family Law Quarterly, 24*(2), 176–198.

Crawshaw, M., Blyth, E., & van den Akker, O. (2012). The changing profile of surrogacy in the UK – Implications for national and international policy and practice. *Journal of Social Welfare & Family Law, 34*(3), 267–277. https://doi.org/10.1080/09649069.2012.750478

Crossley, T., Fisher, P., Low, H., Benzeval, M., Burton, J., Jäckle, A., & Read, B. (2020). The economic effects (Working Paper No 10/2020). Institute for Social and Economic Research, University of Essex, UK. Retrieved from https://www.iser.essex.ac.uk/files/news/2020/single-mother-income-loss-covid-19/covid-briefing-paper-economic-effects.pdf

Curtice, J., Clery, E., Perry, J., Phillips M., & Rahim, N. (Eds.). (2019). *British social attitudes: The 36th report.* The National Centre for Social Research, London. Retrieved from https://www.bsa.natcen.ac.uk

Curtice, J., Hudson, N., & Montagu, I. (Eds.). (2020). *British social attitudes: The 37th report.* The National Centre for Social Research, London. Retrieved from https://www.bsa.natcen.ac.uk

Dafydd, L., & Taylor, G. (2021). *UK: An overview of adoption and employment law.* Society for Human Resource Management. Retrieved from https://www.shrm.org/resourcesandtools/hr-topics/global-hr/pages/uk-adoption-employment-law.aspx

Daly, M., & Kelly, G. (2015). *Families and poverty: Everyday life on a low income.* Policy Press.

Department for Education. (2021a). Children looked after in England including adoptions. [Data set]. Retrieved from https://explore-education-statistics.service.gov.uk/data-catalogue/children-looked-after-in-england-including-adoptions/2021

Department for Education. (2021b). *Adopted and looked-after children.* Retrieved from https://www.ethnicity-facts-figures.service.gov.uk/health/social-care/adopted-and-looked-after-children/latest

Dermott, E. (2008). *Intimate fatherhood: A sociological analysis.* Routledge.

Donovan, C., Heaphy, B., & Weeks, J. (1999). Citizenship and same sex relationships. *Journal of Social Policy, 28*(4), 689–709. https://doi.org/10.1017/S0047279499005747

Duncan, S., & Phillips, M. (2011). People who live apart together (LATs): New family form or just a stage? *International Review of Sociology, 21*(3), 513–532. https://doi.org/10.1080/03906701.2011.625660

Dunne, G. A. (2000). Opting into motherhood: Lesbians blurring the boundaries and transforming the meaning of parenthood and kinship. *Gender and Society, 14*(1), 11–35. https://doi.org/10.1177/089124300014001003

Dunne, G. A. (2001). The lady vanishes? Reflections on the experiences of married and divorced non-heterosexual fathers. *Sociological Research Online*, 6(3). Retrieved from http://www.socresonline.org.uk/6/3/dunne.html

Esping-Andersen, G. (1990). *The three worlds of welfare capitalism.* Polity Press.

Hudson, N. (2017). Making 'assisted world families'? Parenting projects and family practices in the context of globalised gamete donation. *Sociological Research Online*, 22(2). https://doi.org/10.5153/sro.4246

Human Fertilisation and Embryology Authority (HFEA). (2021). Fertility treatment 2019: Trends and figures, UK statistics for IVF and DI treatment, storage, and donation [Data set]. Retrieved from https://www.hfea.gov.uk/about-us/publications/research-and-data/fertility-treatment-2019-trends-and-figures/

Ipsos Mori. (2020). *Race and ethnicity in Britain.* Retrieved from https://www.ipsos.com/en-uk/attitudes-race-and-inequality-great-britain

Jadva, V., Prosser, H., & Gamble, N. (2021). Cross-border and domestic surrogacy in the UK context: an exploration of practical and legal decision-making. *Human Fertility*, 24(2), 93–104. https://doi.org/10.1080/14647273.2018.1540801

Jarvis, J. A., Otero, C., Poff, J. M., Dufur, M. J., & Pribesh, S. L. (2021). Family structure and child behavior in the United Kingdom. *Journal of Child and Family Studies* (Online first) https://doi.org/10.1007/s10826-021-02159-z

Jones, C., & Hackett, S. (2011). The role of 'family practices' and 'displays of family' in the creation of adoptive kinship. *British Journal of Social Work*, 41(1), 40–56. https://doi.org/10.1093/bjsw/bcq017

Jones, C., & Hackett, S. (2012). Redefining family relationships following adoption: Adoptive parents' perspectives on the changing nature of kinship between adoptees and birth relatives. *British Journal of Social Work*, 42(2), 283–299. https://doi.org/10.1093/bjsw/bcr060

Kalmijn, M., & Rodríguez-García, D. (2015). The children of intermarriage in four European countries: Implications for school achievement, social contacts, and cultural values. *Annals of the American Academy of Political and Social Science*, 662, 246–265. https://doi.org/10.1177/0002716215595391

Kelley, N., Khan, O., & Sharrock, S. (2017). *Racial prejudice in Britain today.* National Centre for Social Research, UK. Retrieved from https://natcen.ac.uk/media/1488132/racial-prejudice-report_v4.pdf

Klett-Davies, M. (2016). Under pressure? Single parents in the UK. Bertelsmann Stiftung. Retrieved from https://www.bertelsmann-stiftung.de/en/publications/publication/did/under-pressure#detail-content-4676-4

Kofman, E. (2018). Family migration as a class matter. *International Migration*, 56(4), 33–46. https://doi.org/10.1111/imig.12433

Kulu, H., & Hannemann, T. (2019). Mixed marriage among immigrants and their descendants in the United Kingdom: Analysis of longitudinal data with missing information. *Population Studies*, 73(2), 179–196. https://doi.org/10.1080/00324728.2018.1493136

Lampard, R., & Peggs, K. (2007). *Identity and repartnering after separation.* Palgrave Macmillan.

Lappegård, T. (2014). Changing European families. In J. Treas, J. Scott, & M. Richards (Eds.), *The Wiley Blackwell companion to the sociology of families* (pp. 20–42). Wiley.

Letablier, M.-T., & Wall, K. (2018). Changing one-parenthood patterns: New challenges for policy and research. In L. Bernardi & D. Mortelmans (Eds.), *One-parenthood in the life course* (pp. 29–53). Springer. https://doi.org/10.1007/978-3-319-63295-7_2

Lewis, J. (2001). The decline of the male breadwinner model: Implications for work and care. *Social Politics*, *8*(2), 152–169. https://doi.org/10.1093/sp/8.2.152

Lucassen, L., & Laarman, C. (2009). Immigration, intermarriage and the changing face of Europe in the post war period. *The History of the Family*, *14*(1), 52–68. https://doi.org/10.1016/j.hisfam.2008.12.001

Macrory, I. (2012). *Measuring national well-being – Households and families, 2012.* Office for National Statistics, Measuring National Well-being Programme.

Matheson, J. (2009). National Statistician's annual article on the population: A demographic review. *Population Trends*, *138*, 7–21. https://doi.org/10.1057/pt.2009.43

Migration Watch. (2020). *The history of immigration to the UK* (History & Miscellaneous: MW 437). Retrieved from https://www.migrationwatchuk.org/briefing-paper/437/the-history-of-immigration-to-the-uk

Millar, J. (2010). Lone mothers, poverty and paid work in the UK. In S. Chant (Ed.), *The international handbook of gender and poverty: Concepts, research and policy* (pp. 147–152). Edward Elgar.

Millar, J. (2019). Self-responsibility and activation for lone mothers in the United Kingdom. *American Behavioral Scientist*, *63*(1), 85–99. https://doi.org/10.1177/0002764218816804

Muttarak, R. (2010). Explaining trends and patterns of immigrants' partner choice in Britain. *Journal of Family Research*, *22*(1), 37–64.

Muttarak, R., & Heath, A. (2010). Who Intermarries in Britain? Explaining ethnic diversity in intermarriage patterns. *The British Journal of Sociology*, *61*(2), 275–305. https://doi.org/10.1111/j.1468-4446.2010.01313.x

Narey, M., & Owers, M. (2018). Foster care in England – A review for the department for education. Retrieved from www.gov.uk/government/publications

Nehring, D., & Sealey, C. (2020). Intimate citizenship and the tightening of migration controls in the United Kingdom. *Social Policy & Administration*, *54*(3), 427–440. https://doi.org/10.1111/spol.12541

Nieuwenhuis, R., & Maldonado, L. C. (Eds.). (2018). *The triple bind of single-parent families: Resources, employment and policies to improve well-being.* Policy Press. Retrieved from http://library.oapen.org/handle/20.500.12657/30531

OECD. (2022). OECD family database. Retrieved from https://stats.oecd.org and https://www.oecd.org/els/family/database.htm

Ofsted. (2021). *Fostering in England 2020 to 2021: Main findings.* Retrieved from https://www.gov.uk/government/statistics/fostering-in-england-1-april-2020-to-31-march-2021

ONS. Office for National Statistics (2013). *Adoptions in England and Wales, 2012.* Retrieved from https://webarchive.nationalarchives.gov.uk

ONS. (2014a). *Stepfamilies in 2011.* Retrieved from http://www.ons.gov.uk/ons/rel/family-demography/stepfamilies/2011/stepfamilies-rpt.html

ONS. (2014b). *2011 Census analysis: What does the 2011 Census tell us about inter-ethnic relationships?* Retrieved from www.ons.gov.uk

ONS. (2015). *Births in England and Wales: 2014.* Retrieved from www.ons.gov.uk

ONS. (2017a). *Marriages in England and Wales 2016.* Retrieved from www.ons.gov.uk

ONS. (2017b). *Births in England and Wales: 2016.* Retrieved from www.ons.gov.uk

ONS. (2019a). *Divorces in England and Wales: 2018.* Retrieved from www.ons.gov.uk

ONS. (2019b). *Number and percentage of households with a grandparent as head of household* [Data set]. Retrieved from www.ons.gov.uk

ONS. (2019c). *Families and households in the UK: 2018.* Retrieved from www.ons.gov.uk

ONS. (2019d). *Families and households in the UK: 2019.* Retrieved from www.ons.gov.uk

ONS. (2020). *Civil partnerships in England and Wales 2019.* Retrieved from www.ons.gov.uk

ONS. (2021). *Vital statistics in the UK: births, deaths and marriages* [Data set]. Retrieved from www.ons.gov.uk

ONS. (2022a). *Families and households* [Data set]. Retrieved from www.ons.gov.uk

ONS. (2022b). *Labour force survey* (Series Id 2000026) [Data sets]. UK Data Service. Retrieved from https://beta.ukdataservice.ac.uk/datacatalogue/series/series?id=2000026#!/access

ONS. (2022c). *Families and households statistics explained.* Retrieved from www.ons.gov.uk

Panico, L., Bartley, M., Kelly, Y., McMunn, A., & Sacker, A. (2019). Family structure trajectories and early child health in the UK: Pathways to health. *Social Science & Medicine 232*, 220–229. https://doi.org/10.1016/j.socscimed.2019.05.006

Panico, L., & Nazroo, J. (2011). The social and economic circumstances of mixed ethnicity children in the UK: Findings from the Millennium cohort study. *Ethnic and Racial Studies, 34*(9), 1421–1444. https://doi.org/10.1080/01419870.2011.556745

Perelli-Harris, B., & Gassen, N. S. (2012). How similar are cohabitation and marriage? Legal approaches to cohabitation across Western Europe. *Population and Development Review 38*(3), 435–467. https://doi.org/10.1111/j.1728-4457.2012.00511.x

Phillips, D., Curtice, J., Phillips, M., & Perry, J. (Eds.). (2018). *British social attitudes: The 35th report.* The National Centre for Social Research, London. Retrieved from https://www.bsa.natcen.ac.uk

Platt, L. (2009). *Ethnicity and family: Relationships within and between ethnic groups.* Equality and Human Rights Commission, London.

Qureshi, K., Charsley, K., & Shaw, A. (2014). Marital instability among British Pakistanis: Transnationality, conjugalities and Islam. *Ethnic and Racial Studies, 37*(2), 261–279. https://doi.org/10.1080/01419870.2012.720691

Ribbens McCarthy, J., Edwards, R., & Gillies, V. (2003). *Making families: Moral tales of parenting and step-parenting.* Sociology Press.

Roantree, B., & Vira, K. (2018). *The rise and rise of women's employment in the UK* (IFS Briefing Note BN234). Institute for Fiscal Studies, London. https://doi.org/10.1920/BN.IFS.2019.BN0234

Ross, H., Gask, K., & Berrington, A. (2011). Civil partnerships five years on. *Population Trends 145*, 172–202. https://doi.org/10.1057/pt.2011.23

Smart, C. (2004). Changing landscapes of family life: Rethinking divorce. *Social Policy and Society, 3*(4), 401–408. https://doi.org/10.1017/S1474746404002040

Smart, C., & Neale, B. (1999). *Family fragments?* Polity Press.

Smith, A. (2002). The new ethnicity classification in the Labour Force Survey. *Labour Market Trends, 110*(12), 657–666.

Social Exclusion Unit (SEU). (1999). Teenage pregnancy (Cm 4342). Her Majesty's Stationary Office. Retrieved from https://dera.ioe.ac.uk/15086/1/teenage-pregnancy.pdf

Stone, J., Berrington, A., & Falkingham, J. (2014). Gender turning points and boomerangs: Returning home in young adulthood in Great Britain. *Demography, 51*(1), 257–276. https://doi.org/10.1007/s13524-013-0247-8

Sumption, M., & Vargas-Silva, C. (2019). Love is not all you need: Income requirement for visa sponsorship of foreign family members. *Journal of Economics, Race, and Policy, 2*(1–2), 62–76. https://doi.org/10.1007/s41996-018-0022-8

The Muslim Council of Britain. (2015). *British Muslims in numbers.* Retrieved from https://www.mcb.org.uk

Tromans, N., Natamba, E., & Jeffries, J. (2009). Have women born outside the UK driven the rise in UK births since 2001? *Population Trends, 136*, 28–42. https://doi.org/10.1057/pt.2009.17

Walsh, P. W. (2021). *Family Migration to the UK* (Briefing, 3rd Edition). The Migration Observatory, University of Oxford. Retrieved from https://migrationobservatory.ox.ac.uk/wpcontent/uploads/2020/04/COMPAS-Briefing-Family-Migration-to-the-UK-2021.pdf

Wasoff, F., & Dey, I. (2000). *Family policy*. Routledge.

Weeks, J., Heaphy, B., & Donovan, C. (2004). The lesbian and gay family. In J. Scott, J. Treas, & M. Richards (Eds.), *The Blackwell companion to the sociology of families* (pp. 342–355). Blackwell.

WhatDoTheyKnow. (2021). *Number of intercountry adoptions into England since 1994* (Department of Education reply to a Freedom of Information request). Retrieved from www.whatdotheyknow.com

Williams, F. (2004). *Rethinking families*. Calouste Gulbenkian Foundation.

Zagel, H., Hübgen, S., & Nieuwenhuis, R. (2021). Diverging trends in single-mother poverty across Germany, Sweden and the United Kingdom: Toward a comprehensive explanatory framework. *Social Forces* (Advance Article). https://doi.org/10.1093/sf/soab142

Zilanawala, A., Chanfreau, J., Sironi, M., & Palma, M. (2020). *Household composition, couples' relationship quality, and social support during lockdown: Initial findings from the COVID-19 Survey in Five National Longitudinal Studies* (Briefing Paper). UCL Centre for Longitudinal Studies, London. https://cls.ucl.ac.uk/covid-19-survey/findings/

10

THE COMPLEXITIES OF FAMILY DIVERSITY IN THE CONTEMPORARY US

Marina A. Adler

The cultural and policy context of doing family

While the US has seen similar family-related changes in recent decades as other advanced nations, various unique demographic and social processes have facilitated the diversification of the population, relationship forms, and living arrangements more than elsewhere. The recent release of the 2020 Census data confirms what William Frey (2021) calls a demographic "diversity explosion" as the US moves toward becoming a majority-minority society in the next few decades. Compared with 2000, the non-Hispanic white population has decreased by 8.6%, and for the first time the share of white Americans has fallen below 60% (Frey, 2021). People of color (POC), including people identifying as "multiracial" or "other race," have experienced major growth, and Hispanics/Latin Americans account for about 50% of the total population growth in the last decade. In addition, the median age of POC is significantly younger (20.9–37.5) than that of whites (47.3). This helps explain why since 2010 annually more nonwhite children were born than white children and why since 2000, the overall growth of the number of children has been due to people identifying as Hispanic, Asian, and multiracial. This multicultural societal context with continued immigration mirrors the rapid diversification observed with regard to family forms, including multiethnic families.

"Post-modern" American families – as opposed to the "Standard North American Family" (SNAF, Smith, 1993) consisting of a heterosexual married couple with biological children and a male breadwinner – are characterized by a high degree of mobility and relationship instability, a high probability of forming one or more reconstituted families over the life course (Seltzer, 2019, and increased diversity of family relationships, including sex gender minority (SGM) and multicultural families. Not only are post-modern families socially and culturally

DOI: 10.4324/9781003193500-10

diverse, their membership is no longer only based on blood or legal relationships (Lamanna et al., 2021). According to Cherlin (2004), these trends reflect a deinstitutionalization of marriage in the US in recent decades. He argues that marriage, divorce, and remarriage are currently incomplete institutions because in times of rapid social change, there are no clear social guidelines on how to have relationships. In "Marriage-Go-Round" (2010), he points out that compared to other nations, Americans tend to marry, divorce, and remarry more often. What makes American family life different, Cherlin argues, is this large amount of fluidity and movement – the many transitions in and out of relationships and the frequent changes in living arrangements over the life course. In addition, the US differs from other countries by only having rudimental family policies that simultaneously encourage legal commitment (marriage) and individual (rather than public) responsibility for the family. While marriage is upheld as a cultural ideal actively promoted by religion, the legal system, and government policy, this pressure to commit to marriage is contradicted by the strong values in individualism, self-realization, and self-expression.

One clear recent demographic trend in the US is a "retreat from marriage," particularly among the younger cohorts, in favor of cohabitation and remaining single (Berger & Carlson, 2020; Smock & Schwarz, 2020). In addition, the normalization of serial union formation and the increased acceptance of relationship forms beyond heteronormativity and biological ties have stretched the definition of what family is. Simultaneously, increases in multi-partner fertility and childbearing outside of marriage have shaped new family constellations. Yet, despite the numerous alternative paths to becoming, being, and doing family, the US Census Bureau clings to the outdated definition of families as: "two people or more (one of whom is the householder) related by birth, marriage, or adoption and residing together" (US Census Bureau, 2022). This means that as long as two or more related people live together, they are family. While families are also family households, households generally can include any group of people who reside together regardless of their relationship. Non-family households are either maintained by someone living alone or the householder shares the home with people to whom they are not related. Obviously, these definitions do not take into account the real variety of living arrangements spanning households and borders or involving the numerous social relationships evident in contemporary American families.

Furthermore, US policies continue to support marriage and biological co-resident parents much more than single or non-resident parents or non-biological parents in reconstituted families (Berger & Carlson, 2020). This is particularly problematic in the context of the observed rising union instability among biological parents, resulting in increases in reconstituted families, high proportions of single mother families, and diversity in the pathways to parenthood. The data show that over their life course, Americans are very likely to co-reside and have children with several partners, who will consequently live in various households with different parental figures. Shared legal and physical custody arrangements following parental union dissolution are now the norm (Cancian et al., 2014). And yet, the US legal system remains biased against multi-partner fertility, and blended families are often stigmatized by various social institutions and policies (Stewart & Timothy, 2020).

The American liberal welfare state lacks a comprehensive family policy, instead targeting low-income families with means-tested, minimal social welfare benefits, and marriage promotion programs. The US also lacks a national statutory paid maternity or family leave, but in the last two decades several US states have enacted some paid leave policies that provide up to eight weeks with a wage replacement of 50–90% (Berger & Carlson, 2020). Overall, because of the notion that family responsibilities are a private issue, the US government only provides family support in the case of families with special needs, those who are married and working (tax benefits), and low-income families. Policy changes regarding marriage equality, child support, and some child care expansion at the federal level have eased some of the barriers faced by families since 2000. However, care sharing remains generally quite difficult in the US. The two-full-time worker model assumed for US family households is related to a neoliberal 24/7 economy and complicated by a privatized child care infrastructure, which creates great time scarcity for parents in all family constellations and prevents parents from achieving work-life balance.

Empirical patterns of various family forms

The data for describing the patterns of family diversity in the US come from national governmental sources like the US Census Bureau and estimates from the Current Population Survey (CPS) and the America Community Survey (ACS). They are supplemented by data collected by other governmental and professional agencies, such as the Migration Policy Institute, the Center for Disease Control and Prevention (CDC), the National Center for Family and Marriage Research (NCFMR), and The National Center for Health Statistics (NCHS), as needed. Although an abundance of quantitative data related to families is available in the US, the way the data are collected and categorized is based on changing measures and definitions of family, which can make it difficult to capture trends accurately. One challenge is to compare decennial Census data with CPS or ACS estimates. Another is to disaggregate data that were published based on differing underlying metrics; for example, the percentage of cohabiting couples can be calculated based on "all couple households" or on "all households," resulting in very different numbers.

Union formation and dissolution

While the data presented here focus on the last two decades, the observed trends started long before the turn of the century. In fact, many of the shifts had their origin in the 1960s and 70s. However, the trends reflect an acceleration in recent decades. Table 10.1 shows dramatic changes in union formation and dissolution patterns for different-sex partners in the last 20 years. The crude marriage rate (CMR) decreased from 8.2 in 2000 to 5.1 in 2020. Although over time about 68% of all American adults eventually marry (US Census Bureau, 2018), marriage has lost in popularity, especially among the younger cohorts (Sassler & Lichter, 2020). Overall, more young Americans postpone marriage and only about 29% of young adults aged 18–34 are currently married. According to Smock and Schwartz (2020), there are clear patterns by birth cohort. For women of Generation X (cohort born between 1966 and 1972), 82% were married by age 40. This percentage is expected to decline to 70–75% among Millennials (born between 1980 and 2000) (see Martin et al., 2014). As shown in Table 10.1, the median age at first marriage for women has increased by three years (from 25.1 to 28.1) and that for men by over 3.5 years (from 26.8 to 30.5) in the last two decades (US Bureau of the Census, 2020).

This "retreat from marriage" is reflected not only in the overall reduction of crude marriage rates, but also in the decrease of remarriage rates. Since World War II, the remarriage rate in the US has decreased dramatically for both sexes. They have been cut in half since then, to only 25.1 remarriages per 1,000 previously married persons in 2019, and down from 29.2 in 2000. The remarriage rate for men has remained almost double that of women over time: in 2019, it was 35.1 for men and 19.4 for women (Reynolds, 2021). However, because of overall declining first marriages, the proportion of new marriages that are remarriages for one or both partners has actually increased (Rayley & Sweeney, 2020). The median age at remarriage in 2019 was 48 for men and 44 for women (Reynolds, 2021).

The observed retreat from first marriage does not, however, mean a retreat from pairing up. It mainly signals a weakening of the status of marriage as the most important intimate partnership and indicates that different-sex marriage is being deinstitutionalized (Cherlin, 2020). However, as the struggle for marriage equality indicates, marriage continues to be regarded as symbolically important and beneficial. But it appears that for many young adults, early marriage has been replaced by cohabitation. In the last two decades, the percentage of adults of traditional first marriage age (those aged 25–34) who are living with an unmarried partner has approximately doubled to 14.8% (US Census Bureau, 2018), and about 75% of adults in their early 30s have cohabited at some point (Sassler & Lichter, 2020). Unlike the median age of first marriage, the median age for first cohabiting unions has remained stable (Manning et al., 2014).

Interestingly, American marriage dissolution patterns also show a strong downward trajectory in the last two decades (see Table 10.1). While in 2000 the divorce rate was 4.0, in 2020 it was only 2.3. It appears that once married, couples are more likely to stay together than in the past. About 39% of marriages end in divorce, which suggests a high degree of relationship instability. According to Cohen's (2019) multivariate analysis of age-specific divorce data from the American Community Survey (ACS), this downward trend is mainly driven by

TABLE 10.1 Selected demographic indicators for the US, 2000 and latest available data

	2000				latest available data				
	Total	**Black**	**White***	**Hispanic****	*Year*	*Total*	**Black**	**White***	**Hispanic****
Crude marriage rate	8.2				2020	5.1			
Mean age at first marriage									
of women	25.1				2020	28.1			
of men	26.8				2020	30.5			
Crude divorce rate	4.0				2020	2.3			
Remarriage rate									
of women	29.2				2019	19.4			
of men	63.9					35.1			
% of adults >15 never married	27.1				2021	34.0			
of women	25.1	42.4	22.2	28.8		30.6	48.3	27.1	38.4
of men	31.3	44.9	29.1	37.5		36.6	51.8	33.6	46.6
Total fertility rate	2.06	2.10	2.00	2.70	2020	1.64	1.78	1.61	1.94
General fertility rate	65.0	71.4	58.5	95.9	2020	55.8	59.0	53.2	62.8
Mean age at first birth									
of women	24.9	22.3	25.9	24.0	2020	27.1	25.2	27.8	25.1
% non-marital births	33.2	68.5	22.1	42.7	2019	40.0	68.2	28.2	51.8
% of women aged 40–44 who have born no children	19.0	17.7	20.3	10.9	2018	15.6	16.0	16.0	11.0
Cohorts	**1950**					**1970**			
Completed fertility/cohort	2.00					2.13			
% of women aged 40–44 who have born no children for cohorts	15.1					11.9			

Notes: *White refers to non-Hispanic white. **average of Central/South American, Cuban, Mexican, and Puerto Rican women.
Sources: CDC/NCHS National Vital Statistics System (2021); Guzzo and Schweizer (2020); Martin et al. (2019); Curtin and Sutton (2020); US Census Bureau (2000, 2021b).

Americans under the age 45. Younger cohorts are more likely to hesitate to get married, but then they remain married. The percentage of adults who never marry has also increased from 27.1% (25.1% for women and 31.3 for men) to 34% (30.6 and 36.6, respectively). This trend is particularly noticeable for POC, resulting in around half of all African Americans and Hispanic men never marrying by 2021.

Fertility patterns

While US fertility rates have been declining, they remain higher than those in most other advanced countries (Smock & Schwarz, 2020). Table 10.1 shows that the total fertility rate (TFR) fell from 2.06 in 2000 to 1.64 in 2020, as reported by the US Census Bureau. The general fertility rate (the GFR is the ratio of the number of live births in a given year for every 1,000 women who are aged 15–45 during that year) was 65.0 in 2000 and was reduced to 55.8 in 2020. However, the completed fertility rate (the CFR is the total number of children a woman has at the end of her reproductive age) actually increased from 1.90 to 2.04 in the same time period. This trend can also be illustrated for the specific cohorts of 1950 and 1970: the rate was 2.00 and 2.13, respectively. However, according to Guzzo and Hayford (2020), these cross-sectional fertility measures do not capture any "delay and recuperation" effects and thus may underestimate completed childbearing at the end of the reproductive years. For example, the mean age at first birth climbed to 27.1 in 2020, which represents an increase of two years since 2000. Thus, women are delaying childbearing to later on in their life course, which is reflected in rising birth rates at older ages (Hamilton et al., 2019). In other words, the decline in birth rates has been concentrated among younger women: while the US teen birth rate remains higher than those in Europe, it fell by about 58% since 2007 (Hamilton et al., 2019). The US does not collect official statistics on the age of men at first birth, but data from the National Survey of Family Growth suggests that White men and men with higher education are much older when becoming fathers than men of color and those with less education (Schweizer, 2019). It is also shown that for the cohort of 40- to44-year-old men, the age gap by gender has consistently been about three years over time.

In addition, since the year 2000, the percentage of non-marital births has increased from 33.2% to 40%, indicating an increasing decoupling of marriage and parenthood similar to trends observed in Europe. However, unlike in other advanced nations, the percentage of women who by age 40–44 have born no children has declined from 19% of women in 2000 to 15% in 2018.

There are also major differences in fertility-related patterns by race/ethnicity. Table 10.1 shows that women of color generally have higher fertility rates than non-Hispanic White women. Among African American women, the drop in total fertility rates was least dramatic, and among Hispanic women, it was the highest. Thus, the TFR fell from 2.1 to 1.78 among African American women, compared to a reduction from 2.0 to 1.64 for white women and from 2.7 to

1.94 among Hispanic women. However, the trend with the GFR from 2000 to 2020 is somewhat different: among African Americans, it fell by 12 points to 59, while it fell by only 5 points to 53.2 among White women and by an astonishing 33 points among Hispanic women.

Furthermore, the average age at first birth has increased by almost three years among African American women from 22.3 to 25.2 and by almost two years among non-Hispanic White women from 25.9 to 27.8. However, the postponement was only about one year among Hispanic women – from age 24.0 to 25.1. Dramatic differences by race/ethnicity are also observed for non-marital childbearing. While the percentage of non-marital births remained high and unchanged among African American women between 2000 and 2019 (68.5% and 68.2%), that for non-Hispanic White women and Hispanic women increased. The increase was by about 6 points for White women (22.1–28.2%) and about 9 points for Hispanic women (42.7–51.8%). The observed differences between white and Hispanic women's fertility have increased over time because the proportion of non-marital births grew faster among Hispanic women (Smock & Schwarz, 2020). Overall, the gap between African American and White marital fertility rates and timing is also shrinking. In addition, in 2000, the percentages of women who did not bear any children by the end of their reproductive life were 20.3% for non-Hispanic White women, 17.7% for African American, and 10.9% for Hispanic women. In 2018, comparable statistics were 16%, 16%, and 11%, respectively. So, media reports decrying a rise in "childless USA" appear to be premature (Stone, 2020).

Changes in household composition and living arrangements

Tables 10.2 and 10.3 show that family and non-family household composition in the US has continued to change in the last 20 years. The share of family households has been decreasing since long before the turn of the century. Only 65% of all households are currently considered to be family households. Specifically, the percentage of married-couple households with children has seen a decline from 24.1% to 19% and married couples without children are increasing. In contrast, non-family households have increased from 31.2% to 35%; in particular, more people are living alone.

Table 10.2 presents data on changes in the living arrangements by age and gender, and household composition by race/ethnicity. The proportion of US adults living with a spouse has been shrinking for decades (Smock & Schwartz, 2020). While in 1967, about 70% of Americans were living with a spouse, now just over half of adults do so (Smock & Schwartz, 2020). This also represents another decline since 2000 (from 56.0%). This trend is particularly evident among those aged 18–24, whose percentage living with a spouse was cut in half. Among those aged 25–34, the drop was slightly higher among men (15.8 points) than among women (13.9 points). This age-group is increasingly living with a partner rather than a spouse: among women the increase is from 6.8% to 15.5% and among men

TABLE 10.2 Population in living arrangements in the US, 2000 and latest available data

% of adults are living	2000			2020		
	Total	Age 18–24	Age 25–34	Total	Age 18–24	Age 25–34
With spouse	56.0			51.5		
women		17.7	57.0		8.0	43.1
men		9.8	50.1		4.2	34.2
With partner	3.9			7.3		
women		7.0	6.8		9.8	15.5
men		4.5	8.0		7.1	13.8
Child of householder	10.5			11.5		
women		46.7	7.6		55.6	12.6
men		56.8	12.4		59.3	20.8
alone	13.3			14.4		
women		4.4	8.2		4.5	9.3
men		4.2	12.3		4.8	11.0
With other relatives	11.4			11.8		
women		14.0	15.4		13.7	14.6
men		11.7	7.2		15.6	10.8
With non-relatives	4.9			3.5		
women		10.2	5.0		8.4	4.9
men		12.9	10.0		8.9	8.4

Sources: US Census Bureau (2000, 2020, 2021a); Fields and Casper (2001); Hobbs (2005); Simmons and O'Neill (2001); Simmons and O'Connell (2003).

from 8% to 13.8%. More men in both age-groups still live at home, and this trend has increased among the 25–34 age-group. There have been no major changes in living alone and living with other relatives or non-relatives.

Table 10.3 shows patterns in household composition by race/ethnicity. Overall, the proportion of different-sex spouse households declined from 76.8% to 72.4% and this downward trend is also apparent for households involving parents. At the same time, the percentage of married couple households without children increased from 41.7% to 44.9%. The proportion of all family households that are mother-only and father-only households increased somewhat. In 2020, only 0.7% of households were married same-sex couples and 1.9% were unmarried parent couples. No comparable data are available in 2000.

Cherlin (2020) reported that based on 2018 Census data, about 60% of all African American households with children under 18 were headed by an unpartnered parent, compared with 26% of non-Hispanic White and 33% of Hispanic households. The trends in Table 10.2b by race/ethnicity show that households

TABLE 10.3 Households in the US, 2000 and latest available data

% of households consist of	2000				2020			
	Total	Black	White	Hispanic	Total	Black	White	Hispanic
Different-sex spouses	52.8	32.3	55.6	55.1	46.8	27.2	50.0	46.4
with kids <18	24.1	24.1	24.9	34.6	17.7	10.7	16.7	24.7
w/out kids <18	28.7	8.2	30.7	20.5	29.1	16.5	33.3	21.7
Different-sex partners	5.2	NA	NA	NA	6.8	6.2	6.8	8.7
with kids<18	2.1	NA	NA	NA	2.2	2.6	1.8	4.3
w/out kids>18	3.1	NA	NA	NA	4.6	3.6	5.0	4.4
Mother-only with kids	7.2	27.8	8.1	15.1	9.7	24.4	6.0	15.0
Father-only with kids	2.1	3.2	2.4	3.3	2.4	3.3	2.1	3.0
Married same-sex couple					0.7	<0.1	0.8	0.5
Unmarried same-sex couple	1.0	1.4	0.5	1.3	1.9	2.2	1.4	3.7
Other family/non-family group	12.2	NA	NA	NA	16.0	NA	NA	NA
One person living alone	25.5	28.1	26.7	13.9	28.3	35.6	29.8	19.1

Sources: US Census Bureau (2000, 2020, 2021a); Fields and Casper (2001); Hobbs (2005); Simmons and O'Neill (2001); Simmons and O'Connell (2003).

with different-sex couples are trending downward for all three groups. For African American couple, households with children the percentage fell from 24.9% to 18.8%, and for comparable Hispanic households, the decrease was from 34.6% to 32.5%. However, among non-Hispanic White couple households, the trend is different: 24.9% had children in 2000 and 26.6% in 2020. In addition, while the proportion of mother-only households has decreased among African Americans (from 27.8% to 24.4%) and among Whites (8.1% to 6.0%), the percentage among Hispanics has stayed stable at around 15%. The percentage of father-only households remains small for all groups – between 2% and 3%. The same is true for married same-sex couples and unmarried parent couples.

Current empirical research on the various family forms

Reconstituted families (stepfamilies)

The US has the highest rates of union dissolution and remarriage among advanced countries, and multiple partner fertility (MPF) has proliferated so that stepfamilies have become more visible than ever before (Monte, 2019; Steward & Timothy, 2020). Estimates from the US Census Bureau suggest that one in 10 adults has experienced MPF and about one third of all Americans are part of a stepfamily (Monte, 2019). In addition, over 30% of stepchildren will experience the divorce of their custodial and stepparent (Jones, 2003). Due to families being assembled, disassembled and then reconstituted in new constellations, family complexity has increased, but its measurement remains difficult. In addition, due to ethnic/racial diversity and the many ways of becoming part of a reconstituted family (divorce, remarriage, cohabitation, birth), the stepfamilies themselves are very diverse.

Reconstituted families vary in structure, and the term stepfamily refers to families that are re-partnered and include a child/ren from at least one partner (see Raley & Sweeney, 2020 for a review). The term "blended family" has been used for families that include stepparents and step- or half-siblings, but this term has been criticized because some argue that the family members in these families do not necessarily "blend" (Lamanna et al., 2021). Stepfamilies can be created through remarriage after divorce or widowhood and through cohabitation and non-marital childbearing. They may involve adoption or same-sex couples; in fact, most parenting in same-sex families is done in stepfamilies.

Stepfamilies can reside in one household or span several households in various living arrangements that are not captured in official statistics. While tradition-ally, child custody was assigned to mothers, since the turn of the century the custody arrangements after union dissolution are increasingly shared. This has consequences for parental eligibility for tax and transfer payments, which are cal-culated on the basis of household membership (Berger & Carlson, 2020). Stewart and Timothy (2020) note that three legal concepts are central to understanding US policies regarding stepfamilies: (1) stepchildren and stepparents are "legal strangers" and thus do not have any of the legal rights of biological or adoptive parents and children; (2) stepfamilies are subject to the "rule of two," meaning that children can have no more than two legal parents; and (3) the "de facto" parent concept refers to a co-residing, legally married stepparent, who provides significant support for the child. Resulting ambiguities in how these stepfamily relationships are treated by the legal system can have negative consequences for all family members, especially children.

Stepfamilies are still confronted with negative stereotypes in American cul-ture, media, and society. Members of African American stepfamilies can even face double stigma as they combine minority and stepfamily status (Lamanna et al., 2021). The continued emphasis on the SNAF means that American step-families remain relatively ignored in mainstream culture and face complex and often conflicting laws at the federal, state, and local level. Ambiguous defini-tions of "family," "parent," and even "child" can bias policies and institutional processes against stepfamilies (Stewart & Timothy, 2020). In addition, norma-tive expectations regarding the obligations involved in stepfamily relationships remain unclear (see Berger & Carlson, 2020; Raley & Sweeney, 2020). Hence, doing family in American stepfamilies is complicated as the social script for step-parenting remains underdeveloped and leaves much room for interpretation and ambiguity. In fact, the nature, perceptions, and labels for step-kin relationships vary by age, gender, and custody arrangements. Thus, most stepfamilies end up defining their own language (parental names), boundaries (duties and responsibilities), and relationships in order to create their stepfamily identity (Lamanna et al., 2021). "Shared children" in these hybrid family structures often experience the ambiguity surrounding their re-partnered family's complex history and sibling relationships as stressful (Sanner, Ganong & Coleman, 2021).

One-parent and cohabiting families

Cohabitation has become a more common family form in the US in recent decades, most likely due to decreased stigmatization. In general, while the duration of cohabitation is relatively short in the US, the time interval has increased in recent decades and cohabitation has become less likely to be a precursor of marriage (Mernitz, 2018). Manning & Smock (2005) argue that single Americans are often "sliding" into cohabitation rather than engaging in the deliberate process involved in marriage planning. Marriage may no longer be the goal of couples living together, particularly among African Americans, for whom cohabitation is not necessarily just part of a dating process that leads to marriage after co-residence (Reid & Golub, 2015). While 57% of non-Hispanic White adults were married in 2017, only 33% of African Americans were (Cherlin, 2020). Furthermore, African American women tend to marry later or not at all, and are more likely to divorce than other groups of women. In fact, only 51% of African American women are projected to ever marry, compared to 84% of non-Hispanic white women and 70% of Hispanic women (Martin et al., 2014). According to Council (2021), this "marriage squeeze" is experienced by Black women of all economic backgrounds. This also means that women of color who want to become mothers often do so unmarried. Thus, it appears that the deinstitutionalization process of marriage has advanced the most among African Americans.

Most one-parent families are headed by single mothers (about 80% in 2021), and women of color are more likely to be unmarried mothers. In 2018, about 22% of all US children lived in mother-only families (Smock & Schwartz, 2020), and it is estimated that about 50% of all births outside of marriage were to cohabiting mothers (Heuveline & Timberlake, 2004). Unmarried mothers may cohabit with partners for certain periods of time and consequently their children live part of their lives in such living arrangements with frequent transitions. Reid & Golub (2015) found that low-income African American unmarried mothers first vet their potential partners, whereby child well-being is central to their decision to cohabit with a partner.

In addition, it is estimated that about 10% of US children live in multigenerational households (Pilkauskas & Cross, 2018), and almost 30% of children will be raised by their grandparent(s) at least temporarily during childhood (Amorim et al., 2017). According to the 2018 ACS annual estimate, about 2.3 million grandparents, or about 43% of American grandparents living with their grandchildren, take responsibility for their grandchildren's basic needs (US Census Bureau, 2018). Reliance on grandparents and so-called othermothers (James,

1993), who help mothers with caregiving, is a practice rooted in African tradition common among unmarried mothers in the Black community and among economically disadvantaged families. In general, multigenerational households with flexible family structures providing kindship care are characteristic of the Black community and have historically served to stabilize living arrangements and support children in times of need (Henderson & Bailey, 2015).

Sex gender minority families (SGM)

Since 2000, the SGM population in the US has grown significantly and has diversified more than in previous decades (Bridges & Moore, 2018). Most research on SGM families focuses on same-sex families, mainly because of a lack of data on other non-gender conforming families. Census and Gallup estimates of the number of same-sex couples in the US are far more than 1 million, with same-sex married households exceeding 900,000 by 2019 (US Census Bureau, 2019a). About 50–60% are married couples. While the data show a relatively even split between the number of lesbian and gay couples, over twice as many lesbian couples have children (24%) than gay couples (9%) (Smock & Schwartz, 2020). Overall, it is estimated that about 13% of unmarried same-sex couples and 19% of married same-sex couples are raising children (see Smock & Schwarz, 2020). In addition, African Americans and Hispanics in same-sex couples are more likely to raise children than whites (Moore & Stambolis-Ruhstorfer, 2013; Reczek, 2020). According to Gates (2015), African American same-sex couples are 2.4 times more likely and Hispanics 1.7 times more likely than whites to raise children.

The policy context for becoming parents has recently changed for American SGM families. On June 26, 2015, in Obergefell v. Hodges, the Supreme Court ruled in favor of marriage equality. Specifically, same-sex marriage was legalized in all US states. While this historic legislation has brought increased same-sex marriages and social acceptance of same-sex couples, other policies, such as the transgender military ban and so-called bathroom bills have turned the clock back on recent gains made. Although SGM families experience persistent stigma, marginalization, and discrimination, a recent survey (Family Equality, 2019) indicates that about 63% of SGM aged 18–35 want to become parents for the first time or want to have additional children. Nevertheless, based on a number of studies, it appears that same-sex relationships – married or unmarried – are less stable and have higher dissolution rates than different-sex ones (Smock & Schwarz, 2020).

SGM couples have always encountered legal obstacles to becoming parents, which vary by US state. Same-sex couples' parental rights depend on the recognition of one or both adults as the legal parents of the child (Shapiro, 2013). In some states, only the biological parent in same-sex couples is considered the legal parent, which means that the non-biological parent often will opt for second-parent adoption to become a legally recognized parent. The marital status of the couple also affects the ability to foster or adopt children. The legal system in various states requires same-sex (and in some cases even different-sex) couples to be legally married before they are eligible to jointly become parents through foster care or private adoption (Shapiro, 2013).

There are numerous pathways to parenthood for SGM couples. They can have children from a prior relationship with a different-sex partner, through foster care and adoption, MAR or surrogacy, or partnering with a parent. Nevertheless, becoming an "intentional family" can be quite complicated for same-sex couples. Legal barriers and difficult access to adoption, discrimination and the costs associated with MAR and surrogacy often constitute a hostile climate for potential SGM parents (Baumle & Compton, 2015; Reczek, 2020). The most common path to parenthood is through a previous different-sex relationship, but having children outside of heteronormativity has become more prevalent in recent decades (Moore & Stambolis-Ruhstorfer, 2013). Unlike older cohorts, who mainly became parents in different-sex relationships (Goldberg et al., 2014), survey data now indicate that the majority of young SGM people are expecting to use MAR, foster care, or adoption to become parents (Family Equality, 2019). However, depending on the type of MAR chosen, these procedures can be cost prohibitive for couples. Commercial surrogacy is the most expensive option and therefore used primarily among gay fathers, who tend to have higher incomes (Pachankis et al., 2018), and by higher socioeconomic status (SES) couples (Carroll, 2018). According to Goldberg and Conron (2018), about 20% of same-sex couples have adopted children and 3% are foster parents. Moore and Stambolis-Ruhstorfer (2013) locate the origin of the institutional change in attitudes toward the acceptability of same-sex couples fostering or adopting children in the 1980s. At that time the deinstitutionalization process had rapidly overwhelmed the foster care system with increasing numbers of children. Gay men and lesbians quite quickly became considered to be "suitable" as parents for the many children in need of families.

Recent research on SGM families has mainly focused on the dynamics and experiences of parenting in same-sex families and the effects parenting on children in these families. In particular, the role of social support in mediating the negative effects of social stigma and mental health stress among same-sex parents has been studied. Results indicate that parental stress levels in same-sex families may be higher because they receive less social support than different-sex families (Carroll, 2018; Tornello et al., 2011). In particular, non-coupled gay fathers, those who are of lower socioeconomic status, and African American gay fathers feel marginalized in their communities (Carroll, 2018). Bisexual and transgender families and parenting remain under researched. However, exploratory qualitative research shows that parents in these families make efforts to normalize their sexual minority status and to deemphasize their bisexual or trans identity markers when caring for their children (Kuvalanka et al., 2017; Tasker & Delvoye, 2015).

Research conducted over the last few decades has also consistently shown that children raised in same-sex families experience similar health, education, and behavioral outcomes as children raised by cisgender different sex couples when controlling for SES (see review in Reczek, 2020). These studies use nationally representative surveys to show there are no differences in child well-being measures between children growing up in SGM families and those living in other family structures.

Adoptive and foster families

In addition to other forms of family adoption (grandparents or other kin), it is estimated that annually about 100,000 children are adopted via stepparent or "second parent" adoption in the US. While family adoptions are the most common type of adoption, no nationally representative data are collected regularly on these adoptions and estimates are based on surveys. Census data from 2010 show that about 1.5 million adopted children, or 2.4% of children under 18, live in US households (compared to 4.3% stepchildren) (Kreider & Lofquist, 2014). In the US there are three options for non-family member adoption: (1) private domestic adoption via an agency or attorney; (2) adoption from the foster care system after the parental rights of the biological parents have been terminated; and (3) transnational adoption through professional organizations (Pinderhughes et al., 2015). There are also clear distinctions between, and different trends in, the number of domestic adoptions and intercountry adoptions. For example, because private or intercountry adoption is more expensive than public foster care adoption, only those with higher socioeconomic status can afford this path to parenthood. Recent estimates based on nationally representative data show that about 38% of children were privately adopted, about 37% were placed via foster care, and about 25% were adopted internationally (Vandivere et al., 2009). The number of children who were adopted through public welfare agencies increased from 51,000 in the year 2000 to 57,881 in 2020, while the number of intercountry adoptions fell from 18,854 to 1,622 in 2020 (Department of State, 2021; DHHS, 2021). This rapid decline in intercountry adoptions (from a high of 22,986 in 2004) is due to the reduction of adoptions from Eastern Europe, especially Russia and from Asia, particularly China, because of more restrictive policies. Private domestic adoptions and intercountry adoptions are most likely to involve infants and most intercountry adoptions involve Asian children. The large majority of intercountry adoptions are also transracial adoptions (Pinderhughes et al., 2015).

Only approximately 2–7% of all American children have at least one adoptive parent (Lamanna et al., 2021; Vandivere et al., 2012). About 54% of the children adopted from the foster care system were adopted by their foster parents in 2020, down from 61% in 2000 (DHHS, 2021). There were about 424,000 children in foster care in 2020, with 117,470 waiting to be adopted (DHHS, 2021). Unfortunately, most children in the foster care system have to wait 2–5 years before being adopted (Coughlin & Abramowitz, 2004). Research shows that care giving in foster families is complicated by occurring in a "triangular" relationship among the child welfare system, the birth parents, and the foster arrangement. Having to deal with the demands of the courts, social service providers, the school system, the wider community, and the special needs of the child can pose additional challenges that may strain existing family relationships (Berrick, 2015). In particular, research indicates that foster parents worry about the competing demands of caring for, and attention paid to, both the foster children and their own children.

There are some differences in the characteristics of adopted children. The distribution by sex is about even, and the percentage of the children who were between ages 1 and 6 at the time of public adoption increased from 45% in 2000 to 63% in 2020. Most of this increase occurred for 1- to 3-year-old children (from 17% to 39%). More White children are adopted through private agencies, and more African American children are placed through public channels (Pinderhughes et al., 2015). While an equal proportion of domestically adopted children were White and African American in 2000 (about 38%), in 2020, the proportions changed to 51% white and 17% African American, indicating a significant shift in racial/ethnic composition toward overall racial representation of the US (DHHS, 2021).

There is also variation in the characteristics of adoptive families. In general, those who adopt from foster care are socioeconomically more diverse than those who adopt privately and internationally (Vandivere et al., 2009). About 68% of all parents adopting with public agency involvement were married couples in 2020, about 25% were unmarried women, and 3% unmarried couples. These numbers were 66%, 31%, and 1% in 2000, respectively (DHHS 2021). Private adoption can be quite expensive, and therefore, these parents tend to be older, more educated and of higher socioeconomic status than other parents (see Lamanna et al., 2021). In the African American, Hispanic, and Native American communities, informal adoption, which involves taking in a child without legal formalities, is practiced.

Open adoption is a relatively new phenomenon in the US, breaking a long tradition of secrecy surrounding the adoption process (Pinderhughes et al., 2015). Openness involves communicating with the child about their adoptive status and providing information about birth parents. Due to a movement against sealed birth records of adopted children in the 1970s, the trend toward openness has prevailed and now most adopted children know that they are adopted. There remains some controversy about the degree of information and contact with birth parents because of the level of complexity involved in this process as well as unease about potential interference in the lives of all involved (Pinderhughes et al., 2015).

Families created by medically assisted reproduction (MAR)

The number of births based on MAR (also known as Assisted Reproductive Technology, ART) in the US doubled since the year 2000 (35,025) to 73,831

(CDC, 2021). Thus, overall, the number of live infants born via MAR (81,478) continues to be very small and the percentage of MAR births of all births only rose from 0.9% to 1.9% since 2000 (CDC, 2021). Medical fertility interventions, such as ovulation stimulation, intrauterine insemination, and interventions to prevent miscarriage, are more commonly used than in vitro fertilization (IVF). However, fewer than half of all American women experiencing difficulty conceiving or carrying a child (aged 25 to 44) have used any fertility treatment at all (Chandra et al., 2014).

There is no federal law against commercial surrogacy in the US and thus, surrogacy, oocyte donation, and even sex selection are currently legal in most states in the US (see Box). The distinction between a traditional surrogate and a so-called gestational carrier is that a surrogate donates her own egg and carries a pregnancy for another parent, while a "gestational carrier" (also called a gestational surrogate) refers to a woman who carries an embryo from the egg of another woman for her (CDC, 2019). There are no accurate data available, but estimates suggest that around 1,500 babies are born via surrogacy every year (Jacobson, 2016). The number of embryo transfers using a gestational carrier in the US has tripled from 1,957 in 2007 to 6,556 in 2017. In addition, the percentage of all transfers that are using gestational carriers has doubled during this time, from less than 2% to 4.2%, and the percentage of single embryo transfers (SET) has increased sixfold, from 11.6% in 2007 to 64.2% in 2017 (CDC, 2019).

Roe v. Wade, which granted women the right to an abortion, was overturned by the conservative US Supreme Court on June 24, 2022. This decision allows the individual states to ban or restrict women's ability to terminate a pregnancy, and about half of the states are poised to do so. This also raises renewed concern about the legal status of MAR treatments, such as IVF, in terms of the "rights of embryos" and the liability of doctors in providing reproductive care involving "unborn life." In addition, the decision could signal a general unraveling of marital and adoption rights gained by SGM and other non-standard families.

BOX: Surrogacy as a path to parenthood

The commercial surrogacy model in the US, as opposed to the "altruistic surrogacy model" practiced in some European countries, is quite controversial. The US is among only 11 countries that do not prohibit commercial surrogacy (IFFS, 2019). Various ethical considerations related to the commodification of motherhood for the benefit of wealthy couples (in the US surrogacy costs are estimated to be between $100,000 and $150,000, including $25,000–35,000 for the mother; see Smietana, 2017), such as human rights violations and the potential exploitation of low-income women (for example, surrogates in India receive only around $12,000-$25,000), led to strict regulations and monitoring of surrogacy exist in most countries (Lamanna et al., 2021). The degree of "surrogate-friendliness" of regulations varies by US state from very liberal in California to very restrictive in New York (Twine, 2015). Commercial surrogacy has been legally available in the US disregarding parental gender, sexuality, civil status, or citizenship for more than three decades (Smietana, 2017).

There has been relatively little research on the relationship between parents of children conceived via surrogacy and the surrogates, or on how the families of surrogate mothers deal with a pregnancy carried for others and how their sense of family identity and belonging is affected (Teman & Berend, 2020). Nevertheless, qualitative research by Smietana (2017) shows that in the narratives of surrogates and intended parents in the US, the boundaries between gift giving and exchange of commodities, a sense of altruism and commercialism, emotions and economics, are blurred. Notions of kin-like relationships and affective aspects of economic transactions were intertwined in the narratives and reflected that "a commodity can be a gift and vice versa" (Smietana, 2017, p. 172).

It has also consistently been shown that surrogates have a clear understanding of boundaries and that not they, but the intended parents, are the parent of the child they are carrying (Berend, 2016; Jacobson, 2016). In other words, those who will nurture and raise the child rather than those related by the pregnancy process, are family. This and the temporary nature of the surrogacy are communicated to the rest of the receiving family. Another interesting finding is that surrogates, similar to lesbian adoptive mothers, use symbols and rituals in order to reassure their own children and relatives of the permanence of their family identity and their commitment to their family (Teman & Berend, 2020). Ziff's (2019) research on military spouses, who by some estimates make up about 20% of all US surrogates, shows how these couples negotiate and experience surrogacy within the institutional context of the military and contractual surrogacy arrangements. The decision to become a surrogate was typically a joint one, arrived at collaboratively and seen as a "family project."

Multicultural and migrant families

As has been shown throughout this chapter, racial/ethnic and cultural diversity are an important feature in understanding the trends in US family diversity and the relevant trends have been addressed in each subsection. Thus, the focus here will be on diversity related to migrant and transnational families. In 2019, immigrants made up about 14% of the US population. The US Census Bureau (2019b) treats the terms "immigrant" and "foreign-born" as synonymous and referring to persons without US citizenship at birth, i.e., first generation. This includes permanent residents, naturalized citizens, refugees, and undocumented immigrants. Since 2000, about half of all immigrants came from Latin America and over a quarter from South and East Asia (Radford & Noe-Bustamante, 2019). In terms of marital status, about 61% of the foreign-born are currently married, compared to only about 48% of those born in the US (Radford & Noe-Bustamante, 2019). Furthermore, over the last three decades, divorce and separation has increased among those who were born outside the US. Multicultural families can be transnational and/or binational. Transnational families are those where family members maintain relationships across countries while binational families are composed of members belonging to two nationalities.

Fertility trends among immigrants reflect the impact of the great recession between 2007 and 2009 on Latin American immigration. While about 23% of all babies born in the US have immigrant mothers, after 2007 the birth rates fell more dramatically among Latin American immigrants than the US-born population (Livingston, 2016). This has significantly contributed to the overall fertility decline in the US. In 2019, about 26% of American children were part of "immigrant families," i.e. families that have one or more members who were born outside the US (American Community Survey, US Bureau of the Census, 2019b). The number of first-generation immigrant children has declined since 2000, while the number of second-generation immigrant children has increased (see Migration Policy Institute, n.d.). A sizeable and increasing proportion of immigrant families are "mixed status families," which can include persons with US citizen status, those with US legal residency status, and those who are in the US without documentation. While almost 91% of children in immigrant families are US citizens (National Academies of Science, Engineering and Medicine, 2019), about 30% of them live with an undocumented parent (Capps et al., 2016).

Since the late 1990s, US immigration policies have increasingly focused on criminalizing, detaining, and deporting undocumented migrants, particularly at the Southern border. Forced displacement, border militarization, immigration enforcement by ICE, and increased internal policing have acerbated hardships for transnational families. Parallel to the unprecedented numbers of arrests and deportations, media images of walls being built to protect from "criminal immigrants" have also increased general animosity toward immigrant families in recent years. As a consequence, families that include undocumented people constantly fear discovery and family separation. Fear of detention leads to having to live under the radar of law enforcement, which restricts mobility and causes feelings of entrapment. Short- and long-term consequences for families include disruption of daily routines, economic instability, and emotional distress (Dreby, 2015).

As a consequence of family separation due to deportation, migrant families also suffer from weakened family ties, union dissolution, trauma for children (Van Hook & Glick, 2020), and negative mental well-being for parents (Arenas et al., 2021). Based on interviews with undocumented Latin American families, Berger Cardoso and colleagues (2018) identified three areas of parenting stress due to the risk of deportation: trapped parenting, threat of family separation, and altered family processes.

Transnational migration puts major strains on family members in both migrant-sending and migrant-receiving countries (Montero-Sieburth & Mas Giralt, 2021). Recent studies describe the process of family separation at the US-Mexican border, and on how US border militarization affects children with migrating Mexican parents, family structures and parenting practices (Hamilton & Hale, 2016). Border enforcement policies and practices are weaponizing the family attachments of migrants as a deterrence strategy intended to destroy the immigrant family unit (Coddington & Williams, 2022). In fact, Wessler (2011) shows that a large number of children separated from their parents end up in the US foster care system.

Scholars also focus on undocumented or mixed-status families in which children grow up with fears of deportation and family separation (Dreby, 2015), including the DACA (Deferred Action for Childhood Arrivals) policy that intended to protect these children (Abrego, 2018). In addition, research on "transnational motherhood" (Parreñas, 2017) and parenting at a distance examine the consequences of migrating mother-child separation and the issue of substitute care for children left behind (Zentgraf & Chinchilla, 2012). These families practice doing family while in motion or while living in separate locations across borders.

Conclusion and recommendations

This chapter has provided an overview of the major changes related to the rapid diversification of US American families in the last few decades in the context of a multicultural society that provides minimal support for families. Fewer American couples expect permanence of their different-sex or same-sex relationships, and living alone or remaining single, living with friends or apart together, being unmarried mothers by choice or MAR, and families of choice have replaced the SNAF as lifestyle options. Yet it is clear that the US legal system, government agencies, and private organizations like insurance companies have yet to take these increasingly diverse family forms into account in their policies (Lamanna et al., 2021). In fact, the unique power of the US Supreme Court in determining family-related rights means that the current right-wing majority of judges can reverse the progress made in a more inclusive framing of non-standard families.

Yet, in the face of changing realities, definitions, and rights of family members have to become more flexible and visible – including issues related to how families are created, the number of legal parents, multilocality of living arrangements, marital status and sexual orientation of couples, legal employee benefits, family identity, and legal obligations. Public perceptions of family diversity have changed – according to representative PEW surveys, a majority of Americans now consider divorce, childbearing outside of marriage, cohabitation, same-sex, and interracial marriage as acceptable. Thus, the new variety of family forms has to be supported equally rather than privileging a minority form, such as SNAF. Statutory paid family leave like that offered in the EU remains elusive in the US, mainly because the US considers the "family realm" an individual and private rather than societal responsibility. Discriminatory policies that do not recognize or disadvantage members of SGM, multicultural, and reconstituted families have dramatic negative effects, particularly on children. Hence, mainstreaming post-modern family forms should be a key family policy goal.

Official statistics exclude an accounting of stepfamilies spanning several households, former stepfamily members, and same-sex couples with stepchildren. Furthermore, current US measures of family composition exclusively focus on parent-child relationships and do not account for sibling relationships in stepfamilies (Sanner & Jensen, 2021). Thus, complex stepfamilies are still treated as though they are expanded versions of the SNAF even though they include numerous members who are not part of the original biological parent-child relationship. This conceptual error results in misclassifications of people in stepfamilies, and missed opportunities for researching changing family structures and for analyzing the nature and dynamics of doing family in these complex family constellations. Hence, we need surveys that ask specific questions about the wide range of possible family relationships spanning households and borders, including children with various partners residing elsewhere, siblings, half- and step-siblings, grandparents, cohabiting partners, and chosen or fictive kin who play family roles.

The COVID-19 pandemic has highlighted existing social and health disparities among families in the US. COVID-19-related orphanhood and caregiver loss have affected certain families disproportionately, depending on family size, household structure, and race/ethnicity and age of family members. According to estimates by Hillis and colleagues (2021), about 142,637 US children experienced the death of a primary or secondary caregiver due to COVID-19 in a 15-month period, among them about 91,256 non-White children. Rates of loss of parent or grandparent caregivers were significantly higher for Native American children, Black children, and Hispanic children than for non–Hispanic White children. A bereavement experience can have profound long-term effects on the mental health, education, financial stability, and overall well-being of children. Therefore, families experiencing COVID-19 deaths need additional supports, including an expansion of kinship or foster care services.

The pandemic has disrupted life in the public and family spheres and suspended work and family routines for everyone. By moving most activities (work, school, child care, shopping) online and to the home, it has changed the way family is done in all family forms, particularly for mothers. However, low-income parents with essential jobs or without internet access, women seeking MAR at fertility clinics, foster parents dealing with the child welfare bureaucracy, employed parents of children requiring remote schooling, multilocal stepfamilies, and single mothers, all faced additional financial and caregiving challenges. The pandemic restrictions have revealed an acerbation of existing work-family inequalities by gender, race/ethnicities, family composition, and social class. COVID-19 also closed borders and increased xenophobia, trapping migrant family members in detention facilities and refugee camps.

References

Abrego, L. J. (2018). Renewed optimism and spatial mobility: Legal consciousness of Latino Deferred Action for Childhood Arrivals recipients and their families in Los Angeles. *Ethnicities, 18*(1), 1–16.

Amorim, M., Dunifon, R., & Pilkauskas, N. (2017). The magnitude and timing of grandparental coresidence during childhood in the United States. *Demographic Research, 37,* 1695–1706.

Arenas, E., Yahirun, J., Teruel, G., Rubalcava, L., & Gaitán-Rossi, P. (2021). Gender, family separation, and negative emotional well-being among recent Mexican migrants. *Journal of Marriage and Family, 83*(5), 1401–1419. https://doi.org/10.1111/jomf.12776

Baumle, A. K., & Compton, D. R. (2015). *Legalizing LGBT families: How the law shapes parenthood.* New York University Press.

Berend, Z. (2016). "We are all carrying someone else's child!": Relatedness and relationships in third-party reproduction. *American Anthropologist, 118*(1), 24–36.

Berger, L. M., & Carlson, M. J. (2020). Family policy and complex contemporary families: A decade in review and implications for the next decade of research and policy practice. *Journal of Marriage and Family, 82,* 478–507.

Berger Cardoso, J., Scott, J. L., Faulkner, M., & Barros Lane, L. (2018). Parenting in the context of deportation risk. *Journal of Marriage & Family, 80*(2), 301–316. https://doi.org/10.1111/jomf.12463

Berrick, J. D. (2015). Research and practice with families in foster care. In S. Browning & K. Pasley (Eds.), *Contemporary families: Translating research into practice* (pp. 54–69). Routledge.

Bridges, T., & Moore, M. R. (2018). Young women of color and shifting sexual identities. *Contexts, 17,* 86–88.

Cancian, M., Meyer, D. R., Brown, P. R., & Cook, S. T. (2014). Who gets custody now? Dramatic changes in children's living arrangements after divorce. *Demography, 51*(4), 1381–1396.

Capps, R., Fix, M., & Zong, J. (2016). *A profile of US children with unauthorized immigrant parents.* Migration Policy Institute.

Carroll, M. (2018). Managing without moms: Gay fathers, incidental activism, and the politics of parental gender. *Journal of Family Issues, 39,* 3410–3435.

CDC/NCHS National Vital Statistics System. (2021). National marriage and divorce rates 2000–2020. Retrieved from https://www.cdc.gov/nchs/data/dvs/national-marriage-divorce-rates-00-20.pdf

Centers for Disease Control (CDC). (2019). *ART-2017 report.* Retrieved from https://www.cdc.gov/art/pdf/2017-report/ART-2017-National-Summary-Figures_508.pdf

Centers for Disease Control and Prevention. (2021). *2019 assisted reproductive technology (ART) fertility clinic and national summary report.* Retrieved from https://www.cdc.gov/art/reports/2019/fertility-clinic.html

Chandra, A., Copen, C. E., & Stephen, E. H. (2014). *Infertility service use in the United States: Data from the National Survey of Family Growth, 1982–2010 (No. 73).* US Department of Health and Human Services, Centers for Disease Control and Prevention, National Center for Health Statistics.

Cherlin, A. J. (2004). The deinstitutionalization of American marriage. *Journal of Marriage and Family, 66*(4), 848–861. Retrieved June 22, 2021 from http://www.jstor.org/stable/3600162

Cherlin, A. J. (2010). *The marriage-go-round: The state of marriage and the family in America today.* New York: Vintage.

Cherlin, A. J. (2020). Degrees of change: An assessment of the deinstitutionalization of marriage thesis. *Journal of Marriage and Family, 82,* 62–80.

Coddington, K., & Williams, J. M. (2022). Relational enforcement: The family and the expanding scope of border enforcement. *Progress in Human Geography.* https://doi.org/10.1177/03091325211044795

Cohen, P. N. (2019). The coming divorce decline. *Socius, 5,* 1–6. Retrieved from https://osf.io/preprints/socarxiv/h2sk6/

Coughlin, A., & Abramowitz, C. (2004). *Cross-cultural adoption.* Lifeline Press.

Council, L. D. (2021). Marriage matters for Black middle-class women: A review of Black American marriages, work, and family life. *Sociology Compass, 15.* https://doi.org/10.1111/soc4.12934

Curtin, S. C., & Sutton, P. D. (2020). Marriage rates in the United States, 1900–2018. NCHS Health E-Stat. 2020. Retrieved from https://www.cdc.gov/nchs/data/hestat/marriage_rate_2018/marriage_rate_2018.htm

Department of State. (2021). *FY 2020 Annual report on intercountry adoption.* Retrieved from https://travel.state.gov/content/dam/NEWadoptionassets/pdfs/FY%202020%20Annual%20Report%20(V2.1).pdf

Dreby, J. (2015). *Everyday illegal: When policies undermine immigrant families.* University of California Press. https://doi.org/10.1086/685718

Family Equality. (2019). *LGBTQ family building survey.* Retrieved from https://www.familyequality.org/fbs

Fields, J., & Casper, L. M. (2001). America's families and living arrangements: March 2000. Current population reports, P20–537. U.S. Census Bureau, Washington, DC. Retrieved from https://www.census.gov/content/dam/Census/library/publications/2001/demo/p20-537/p20-537.pdf

Frey, W. H. (2021). *New 2020 census results show increased diversity countering decade-long declines in America's White and youth populations.* Washington, DC: Brookings Institution.

Gates, G. J. (2015). Marriage and family: LDBT individuals and same-sex couples. *The Future of Children, 25,* 67–87.

Goldberg, A. E., Gartrell, N. K., & Gate, C. (2014). Research report on LGB-parent families. *UCLA: The Williams Institute.* Retrieved from https://escholarship.org/uc/item/7gr4970w

Goldberg, S. K., & Conron, K. J. (2018). *How many same-sex couples in the US are raising children?* UCLA: The Williams Institute. Retrieved from https://williamsinstitute.law.ucla.edu/publications/same-sex-parents-us/

Guzzo, K. B., & Hayford, S. R. (2020). Pathways to parenthood in social and family contexts: Decade in review. *Journal of Marriage and Family, 82,* 117–144.

Guzzo, K.B., & Schweizer, V. J. (2020). FP-20-04 number of children to women aged 40-44, 1980-2018. *National Center for Family and Marriage Research Family Profiles, 218.* Retrieved from: https://scholarworks.bgsu.edu/ncfmr_family_profiles/218?utm_source=scholarworks.bgsu.edu%2Fncfmr_family_profiles%2F218&utm_medium=PDF&utm_campaign=PDFCoverPages

Hamilton, B. E., Martin, J. A., Osterman, M. J., & Rossen, L. M. (2019). *Births: Provisional data for 2018. Vital Statistics.* National Center for Health Statistics.

Hamilton, E. R., & Hale, J. M. (2016). Changes in the transnational family structures of Mexican farm workers in the era of border militarization. *Demography, 53*, 1429–1451.

Henderson, T. L., & Bailey, S. J. (2015). Grandparents rearing grandchildren: A culturally variant perspective. In S. Browning & K. Pasley (Eds.), *Contemporary families: Translating research into practice* (pp. 230–247). Routledge.

Heuveline, P., & Timberlake, J. M. (2004). The role of cohabitation in family formation: The United States in comparative perspective. *Journal of Marriage and Family, 66*(5), 1214–1230.

Hillis, S. D., Blenkinsop, A., Villaveces, A., Annor, F. B., Liburd, L., Massetti, G. M., Demissie, Z., Mercy, J. A., Nelson III, C. A., Cluver, L., Flaxman, S., Sherr, L., Donnelly, C. A., Ratmann, O., & Unwin, H. J. T. (2021). Covid-19-associated orphanhood and caregiver death in the United States. *Pediatrics, 148*(6). https://doi.org/10.1542/peds.2021-053760

Hobbs, F. (2005). Examining American household composition: 1990 and 2000. Census 2000 Special Report, CENSR-24, U.S. Census Bureau, U.S. Government Printing Office, Washington, DC. Retrieved from https://www.census.gov/library/publications/2005/dec/censr-24.html

International Federation of Fertility Societies (IFFS). (2019). *Global trends in reproductive policy and practice, 8th Edition.* Retrieved from https://journals.lww.com/grh/Fulltext/2019/03000/International_Federation_of_Fertility_Societies_.3.aspx

Jacobson, H. (2016). *Labor of love: Gestational surrogacy and the work of making babies.* Rutgers University Press.

James, S. (1993). Mothering: A possible black feminist link to social transformation? In J. Stanlie and A. P. A. Busia (Eds.), *Theorizing Black feminisms: The visionary pragmatism of Black women* (pp. 44–54). Routledge.

Jones, A. C. (2003). Reconstructing the stepfamily: Old myths, new stories. *Social Work, 48*(2), 228–236.

Kreider, R. M., & Lofquist, D. A. (2014). Adopted children and stepchildren: 2010. *Current Population Reports*, P20–572, U.S. Census Bureau, Washington, DC.

Kuvalanka, K. A., Weiner, J. L., Munroe, C., Goldberg, A. E., & Gardner, M. (2017). Trans and gender-nonconforming children and their caregivers: Gender presentations, peer relations, and well-being at baseline. *Journal of Family Psychology, 31*, 889–899.

Lamanna, M. A., Riedmann, A., & Stewart, S. D. (2021). *Marriages, families, and relationships: Making choices in a diverse society.* Cengage Learning, 14th edition.

Livingston, G. (2016). *Births outside of marriage decline for immigrant women.* Washington, DC: Pew Research Center.

Manning, W. D., & Smock, P. J. (2005). Measuring and modeling cohabitation: New perspectives from qualitative data. *Journal of Marriage and Family, 67*(4), 989–1002.

Manning, W. D., Smock, P. J., Dorius, C., & Cooksey, E. (2014). Cohabitation expectations among young adults in the United States: Do they match behavior? *Population Research and Policy Review, 33*(2), 287–305.

Martin, J. A., Hamilton, B. E., Osterman, M. J. K., Driscoll, A. K. (2019). *Births: Final data for 2018.* National Vital Statistics Reports; vol. *68*, no 13. Hyattsville, MD: National Center for Health Statistics (NCHS). 2019. Retrieved from https://www.cdc.gov/nchs/data/nvsr/nvsr68/nvsr68_13-508.pdf

Martin, S. P., Astone, N. M., & Peters, H. E. (2014). *Fewer marriages, more divergence: Marriage projections for millennials to age 40.* Urban Institute.

Mernitz, S. E. (2018). A cohort comparison of trends in first cohabitation duration in the United States. *Demographic Research, 38*, 2073–2086.

Migration Policy Institute. (n.d.) *Migration data hub*. Retrieved from https://www.migrationpolicy.org/programs/migration-data-hub

Monte, L. M. (2019). Multiple-partner fertility in the United States: A demographic portrait. *Demography, 56*(1), 103–127.

Montero-Sieburth, M., & Mas Giralt, R. (2021). Introduction. Family practices in migration: Everyday lives and relationships. In N. Garcia-Arjona & J. Eguren (Eds.), *Family Practices in Migration* (pp. 1–24). Routledge.

Moore, M. R., & Stambolis-Ruhstorfer, M. (2013). LGBT sexuality and families at the start of the twenty-first century. *Annual Review of Sociology, 39*, 491–507.

National Academies of Sciences, Engineering, and Medicine. (2019). *A roadmap to reducing child poverty*. National Academies Press.

Pachankis, J. E., Sullivan, T. J., & Moore, N. F. (2018). A 7-year longitudinal study of sexual minority young men's parental relationships and mental health. *Journal of Family Psychology, 32*, 1068–1077.

Parreñas, R. S. (2017). Love's labor's cost: The family life of migrant domestic workers. *World Policy Journal, 34*(3), 16–20.

Pilkauskas, N. V., & Cross, C. (2018). Beyond the nuclear family: Trends in children living in shared households. *Demography, 55*(6), 2283–2297.

Pinderhughes, E., Matthews, J. A., & Zhang, X. (2015). Research on adoptive families and their 21st-century challenges. In S. Browning & K. Pasley (Eds.), *Contemporary families: Translating Research into Practice* (pp. 14–34). Routledge.

Radford, J., & Noe-Bustamante, L. (2019). *Facts on US immigrants, 2017: Statistical portrait of the foreign-born population in the United States*. Pew Research Center, 3.

Raley, R. K., & Sweeney, M. M. (2020). Divorce, repartnering, and stepfamilies: A decade in review. *Journal of Marriage and Family, 82*, 81–99.

Reczek, C. (2020). Sexual- and gender-minority families: A 2010 to 2020 decade in review. *Journal of Marriage and Family, 82*, 300–325.

Reid, M., & Golub, A. (2015). Vetting and letting: Cohabiting stepfamily formation processes in low-income Black families. *Journal of Marriage and Family, 77*(5), 1234–1249.

Reynolds, L. (2021). The U.S. remarriage rate, 2019: Trends and geographic variation by gender. *Family Profiles*, FP-21-18. National Center for Family & Marriage Research. Retrieved from https://doi.org/10.25035/ncfmr/fp-21-18

Sanner, C., Ganong, L. H., & Coleman, M. (2021). Families are socially constructed: Pragmatic implications for researchers. *Journal of Family Issues, 42*, 22–444.

Sanner, C., & Jensen, T. M. (2021). Toward more accurate measures of family structure: Accounting for sibling complexity. *Journal of Family Theory & Review, 13*, 110–127.

Sassler, S., & Lichter, D. T. (2020). Cohabitation and marriage: Complexity and diversity in union-formation patterns. *Journal of Marriage and Family, 82*, 35–61.

Schweizer, V. (2019). 30 years of change in men's entry into fatherhood, 1987–2017. *Family Profiles*, FP-19-28. National Center for Family & Marriage Research. https://doi.org/10.25035/ncfmr/fp-19-28

Seltzer, J. A. (2019). Family change and changing family demography. *Demography, 56*(2), 405–426.

Shapiro, J. (2013). The law governing LGBT-parent families. In A. E. Goldberg & K. R. Allen (Eds.), *LGBT-parent families: Innovations in research and implications for practice* (pp. 291–304). Springer.

Simmons, T., & O'Connell, M. (2003). Married-couple and unmarried partner households: 2000, census 2000 special report, CENSR-24, U.S. Census Bureau, U.S. Government Printing Office, Washington, DC. Retrieved from https://www.census.gov/content/dam/Census/library/publications/2003/dec/censr-5.pdf

Simmons, T., & O'Neill, G. (2001). Households and families 2000. Census 2000 Brief. Retrieved from https://www2.census.gov/library/publications/decennial/2000/briefs/c2kbr01–08.pdf

Smietana, M. (2017). Affective de-commodifying, economic de-kinning: Surrogates' and gay fathers' narratives in US surrogacy. *Sociological Research Online, 22*(2), 163–175.

Smith, D. (1993). The standard North American family: SNAF as an ideological code. *Journal of Family Issues, 14*, 50–65.

Smock, P. J., & Schwarz, C. R. (2020). The demography of families: A review of patterns and change. *Journal of Marriage and Family, 82*, 9–34.

Stewart, S. D., & Timothy, E. E. (2020). Stepfamily policies and laws in the United States: Lessons from the West. *Journal of Family Issues, 41*(7), 891–912.

Stone, L. (2020). The rise of childless America, Institute for Family Studies. June 4, Retrieved from https://ifstudies.org/blog/the-rise-of-childless-america

Tasker, F., & Delvoye, M. (2015). Moving out of the shadows: Accomplishing bisexual motherhood. *Sex Roles, 73*, 125–140.

Teman, E., & Berend, Z. (2020). Surrogacy as a family project: How surrogates articulate familial identity and belonging. *Journal of Family Issues, 42*(6), 1143–1165.

Tornello, S. L., Farr, R. H., & Patterson, C. J. (2011). Predictors of parenting stress among gay adoptive fathers in the United States. *Journal of Family Psychology, 25*, 591–600.

Twine, F. W. (2015). *Outsourcing the womb: Race, class, and gestational surrogacy in a global market.* Routledge.

U.S. Census Bureau. (2000). America's families and living arrangements: 2000. Current Population Survey, 2000 Annual Social and Economic Supplement. Retrieved from https://www.census.gov/data/tables/2000/demo/families/families-living-arrangements.html

U.S. Census Bureau. (2018). *Grandparents living with their own grandchildren.* 2018: ACS 1-Year Estimates Detailed Tables. Retrieved from https://data.census.gov/cedsci/table?q=ACSDT1Y2018.B10056&g=0100000US, %2404000%24001&tid=ACSDT1Y2019.B10056&tp=true&hidePreview=true

U.S. Census Bureau. (2019a). *U.S. census bureau releases CPS estimates of same-sex households,* November 19 Press Release. Retrieved from https://www.census.gov/newsroom/press-releases/2019/same-sex-households.html

U.S. Census Bureau. (2019b). *ACS migration/geographic mobility data tables.* Retrieved from https://www.census.gov/topics/population/migration/data/tables/acs.html

U.S. Census Bureau. (2020). *Census bureau releases new estimates on America's families and living arrangements.* December 2 Press Release. Retrieved from https://www.census.gov/newsroom/press-releases/2020/estimates-families-living-arrangements.html

U.S. Census Bureau. (2021a). America's living arrangements: 2021. Current Population Survey, 2021 Annual Social and Economic Supplement. Retrieved from https://www.census.gov/data/tables/2021/demo/families/cps-2021.html

U.S. Census Bureau. (2021b). Historical marital status tables. Estimated Median Age at First Marriage, by Sex: 1890 to the Present. Retrieved from www.census.gov/data/tables/time-series/demo/families/marital.html

U.S. Census Bureau. (2022). Subject definitions. *Family.* Retrieved from https://www.census.gov/programs-surveys/cps/technical-documentation/subject-definitions.html#:~:text=Hispanic%20White%20origin.-, Family, as%20members%20of%20one%20family

U.S. Department of Health and Human Services (DHHS). (2021). Administration for children and families, administration on children, youth and families, children's bureau. *AFCARS Report #28 for Preliminary Estimates for FY 2020*. Retrieved from https://www.acf.hhs.gov/cb/research-data-technology/statistics-research/afcars

Vandivere, S., Malm, K., & Radel, L. (2009). *Adoption USA: A chartbook based on the 2007 national survey of adoptive parents*. US Department of Health and Human Services.

Vandivere, S., Yrausquin, A., Allen, T., Malm, K., & McKlindon, A. (2012). Children in nonparental care: A review of the literature and analysis of data gaps. *Children, 12*(1). Retrieved from: https://aspe.hhs.gov/reports/children-nonparental-care-review-literature-analysis-data-gaps-0

Van Hook, J., & Glick, J. E. (2020). Spanning borders, cultures, and generations: A decade of research on immigrant families. *Journal of Marriage and Family, 82*, 224–243.

Wessler, S. (2011). *Shattered families: The perilous intersection of immigration enforcement and the child welfare system*. New York: Applied Research Center. Retrieved from http://arc.org/shatteredfamilies

Zentgraf, K. M., & Chinchilla, N. S. (2012). Transnational family separation: A framework for analysis. *Journal of Ethnic and Migration Studies, 38*(2), 345–366.

Ziff, E. (2019). "Honey, I Want to Be a Surrogate": How military spouses negotiate and navigate surrogacy with their service member husbands. *Journal of Family Issues, 40*(18), 2774–2800.

11

DIVERSIFICATION IN FAMILY FORMS IN NINE OECD COUNTRIES – CHALLENGES FOR POLICY AND RESEARCH

Marina A. Adler and Karl Lenz

We began this project by asking who is considered part of a family in the 21st century in nine OECD countries (Canada, France, Germany, Japan, Lithuania, Spain, Sweden, the UK, the US) and what policies may facilitate or inhibit the observed patterns regarding family diversification. The country cases reflect the current state of knowledge regarding dominant definitions of family and the extent to which living arrangements and doing family have become detraditionalized. The selected countries are characterized by different welfare state, gender, and family policy regimes. We will first present a comparative overview of the observed changes in the demography and living arrangements in the countries and the current patterns related to the trends regarding "non-standard" families. We then discuss how family diversity is promoted and curtailed in the laws and family policies of the different welfare states, with a particular interest in changes in gender regimes and policies that move beyond heteronormativity, biological reductionism, and ethnic homogeneity. Finally, based on the lessons learned from the comparisons, we make recommendations for new developments in family policy and research.

Focusing on the last two decades, the data for the nine countries show dramatic changes in family forms, related policies, and the process of doing family in this context (Widmer, 2021; Sobotka & Berghammer, 2021). It is also clear that this transformation has been ongoing since the last third of the 20th century. The cultural hegemony of one standard family form, composed of a married couple living together in one household with their biological children, has been eroded by a diversification of family forms. In the 1950s and 1960s, the hegemony of this living arrangement was quite clear in OECD nations. Incorrectly glorified as the "golden age of family" (Vilhena & Oláh, 2017, p. 2), this era perpetuated the claim that this family form was the only proper family to aspire to. This

DOI: 10.4324/9781003193500-11

cultural normative standard was accompanied by the devaluation – in public discourse and family research – of all other family forms as deficient, deviant, or incomplete. Critical analysis reveals, however, that rather than being a historical constant, this family form emerged as part of an ongoing process of social and cultural change (Ehmer, 2021).

As the country cases examined here demonstrate, different social processes have advanced the destandardization of this family form and the diversification of families. While clear changes occurred in relationship patterns, couple stability, and fertility, these demographic factors alone are not sufficient to explain the phenomenon. The growing acceptance of non-binary gender identities and relationships beyond heteronormativity, increased ethnic heterogeneity in the population due to global migration processes, and advances in reproductive medicine have contributed to a growing variety of alternative paths to being and doing family.

Changes in the demography and living arrangements in OECD countries

The central results for the nine countries are presented in a comparative manner with regard to relevant dimensions, highlighting both similarities and differences in Table 11.1. In order to contextualize the patterns of union formation, union dissolution, and fertility, data from the OECD Family Database (https://www.oecd.org/els/family/database.htm) are used to compare the demographic trends to average values for all OECD countries.

The comparisons of union formation patterns are shown in Table 11.1, using the crude marriages rate (CMR) and the age at first marriage. The values shown for 2000 and the most recently available year indicate a continued decline for France, Japan, Spain, the UK, the US, and Canada (data only available up to 2008), a trend that already began in the early 1970s (OECD, 2022i). In Germany, the CMR has remained largely constant over the past two decades. However, this development is embedded in a longer-term decline that began in the early 1960s. Sweden had a particularly low marriage rate for a long period in the late 20th century after which the CMR increased slightly. Lithuania's development is typical of Eastern European countries, where the decline in the frequency of marriages began much later than in the West. In 1990, Lithuania still had a CMR of almost 10, which rapidly reached a low of 4.5 after the collapse of the Soviet Union. Since the new Millennium, it has rebounded over several years with a new peak in the mid-2010s.

The CMR values for 2020 are significantly lower than for 2019 in all nine countries. This difference is particularly pronounced for Spain, where the CMR was almost cut in half (from 3.5 to 1.9). It is reasonable to attribute this decline to the COVID-19 pandemic, but the pattern varies by country, and thus, it is advisable to use the 2019 data for comparisons. The OECD 32-average CMR was 3.7 in 2020 and 4.6 in 2019. Using OECD averages as a benchmark, it can

TABLE 11.1 Selected indicators of union formation, union dissolution, and fertility in nine OECD countries

	Canada	France	Germany	Japan	Lithuania	Spain	Sweden	UK	US
Union formation pattern									
Crude marriage rate (CMR) trends and vs OECD average	Decline (data only until 2008)	Strong decline, below average	Largely constant, Long term decline, at average	Strong decline, at average	Strong decline in 1990s, then strong increase; above average.	Strong decline, below average	Particularly low since the 1960s, 2000–19: largely constant; now at average	Strong decline, below average	Strong decline, above average
Mean age at first marriage trends and vs OECD average	Increase (data only upto 2008)	Very strong increase for woman, strong increase for men, significantly above average	Strong increase, Above average	Strong Increase, woman below average, mean significantly below average	Very strong increase, significantly below average	Very strong increase, significantly above average	Strong increase, significantly above average	Strong increase, at average	Strong increase, significantly below average
Union dissolution pattern									
Crude divorce rate (CDR)	Increase until 1987, decline until end of the 1990s, long period of stagnation, 2000–2020: strong decline, below average	Long-term increase until 2005, till 2016: largely constant, at average	Long-term increase until 2004, till 2018: decline, average	Long-term increase until early 2000s, till 2019: largely constant, at average	Very strong increase until 1991, then sharp drop variations at a high level since the end of the 1990s, till 2019: largely constant; above average	Strong increase until 2006, till 2019: decline, below average	Increase until the mid-1970s, then since the 1980s variations at a high level, above average	Increase until mid-1990s then falling with short interruption, at average	Strong increase until 1980s, since then strong decline; above average
Fertility Pattern									
Total fertility rate (TFR) trends vs OECD average	Back to 2000 level after temproray decline, below average	Declining after temporay increase, significantly above average	Long-term constant, slight increase in recent years, below average	Constant with slight varriations, significantly below average	Strong decline until 2006, then increase above 2000 level, below average	Strong decline until 2006, then increase with variations, significantly below average	Significantly increase in recent years, now declining above average	Intial increase, now declining at average	Continuous and strong decline, at average

(Continues)

	Canada	France	Germany	Japan	Lithuania	Spain	Sweden	UK	US
Mean age at first birth trends and vs OECD average	Strong increase, at average	Increase, at average	Increase, above average	Increase, significantly above average	Very strong increase, above average	Strong increase, significantly above average	Increase, at average	Strong increase, at average	Strong increase, below average
Share of births outside of marriage trends and vs OECD average	Increase, significantly below average	Strong increase, significantly above average	Increase, below average	Largely constant, very rare	Increase, significantly below average	Very strong increase, above average	Largely constant, significantly above average	Increase, above average	Increase, at average

Additional sources: OECD Family Database, 2022f, g, h, i;

Notes:

Crude marriage rate (CMR)

Development trend (2000–2019): Largely constant: less than plus/minus 0.5; decline: −0.5 to −1.5; strong decline: minus 1.5 and more; increase: 0.5–1.5; strong increase: 1.5 and more.

Comparison (OECD-average 2019: 4.6): Average: within plus/minus 0.5 of average; below average: 0.5 and more below; above average: 0.5 and more above.

Mean age at first marriage

Development trend (2000–2018/2020): strong increase: more than 2 years; very strong increase: more than 4 years.

Comparison: (OECD-average 2020: W 31.4; M: 33.8): At average: within plus/minus 1 year; below average: 1–2 years below; significantly below average: 2 years and more below; above average: 1–2 years above; significantly above average: 2 years and more above.

Crude divorce rate (CDR)

Development trend: Indication of when the decline began; Since then until 2016/2020: Largely constant: within plus/minus 0.5; decline: 0.5–1.5 lower; strong decline: 1.5 and more lower; increase: 0.5–1.5 higher; strong increase: 1.5 and more higher.

Comparison: (OECD-average 2020: 1.9): Average: less than plus/minus 0.2; below average: 0.2 and more below; above average: 0.2 and more above.

Total fertility rate (TFR)

Development trend: Description of the development since 2000; in the case of striking development, also beyond this date.

Comparison (OECD-average 2020: 1.59): Average: within plus/minus 0.05; below average: 0.05–0.15 below; significantly below average: 0.05–0.15 and more below; above average: 0.05–0.15 above; significantly above average: 0.15 and more above.

Mean age at first birth

Development trend: increase: up to 2 years; strong increase: up to 3 years; very strong increase: more than 3 years.

Comparison (OECD-average 2020: 29.2): Average: within plus/minus 0.5 year; below average: 0.5–1.5 years below; significantly below average: 1.5 years and more below; above average: 0.5–1.5 years above; significantly above average: 1.5 years and more above.

Share of births outside of marriage

Development trend: Largely constant: within plus/minus 2%; increase: 2–10% higher; strong increase: 10%–20% higher; very strong increase: 20% and more higher.

Comparison (OECD-average 2018: 40.7%): Average: within plus/minus 5%; above average: 5–10% above; significantly above average: 10% and more above.

Additional sources: OECD Family Database (2022f, 2022g, 2022h, 2022i).

be seen that the CMR is lower in France, Spain, and the UK. In Lithuania and the US, the CMR remains higher, and the current values for Sweden, Japan, and Germany are at the average level.

A more uniform pattern emerges in the development of the age at first marriage. In all nine countries, the average age at marriage of both women and men has risen as part of a long-term trend that began in the 1970s (OECD, 2022i). Spain has seen the largest increase, with 7 years for men and 6.8 years for women, and Lithuania also records a very large increase. In France, this is only true for women (+5.1 years). Excluding Canada, for which no recent data are available, all countries show a large or very large age increase. The smallest increase, 2.6 and 2.4, is reported in Japan. The marriage age of women has increased more than that of men in France, the UK, and Germany. Observed gender differences in age are smallest (less than two years) in Canada, Japan, and the UK.

In 2020, the OECD average age at marriage was 31.4 for women and 33.8 for men (2019: 33.5 and 31.2 years, respectively). Spain and Sweden have the highest age at marriage, France is significantly above the OECD average, and Germany is also above average. Significantly below average is the age at marriage in Lithuania, the US, and among Japanese men. The UK (and also Canada according to 2008 data) has a marriage age at the OECD average level.

Declining marriage frequency and rising marriage age do not mean that couple relationships are declining overall or in specific age-groups. The decline of marriages is compensated or even surpassed by increases in other relationship forms, such as non-marital cohabitation and living apart together (LAT) (Sobotka & Berghammer, 2021). While in the case of cohabitation, the unmarried couple has a joint household, in LAT relationships, the individuals continue to live in separate households. In France, the "pacte civil de solidarité" (PACS), an alternative form of state-registered partnership, is available to all couples since 1999. The PACS establishes a clear legal framework for couples with mutual rights and obligations and offers more flexibility than marriage, especially with regard to separation. In 2018, different-sex couples entered into more PACS than marriages for the first time (Papon, 2022). Such a legal partnership now also exists in the UK, where civil partnerships that were initially introduced only for same-sex couples were extended to different-sex couples in 2019 (in England and Wales) and 2020 (in Northern Ireland and Scotland). The notion of "common law marriage" has a long history in English-speaking nations and is roughly defined as two people living together in a committed "marriage-like" relationship without a marriage license. This arrangement is still legally recognized in ten American states and in Canada. The requirements for recognition as a common law marriage and the rights associated with it vary among US states and Canadian provinces. In Canada, common law marriage is also available to same-sex couples; in the US, this is the case only in three of the ten states.

Non-marital cohabitation is particularly popular in Sweden – over 18% of the adult population lived in such partnerships in 2018. Compared with the turn of the century, this is actually a slight decrease. In France, the UK, and Canada, non-marital cohabitation – already at a high level – has continued to increase significantly over the past two decades. In France, the increase occurred despite the availability of the PACS. In the UK, marriages and non-marital partnerships are almost equally prevalent in the 25–34 age group. In Germany and the US, the prevalence of cohabitation has continued to increase, but it remains significantly lower than in the countries already mentioned. In Spain and Lithuania, the increase in non-marital cohabitation began much later. In Spain, however, cohabitation levels have already caught up with Germany and the US. Due to the lack of current Census data, it is unclear whether the same is happening in Lithuania. Japan is a special case because non-marital cohabitation is not reported in official statistics. In fact, cohabiting couples with or without children seem to be rare in Japanese society.

Not only fewer marriages and the embrace of alternative non-marital life styles, but increased marriage instability patterns indicate that the institution of marriage has lost popularity. The crude divorce rate (CDR) is the number of annual divorces per 1,000 inhabitants and is widely used for international comparisons because of its ease of calculation. While the total divorce rate (TDR) would be better suited for comparison, this indicator is not reported on an ongoing basis for the selected countries. In addition, due to the sharp increase in non-marital relationships, divorce rates are becoming less appropriate for providing an accurate estimate of union instability.

For all nine countries, the CDR reveals that the divorce frequency has been rising sharply for a long time (OECD, 2022i). In the US, the CDR reached its highest level at the beginning of the 1980s with a value of over 5 and has been falling since then. Despite this decline, the American rate remained significantly above that of the other countries. However, since 2012, it has been surpassed by Lithuania. In Sweden, the CDR has remained virtually unchanged during the first two decades of the new century, after rising sharply until the mid-1970s. In the other countries, the increase in divorce lasted much longer. In Canada, with a sharp drop until 1987, and in the UK until the mid-1990s. In the remaining four countries, the peak in CDR was reached after 2000: in Japan in 2001, in Germany after two marked slumps (due to the divorce reform in the 1970s in West Germany and unification in the early 1990s in East Germany) in 2004, in France after a long-term increase in 2005, and in Spain in 2006. Spain, which had a very low divorce rate for a long time, saw a sharp increase at the beginning of the new century when the CDR briefly even exceeded that of Sweden. Now it remains above that of Japan, the UK, France, and Germany.

While in Lithuania and Sweden the CDR fluctuates at a relatively stable level, the data for the other countries show a downward trajectory. However, this should not be interpreted as a trend toward greater relationship stability. Rather, the declining divorce frequency is primarily related to fewer and later marriages.

High union instability also affects the usefulness of conventional indicators. It is increasingly uncommon that the first committed couple relationship is a lifelong one, and relationship biographies are likely to involve a number of partners and various relationship forms of different durations over the life course. In between, there can be temporary or permanent phases of living alone. A single measure cannot capture this sequence of relationship statuses in biographies. At any given time, persons may be living alone, but it remains invisible whether they have just left a living arrangement of a married couple with a child or entered a part-time stepparent situation. Thus, longitudinal data are required to adequately capture the diversity in dynamic relationship biographies.

To compare fertility trends, the total fertility rate (TFR), mean age at first birth, and the proportion of births outside marriage are presented. Taking 1960 as the reference year, all nine countries show significant fertility declines; most sharply Canada – from 3.9 to 1.5 (OECD, 2022f). In Canada and the US, the decline began in the early 1960s, in France, Germany, Sweden, and the UK in the mid-1960s, and in Lithuania, Spain, and Japan in the early 1970s. In the last two decades, the countries show quite different trends. The TFR is currently lowest in Japan (1.33) and Spain (1.36), and highest in France (1.79). The American TFR has been declining sharply since 2008 (2020: 1.64) after a long period of stability and registering at the highest rate of all countries (2.06) in 2000. The TFRs fell sharply in Spain until 2000 and in Lithuania until 2006, but currently they are rising again: in Spain slightly and in Lithuania more strongly. Germany has also seen a slight increase in recent years, even though the German TFR (1.53) remains slightly below the OECD average (1.59). Canada, France, Sweden, and the UK all experienced brief increases during these two decades, but currently their TFR has declined again to at or below values in 2000. In Japan, fertility has been very low with only minimal fluctuations. Unlike the marriage rate, the TFR does not reflect a "pandemic effect" for the 2020 rates.

In all nine countries, women's age at first birth increased between 2000 and 2020 (OECD, 2022g). The increase is strongest in Lithuania, where the age has risen by 4.3 years. However, despite this increase, Lithuanian women have the lowest average age at first birth (28.2) among the countries, which is also one year below the OECD average (2020: 29.2 years). The smallest increase in age is 1.1 years for German women. Spanish and Japanese women are the oldest at the birth of their first child, at 31.2 years and 30.7 years, respectively.

There are also major cross-national differences in the proportion of children born to unmarried women (OECD, 2022h). In Japan, the proportion of births outside of marriage was just 2.3% in 2015, and this is apparently due to strong pressure to get married before the birth occurs. This contrasts dramatically with France, where 59.6% of children were born outside of marriage in 2020. High proportions of non-marital births are also reported in Sweden (54.5%), and also in the UK (48.2%) and Spain (47.3%). The US has a value in the range of the QECD average, but the proportions are significantly higher for Women of Color than White women. Spain shows an extremely large increase of almost

30 percentage points in the last two decades. The proportion of non-marital births is comparatively low in Germany (33.3%), Canada (29.7%) and Lithuania (27.0%). There are, however, large regional differences within Germany. While non-marital birth rates are low (28.9%) but rising in West Germany, those in East German are 53.3%, which is comparable to Sweden's.

Changes in living arrangements confirm the demographic trends – we compare them in terms of households in Table 11.2. Available statistics usually distinguish between married couples with and without children, unmarried cohabiting couples with and without children, single parents (by gender), and those living alone. In all countries with available data, it is clear that households with different-sex spouses have been declining in the first two decades of the 21st century. This decline is particularly pronounced in Spain (−8.6%) and Germany (−8.3%). The share of different-sex married couple households is lowest in Sweden, where fewer than one in three households involve a married couple. Their share is also low in Lithuania and France. In eight countries (for Japan no data are available), the number of unmarried couples has increased. There has been a particularly large increase in the number of these couples in Spain and the UK. They are most prevalent in Sweden; the share is also high in France, Canada, and the UK. In all countries except the UK, the number of people living alone has also increased; in Germany and Spain, their share has risen very sharply. Germany, Sweden, and France report the highest proportion of people living alone.

With the exception of Japan, households with a married different-sex couple that include children also have declined. In Spain, the proportion has been cut in half from 43.4% to 20.9%. Lithuania and the US also report a very sharp decline. The proportion is again particularly low in Sweden, where fewer than one in eight households involve a married couple with kids. These figures do not indicate whether the children are joint biological, or stepchildren, adopted children, or foster children. Thus, the proportion of "standard families" is even smaller than these percentages indicate. Except for the US, households with cohabiting couples with children have increased in all countries with available data, and particularly so in Spain. The percentage of one-parent families has remained stable over these two decades. Only the US and France have seen a large increase in these households. Their share is high in the US, Canada, Spain, and France. In Sweden and France, there are more households with cohabiting couples with children and single parents than there are with married couples and children. In contrast, married–couple families still predominate in Japan and Germany. In Germany, however, there is a clear difference between the West and East: in East Germany, the move away from the standard family is much more advanced.

Changes beyond heteronormativity, biological reductionism, and ethnic homogeneity

Significant progress has taken place in the last two decades in the recognition of same-sex relationships and in the weakening of heteronormativity. The

TABLE 11.2 Living arrangements in households, 2000 and most recent year available

Living arrangements	Canada	France	Germany	Japan	Lithuania	Spain	Sweden	UK	US
Period	2001–2016	2005–2019	2000–2020	2005–2015	2000–2011	2001–2020	only 2018	2000–2017/2020	2000–2020
Living without children									
Married different-sex couples	Strong decline, medium share	Strong decline, low share	Very strong decline, medium share	Decline, medium share	Decline, low share	Very strong decline, high share	NA, low share	Strong decline, medium share	Strong decline, medium share
Cohabiting couples	Strong increase, high share	Increase, high share	Strong increase, medium share	NA	Increase, low share	Very strong increase, medium share	NA, high share	Very strong increase, high share	Increase, low share
Living alone	Increase, medium share	Strong increase, high share	Very strong increase, high share	Very strong increase, medium share	Increase, medium share	Very strong increase, medium share	NA, high share	Almost unchanged, medium share	Increase, medium share
Living with children									
Married couple with children	Strong decline, high share	Strong decline, low share	Decline, high share	Almost unchanged, high share	Very strong decline, low share	Very strong decline, high share	NA, low share	Decline, medium share	Very strong decline, medium share
Cohabiting couple with children	Increase, high share	Increase, high share	Increase, high share	NA	Increase, low share	Very strong increase, high share	NA, high share	Increase, medium share	Almost unchanged, low share

(*Continues*)

TABLE 11.2 (Continued)

Living arrangements	Canada	France	Germany	Japan	Lithuania	Spain	Sweden	UK	US
Period	2001–2016	2005–2019	2000–2020	2005–2015	2000–2011	2001–2020	only 2018	2000–2017/2020	2000–2020
One-parent with children	Almost unchanged, high share	Strong increase, high share	Almost unchanged, medium share	Increase, medium share	Almost unchanged, low share	Almost unchanged, high share	NA, medium share	Decrease, low share	Very strong increase, high share

Notes:

Living without children

Married different-sex couples

Development trend: decline: less than 4% lower; strong decline: 4%–7 % lower; very strong decline: 7% and more lower.

Comparison: low share: less than 40%; medium share: 40–50%; high share: 50% and more.

Cohabiting couples

Development trend: increase: less than 2%; strong increase: 2–3.5%; very strong increase: 3.5% and more.

Comparison: low share: less than 7%; medium share: 7–11%; high share: 11% and more.

Living alone

Development trend: almost unchanged: less than +/−1%; increase: 1–3%; strong increase: 3–5%; very strong increase: 5% and more.

Comparison: low share: less than 25%; medium share: 25–35%; high share: 35% and more.

Living with children

Married couple with children

Development trend: almost unchanged: less than +/−1%; decline: 1–3%; strong decline: 3–6% lower; very strong decline: 6% and more lower.

Comparison: low share: less than 15%; medium share: 15–20%; high share: 20% and more.

Cohabiting couple with children

Development trend: almost unchanged: less than +/−0.5%; increase: 0.5–1.5%; strong increase: 1.5–2.5%; very strong increase: 2.5% and more.

Comparison: low share: less than 3%; medium share: 3–5%; high share: 5% and more.

One-parent with children

Development trend: almost unchanged: less than +/−0.5%; increase: 0.5–1.5%; strong increase: 1.5–2.5%; very strong increase: 2.5% and more; decrease: 0.5–1.5% lower.

Comparison: low share: less than 6%; medium share: 6–9%; high share: 9% and more.

prerequisite for this development was the legalization of same-sex relationships, which was implemented at very different times in the selected countries. In Germany and Lithuania, legalization did not take place until the 1990s. In the US, criminal penalties against homosexual acts still existed in some states until 2003. In contrast, the recognition of homosexuality as a sexual behavior has a very long tradition in Japan. It has also never been considered a sin by religion. In France, legalization dates back to the French Revolution, but during the Vichy regime, the age of consent for homosexual relations was raised. This regulation was eliminated in 1982, and since then, a common age of consent has applied to heterosexual and homosexual contacts.

Another essential step on the way to normalization of SGM families is access to marriage for same-sex couples. This was preceded in most countries by a registered partnership option. Canada and Spain took this step in 2005 and Sweden, France, the UK, the US, and most recently Germany followed suit. However, same-sex couples still cannot marry in Japan and Lithuania. In Lithuania, there have been attempts to introduce a registered partnership for same-sex couples for some time, but as of 2022, these attempts have failed. In Japan, same-sex marriage is only possible in a few districts; however, there are plans to introduce it nationwide. The percentage of same-sex marriages of all marriages in the countries varies between 2% and 4%. The right to marry is also linked to the possibility of jointly adopting a child. It appears that in those countries that allow same-sex marriage, these couples also can adopt children. The regulations also vary in terms of same-sex couples' access to MAR – in France, Lithuania and Japan same-sex couples and single persons do not receive MAR treatments. In general, single men and gay couples still seem disadvantaged in access to MAR. In addition, there are also differences in whether the same-sex partner can be recognized as a parent. This is only the case in Canada, Spain, Sweden, the UK, and the US. While in all nine countries, the acceptance of same-sex couples in society has greatly increased in recent decades, discrimination and disadvantages still remain. Some of the countries have legal regulations against such discrimination; in some cases, these even have constitutional status, but the road to equality in everyday life is still long (ILGA Europa, 2022) (see Table 11.3).

Reproductive medicine has expanded the possibilities for family formation, but these biotechnological innovations are regulated differently in the nine nations. Only the US allows commercial surrogacy; non-commercial surrogacy is also allowed in Canada and the UK; and Japan has no official regulations. There are other differences in the forms and techniques permitted, such as the licensing of egg donation. In addition, there are regulations concerning who has access to MAR. In Japan and Lithuania MAR is available only to married couples. In Germany, a regulation by the German Medical Association no longer excludes unpartnered women from MAR. However, this is currently applied differently by state and doctor. Sweden, Spain, Canada, the US, the UK, and France have gradually extended the availability of MAR to unpartnered women and same-sex couples. The question of cost coverage is also highly relevant:

TABLE 11.3 Policies and laws related to SGM, MAR, step-, and migrant families

	Canada	France	Germany	Japan	Lithuania	Spain	Sweden	UK	US
Rights of SGM families									
Year of legalization/ decriminalization of homosexuality	1967	1791; 1982 Elimination of the higher age of consent introduced by the Vichy regime	1994 (West) and 1988 (East)	Historically accepted sexual behavior; mostly legal for centuries	1993; but cannot be taught about in schools	1978	1944	1967 in England and Wales, 1981 in Scotland, 1982 in Northern Ireland	2003; Supreme Court decriminalized homosexual acts
Marriage equality? Year	Yes, 2005	Yes, 2013	Yes, 2017	No, also no civil partnership	No, also no civil partnership	Yes, 2005	Yes, 2009	Yes, 2014, 2020 in Northern Ireland	Yes, 2015 nationwide, previously only in certain states
Can adopt children?	Yes	Yes	Yes, married couples	No	No	Yes	Yes	Yes	Yes
Legal parental status of same-sex partner in case of MAR?	Yes	No	No	No	No	Yes	Yes	Yes	Yes
Regulations re MAR									
Surrogacy legal?	Yes, non-commercial	No	No	No regulation	No	No	No	Yes, non-commercial	Yes

Oocyte donation legal?	Yes	Yes	No	Yes	Yes	Yes	Yes	Yes	Yes
Health insurance coverage for MAR?	Yes, complete coverage at the state level	Yes, complete coverage at national level, with maximum age	Yes, partial coverage at national level, with maximum age	Yes, partial coverage at state level	Yes, complete coverage at national level, with maximum age	Yes, partial coverage at national level, with maximum age	Yes, complete national coverage, with maximum age	Yes, complete coverage at national level, with maximum age	Yes, partial coverage at state level/private insurance
Can non-standard families get MAR?	Yes: Single women and lesbian couples, single men and gay couples, transgender and intersex	No	Yes: Single women, lesbian married couples, trans and intersex	No	No	Yes: Single women, lesbian married couples, trans and intersex	Yes: Single women, lesbian married couples, trans and intersex	Yes: Single women, lesbian married couples, trans, intersex	Yes: Single women and lesbian married couples, single men and gay couples, transgender and intersex
Rights of Stepfamilies									
Regulation of legal child custody or in divorces	Parents can obtain sole or joint custody, confirmed by court decision	Continuation of joint responsibility; modalities are determined by agreement and, in dissent, by court.	Continuation of joint responsibility	Only one parent is allowed to maintain custody	Parents can obtain sole or joint custody, confirmed by court decision	Parents can obtain sole or joint custody, confirmed by court decision	Continuation of joint responsibility	Continuation of joint responsibility	Parents decide on custody arrangements; court decides in disputes; sole custody is rare

(Continued)

TABLE 11.3 (Continued)

	Canada	France	Germany	Japan	Lithuania	Spain	Sweden	UK	US
Possibility of custody modification	Yes, parents and spouses can apply for changes to the court	Yes, transfer to one parent is possible by mutual agreement or by court order	Yes, upon request, with the consent of the other parent or based on the best interests of the child – transfer custody to one parent		Yes., based on the child's best interests, custody may be transferred by court to one parent	Yes, by court may order custody rights can be restricted or withdrawn	Yes, change of custody is possible by consensus of parents without court; the court can order sole custody	Yes, by voluntary agreement or withdrawal of custody by court based on the best interests of the child.	Yes, transfer to one parent is possible by mutual agreement or by court order

Trends re multicultural & migrant families

	Canada	France	Germany	Japan	Lithuania	Spain	Sweden	UK	US
Historical trends are migration and diversity	Long history of immigration; very high ethnic diversity and intermarriage	High level of immigration; high ethnic diversity and intermarriage	Strong immigration in the last decades; increasing ethnic diversity	Very low ethnic diversity, intermarriage and transnational families	Very low ethnic diversity and intermarriage; increasing transnational families	High level of immigration in the last decades; increasing ethnic diversity and intermarriage	High level of immigration in the last decades; increasing ethnic diversity; low intermarriage	High level of immigration; high ethnic diversity and intermarriage	Long history of immigration; very high ethnic diversity, intermarriage, and transnational families
% Foreign-born population 2019	21.0 (2016)	12.8	16.1	2.3	5.0	14.0	19.6	14.0	13.6

Additional sources: Passet-Wittig and Bujard (2021); IFFS (2022); OECD International Migration Database (2022); OECD Family Database (2022); European Commission (2018); European Justice (2022a, 2022b).

while for those who are eligible for MAR, these costs are covered in part or in full by health insurance in all nine countries, non-standard families are not eligible in three countries.

Today, most stepfamilies come about through separations and divorces. Thus, it is important to understand how the different divorce laws regulate relationship dissolution and custody issues in the nine countries. Divorce is considered a free decision of the spouses in Sweden and Spain. In Canada, Germany, and the UK, divorce is tied to the breakdown of a marriage, which is determined by a court. While in the US, France, and Lithuania divorce can still be granted based on misconduct (fault principle), this is only one of several legal grounds for divorce.

In five of the nine countries (France, Germany, Sweden, and the UK), child custody is anchored in the law that parents continue to have joint responsibility for their children even after a divorce. Only in exceptional cases, related mainly to the best interests of the child, will custody be awarded to only one parent due to a court decision or the request of a parent. In the US, divorce is not regulated by federal law, but falls under each state's jurisdiction. However, in all states, parents must settle child custody and visitation rights either in a written agreement or in a court hearing. In Lithuania and Spain, too, parents are expected to agree independently on custody and all other arrangements in an agreement in the event of divorce; if the parents do not agree, then the court decides. Joint custody can be agreed upon. In contrast, in Japan, custody is generally awarded to only one parent, typically now the mother.

Traditionally, the rule of two parents was applied in all countries. Recently, the possibility of assigning legal custody to more than two parents has opened in some nations. Multi-parent families are those where three or more parents are legally recognized as responsible for the care of a child. Most of the nine countries still only recognize two parents; for example, Germany's and Sweden's parental custody law remains based on a maximum of two parents. By contrast, in Canada and in more than 12 states in the US, multiple parents can be assigned legal parenthood for a child.

Migration and the associated ethnic heterogeneity of the population make an important contribution to family diversification. If we take the proportion of the population born abroad as a benchmark, we find that this is particularly high in Canada and Sweden. The most important immigrant groups in Canada are South Asians, Chinese, and Blacks. In Sweden, the majority of immigrants come from outside Europe. In contrast, there is comparatively little multiculturalism in Japan and Lithuania. These countries continue to have very low immigration and are still quite homogeneous with respect to ethnicity and religion. The UK and France were colonial empires into the postwar period and already have a long history of immigration. However, they are now surpassed by Germany and Spain in the proportion of the population that is foreign-born. Despite its history of being a nation of immigrants, due to restrictive immigration regulations, the contemporary US has a proportionally smaller foreign-born population than

Canada and Sweden. The US – like Canada – was founded by emigrants from Europe who invaded a continent with an indigenous population that is now relegated to living as minorities. Quite significantly contributing to ethnic heterogeneity in the US was the mass enslavement of Africans since colonialization. The descendants of African slaves and also new immigrants from Latin America and Asia, are the people of color constituting an increasingly large share of the population. The proportion of White Americans has now fallen below 60%, and continues to shrink.

This growing ethnic heterogeneity means that in at least seven of the nine countries considered, an increasing proportion of families are multicultural. These multicultural families may share a common cultural context of origin as well as different ones. Transnational families, where individual family members (father or mother or both) work in other countries as part of labor migration, are increasingly common. It is reported from Lithuania that in the last three decades, the proportion of transnational families has increased significantly. The seven countries with high immigration also have transnational families, but they are the receiving countries for labor-migrating family members.

Changes in gender regimes and family policies

The comparison of the current legal and policy context relating to the detraditionalization of family forms in the OECD countries reflects several patterns (Table 11.4). Family policy is progressing in all nine countries by moving away from the primary focus on supporting the standard family and increasingly recognizing the diversity of family forms. A major reason for this is a shift in gender regimes. The male breadwinner model is increasingly being pushed back in favor of a model with two (often full-time) employed parents. In the nine countries, between 67.5% (Spain) and 80.8% (Lithuania) of mothers with at least one child younger than 14 (or 17) were employed. Three-quarters of mothers in Lithuania and Sweden are employed full-time. Also in the US, Canada and France, significantly more mothers are employed full-time than part-time. In the UK, the share of full-time working mothers is slightly larger than that of part-time workers. Apart from Japan, where there is no breakdown by full-time and part-time employment, Germany is the only country where there are still more mothers working part-time than full-time. In addition, there again are clear differences between East and West Germany; in East Germany, full-time employment continues to be much more widespread among mothers.

The number of children in daycare facilities from an early age has increased sharply in parallel with the growth of dual earner families. With the exception of Lithuania and the US, over 90% of 3- to 5-year-olds are in daycare. This proportion is lowest in the US at 66%, which is a consequence of the lack of affordable daycare. There has also been a significant increase in the proportion of children aged up to two years in care. Among the selected countries, this is highest in France at 57.5%, well ahead of Sweden and the UK.

TABLE 11.4 Gender regimes, family policies, and laws

	Canada	France	Germany	Japan	Lithuania	Spain	Sweden	UK	US
Gender regime	Dual earner	Dual earner	1.5 earner – regional variation	Male bread winner	Dual earner	1.5 earner, moving toward dual earner	Dual earner	1.5 earner	Dual earner
Percent mothers employed, 2019 (at least 1 child aged 0–14)									
Total	76.8	73.0	73.2	70.6	80.8	67.5	86.1	74.2	70.0
Full-time	60.7	57.2	35.7	NA	74.0	50.1	76.7	39.7	58.1
Enrolment rates in early childhood education, 2018									
0–2 year olds	NA	57.5	37.7	32.6	28.3	38.2	46.3	45.1	NA
3–5 year olds	NA	100.0	94.2	91.8	86.2	97.5	93.8	100.0	66.0
Statutory policy re parental leave									
Statutory maternity leave entitlements	16 to 19 weeks, 14 weeks thereof paid; 55% of salary, with income limit; minimum insurance period as a prerequisite	16 weeks for 1st and 2nd child, then 24 weeks; 100% of salary; all employed and self-employed women	14 weeks; 100% of salary; all insured women employees	14 weeks; 87% of salary with income limit; insured women employees (excluding self-employed, part-time or casual employees)	18 weeks (126 calendar days); 100% of salary with income limit; all insured women employees with minimum insurance period	16 weeks; 100% of salary with income limit; All currently insured women employees and self-employed	14 weeks; all employed women.	52 weeks; 90% of salary, from the 7th week with income limit; all women with a minimum period of employment with the company	None
Statutory paternity leave entitlements	None	14 working days; 100% of salary with income limit	None. But partner months for parental allowance	None	4 weeks; ca. 76% of salary with income limit and benefit minimum	16 weeks; 100% of salary with income limit;	10 calendar days; ca. 76% of salary with income limit	2 weeks; 90% of salary with income limit	None

(Continued)

TABLE 11.4 (Continued)

	Canada	France	Germany	Japan	Lithuania	Spain	Sweden	UK	US
Gender regime	Dual earner	Dual earner	1.5 earner – regional variation	Male bread winner	Dual earner	1.5 earner, moving toward dual earner	Dual earner	1.5 earner	Dual earner
Statutory parental leave entitlements	35–week parental leave or up to 37 weeks. Two options: 35 weeks at 55% with income limit or one or both parents can share extended leave entitlements.	Until the child is three years old. Payment for one child: ca. 400 per month for 12 months. For two or more children: ca. 400per month paid until a child is three years old.	12 months of parental leave, plus 2 months for the other parent. The payment is a family entitlement: 67% of income, max. €1,800. Special regulation for the promotion of employment.	Until the child is 12 months old. One parent can take their leave up until the child is 14 months old if both parents take some of the leave.	Until the child is 3 years old. C.a. 76% or 55% of salary with different time periods. Parental leave is fully flexible.	Parental leave is non-transferable	Until the child is 3 years old. Family entitlement for 480 days; ca. 90 days are reserved each parent. First 390 days: ca. 79% of salary with income limit. Parental leave is fully flexible.	18 weeks, unpaid leave; a maximum of 4 weeks can be taken in any one year unless the employer agrees to more.	12 weeks unpaid leave for qualified individuals. States and employers can provide payment compensation

Family benefits and tax system

Public spending on family benefits (% of GDP)

	Canada	France	Germany	Japan	Lithuania	Spain	Sweden	UK	US
Total	1.77	3.60	3.17	1.79	2.08	1.31	3.40	3.23	1.08
Cash	1.43	1.42	1.08	0.65	0.86	0.51	1.24	2.12	0.07
Services	0.23	1.46	1.25	0.93	0.91	0.68	2.15	1.12	0.56
Tax-break	0.11	0.72	0.84	0.20	0.31	0.12	0.00	0.00	0.46

Tax systems	Individual taxation, favoring equal dual-earner couples	Optional joint taxation for families, favoring single-earner couples	Optional joint taxation for married couples, favoring single-earner couples, especially with higher incomes	Individual taxation, favoring equal dual-earner couples	NA	Optional joint taxation for families	Individual taxation, strongly favoring equal dual-earner couples	Individual taxation, strongly favoring equal dual-earner couples	Optional joint taxation for married couples; tax neutrality

Beyond binary gender and heterosexuality

Legal recognition of non-binary gender and ability to change binary gender	Yes. Since 2019, "X" gender marker on official documents	No non-binary "X" gender marker. Since 2016, Transgender individuals can change their gender marker	Yes. Since 2018, "diverse" and "no gender marker" are options.	No non-binary "X" gender marker. Since 2004, Transgender individuals can change their gender marker on legal documents.	No non-binary "X" gender marker. Since 2022, Transgender individuals can change their legal name and/or sex without sex reassignment surgery	No non-binary "X" gender marker. Since 2007, Transgender individuals can change their legal gender without the need for sex reassignment surgery or sterilization. Since 2022 people over age 16 can determine their own sex on official documents.	No non-binary "X" gender marker. Since 1972, individuals can change their binary gender marker. The restrictions regarding age, marital status, sterilization and sex reassignment surgery were removed in 2007.	Yes. Since 2020, non-binary gender marker "X" officially available	Yes. Since 2022, non-binary gender marker "X" is allowed on official documents

(Continued)

TABLE 11.4 (Continued)

	Canada	France	Germany	Japan	Lithuania	Spain	Sweden	UK	US
Gender regime	Dual earner	Dual earner	1.5 earner – regional variation	Male bread winner	Dual earner	1.5 earner, moving toward dual earner	Dual earner	1.5 earner	Dual earner
Conditions for non-binary / different gender recognition	Medical or parental consent is required in some states	Reform of gender recognition law 2016 removes sterilization and diagnosis, but no right of self-determination of the persons concerned	Diagnosis as a mandatory precondition; introduction of a right of self-determination planned	Must be over 22 years old, unmarried, undergoing sex reassignment surgery, sterilization, and having no children under 20.	Sterilization (without existing regulation) and diagnosis as mandatory precondition	Diagnosis as a mandatory precondition	Diagnosis as a mandatory precondition	Diagnosis as a mandatory precondition	Varies by state– some states require gender affirmation surgery, others require evidence of steps taken toward transition (psychological therapy, hormone therapy)

Additional sources: OECD Family Database (2022a, 2022b, 2022c, 2022d, 2022e); European Commission (2018).

There are also major differences in the legal entitlements to parental leave in terms of duration and financial support, as well as whether the leave is exclusively for mothers, shared by parents, and includes social parents. Some countries have regulations stipulating that other persons who provide childcare (e.g., the mother's new partner, grandmother) can also claim these benefits. In order to promote greater participation by fathers in the care of young children, well-compensated leave can be specifically aimed at fathers. The Spanish arrangement is interesting in this respect: mothers and fathers each have 16 weeks leave at their disposal, for which they receive full wage compensation. These periods are not transferable. While the federal 12-week non-paid leave (FMLA) in the US has been lauded because it is a gender-neutral policy that applies to all types of parents, not all Americans are covered and only few can afford to take it because it is unpaid. Germany also does not have paternity leave, but it does provide for two "partner months," which target fathers and thus have become known as "father months" in popular discourse. At 480 days, parental leave is the longest in Sweden, plus other exclusive periods for mothers and fathers. Of the 480 days, 90 are also reserved for each parent.

A key indicator of general family-friendliness of welfare states is the share of public spending on family benefits as a percentage of gross domestic product (GDP) (OECD, 2022b). Public spending on families can be distinguished into (1) child-related cash transfers to families (e.g., public income support payments during parental leave), (2) public spending on services for families (e.g., direct financing or subsidization of childcare facilities), and (3) financial support for families through the tax system. Briefly, these three forms of public spending are shown in Table 11.4 as "cash," "services," or "tax-breaks." At 3.6% of GDP, the share is highest in France, followed by Sweden, and the UK. At 1.08% of GDP, the share is lowest in the US. In the expenditure structure, service and cash are almost equal in France and significantly larger than tax support. Sweden and the UK dispense entirely with support from the tax system. Sweden clearly dominates with public spending on services while the UK mainly uses cash transfer to families. Support from the tax system is most significant in Germany, higher even than in France.

Tax systems can affect gender regimes and diverse families, for example, depending on whether there is joint taxation of married couples or whether each person is taxed separately regardless of marital status and family circumstances (individual taxation). In the case of joint taxation and a progressive tax system, the tax on the second income, usually that of the lower-earning spouse, is higher than it would be for a single person with the same income. This creates a negative incentive to be employed for one spouse and single-earner households are favored. This is particularly the case if a household can switch to a more favorable tax bracket, as is the case in Germany with "spousal splitting." Canada, Spain, Sweden, and the UK have individual taxation. In Sweden and the UK in particular, dual-earner couples in which both partners earn similar amounts benefit significantly from the tax system. Germany and the US have joint taxation of married couples; in France and Spain families are taxed jointly. The German tax system benefits single-earner households, and these advantages are particularly large in the higher income groups (OECD, 2022c).

There are clear trends away from the rigid gender binary in the legal systems. This was preceded by a significant weakening of the polarization of gender norms between men and women that lasted well into the 20th century. The progressive normalization of same-sex relations and the recognition of sexual diversity have contributed to the erosion of the gender binary. In this regard, North American nations have traditions in their indigenous cultures that recognized more than two genders and gender fluidity. Historically, European conquest and oppression of indigenous peoples has marginalized these multiple gender systems (Eidinger, 2021). In recent years, four of the nine countries (Canada, Germany, the UK, and the US) have introduced the possibility of registering a non-binary gender other than male or female in official documents, such as an "X" marker. There have also been changes in the legal requirements for changing one's gender. Surgery or sterilization as a prerequisite for gender change has been eliminated in most of the countries. The UK was the first European country to allow legal gender recognition without the requirement of medical intervention in 2004. Quite overwhelmingly, these countries continue to require the applicant to have a diagnosis of gender dysphoria, gender identity disorder, or transsexualism. Currently, there are strong efforts to achieve a right to self-determination in regard to gender identity. From the perspective of trans and intersex people, a self-determination model offers decisive advantages, such as a streamlined procedure without the difficulties of meeting any medical requirements. Above all, the symbolic meaning of determining one's own gender independently without the consent of others is empowering. Even though there are discussions about reforms, none of the nine countries has enacted a right of self-determination. The most far-reaching movement toward self-determination occurred in France, where a court has to recognize the gender change (European Commission, 2018). Largely unaddressed is the need to replace the binary patterning of parenthood in the form of motherhood and fatherhood with gender neutrality at the legal level.

In general, the selected countries show significant differences in the recognition and consideration of family diversity. The orientation of family policy toward family diversity and the dual-earner model has been longest established and most pronounced in Sweden. This reorientation is also strong in France, which has a tradition of family policy motivated by pronatalism. In recent decades, this tradition has shifted toward prioritizing gender equality and family diversity, which has resulted in political debates. In contrast, Japan's and Lithuania's family policies are still primarily oriented toward a traditional understanding of the standard family. In Japan, the family and the gender-specific division of labor are deeply rooted in the traditions of Confucianism and a family ideal involving a multigenerational household. However, these three-generation households are decreasing and the birth rate is extremely low with a high level of female employment. Non-marital births, however, continue to be almost non-existent, and non-marital living arrangements do not appear at all in family statistics. While the diversification of family forms has become an important topic in Japanese family research, policy-makers are only slowly beginning to recognize this as a basis for political action. Similarly, Lithuania is an agrarian society in which three-generation families also have a long tradition. The high divorce rate and the significant drop in fertility also indicate that families are undergoing changes. Due to the loss of national independence under Soviet rule and later the abrupt transition to neoliberalism, the observed adherence to traditional family ideals is widespread, but becoming less appropriate. In Germany, too, the shift away from the model of the standard family took a long time, much longer than in the other neighboring European countries, and only gained momentum after unification.

Another country that stands out is the US: while it has legalized same-sex marriage, same-sex adoption rights and extensive MAR access, including surrogacy, the American legal and policy framework does not include federal support for families, except via taxation. Statutory paid parental benefits are not available for families in general, making it difficult to argue that non-standard families are supported less than traditional ones. Canada, also part of the liberal welfare state cluster, also does not feature paid paternity leave; however, it does provide other supports to families, including non-standard families.

However, a more progressive orientation of family policy is not an irreversible process. The recent decision of the US Supreme Court to overturn the right to abortion and thus, allow each US state to ban or severely restrict access to abortion makes this immediately clear. Similarly, in Europe, the far-right and right-wing populist parties promote a patriarchal image of the family and reject any attempt to reduce the dominance of heteronormativity.

Addressing family diversity in policy

As we compared the nine countries, we asked ourselves: can we construct a "best practices" scenario that can guide policies to support increasingly diverse family forms in advanced nations? What policies are needed to support and promote diversity and how should they be framed (see also Neyer et al., 2016; Vilhena & Oláh, 2017)?

When examining the trends in the four tables together, several connections can be made. The detraditionalization of families and living arrangements is progressing in all countries covered here, albeit at a differing pace. Policy-makers are increasingly recognizing the changing nature of families and the growing diversity of family forms. This is clearly reflected in the basic principles of family policy as well as in legal reforms. However, there is a need for action in all countries. In Japan, this process of reorienting family policy is still in the beginning stages. In Lithuania, too, the orientation toward the traditional family model is still dominant, although there is now a reform debate, illustrated by the so far unsuccessful attempts to introduce state registration of same-sex couples.

Germany has also clung to a conservative family policy for a very long time, and only after unification a reorientation of family policy and the introduction of same-sex marriage was initiated. Even in Sweden, which can be considered a trail blazer in linking family policy with gender equality, the process of change is still in progress and the task to overcome the heteronormative coding of family law remains.

It is urgently necessary for family policy to move away from outdated understandings of family. In today's world, parents do not have to have biological children, be married, be of different genders, or live together in a common household. Because family diversity is not an exceptional circumstance, it should be considered the starting point of family policy. There is not one normal, "true," and "only desirable" family, but a multitude of family constellations, which policy must recognize as a given fact. The goal would be to remove inherent biases favoring the outdated "heteronormative, standard two-biological parents in one location model" of the family in existing laws, family policies, and related terminology. At the center of policy changes would be the general well-being of all families in order to ensure currently disadvantaged and marginalized family forms are supported and can thrive without stigma and exclusion. Parents in reconstituted families, one-parent families and cohabiting families, adoptive families, SGM families, and multicultural and migrant families must have equal rights under family law and policies. What is needed are policies that actively strive to eliminate discrimination against and disadvantages of individual family forms. This applies to the design of policy measures as well as to the formulation of legal regulations.

Along with that of family, the cultural coding of gender has undergone a sustained change. The male breadwinner model constitutive of the bourgeois family ideal, which is inextricably linked to structural gender inequality, has been replaced by a dual-earner model. Family policy must be geared to enabling and promoting gainful employment for parents in general. Countervailing incentive structures must be eliminated, such as the marital splitting tax system in Germany. Parallel to integrating women into the workforce, however, it is also necessary to provide incentives for men to take on a greater share of the care work in families. A broad range of public childcare facilities and a school system that is adapted to the requirements of parental employment are indispensable for families to reconcile family and career. Family responsibilities also require as much flexibility as possible in terms of time spent at work, either for a specific phase of life or as needed. Flexible parental leave and workplace policies must allow biological and social parents in all family forms to participate in employment and care. This includes options for shared leave taking, well-compensated leave, as well as workplaces encouraging the use of leave. Dedicated leave periods for each parent, extensive affordable high-quality daycare, and the option to reduce working hours are crucial.

Some steps have also been taken to recognize non-binary gender diversity, such as the legal recognition of a non-binary gender marker "X". In addition, the restrictive conditions regarding changing one's gender, such as reassignment surgery and sterilization are beginning to be lifted. However, policies regarding parenthood remain fundamentally binary and gendered by distinguishing between motherhood and fatherhood. What is needed is a degendered conception of person- and parenthood, implemented by law and supported by social acceptance. In addition to legal reforms allowing the possibility to determine one's own binary and non-binary gender, gender-neutral terminology is needed in laws and policies related to all families. In particular, gender biases in policies related to care-giving must be removed; rather than mother and father, the term *parent* describes the relevant social or biological relationship. Spain can serve as model of having parental leave policies that do not distinguish between different-sex and same-sex parents. While France refers to parental leave in gender-neutral terms so that the partner (disregarding gender) of the mother giving birth can take leave, Sweden's parental leave policy is also framed in a gender-neutral way.

Clearly access to well-compensated parental leave is important to family well-being, disregarding whether a family is a heteronormative nuclear family or not. Policies need to ensure that parents and partners in all families can access parental benefits to the same extent. However, this requires changes in definitions of family membership and adjustments of policies so that the legal relationships to children are clear. While this may be the case for fostering and adoption, the insistence on a maximum of two legal parents can prevent members in stepfamilies, same-sex and migrant families from accessing parental rights and benefits. While various EU directives, the UN Convention on the rights of the child, and changing ideas regarding gender are moving toward greater acceptance of diversified ways of doing family, an uneven development and lack of coherence of national policy and legal responses supporting all families can be observed across advanced countries.

Reconstituted families are increasing in all societies, and yet, they are underreported or misclassified in official statistics. Limited data collection on family relationships prevents a clear accounting of the characteristics of step families. There is also variation in the extent to which countries recognize the parental rights of non-parents in new marriages, cohabiting unions, or multi-local living arrangements. The separation of biological and social parenthood makes it necessary to take into account the fact that a child may have more than two parents or, better, two primary caregivers. In most countries, a social parent can only acquire custody through adoption, which means that the biological parent loses custody. However, there are more and more multi-parent families, i.e., family constellations in which more than two persons (want to) jointly assume parental responsibility for one or more children. This is often found in multilocal families and also in same-sex families. The expansion of legal parenthood to more than two persons, such as is Canadian policy, is needed. First steps on this path could be assigning legal rights to co-care to social parents.

So far, biological parenthood has been strongly privileged and social parenthood has received little legal recognition. After separation from the legal parent, stepparents lose any rights of custody, even if they helped raise the child since infancy. On the other hand, biological parents, usually biological fathers, can claim joint custody even if they have hardly been involved in parenting before. Rather than a rigid focus on biological parenthood, the best interests of the child and existing childcare practices should be the determining factors in the allocation of parental rights and responsibilities. Parental care is exercised within and outside of marriage, by different-sex and same-sex couples, women, men, or non-binary individuals. The law must create the conditions that do justice to this diversity of lived and desired parenthood.

MAR is certainly not an important means of increasing low fertility rates. However, reproductive medicine can fulfill the desire to be a parent despite infertility of a partner or living in a non-standard living arrangement. The policy goal should be to make assisted reproduction measures open to all, regardless of marital status, sexual orientation, and income. Egg donation as well as anonymous sperm or a mixture of sperm should be legally accessible and covered by health insurance for everyone. Surrogate motherhood, designed according to social and ethical considerations, should also be permissible. However, starting a family is optional, not mandatory. The norms of responsible parenthood include the option of deciding against becoming a parent oneself. The fundamental right to decide freely whether to become a parent or not is enshrined in the Convention on Human Rights. A living arrangement without children can be chosen just as freely as any of the other family forms described above.

A particular challenge for policy and law is how to reduce vulnerability among families. One-parent families are widely agreed to be a particularly vulnerable family type because they are at higher risk for various economic disadvantages. In order to allow solo parents to avoid poverty and participate in the labor market, provisions like affordable daycare and flexible work arrangements must be a priority. But families with disabled members, families affected by violence, and even large or migrant families also face particular risks. It is important to recognize that diversity may not always result in a freely chosen family. It can also be the result of constraints, when couple relationships receive too little support and break under the pressure of everyday life.

Current family policies may be biased against families that include immigrants and people of color because they may be one-parent, large, multigenerational, or transnational. Non-discriminatory treatment and access to social assistance, educational opportunities, and housing should be a priority to counteract any potential disadvantages. This includes framing laws and policies in culturally sensitive language that respects socio-cultural differences. With increasing globalization and related migration, the social integration of migrant and multicultural families must become a priority. A key policy goal relates to recognizing the unique challenges of doing family across boundaries and cultures. Migrant and multicultural families must be provided with the resources that facilitate family connections rather than divisions.

Recommendations for future research

Doing family in diverse family forms is a challenge not only to parents and policy-makers, but also to researchers, who try to accurately analyze related trends and relationships. As concepts like gender, family, household, and even parenthood become more fluid and inclusive, researchers are encountering difficulties in finding comparable measures for analyses across countries and time. As diverse family forms are becoming more visible in societies, data collection has to catch up so as to reflect the growing complexity of family life.

The available research in the nine countries is by no means sufficient to adequately assess and compare the existing diversity of family forms. A particular deficit is the focus on the household, however defined. This does not capture LAT relationships with and without children or multilocal post-separation families. At the same time, single parents and those living alone are overestimated because of this measurement deficit. It is also essential to record the respective child relationships within families, i.e., whether the child lives with both of its biological parents, is an adopted or foster child, or has stepchild status with one or more adults. Information on the relationship to other children in the household would also be helpful in capturing the complexity of family forms. In addition, it is problematic that data on fertility are still mainly related to women and not men or non-binary individuals. Further, the high instability of couple relationships cannot currently be adequately assessed in cross-sectional studies (Konietzka & Kreyenfeld, 2021) because they only map the probability that a person will be living in a particular family form at some point in their life course. "However, the probability of experiencing a living arrangement beyond the classic nuclear family at some point in the life course is significantly higher than at a specific point in time" (Bastin et al., 2013, p. 143; our translation).

There is certainly potential for the improvement and further development of official family statistics to account for the growing diversity of family forms. For instance, current household statistics could be replaced by recording family membership and special parent-child statuses. For the most comprehensive overview possible, however, the official family statistics always need to be supplemented by family surveys, if possible, with a panel design, and collected cross-nationally. A good model for this is the continuation of the relationship and family panel (pairfam) from Germany, the "Family Research and Demographic Analysis" (FReDA) study based at the Federal Institute for Population Research (Schneider et al., 2021). However, the problem arises that the number of cases for some family forms (e.g., SGM, MAR, adoption or foster families) is too small for generalizability. Thus, large representative samples for these family forms are necessary. Qualitative studies can also make an important contribution, especially in order to study the ongoing practices and challenges of doing family in the different family forms (Bernardi, 2021). In order to incorporate data on smaller countries with insufficient research capacity, international research networks could be a useful addition.

For international comparisons in particular, a broader data base with more complex, comparable measures is needed. Simple measures, such as the crude divorce rates (CDR) are not sufficient for recording and comparing union dissolution. Also lacking are measures to address relationship instability in general. The measures should be supplemented by relationship dissolution measures and replaced by the total divorce rate (TDR). That this is possible is shown by the recording of fertility; here, the total fertility rate (TFR) has replaced the crude fertility rate (CFR) and non-marital childbearing is measured as well. It is particularly problematic, and an obstacle to international comparisons, when individual indicators are no longer compiled at the national level – as has been the case in Canada since 2008 – or when data are only accessible to a very limited extent – as is the case in France with same-sex couples. For international comparisons, it is important to have central data points, such as those already offered in part by the OECD and Eurostat.

Migrant families pose another special challenge for researchers because, as they do not reflect an independent family form, they cannot be studied as a homogenous group. Rather, it is necessary to view migration or geographic origin as a feature that intersects with gender, age, heritage, and social class (Baykara-Krumme, 2015). Migrant families can take on all family forms and the large number of immigrant families or migrant family members necessitate that this structural feature is anchored in family research and data collection. It will be important to pay more attention to cultural differences and variation in family forms within this group (Andersson, 2021).

In the end, anyone who takes on care work, economic support, and responsibility for the well-being of family members is part of family, disregarding where they live and how they are related. That can include grandparents, extended family, and even fictive kin. In post-industrial times, it is abundantly clear that nuclear families cannot take on all the necessary care tasks to raise families. In the face of increasing family diversity, more appropriate measures must be developed and more diversity-sensitive research is needed.

Ultimately, a new and broader concept of family is necessary to adequately capture family diversity within and among countries. As has been shown in detail, it is not enough to limit family to one household or to two biological parents. Defining two generations in direct relationship also falls short because in some countries there is a long tradition of families spanning more than two generations. What distinguishes families is rather the performance of care work in the private sphere. This care work can be done not only for children, but also for older persons or peers. How many people share this care work can vary, as can the gender of the care givers. Only when family is understood as informal care structure will it become possible to comprehensively grasp the diversity of families. Research in this area is only just beginning.

References

Andersson, G. (2021). Family behaviour of migrants. In N. F. Schneider & M. Kreyenfeld (Eds.), *Research handbook on the sociology of the family* (pp. 253–276). Elgar.

Bastin, S., Kreyenfeld, M., & Schnor, C. (2013). Diversität von Familienformen in Ost- und Westdeutschland. In D. Krüger, H. Herma, & A. Schierbaum (Eds.), *Familie(n) heute: Entwicklungen, Kontroversen, Prognosen* (pp. 126–145). Beltz Juventa.

Baykara-Krumme, H. (2015). Migrantenfamilien. In P. B. Hill & J. Kopp (Eds.), *Handbuch Familiensoziologie* (pp. 709–736). Springer.

Bernardi, L. (2021). Qualitative longitudinal research in family sociology. In N. F. Schneider & M. Kreyenfeld (Eds.), *Research handbook on the sociology of the family* (pp. 109–124). Elgar.

Ehmer, J. (2021). A historical perspective on family change in Europe. In N. F. Schneider & M. Kreyenfeld (Eds.), *Research handbook on the sociology of the family* (pp. 143–162). Elgar.

Eidinger, A. (2021). History of gender roles in Canada. The Canadian encyclopedia. Retrieved from https://www.thecanadianencyclopedia.ca/en/article/history-of-gender-roles-in-canada#

European Commission. (2018). *Trans and intersex equality rights in Europe – A comparative analysis*. European network of legal experts in gender equality and non-discrimination. Written by Marjolein van den Brink Peter Dunne. Publications Office of the European Union. Retrieved from https://ec.europa.eu/info/sites/default/files/trans_and_intersex_equality_rights.pdf

European Justice. (2022). Divorce and legal separation. Retrieved from https://e-justice.europa.eu/45/DE/divorce_and_legal_separation

European Justice. (2022). Parental responsibility – Child custody and contact rights. Retrieved from https://e-justice.europa.eu/302/DE/parental_responsibility__child_custody_and_contact_rights?

ILGA Europa. (2022). Annual review of the human rights situation of lesbian, gay, bisexual, trans and intersex people in Europa and Central Asia. Retrieved from https://www.ilga-europe.org/report/annual-review-2022/

International Federation of Fertility Societies' Surveillance (IFFS). (2022). *Global trends in reproductive policy and practice*, 9th Edition Editors: Steven J. Ory, Kathleen Miller, Marcos Horton. Retrieved from https://journals.lww.com/grh/Fulltext/2019/03000/International_Federation_of_Fertility_Societies_.3.aspx

Konietzka, D., & Kreyenfeld, M. (2021). Life course sociology: Key concepts and applications in family sociology. In N. F. Schneider & M. Kreyenfeld (Eds.), *Research handbook on the sociology of the family* (pp. 73–87). Elgar.

Neyer, G., Thévenon O., & Monfardini, C. (2016). Policies for Families: Is there a best practice? *Families and Society. European policy brief*. Retrieved from https://population-europe.eu/files/documents/policy_brief_final.pdf

OECD Family Database. (2022a). *LMF1.2: Maternal employment*. Retrieved from https://www.oecd.org/els/family/LMF1_2_Maternal_Employment.pdf

OECD Family Database. (2022b). *PF1.1: Public spending on family benefits*. Retrieved from https://www.oecd.org/els/soc/PF1_1_Public_spending_on_family_benefits.pdf

OECD Family Database. (2022c). *PF1.4: Neutrality of tax-benefit systems*. Retrieved from https://www.oecd.org/els/soc/PF1_4_Neutrality_of_tax_benefit_systems.pdf

OECD Family Database. (2022d). *PF2. 1: Parental leave systems*. Retrieved from https://www.oecd.org/els/soc/PF2_1_Parental_leave_systems.pdf

OECD Family Database. (2022e). *PF3_2_Enrolment_childcare_preschool*. Retrieved from https://www.oecd.org/els/soc/PF3_2_Enrolment_childcare_preschool.pdf

OECD Family Database. (2022f). *SF2.1: Fertility rates*. Retrieved from https://www.oecd.org/els/family/SF_2_1_Fertility_rates.pdf

OECD Family Database. (2022g). *SF2.3: Age mothers childbirth*. Retrieved from https://www.oecd.org/els/family/SF_2_4_Share_births_outside_marriage.pdf

OECD Family Database. (2022h). *SF2.4: Share births outside marriage*. Retrieved from https://www.oecd.org/els/family/SF_2_4_Share_births_outside_marriage.pdf

OECD Family Database. (2022i). *SF3.1: Marriage and divorce rates*. Retrieved from https://www.oecd.org/els/family/SF_3_1_Marriage_and_divorce_rates.pdf

OECD International Migration Database. (2022). *Stocks of foreign-born population*. Retrieved from https://www.oecd.org/els/mig/keystat.htm

Oláh, L. Sz. (2015). Changing families in the European Union: Trends and policy implications. Prepared for the United Nations Expert Group Meeting. *Family policy development: Achievements and challenges*. New York. Retrieved from https://www.semanticscholar.org/paper/Changing-families-in-the-European-Union%3A-trends-and-Sz/7fc0a81f87109de43d55a86c7dd1f7be7d34eab2

Papon, S. (2022). Bilan Démographique 2021. La fécondité se maintient malgré la pandémie de Covid-19. *Insee Première*, No. 1889. Retrieved from https://www.insee.fr/fr/statistiques/6024136

Passet-Wittig, J., & Bujard, M. (2021). Medically assisted reproduction in developed countries: Overview and societal challenges. In N. F. Schneider & M. Kreyenfeld (Eds.), *Research handbook on the sociology of the family* (pp. 417–438). Elgar.

Schneider, N. F., Bujard, M., Wolf, C., Gummer, T., Hank, K., & Neyer, F. J. (2021). Family research and demographic analysis (FReDA): Evolution, framework, objectives, and design of "The German Family-Demographic Panel Study". *Comparative Population Studies*, *46*, 149–186.

Sobotka, T., & Berghammer, C. (2021). Demography of family change in Europe. In N. F. Schneider & M. Kreyenfeld (Eds.), *Research handbook on the sociology of the family* (pp. 162–186). Elgar.

Vilhena de, D. V., & Oláh, L. Sz. (2017). Family diversity and its challenges for policy makers in Europe. Evidence and recommendations from the FP7 project FamiliesAndSocieties. Discussion Paper. Berlin. Retrieved from https://population-europe.eu/files/documents/famsoc_discussionpaper5_final_web.pdf

Waaldijk, C. (2017). Legal family formats for same-sex and different-sex couples in European countries. Comparative analysis of data in the *LawsAndFamilies database*. *FamiliesAndSocieties*. Working Paper Series 75. Retrieved from https://www.semanticscholar.org/paper/Legal-Family-Formats-for-(Same-Sex)-Couples-Waaldijk-Casonato/e1206035675bc755c3b975976f6f3b181dec0dda

Widmer, E. D. (2021). Family diversity in a configurational perspective. In N. F. Schneider & M. Kreyenfeld (Eds.), *Research handbook on the sociology of the family* (pp. 60–72). Elgar.

INDEX